Beyond Suspicion

Penn Studies in Contemporary American Fiction
A Series Edited by Emory Elliott,
University of California at Riverside

Dennis Barone, ed., *Beyond the Red Notebook: Essays on Paul Auster.* 1995
Herman Beavers. *Wrestling Angels into Song: The Fictions of Ernest J. Gaines and James Alan McPherson.* 1995
Alicia Borinsky. *Theoretical Fables: The Pedagogical Dream in Contemporary Latin-American Fiction.* 1993
Marc Chénetier. *Beyond Suspicion: New American Fiction Since 1960.* 1996
Silvio Gaggi. *Modern/Postmodern: A Study in Twentieth-Century Arts and Ideas.* 1989
John Johnston. *Carnival of Repetition: Gaddis's* The Recognitions *and Postmodern Theory.* 1990
Paul Maltby. *Dissident Postmodernists: Barthelme, Coover, Pynchon.* 1991
Ellen Pifer. *Saul Bellow Against the Grain.* 1990
Arthur M. Saltzman. *Designs of Darkness in Contemporary American Fiction.* 1990
Brian Stonehill. *The Self-Conscious Novel: Artifice in Fiction from Joyce to Pynchon.* 1988
Patricia Tobin. *John Barth and the Anxiety of Continuance.* 1992
Alan Wilde. *Middle Grounds: Studies in Contemporary American Fiction.* 1987

Beyond Suspicion

New American Fiction Since 1960

Marc Chénetier

Translated by
Elizabeth A. Houlding

University of Pennsylvania Press

Philadelphia

*This work has been published with the assistance of the
French Ministry of Culture.*

First published in France as *Au-delà du soupçon: La nouvelle fiction américaine de 1960 à nos jours.* © Editions du Seuil, 1989.

Library of Congress Cataloging-in-Publication Data

Chénetier, Marc, 1946–
  [Au-delà du soupçon. English]
  Beyond suspicion : new American fiction since 1960 / Marc Chénetier ; translated by Elizabeth A. Houlding.
    p. cm. — (Penn studies in contemporary American fiction)
  Includes bibliographical references (p.   ) and index.
  ISBN 0-8122-3059-0 (alk. paper)
  1. American fiction — 20th century — History and criticism.   I. Title.   II. Series.
PS379.C4713   1996
813'.5409 — dc20   95-38105
                                                    CIP

. . . the first half of our century under [our] belt, but not on [our] back.

—John Barth, "The Literature of Replenishment"

. . . to avoid false innocence, having once clearly said that one can no longer speak innocently . . .

—Umberto Eco, afterword to *The Name of the Rose*

This book is for Nathalie Sarraute, with gratitude and respect.

It owes much to André LeVot, who would have written it better than I, and to the American writers who have welcomed me, helped me, and honored me with their friendship over the past twenty years.

As for you, Claude, if you weren't with the wind, laughing, how could I thank you?

*   *   *

I would like to thank the University of Orléans for granting me the sabbatical leave necessary to finish this work; Princeton University for welcoming me at crucial stages in my research; the Franco-American Commission for University and Cultural Exchange for material support; Thomas Pughe, accomplice and work companion in hours of solitude; Pierre Fresnault-Deruelle for his friendship, his advice, and his time.

Contents

III. The Age of American Fiction

Foreword

> Our critics . . . get excited only about classified matters, closed
> quarrels, stories whose ends are known. They never bet on
> uncertain issues, and since history has decided for them, since the
> objects which terrified or angered the authors they read have
> disappeared, since bloody disputes seem futile at a distance of two
> centuries, they can be charmed with balanced periods, and
> everything happens for them as if all literature were only a vast
> tautology and as if every new prose-writer had invented a new way of
> speaking only for the purpose of saying nothing.
>
> Jean-Paul Sartre, *What Is Literature?*[1]

Henri Bergson, a "serious" man, said: "One never *has* to write a book."
And H. L. Mencken, a famous "humorist": "Criticism consists in making
plausible one's own prejudices."

Which is to be trusted? And given these two invitations to renounce
such a project, why go on? Writing literary history in the present tense is
never the least of wagers; recent years cannot be pictured in the same way
as those great literary highways bordered by clean century breaks. Instead we have a single period, a mere bypass road perhaps, along which
we can still make out a faded sign that reads "Soft Shoulder," an en-
ticing expression that warns of pertinent, enjoyable, and unavoidable
slippages — those that separate textual analysis from the sensuous pleasures of reading, those that the perceived, substantial effects of sounds
and semantic harmonics forbid us from ever really "translating," render
the gap between lands, continents, and languages irremediably large.
Since America and France weren't much made for mutual understanding, their only chance is to try and love each other. To that purpose, their
recent literatures could be instrumental.

But making the necessary introductions is by no means simple. They
have to be performed as if one were suspended between two stages on

which the respective dramas multiply the difficulties rather than resolve them, stuck between a gamut of occultations and a series of classifications.

In the United States, the fiction that has renewed the literary landscape since 1960 is far from being the most popular or the most widespread. The luckiest among its writers belong to a cohort of famous unknowns. With some exceptions, the works that continue to dominate sales and the bookstands in supermarkets, train stations, and airports are those on which time has little effect: either their respectability is well established (the realization that Faulkner and Fitzgerald are worth reading eventually comes across), or else their constitutive ephemeral status requires that their obsolescence be planned within a perpetually renewable series in the commodities market.

Between readily mummified classics and necessarily classified mummies, few are the shelves stocked with recent literature of quality. What is more, a certain stereotype of the "mainstream" acts as a formidable obstacle to innovative literature. The economic conditions governing the production of books are not of the sort to lessen this fact.

In France, American literature remains associated in the minds of a large majority with the names of such writers as Hemingway and Steinbeck. But over the last twenty years or so the number of translations has increased and the image of American literature has been enriched. This spread of American fiction has occurred despite the sometimes harmful effects of a certain disorder — a publisher's personal whimsy or the lack of editorial constancy can damage a writer's fate. It is becoming less rare to hear the names of writers mentioned as a result of their recent critical reputation in the United States, or to hear of writers whose exoticism pleases the consumers of a season's literary fashion. Henry Miller titillated the bourgeoise grown tired of Lady Chatterley and jammed traffic in the Latin Quarter when he came to Paris. Charles Bukowski now thrills the "in-crowd" of Kenzo-clad slumming loft-dwellers, those who are "plugged into the States." Unfortunately, France doesn't unearth a Faulkner to reintroduce to the Americans everyday. Although when it came to John Hawkes or Paul Auster . . .

No one is to blame, but it is hardly possible to get an overall picture. In the best of cases, publishing houses will follow up on their authors' works; but even literary journalists familiar with the author's books have to discuss the works in the order in which they are translated. Still, when books do not sell, they will be returned to the warehouse and then turned into pulp, and, to adapt George Ade's saying on the daily press, soon there will be "nothing as dead as yesterday's contemporary fiction." It is without scruple, then, and with a fair share of rashness that I attempt this global presentation of fiction in the United States over the last thirty years. When few maps exist, one may be forgiven for having a vision less accurate than Mercator's and for proposing clumsier and less rigorous distortions.

Or for disturbing somewhat, if possible, since talking about contemporary fiction necessarily means to shake up a number of overly simple viewpoints, to simplify that which by rights ought to remain complex, to go against the grain of received ideas, to shamelessly display one's prejudices, to play the iconoclast. *Necessarily so,* because if choices had to be made here, they were made reluctantly. To satisfy my wishes would have meant devoting a great number of pages to each of the almost three hundred writers I find interesting, in different ways and to differing degrees, in the United States today. It would also have meant satisfying the demands of honesty and rigor; but establishing a corpus according to the limits and demands of a critical form means giving it a profile that cannot faithfully be its own. We know what can happen to the image of great poets as long as we can only judge them by fragments of their work. Wallace Stevens and Vachel Lindsay forgive us. Such a "selection of facts" is unavoidable, even if it is one that Raymond Poincaré could not mistake for his own definition of a "method." One has to assume responsibility both for it and for the criteria used to put it into effect. Pound said that a critic is judged by his selections rather than by his endless palavers. Faced with the present, the problem is severe. To make such choices *in medias res* verges on aporia. The uncomfortableness of the position is matched only by that in which it is bound to place my reader. Such perturbations of the channel, then, according to the logics of communication, will have to be shared.

Too much simplification ensures that we can no longer understand anything. "If you're not confused, you don't know what's going on!" The worst scenario of all would be if the reader were to reach the end of this study and feel that everything had become clear. I hardly have the means to convince my reader anyway, and such an impression is not to be wished for, nor is it justified by a situation that is fluid, plural, full of contrasts, even contradictory, mobile, impossible to block or seize between the artificial limits of relatively arbitrary dates. One of the observations on which this study is based is that the old categories have had their day and can no longer account for the American fiction of our time; with the evolution in aesthetics, the slots and drawers conceived in response to preoccupations of long ago no longer fit. We cannot wish then to artificially pin down in one place that which can only be grasped in its life and movement beyond all the usual constraints. For this reason I will take the risk — a conscious infraction of the laws of the genre — of condemning certain works to the form of oblivion with which Paul Valéry, tongue in cheek, threatened insufficiently simple works and artists whose "character" cannot be readily ascribed:

Indefinable. Fame is not easily come by in the case of works that do not fall into some simple category; works that the public feels at a loss to classify. . . . Implicit in our judgments is an unvoiced postulate: "Every personality and every book can be defined by a small number of epithets." And if the number is increased, the existence of the book, or of the man, is imperiled (in the world of opinion).[2]

Better to take this sort of risk, it seems to me, than to resort to the logic of preserves and sterilize all the readings through a liberal use of labels. Since I already wore my prejudices on my sleeve, I thought it best not to increase them by locking up each author in one paragraph or chapter where he or she would be summed up. I have chosen a multiplicity of mentions within different thematic fields and formal concerns over a systematic classification by means of an adjective or a thumbnail sketch. This literary cartography — history requires more time — relies less on the limits traced by my own choices and tastes than on the shadings that define the relative importance of the authors under consideration. A frequency of recurrences and the superimposing of layers have been chosen over the juxtaposition of isolated summits as a means of establishing a kind of relief map. The works, variously diffracted by the different lights, will reconstitute themselves as a whole as the reading proceeds.

One could of course follow the rules for the packaging of cultural merchandise and force one author or another into one neat, ready-made procrustean category or another. I have done my best to avoid this, although the demands of logic and of reading have sometimes obliged me to do so. Not only are the usual groupings not found here, there are few fixed groups of any kind. There are movements, but there are no schools. There are schools, as fish would say, but their edges are fragile: grouped as they are by affinity or by their search for the same food, gatherings formed against the currents of a poorly understood tradition. When it comes to the best writers, the notion of a school or group is of little use, outmoded or artificial. It may also be foreign to our times. On the other hand, the possibility existed to point out certain forms, practices, or fields within the imaginary, to regroup by chapter a certain number of writers around one pole only to find others assembled around a different one, just as unstable and volatile. My attempts to group them together sometimes forced their hand. At least one will grant that I have substituted more courteous activities for those lexical power plays in which all too often, in the name of theory, willful labels are attached to objects for whose specificity they can then no longer account. Analysis then becomes replaced by mere synecdoche. Such is the case in the use of the phrases "Jewish," "woman," "realist," "black humorist," "fantastic," or "postmodern(ist)." I have sometimes resorted to these shorthand distinctions — one will judge with what reticence, what guilty elasticity, what unwillingness to do so.

At best I could have proceeded in the manner of certain biologists, partisans of a "systematic phylogenetics" — and said of the authors chosen that they present "plesiomorphic" traits. Willi Hennig, a biologist, would tell us that they are found more broadly spread than in the one examined group: all primates have hair, but so do most mammals; all our writers create fictions, but so do others. Or again I could have sacrificed categories and distinctions (without owing more to Linnaeus than to Lanson) by turning to the magic notion of paraphilia in order to define my corpus through negation, in terms of gaps, blurring, or vagueness: there are animals with feathers that we call birds; there are other creatures without feathers that are everything but birds. Hennig calls such groups as are formed in nature by their absence of characteristics "paraphyletic." Such is the case for the writers I speak of, identified as representative of the period in opposition to others who do not appear to be such. My method, as subjective as can be, can be compared to what William Gaddis has magnificently named "disciplined recognitions." Another William, by the last name of James, claimed that wisdom consists in knowing what we need not worry about.

In reading this work, one can judge whom I have chosen not to discuss or whom I was forced to omit due to lack of space, and one can guess my avowable reasons. Let me confess the unavowable ones here: there is no consideration of science fiction in this book. My reasons being: my own ignorance of the field and lack of personal interest.[3] (There is also Don DeLillo's suggestion in *The Names* that we read "slightly *facetious*" under the *s* and the *f* of the name by which the genre is known.) Nor is there any discussion of best-sellers or of "popular" novels. My reasons for this being: what I know of the field and the ensuing lack of personal interest — an effect of that skepticism George Santayana called "the chastity of the mind." Finally, there is no consideration of authors who write like those of periods preceding the one in question here. The survivors of a naive or sophisticated realism need fall victim to the immense richness of a corpus that demands that those usually least discussed be favored here. I borrow my main dividing line from Conrad Detrez's serene affirmation, a remark heard long ago, and one that keeps on playing its fine song to my ears: "I want a novelist to produce a painting or a movie for me. As for the rest, I've got the telephone." I am not, in other words, overly worried about Singer or Bellow: the Nobel Prize tends to get you noticed.

Those that one might have expected to see discussed here and who are missing have already been the object of studies to which I happily and dutifully refer.[4] I have applied the rules of "affirmative action," otherwise known as "positive discrimination" to the British, by deliberately being unjust in order to establish a chance for equal opportunity after a long period of unfair treatment. Rather than the current litanies and chanting of holy trinities — Malamud-Roth-Bellow or Mailer-Styron-Vidal — I have preferred more risqué adoptions, unconstrained affections, shameless admirations. Over the repetition of known information concerning authors whose names are widely recognized, I have preferred approaches from a critical angle that reveals relief, approaches that go against the grain, against the norm, and may well raise hackles.

In sum, I wanted to paint a canvas that would somewhat resemble a family portrait by Friedrich von Amerling that René Tadlov showed me one day in a museum in Budapest, or Watteau's sketches, or Degas's pastels, all works in which the meticulous attention to detail and to finish accommodates entire sections abandoned to *réserve*. There remains a situation in space, portraits, a contour, a manner and hues. Only here and there have I used the necessary pigments. The canvas is certainly not completed, but the white spaces become the creators I seem to have abandoned, and cannot do them any harm.

In any case, I present my apologies to them. As I do in advance to the reader for my obvious points and my obscurities, to the aficionado who will not fail to be frustrated by the absence of this writer or that one, considered essential, and will vituperate — with good reason — my incompleteness, my superficiality, my arbitrariness. As for those who, on the other hand, find that I have unduly complicated things, that my choices are unwarranted, and that "all this is not very clear," may they think that by the time it *has* become clear, time will have passed its own judgments, both over those it deemed worthy to survive and over the final shape of our own lives.

"Disturbing thoughts" certainly; among which Valéry placed a sobering one: "It's not the bottle labels that get us drunk or that slake our thirst." A lovely metaphor, that, and I steal it from him: decantation takes time, new wine is never clear, and my filters are made of coarse fabric. "Never read a book that is less than a year old," wrote Emerson. I never stop breaking his rule, having inherited a taste for the "recent pressing" from my winegrower grandfather. To each his own intoxications. Even though, a fervent convivialist, I would rather share them with others.

Part I
"New Directions"

Chapter 1
Traditions

The notion of "contemporaneity" is very imprecise. Authors who have published during the period under consideration are obviously "contemporaries." We could thus argue that the work begun in France by Pierre Dommergues in *L'Aliénation dans le roman américain contemporain, 1940–1965* and *Les USA à la recherche de leur identité,* by Rachel Ertel in her meticulous study of the Jewish American novel,[1] or by specialists in African American literature needs to be continued here since their corpus does not cover all of the 1960s nor do they fully account for the production of writers who are still active. However, to the extent that recent work by the same authors would only explore further or probe more deeply, but in a largely unaltered manner, the thematic that allowed for these groupings in the first place, one might make the Orwellian suggestion (which remains to be proven) that some writers are "less contemporary than others," and that an identical treatment of their more recent works would not cast a radically different light upon the scene. For this reason, we will place the work of such novelists as Norman Mailer, Gore Vidal, John Updike, Philip Roth, or William Styron in the background of the period under consideration here, without completely neglecting their contributions to a contemporaneity that they too represent, but that seems, in the last analysis, to rely on other factors.

A strict respect of chronology cannot faithfully reflect what we perceive as the specific production of a "time." Paul Bourget's survival into the 1920s did not make him a "modern"; Laurence Sterne's presence at the heart of the eighteenth century does not make him a "classic." The same holds true today. Some works that were begun during the 1940s and the immediate postwar years, while brilliantly illustrating their "givens" (H. James), have barely evolved since and are not noteworthy for their ability to define fiction writing of the last quarter century. For example, after the publication of *Go Tell It on the Mountain* and *Augie March,* neither

James Baldwin nor Saul Bellow changed his manner of writing so markedly that his more recent books could be said to be emblematic of a period different from that of his earlier greatness. It could even be argued in both cases that they have more to gain from being measured by the standards of a period preceding the one covered in this work. While the waves of their respective impacts remain perceptible, it would be overstating the case to say that the contemporary landscape has been affected by their latest novels. Certain novels published after 1960 were essentially conceived through aesthetic schemata that belong to the 1950s and reflect that decade's values: this holds true for Philip Roth's *Letting Go,* Saul Bellow's *Herzog,* and Bernard Malamud's *A New Life.*[2]

Inversely, and this problem is less easily defined, the appropriate weight to be granted to newly undertaken bodies of work remains a matter of reasoned conjecture (the writer's age is not necessarily a factor here). Grace Paley emphasizes this point ironically in "Friends": "hindsight, usually looked down upon, is probably as valuable as foresight, since it does include a few facts."[3] Unfortunately, my own work cannot benefit from such a vantage point. Consequently, it is indispensable to draw out the period's "dominant features" (Tynyanov) as well as the specificity of the corpus that seems best to illustrate it. (This will be the task of the three chapters to follow.) This is, of course, a syllogism, when one thinks about it; the price to be paid by any literary history that dares to write itself in the present tense. But it is also a conscious orientation of a field that would not exist without it, the application of a charged undercurrent to the discrete elements in question, magnetizing them from below, causing them to shape themselves into arcs whose various shapes result from the fact that some filings are raised and others are not.

I believe that the years 1960 to 1990 have a specific profile that can be contrasted with that of preceding decades, and that allows us to raise questions about the nature and validity of the notion of the "mainstream" as used by historians of American literature, and to propose that we switch from a conservative meaning to a more "anarchic" one, aligning our interpretation with the "tuning fork" of contemporary epistemology, as the works of Thomas Kuhn and Paul Feyerabend sound it. Short of postulating a literary telos that would relativize the differences within what could then be seen as a predefined course—American millenialism and eschatology certainly lend themselves to this, as Pierre-Yves Pétillon has so admirably shown[4]—any period added to the tiled structure of the evolution in literary forms and themes will throw off the totalizing visions that were elaborated a posteriori, but before its advent. As the proverb goes, the first step is the hardest, but it is always the last step that gives the itinerary its shape.

The "Mainstream"

There is something resembling the irresistible flow of the Mississippi toward the sea in the notion and use of the term "mainstream." The indecision of the present translates as the ultimate hesitations of a delta, but the pull of origins and ends transcends muddy waves, shallows, seasonal flooding, and low water, drawing an essential and irresistible curve whose eventual tributaries, far from modifying its course, reinforce and nourish it. The "Father of the Waters," a native and therefore privileged metaphor of causality and becoming, is indissolubly both a source and an end. We read nature into "mainstream" as though it were inevitable, while everything about it is cultural and ideological, the result of privileged hierarchies and power structures. From the first streams with their uncertain direction[5] we readily infer a necessity, a past, and consequently, a future, just as one did not fail to do with the lines of that huge palm called "America." A kind of literary "manifest destiny," or better, a *tradition* — a key word that is too often superimposable on "mainstream," too often set up as an unalterable norm. The first syllable of the word tells us in what low and paternal esteem the lesser orders are held, how much respect is owed to riverbanks, and of the insignificance of minor arms.

Yet, the assurance with which this term is used is equaled by its chronic imprecision; I was going to say, as I will say, by its *constitutive, functional* imprecision. And, since the hierarchies, classifications, and value judgments depend upon this, one will forgive a few remarks and questions.

Until the "declaration of intellectual independence" that Emerson's "The American Scholar" is said to have constituted in 1837, the United States sought legitimacy for its literary enterprises through England.[6] Should we, for all this, consider that the American mainstream was born through the aberration called the "romance," in direct contradiction of Tocqueville ("They put the Real in the place of the Ideal"), or in complete agreement with him ("the fantastic beings of their imagination will perhaps make us regret the world of reality")?[7] Herman Melville, a representative of the mainstream in its present academic configuration if ever there was one, still remained an outcast in the eyes of his country, an exotic, minor writer, quite like Walt Whitman, that other unbearable man, until Europe chose to see the American in him. Is the mainstream so broad that the distance of an ocean is needed in order to observe its flow? From Mark Twain to Stephen Crane and from Emily Dickinson to Henry James, can it be crossed on such pitiful sandbanks that these giants were unable to alter its course before constituting it? What Bunyanesque leaps must we perform to get from a mainstream nourished on the "romance" and the "American grain" of Crane's "The Bride Comes to Yellow Sky" or Twain's "The Celebrated Jumping Frog of Calaveras County" to the mainstream whose flow is regulated and whose locks are watched over by William Dean Howells from his editor's chair on high at *Harper's* at the beginning of the century? And what about William Faulkner, that redneck, that incomprehensible bumpkin, that writer from the sticks whose sound and fury bowl us over, and whose monstrous book no editor would take the risk of reprinting until Jean-Paul Sartre and André Malraux universalized him for us—which swamp boat did he use to rejoin the great river? And how many ships do the expatriates of the 1920s have to take in order to meet up with the distant tributaries that will float them back to the father-river? The incoherence can be seen in the ideological gesticulations required to lead each one of them back into the straight and narrow. Jacques Derrida may well be correct in likening literary history to the policing of borders.

The mainstream is the image that we form of the "supply" available at a given moment in time to serve the intellectual comfort of the "demand." It could be the always new charted line along the graph, the product of a Gestalt for astigmatics. In a more general and more serious way, the mainstream seems to be perpetually in the process of reconstituting itself, shaping its meanders under the influence of recognizable and desired currents; it appears to be the shifting geometrical locus of such ideological demands as are formulated by the image that the literary establishment wants to give of its field. The integration and gradual activation of elements from a past that was excluded at the outset can be documented step by step. In this way, an author who was initially "neglected" or dismissed for not having displayed the qualities of a preconceived "tradition" can become more visible, more remarked upon, and more essential over time. Sarah Orne Jewett, a "regionalist" and "minor" writer, certainly constitutes a model for Willa Cather in the 1920s. But at the time this influence was only recognized in the name of "regionalism." Only when feminist criticism thought it could discern a potentially allied production in Cather's work could Jewett, by rebound, so to speak, take her place beside Edith Wharton and other women who had remained in the shadows of the great James, thereby affirming the central importance of a tributary previously held in small esteem. Or let Djuna Barnes be revealed to have had an influence on the genesis of the works of John Hawkes, let the presence of Nathanael West now grow increasingly insistent, and it is three new streams we have, rising in importance and in respectability, even if sometimes for all the wrong reasons. Would Willa Cather, the prodigious stylist, have "made it" if her sexuality had not drawn critics to her work for reasons extraneous to what makes her great?

Eminently fluid and dialectical, as though engendered by its eddies, the mainstream finds itself today at the center of virulent, often comical, and not seldom scotomizing debates among American historians of literature on the nature of the canon; for all that, curiously enough, the icon of the great American literary work seldom seems to come under direct attack, recent silly attempts at surgically purging it of its nefarious Eurocentric core notwithstanding. The publication or preparation of new literary histories, the challenges of F. O. Matthiessen's *American Renaissance* and the great panoramic studies of the forties and fifties, the increasingly critical look at the founding discourses of Henry Nash Smith, Granville Hicks, Van Wyck Brooks, Edmund Wilson, Alfred Kazin, and Leo Marx are indication enough of the periodic upheavals to which the perennial notion of the mainstream is subject. The populist guerrilla attacks led for years with very relative success by Leslie Fiedler against the norm equally inspire reflection on the means of integration of successive "revisionisms," helping us to see the mainstream as a structure of progressive recuperation of works that have "proved themselves," after having once been the instrument of their exclusion.

What is evident from these periodic manipulations of the mainstream, and what is of utmost importance here, is that with each revision a kind of consensus is established only on the basis of a weak *thematic,* a game of preoccupations, images, and *ideas* that hold highly uncertain links to literariness. Literary form and the *treatment* of themes barely enter into the notion of the mainstream that privileges contents and messages suited to coddling the consciousness that a nation has of itself at any given moment, what Robert Coover has called the "mythological American serial."[8] The mainstream seems in its very makeup to function as an aesthetic counterpart of the ideology of consensus: it dams up the eruptions of poetic language that are irrecuperable within the accepted discourses, sending them back to the categories of the referential and the mimetic, acting as a security guard to protect against suspicion, permitting the integration of the "literary" within the discursive mechanism of the great founding political texts. The mainstream is to literary history what "the general interest" and "the people" are to political rhetoric: a means of smoothing over differences and adverse discourses, a drowning of delicate musics and shouts of protest under the brass and carnival blares, an affirmation that resemblances, however minimal and lacking in pertinence they might be, are more interesting and more valuable, all things considered, than particularities. This is a literary point of view I do not share.

The 1950s

Closer to home, the general literary categories that exist in the mind of the American public, and *a fortiori* of the European public — with geographical distance, cultural lag time and the phenomena of exoticism all playing a part—were constituted on the whole just after World War II. The break proposed most often by literary historians coincides with the year 1945, mechanically linking in this way literary moments with outside events.[9] Categories proposed during the preceding decades (from the "lost generation" to the "proletarian novel") gave way to divisions in which the tensions and ideological integrations of a period can be perceived, a period whose atmosphere of control and obligatory consensus was suggested by Allen Ginsberg's expression "the syndrome of shutdown." The Cold War; the celebration of the victorious nation's virtues, of its ability to make the tutelary melting pot simmer harmoniously and to hold together the puzzle of a plural identity while being enriched by its differences (provided they proclaimed an unreserved adhesion to the essential principles of the dominant ideology); a hymn to geographical variety and human diversity . . . "My country 'tis of thee"; a general occupies the White House; intellectuals led astray by "foreign ideologies" fall back into line with the fanfare of the *Partisan Review*'s "Our Country, Our Culture" symposium of 1952; a man named McCarthy is preparing to make his name a difficult one to bear for those others — Mary, Cormac, and Eugene — who will become notorious in spite of their sharing it.

Within this context, the categories we know began to function, easily distinguishing between those who were to be granted shelter and those who were kindly asked to remain outside. The latter were dubbed "Beatniks" (Henry Luce's *Time* could be counted on to distill the suffix that would hurry the unacceptable to their place on the margins); the others got asked for their papers, on which their race, religious affiliation, and their place of origin were written. Literary history exhumed a tried and true "sectionalism" to enrich its ethnic and cultural distinctions. The cliché machine was at work. According to literary history, from the end of the war until the beginning of the 1960s, you were either from the South, from New York, Jewish, black, or a "WASP," and you expressed yourself according to these diverse modalities of alienation and belonging, defining yourself through the social, in the telling of your life. It was the time of either the search for or the comfort of identity, of the sharing of experience, of the "message" that had not yet been debunked for the masses through Marshall McLuhan's famous equation. Heterodoxy fell silent or explained itself in appropriate terms. You were requested to present your labels and declare your ideas at the door.

The European public was only too happy to be provided such a clear description of the state of things, prolonging the stereotypes of a "redskin" literature that was much preferred to an all too familiar "paleface" production.[10] European readers sought there the energy of a different world, an exoticism renewed by the diversity of populations, and the places and icons of an Americanness rendered all the more seductive by the fact that America remained far from the eyes but close to the heart of recently liberated populations. Ernest Hemingway, John Dos Passos, and William Faulkner were still alive and were able to provide the necessary sutures through the final products of their considerable bodies of work, although these were almost completed by the end of the 1950s. Replacements were sought for a play that took place on a largely fantasized set in which Jack London and John Steinbeck, Henry Miller and F. Scott Fitzgerald, in chronological and geographical bulk, supplied a supplement for the exhausted European soul. As with the permanent redistribution of the French ministers of the period, entrusting Styron with "Southern Affairs," Vidal with History, and James Jones with the Department of War served as a form of continuity beyond the instabilities of regimes; blacks and Jews can sell well when seen in the light of pious and vicarious contritions; Sartre and Malraux handled the follow-up service; and Claude-Edmonde Magny brilliantly situated the American modern.[11] In brief, the mainstream was even more successful as an export. To this day, it informs the European vision of American fiction more deeply than it manages to do in the United States. Lag time and exoticism, always and forever . . .

Yet literature is ill-mannered enough not to be built according to plans, plebiscites, or market analyses. During the 1960s, a decade rich in revisions if not in "revolutions," literary categories began to jam. Suddenly there were a few too many unclassifiable works for the classifications to hold.

From the 1940s and 1950s on, there were powerful underground works — marginalized, downgraded, little read in any case — that could not be integrated into the mainstream. Certainly, at the turn of the decade, Arthur Miller's *Death of a Salesman* held the stage and John P. Marquand's *Point of No Return* held public attention when John Hawkes published *The Cannibal* in 1949; people were reading Herman Wouk's *The Caine Mutiny* and James Jones's *From Here to Eternity* when J. D. Salinger published *The Catcher in the Rye* in 1951. It was Wouk again, with *Marjorie Morningstar*, who held the honors of the press when William Gaddis's first novel *The Recognitions* appeared in 1955. James Gould Cozzens's *By Love Possessed* made the publication of Jack Kerouac's *On the Road* go practically unnoticed in 1957. Ginsberg's "Howl" received attention in the late fifties, but mostly due to the obscenity trial that followed its 1956 publication. Two years later, Vladimir Nabokov's *Lolita* barely escaped the same treatment, but the success of the year — a dazzling fiction in the paranoid mode — was J. Edgar Hoover's *Masters of Deceit*. Same story in 1962 for William Burroughs's *Naked Lunch*, published three years earlier in Paris, the year in which Philip Roth timidly attempted through Neil

Klugman to bid "goodbye to Columbus" from well within a tradition of Jewish literature dominated by moral earnestness, civic responsibility, and respect for the narrative constraints characteristic of the forties and fifties.

These more or less innocent oversights, a kind of self-defense on the part of the mainstream or a momentary state of self-consciousness on the part of American literature, would not appear in any way surprising, inexact, or damning if something new had not been brewing for some time, lending a somewhat outdated air to the triumphalist obstinacy espoused by the offshoots of that period.[12] They continue to dominate American and international opinion, their reputation fanned by the increasingly autarchic and quasi-incestuous functioning of a chain composed of "publicity/unspecialized-and-hurried journalism/quotation-of-press-reviews-for-previous-books-on-the-cover-of-the-new-book" that only ends up reinforcing resemblances and satisfying expectations.[13]

Outdated Categories

With nostalgia still being what it used to be ("The South obliges," but does it really oblige and whom?), William Styron was quickly brought in to fill Faulkner's still warm boots in order to avoid stock interruptions[14] and was celebrated like an astronaut back from his stay with the Selenites each time he proposed a warmed-over version of public debate seasoned years earlier by the big media show: The civil rights movement in Alabama? The rise of Black Power? *The Confessions of Nat Turner* were delivered in 1967. *Holocaust* in every home? *Sophie's Choice* was made in 1979 (Corneille is still trembling).[15] Anything can lead to the Pantheon, whether on the rue Soufflot or elsewhere, including good intentions — eroticized somewhat to fit the times — and in difficult times America makes do with the intellectual liberals on hand.[16] An appearance on *Apostrophes* is not enough to make Gore Vidal an important writer; the Nobel Prize crowned an embittered and polemical Bellow; Mailer turned to show biz. Complain as one will, the mainstream keeps presenting these as "the greatest American writers of our time," defending as long as possible the configurations of recent decades, a fossilized history for troubled times. If it hiccups somewhat in so doing, it is because works of rupture have been making their presence felt and because the categories that provided the mainstream with its balance have been unseated by such facts as the rise in power of new modes of writing and the Pyrrhic victories of dated classifications.

Concerning Jewish writers, for example, Allen Guttman was able to write in 1971:

The twenty-five years that followed World War II have been both "breakthrough" and climax. The assimilation of the Jewish writer has reached the point where Bellow, Mailer, and Roth can now find a national rather than the largely ethnic audience that Abraham Cahan, Ludwig Lewison, and Meyer Levin were forced to settle for. [. . .] In 1964, I rashly conjectured that the renaissance of Jewish writers had very nearly run its course. [. . .] This does not yet strike me as a foolish remark.[17]

Today, the fact that Stanley Elkin, Mark Mirsky, and Jerome Charyn are Jewish may sometimes affect their choice of subject matter, as in Elkin's "The Condominium" (*Searches and Seizures*) or *The Rabbi of Lud*; Mirsky's *Thou Worm Jacob* or *Blue Hill Avenue*; Charyn's *Secret Isaac* or *Panna Maria*. But it is as *writers* that they seek to situate themselves in regard to their colleagues' practices and aesthetic choices, more than as Jews within a society that seems to have integrated them. A number of Jewish writers no longer define their writing through the tradition that allowed them into the mainstream: Raymond Federman, Jonathan Baumbach, and Peter Spielberg figure within an aesthetic movement largely devoid of considerations of ethnic identity; Bruce Jay Friedman and Cynthia Ozick accomplish more than a mere illustration of a Jewishness whose loss of specificity they also point out.

Regarding African American writers, the modes of writing have become so diverse that to speak of the "black novel" in the United States today without further elaboration no longer makes any sense. Quite different voices have succeeded James Baldwin's and Ralph Ellison's. Baldwin's work was essentially completed in the years preceding the period studied here; Ellison's *Invisible Man* belongs to a bygone era. Yet they both continue to embody the "black novel" such as the mainstream was able to integrate it after Richard Wright. The main responsibility taken on by these new voices, as with Jewish writers, no longer seems to be the promotion of a political and social struggle through ideas. Even though this struggle has not yet been fully won, it would still mean hurling oneself against doors that are half-open for the most part, risking in this way prejudicial imbalances. Instead, they seek to affirm their presence in all varieties of the aesthetic field, to put an end not only to a segregation now condemned by law, but especially to the limitations of artistic practices that would re-ghettoize them through foreseeable and codified recourse to techniques, themes, and voices attributable to (read: reserved for) their cultural community alone. Such was the struggle of Clarence Major's *My Amputations* (1986), whose title sums up the protests of a black writer who wishes to remain loyal to a cultural tradition without sacrificing aesthetic originalities to racial expectations that would program a certain form or a thematic.[18] Ellison is the admired foil for Major's "antirealist" novel. Ishmael Reed considers Ellison a "European" author, and sees his own work as the result of an entirely different tradition, taking its sources from a third-worldism that is not without its ambiguities, and whose forms, far from Ellison's modernism, are fed by the most popular modes of expression. On the other hand, the work of David Bradley or John Edgar Wideman takes its sources from a vision of history influenced by recent historiography. Toni Morrison seems closer to the "magic realism" of Latin American writers than to the black novel of the forties and fifties. The sumptuous effects of Toni Cade Bambara's voice invite comparison with some white writers for whom the glistening of spoken language counts above all. Gloria Naylor and Alice Walker have placed a feminine or a feminist accent on the black tradition.

It seems, finally, rather reductive to continue to group together, whether out of habit or intellectual comfort, "Southern" writers whose modes of expression are beyond comparison. What do Barry Hannah, Larry McMurtry, Fred Chappell, Richard Ford, Michael Malone, and André Dubus have in common, with Dubus's Louisiana origins indicating in a solely derisory manner a production rendered interesting for other reasons?

In an increasingly marked and pronounced way, it is the qualities and the particularities of their writing that make these authors remarkable. These qualities demand that we study their specificities rather than cling to categories whose level of generality removes all pertinence and usefulness. It is only in the case of ethnic groups who have recently reached a level of collective consciousness through a demographic upsurge and a proportionally increased importance within society (Native Americans, Chicanos, or Asian Americans) that we can again legitimately (but carefully) resort to the categories that have been rendered inoperative and obsolete in today's world through the relatively successful emergence and ensuing "banalization" of older ethnic, cultural, and regional groups.

What is more, the *internal* diversity within the bodies of work themselves often keeps us from identifying each author with one "tendency" or another, if the term "tendency" can nuance somewhat the old "categories." Seen close up, then, the present situation constantly poses sharp theoretical problems whose presence is permanent in literary history, but which the study of the present requires us always to keep in sight. This chapter, devoted to placing the corpus in perspective, will close with a brief outline of these problems while proposing a new definition of the mainstream.

The Rebel Tradition

Following the obsolete notion of the "avant-garde," common expressions such as the "advance" or the "progress" of the American novel point symptomatically to the main problem, which is the vision of an "oriented" literature. By this I mean a literature not only subjected to particular ideological demands, but one that is drawn toward an omega of some kind, attainable or not, where it would reveal itself to have arrived at the end of an ascending path, continuous in spite of gaps that are recognizable as such and as passing deviations. This vision does not imply that, platonically, an Ideal has been defined a priori. In this way, Nathalie Sarraute was able to speak of a "continuous relay race"[19] without noticing that races such as these often take place on a circular track. But it is full of a positivism inherited from the nineteenth century that privileged the notion of "progress," and of permanent evolution toward a mysterious "better," linked or not to an absolute telos. According to this vision, the mainstream would naturally privilege — against all evidence, one might say — works that reinforce advances already made in the anticipation of further developments. Along this line, Warner Berthoff wrote that Mailer, Ellison, and Wright were examples of an "effective conservatism" camping on the advanced bastions of modernism to defend it against all relapses.[20] For similar reasons, the term "postmodernism," with its telling prefix, enjoyed great success among those who were attached to defining artistic futures.[21] The image here is one in which the majority of a troop (the mainstream) waits to occupy in one leap the next positions upon the return of its scouts from no man's land; when the time has come, it moves to occupy all of the bridgeheads. Or else the image could be one of an ever-rising tide whose waves overlap and thereby increase in force. Adjacent to this vision is the quantitative, naturally ("the wave swells and gains strength"), but also the qualitative. The "cult of the new" discussed by Irving Howe and Harold Rosenberg maintains that innovation is a step toward the realization of implicit objectives. This teleological and organically cumulative vision of the massive and definitive forward movement of literary progress does not hold up to scrutiny: it lacks undertows and ebb tides, moves at the rhythm of a history necessarily without sense (in both meanings of the term), and is purged of the hazards of power relations. For this reason, Claude Simon brilliantly explained in his Nobel Prize address why the notion of progress in art makes absolutely no sense.

Along with Mikhail Bakhtin, we notice that the novel is particularly "generophagic," feeding on incessant reversals and exotic plunderings; and with Viktor Shklovsky, that it transforms itself by means of crossings and borrowings, so that the notion of "newness" in literature is, at best, necessarily weighted with intertextuality, and at worst, paradoxical. "Revolutions" in the novel are often just as much a "return to" as a "breaking away from"; they are carried out through reworking, fusion, the mutual fertilization of objects distanced by time, the discovery and exploitation of different sedimentations that were previously ignored, the elaboration of new and nourishing filiations or connections that always begins again. Linearity, the founding notion of mainSTREAM, appears to founder here.

Emphasizing the discrete and circumstantial nature of the idea of a "tradition," and the uncertain tactical factors to which reconstructions of literary history forever lend themselves, Paul Valéry wrote that "the duration of works is that of their usefulness," that "there are centuries when Virgil is of no use at all."[22] Wyatt Gwyon, the forger-hero of *The Recognitions,* indirectly illustrates this problem of the dialectical relation between the nature of perceived objects and the perception of these objects' natures:

Most forgeries last only a few generations, because they're so carefully done in the taste of the period, a forged Rembrandt, for instance, confirms everything that that period sees in Rembrandt. Taste and style change, and the forgery is painfully obvious, dated, because the new period has discovered Rembrandt all over again, and of course discovered him to be quite different. That is the curse that any genuine article must endure.[23]

Such is the way with romantic, modernist, and "postmodernist" readings of the Western canon that redesign the contours of the past. The Rabelais-Cervantes-Sterne-Joyce connection that is so meaningful in the eyes of the "postmodernists" was in no way evident to preceding generations. The place allotted to Charles Brockden Brown, Melville, or Henry David Thoreau varies considerably according to whether or not they fall within the privileged line of sight. I do not know whether each age gets the literature that it deserves, but each age always gives itself the literary history it needs. And the flux of the mainstream is very accommodating, in the ethical and optical meanings of the word. What is more, within the same reconstructive movement, divisions can appear and be in more or less direct confrontation. A fringe of "postmodernist" criticism simultaneously sees a large part of today's literary production as a prolongation of modernism and as an almost Oedipal revolt against it. Gilbert Sorrentino suggests that the true birth of "postmodernism" occurred earlier through the intervention of poets, when Williams, Zukofsky, and Olson chose to attack the still fresh monuments of modernism to which they belonged (T. S. Eliot, W. B. Yeats, imagism) in order to deconstruct them; or, looking in another direction, they prefer older and more precious traditions (Melville for Olson, Blake for Ginsberg).[24] The contours of the tradition do not necessarily lie along the same watershed lines, and one can choose to read it from one "fault" to another rather than from one "peak" to the next.

This is the vision of the mainstream proposed by Robert Coover in "On

Reading 300 American Novels."[25] For Coover, the voice of the "mainstream" is not one that generates support for a game of evolutive values, but rather one that challenges György Lukács's "homologous structures." As a necessarily eccentric voice, it "is true mainstream fiction," "emerging from the very core of the evolving form, peculiarly alert to the decay in the social forms that embrace it, early signals of larger mutation to follow."[26] The artist of the real mainstream would be one who, perceiving the dissonances of an era, resolves them by creating new forms, forms previously perceived as strangers to the "state of affairs":

For these writers, the ossified ideologies of the world, imbedded in the communal imagination, block vision, and as artists they respond not by criticism from without but by opposition from within. In effect, in mythopoeic dialogue, they challenge these old forms to change or die.[27]

Seen in this light, the mainstream is *the tradition of rupture* with conventional and admissible discourses, the common ground of articulations and of turning points, that which *pulls away*, at strategic moments of crisis, from an accepted discursive universe. Rather than an ongoing display of the real and of ideas, it is the fertile inventiveness of forms and the surpassing of proposed choices that become the irregular motor of a movement that does not necessarily have a "direction." According to this anarchizing vision that founds a superior and temporary order and harmony, the mainstream forbids the flowering of what Gustave Flaubert termed with his usual cruelty "shameful popularities."[28] It is what gives social power to the experimental "artisan of words," who, according to James Laughlin, has to lead all movements, since language always controls thought.[29]

The American literary tradition is artesian and the mainstream is very rarely a matter of forward flow. As soon as one becomes concerned with "writing in its strictest sense," it is the deed "of the rebel, the iconoclast, the transformer"[30]: a luminous definition for the topic at hand, but one that invites two warnings and a clarification.

First, we must guard against confusing novelty with value. The "cult of the new" that is inherent in American culture calls for prudence on our part, and the authors studied here were not retained simply because of their proclaimed difference. Secondly, any axiology is defined, accompanied, and complicated by a system of valences. Thus, different valences can be attached to equally defined values, depending on whether these values were inherited, imposed, co-opted, discovered, or conquered. Any appreciation of the values at play and under consideration should be modulated by a coefficient resulting from these differentials. Where writing and styles are concerned, the relationship between that which is produced and that which is expected varies according to the surroundings, thereby acquiring relative values that are independent from the intrinsic quality of the gesture performed. So that imitation can be subversive, while revolt can be easily assimilated, perfectly controllable, and harmless. To take up Georges Devereux's expression, "the anxious orthodoxy of the restrictive old guard, in science as well as in the arts, is as sterile as the anxious heterodoxy of the talentless rebel."[31] The "anxiety of influence" dear to Harold Bloom does not authorize every willful attempt at singularization.

The notion of the mainstream and a certain number of conventional hierarchies having been called into question and placed in perspective, I now invite my reader to consider that the choices made here do not arise from a dogged iconoclasm as much as from a desire to reset the balance, broaden the horizons, relativize received ideas, and decenter the vanishing points.

Chapter 2
Transitions

To propose a new vision of a corpus worn down by routine but enforced over time requires calling into question established lineages and descendancies. To do this we must return to those forks in the road where, until now, only one path has been chosen, keeping in mind at each stage the aesthetic and ideological necessities or determinations of the moment, traveling back through the years like a paleologist in order to propose new evolutive directions. Like Robert Frost in "The Road Not Taken," we must consider the paths that were followed *because* they were less traveled as well as those that were not in order to enjoy a different perspective on the landscape. Such an undertaking is not motivated by a desire for originality at any cost. Our corpus can construct itself naturally enough if we truly want to rediscover an ensemble of derivations (partially submerged yet still perceptible throughout the course of the previous few decades) and to juxtapose them, thus demonstrating that the marginalities of the past were paving the way for future evolutions.

In addition to John Hawkes and William Gaddis, privileged here for reasons discussed later, two groups of better known works call for a reconsideration of contemporary fiction's heritage and for its redistribution over a different spectrum. The first group is homegrown for the most part. It is difficult to understand the directions taken by fiction after 1960 without referring to previous advances made by J. D. Salinger, Vladimir Nabokov, Jack Kerouac, and William Burroughs. The second group is foreign to the United States since it includes the French New Novel and a South American contribution.

The Word Catcher

In 1951, under the guise of reworking the trusty thematic of childhood and adolescence, and following in the line of picaresque heroes introduced in the United States by *Huckleberry Finn,* there emerged with the publication of Salinger's *The Catcher in the Rye* a triumphant orality and a montage of dialogues that drew their authenticity from attentiveness to everyday language. Salinger's novel liberated speech and repudiated accepted novelistic discourses. It was the story of a strategic flight into the very grain of language, with language being, truth be told, the novel's true hero. This would be remembered by many when the time came for finding voices for the marginals of a society that reigned supreme over discourses. But it was also — and Salinger's truncated career proves this — an asymptotic turn toward silence, the end of a quest less influenced by Samuel Beckett than by Zen, and by reflection upon the vanities of expression that underpins the koan. *The Catcher in the Rye* figures among a number of works from the fifties that fostered a thematic of alienation and estrangement. It also initiated a transgression of formal conventions. Beyond a certain superficial obedience to the *New Yorker* style to which John Updike, Philip Roth, and Donald Barthelme would each have to adapt in turn, beyond the slickness occasioned by the nature of advertising and a luxurious medium, Salinger became the echo of an uneasiness claimed by later generations of writers and threw suspicion on the capacity of language to render the real in any way. Salinger remains a modernist to the extent that the metaphors of *The Waste Land* inhabit his novel and some of his thematically related short works. He ceases to be a modernist the minute he notices the very slight probability of anyone being able to *communicate* at all. Holden Caulfield constantly suspects that, like his little sister Phoebe, his reader[1] is able only to listen, without understanding, submitting to a flow of language that produces effects distinct from those of meaning: "I'm not too sure old Phoebe knew what the hell I was talking about. I mean she's only a little child and all. But she was listening, at least. If somebody at least listens, it's not too bad."[2] This awareness of language's potential intransitiveness is bolstered by a perception of the real that goes some way toward predicting the point of view shared by later writers.

What is essential for Caulfield is his feeling that existence is a state of flux, that experience cannot be contained within language, that discrete moments can only engender reactions governed by different principles, that the real is a disjunction, a solution of permanent continuity, and that, consequently, language cannot simply attach to the real a constancy or solidity that does not belong to it. As oppressive as this fluidity can sometimes be, even to the point of worsening his feeling of alienation, Holden Caulfield is unable to confer upon it any sort of fixity through discourse, nor does he want to. In his first-person narrative — scarcely objectivizing in itself — facts and feelings, events and internal reactions melt together. From this situation arises a chronic imprecision that is as much due to Holden's inability to understand as to the impossibility of underscoring the real with a thick black stroke. Language is manipulated then like a plumb line, or like a loosely knit net thrown randomly upon reality, a net or a line that can no more serve to measure that reality's depth than to immobilize its movement. At best, spoken language, combined with more traditional narrative elements, makes possible the reconciliation of fluidity with fixity, of stasis with digression, of drilling with exploration, while the real does not allow itself to become either fixed, used up, or analyzed. The net of language yields only language. The feeling of "phoniness" that obsesses Caulfield is not the simple effect of a reality perceived as "fake" or "hypocritical" or "inadequate" according to thematic, moral, or existential terms. The "falseness" that will dominate William Gaddis's *The Recognitions* four years later is part and parcel of language's relation to the real. For this reason, in his transitory, tentative, and not explicitly theorized way, J. D. Salinger inaugurated the era of suspicion on American soil, through a tonality suggestive of a certain uneasiness. He was already looking for ways around it. The sale figures for Salinger's books also suggest that his work truly spoke to the public of the 1960s. The uproar it caused in some circles testifies to its tonal unreceivability.

Vladimir the Magician

When it comes to *Lolita,* we will recall the programmatic value of the story's opening lines: "Lolita, light of my life, fire of my loins. My sin, my soul. Lo-lee-ta: the tip of the tongue taking a trip of three steps down the palate to tap, at three, on the teeth. Lo. Lee. Ta."[3] Truth be told, the heroine is transformed into a princess by the effects of language itself, a language that crowns and creates her at the same time. For the French reader, the ambiguity of the word "palais" (palate or palace) only hurries her metamorphosis along. In addition, for all the novel's concrete descriptions of American landscape, these descriptions constitute a verbal landscape manipulated by the narrator according to his desires, filled with spoonerisms, puns, alliterations, and a characteristic rhythm of its own. Salinger prolonged the tradition's picaresque qualities; here Nabokov inaugurates a verbal version of the genre that would later be taken up by Richard Brautigan.[4] The "erotics of art" Susan Sontag called for in her essay "Against Interpretation" is put into practice here.[5] Not that *Lolita* is the pornographic novel that it was said to be upon publication, but rather, Nabokov, like Joseph Conrad, that other exile within language, revels in the necessary linguistic distance, lovingly caresses with his lips and his pen a form of English that is savored for its sonorities, its games, and its textures. William Gass would do the same later on, drawing upon the examples of Gertrude Stein and Thomas Browne. The sensuous materiality of language, of its figures of style, its syntax, its volumes, and its sounds leaves its transitiveness far behind, happily impugns the univocity upon which an unproblematic referentiality could be founded on a realism conforming to the expectations of the time. One must be very clever to discover in this novel — the judges went to much trouble for nothing — even the slightest breach of lexical manners. However, the text *does* exude a patent eroticism, but always when it is least expected. The narrative and structural games (both instruments and fruits of the uncommon imaginary from which Nabokov produced most of his work) only prolong the attention lovingly paid to the effects of his verbal material: this may mark a violent rupture with the dominant linguistic utilitarianism, or a form of tribute to Edgar Allan Poe's "Annabel Lee" woven through the opening pages. Is there an artist more distanced from the real than the magician,[6] a writer more suspicious than the one who caresses with his gaze the underside of words, the inner lining of a language rendered more sumptuous and desirable, an object much more than an agent? Haughtily denied by those who do not admire him, disdained for his tardy arrival in America in the name of national continuity,[7] Nabokov haunts the lovers of the American language who would have liked to borrow his magic wand in the sixties, seventies, and eighties. Published the same year as *The Recognitions* (1955), *Lolita* also heralded the times we are concerned with here.

Adventure Writing

Written in one draft in three weeks of 1951, if we are to believe the author, *On the Road* did not appear in the United States until 1957. A recent study scrupulously documents the genesis of a work much more labored than Kerouac's essay on the "essentials of spontaneous prose" would have us believe.[8] With revisions, numerous versions, structural changes, and reworkings, *On the Road* appears to have gradually become the book that it is rather than simply having been born that way. "Nascuntur rebels, sed fiunt verbal craftsmen" . . . But apart from revitalizing the picarism deeply anchored in the American imaginary and narrative tradition, this novel placed fiction on the same wavelength as other forms of art. In particular, music and painting found their counterpart in this work at the time of Charlie Parker and bop and Jackson Pollock's "all over." The conventional linearity of language is certainly not as fragmented as in *Mexico City Blues* or *Doctor Sax,* nor as brutalized as in works by William Burroughs. Nonetheless, the existential translation of riffs and of a pictorial dimension established a language of corporeal and visceral rhythms. The text was to be "performed by the mile" in a sort of narrative trance, on a roll of newspaper, transcribing the rattling along of an adventure. It was to make of itself its own adventure, an example before its time of what Jean Ricardou later termed the "adventure of a writing" rather than the "writing of an adventure." Today, some poets, however distant from those for whom (in their longing for the good times at North Beach) the "beatific" image still reigns supreme, will mention, as Clark Coolidge does, the determining influence of this text in their development. At a time when realism held sway, this meant no less than the possibility of a plasticity and of a sound, than the recognition that narrative linearity could also accommodate proliferation, plurivocality, lyricism, and the investment of the body. In other words, this was like discovering a new continent.

The proliferation of pseudo-Kerouacs at the beginning of the sixties, the adoption of his themes and his style by the children of Haight-Ashbury, the exploitation of his rhythms and tonality by a large number of occasional writers attest to his impact and to the fascination exerted by this text over the course of time. Like Salinger, Kerouac contributed to the blossoming of an orality that had previously been held back. He drowned novelistic etiquette in an overflow of language, encouraged the raising of pure energy to a criterion of quality, authorized the testing of one's verbal balance—with speed structuring a space; and each of these contributors would be drawn upon, more or less consciously, but "legitimately" from then on, by more than one successor.

Heroin Language

We must also place William Burroughs's technique in perspective. Burroughs is stereotypically represented as a writer who resorts to absolute arbitrariness in order to liberate himself from the alienations provoked by programmed and authorized discourses. His practice of cut-ups and fold-ins has been discussed many times, all to affirm that Burroughs cut into the paper at random, at Bryon Gysin's urging, without concern for continuity of any kind. Burroughs has himself explained that some mending did take place in order somewhat to repair this series of torn strips. Nevertheless, his conception of language did unsettle and authorize practices that had been considered relatively unacceptable until then. As his most fervent admirers claim, Burroughs's most remarkable formal contributions are not found in *Naked Lunch* (1959); a glance at the typography of that novel suffices to convince us of this, especially when compared to the more chaotic *The Soft Machine* or *The Ticket That Exploded*. But *Naked Lunch* already partakes of a sufficiently tortured form for us to recognize signs of change there.

For Burroughs, language is an absolute evil, the origin of all alienations, the ultimate drug. Within the horrifying thematic universe that they nourish, other drugs are rendered all the less disturbing since to recount their use and their damage necessitates resorting to that even more violent and more widely abused drug, the one that kills minds as surely as heroin does bodies. It is no longer so much a question of using language as of destroying, breaking, and crushing it, so as to extract the virus that lives inside and eats away at us. Its logic is a prison, as Nietzsche showed, and there is no worthy solution but to tear down its walls. Writing is destined to make events happen, rather than to reflect them. In a certain way, it already operates as a kind of "performance"; it constitutes a supplement to the real rather than acts as its image. Tempted by a desire for silence, yet equally constrained by the obligation to speak that language imposes upon us, the paroxysmal pages of Burroughs's writing untiringly explore the ways in which language oppresses us, and the means through which we can combat it, by "counterfeiting rather than by opposition."[9] An entire segment of contemporary American paranoid fiction is filled with variations on Burroughs's suggestions, fed by a conception that works on the other side of suspicion.

Nathalie, Alain, Samuel, Jorge . . .

Of course, suspicion and change had already manifested and exemplified themselves elsewhere as well. The French New Novel was at its peak in the fifties, and the title essay in *The Age of Suspicion* was published in 1956, although it dates from 1950.[10] The French questioning of novelistic conventions, of the "psychological" dimension of the novel, of the notion of character, plot, and point of view, the newly developed relations between voice and narrative did not go unnoticed. While it is more appropriate to speak in terms of parallel evolutions and simultaneous discoveries, these developments were to have some influence on subsequent American fiction. In 1975, Donald Barthelme confessed to me that, whereas he "would no longer cross the street to buy the latest Robbe-Grillet," he had been influenced by Robbe-Grillet's earlier novels, as well as by the philosophical debates of the first half of the century and by the critics of the Geneva School.[11] The debts, paid back with interest, are not forgotten. To steal an expression from John Barth, the lessons of suspicion that were learned in the sixties by a new and relatively insecure American fiction, were quickly taken for granted: with the coming of the seventies, they were "under our belt, and no longer on our back."

Samuel Beckett and Jorge Luis Borges represent essential steps within this evolution. The *Ficciones* date from the forties, even though their impact was delayed by translation. Beckett would have a different influence on the thought and creation of writers such as Robert Coover, Ronald Sukenick, Rudolph Wurlitzer, and John Barth.[12] Both writers profoundly modified the manner in which American creators apprehended what Roland Barthes termed the "logosphere"; they traced paths leading to an escape from a strict form of referentiality toward a "reality" that was becoming increasingly dependent on language to create it. They inflected the conventional ground of "tradition" by referring back to abandoned moments of Western literature, looking to authors previously thought of as "exceptions" — Cervantes, Sterne, Rabelais — in whose work verbal creativity, the space of play, and the breaking down of narrative instances weaken readings merely in search of a mimetic reflection of the real. Without these two authors, "fiction" would no doubt have failed to impose itself as a respectable term after centuries of pejorative connotations.

William Gaddis: The Art of Alchemy

The very name of Wyatt Gwyon, the central character of *The Recognitions,* announces the desire for a return to origins. These two words, borrowed from the Gaelic, both mean "son." From the beginning, they make of this inspired forger a "son of a son," the defiant and deviant heir to a tradition that, as Gaddis wants to demonstrate, cannot be traced back to a locatable origin. At the same time, causal genealogies are both called into question and rendered pointless.

Within the chaotic mess of Western culture that T. S. Eliot tries to shore up in *The Waste Land* to save himself from ruin and that James Joyce tries to reorganize around the myth of Ulysses, Gaddis follows more in Nietzsche's line and in no way attempts to provide a precise explanation or global solution. Art certainly invades the structure and the texture of the novel; but, contrary to modernism, where Art stands as the ultimate metaphor and represents the only remaining hope of finding sense, Art no longer can deliver the secret of origins and ends. It remains a source of value but is no longer a substitute for it. The same is true of religion. For while T. S. Eliot was to place his last chance for salvation in religious faith, in *The Recognitions* it is nothing more than a fragile scaffold of possibilities, the artificially transitive declension of the broader paradigm of a presence that is both unlikely and unlocatable. Any paternal and divine logos having been evacuated toward the perpetual precedents to which logical retrogressions lead, the absolute has fled a work in which absence reigns, where presence exists only for brief moments and in relative degrees. From *The Waste Land* to the *Quartets,* Eliot's work and the cherished themes of European modernism haunt Gaddis's novel, but they do so almost as though to mark a loss; the permanent recurrence of allusions and quotations take the form of questions more than of answers.

Based on *Recognitions,* a third-century "theological romance" attributed to Clement of Rome, Gaddis's *The Recognitions* is one of the furthest advanced bastions of modernism in American territory and goes well beyond the questions it poses. Clement's "recognitions" already explored the ties linking things and events to their origins. They were ways of identifying ultimate truths through intuition, the emptiness of signs by which they were to be transmitted being duly recognized. A paradigm of creation in general — "in God nothing is without meaning" (*Nihil cavum neque sine signo apud Deum*) says the epigraph taken from Irenaeus[13] — this work is "revisited" here in the ironic, disguised, or direct light shed by such "masters of suspicion" as Marx, Nietzsche, Freud, and Saussure.

Wyatt Gwyon is a forger. In addition to works by the masters, he forges right down to his name and his identity: he adopts Joyce's given name of Stephen, but his surname, Ashe, speaks of the ashes to which this myth has been reduced. He lives surrounded by counterfeiters and imitators. Fake surgeons for fake and deadly operations, fake relics and icons for fake saints, fake wounds and fake signs of recognition, real and fake spies, plagiarists: a mass of counterfeiters. Gide is not forgotten; his presence is acknowledged with a sly nod. Wyatt Gwyon is certainly a hero, but a hero of a very different kind since only he is fully conscious of the wild ambition of his actions. These consist in a desire to bridge through permanent regression the space separating him from the sought-after origins, origins that remain as desired and unattainable as those fathers for whom the characters have often renounced their search, or whom they fail to meet when the opportunity arises. Wyatt is alone in understanding that all attempts to return to the sources are irreducible, that there is no original, but always and forever copies and repetitions, that there is only the *pharmakon*,[14] as Derrida and Socrates would say, "a supplement," a poisonous extra. Any imitation and downstream repetition are already a kind of false advertising; what is more, it becomes ontologically impossible to identify the real goods. According to Valéry:

What differentiates a forged bank note from a genuine one depends solely on the forger. At the trial of a man accused of forgery two bills bearing the same number lay on the judge's table and it was quite impossible to detect any difference between them. "What am I charged with?" the man asked. "Where is the *corpus delicti?*"[15]

In his youth, Wyatt Gwyon copied Bosch's *Seven Deadly Sins* and sold the painting to pay for art lessons. Exploited by unscrupulous merchants who ask him for fake Memlings, fake van Eycks, and fake van der Goeses, he renounces creation and ends up scraping off the layers of paint that cover the "original" frescoes in a convent so as to leave only the surface of the stone. The sought-after originality is not invention but the rediscovery of what will later be called the "always already there." The desire for originality, that "romantic affliction," ignores the fact that all work, all figuration and representation, is already a copy. What is more, the world in which Wyatt lives, our world, is a world devalued by the entropic practice of imitation and the double. Between a "real" rendered hypothetical by the perfection of copies and an art whose ontological solidity is unsettled by reproduction, questions of value are brutally raised. (Walter Benjamin can also be found within the secret crowds of quotations and references murmuring through the novel.)

In a world from which transcendence has fled, money inserts itself somewhere between existential value and alienating value, acts as an agent in the destruction of all truth between art and technology, interposing itself between the merchant and the artist. After the Age of Faith and the Age of Reason, we have entered, we are told by the Mr. Pivner of the book, the Age of Advertising in which the sign is triumphant. What do truths matter if their external signs replace them? True alchemy, that of the Great Work to which Clement referred, redeemed the operator more than his objects. For this has been substituted the metamorphosis of the real into merchandise, and all value seeks to ground itself in exchange and to dissolve there. In the absence of any transcendent intervention that would reinstate with each step the value of the act or of the (artistic) object, there is only doubling, repetition, restatement, and stammering, the dissolution of being into appearance. In the novel, the polysemous monikers change frequently, identities are borrowed, values are corrupted, pregnancies are hysterical, suicides are unsuccessful, quid pro quos abound. The entire world is literally *quid pro quo* in that the One, be it Several or Plural, is constantly taken for the Other, for that long lost One, That Which Has Gone Forever. In this world on the make, who is to say where to place the reality of behavior or of perception, that of hallucination or stage setting? Where is madness to be detected and the "sane" to be found? If gold were to emerge from the crucible of the work, no touchstone would be available to prove it. In *The Recognitions,* everyone pretends, imitates, sells, and passes for. Everything communicates because everything is the same and belongs to the world of signs, but nothing is communicated any longer, since there is nothing left to communicate. If "recognition" is the intuition of a contact with the Other, with The Only Truth, there are enough pastors and doctors of religion in the previous six generations of Wyatt's family to point out the disturbing parallels afforded by comparative religion that had already led Melville into a state of doubt and had forbidden him all certainty. For this reason, some have written that, rather than the *Ulysses* of the fifties, *The Recognitions* was perhaps the *Moby-Dick* of our century.

In a work in which icons go so far as to take the place of bodies, as when Wyatt's father brings back pious images from Italy in place of his wife's corpse, the absence of Value and the absence of locatable Origin prevent the endowing of any solidity upon the signs charged to express them. Language, like the broker in paintings who places himself between the fake and the buyer, is utterly corrupt. When Esmé wants to write a poem, she reproduces Rilke's "First Duino Elegy." This is not like Pierre Ménard rewriting *Quixote*; rather, Esmé writes under the dictation of the "always there" of a language she no longer has the means to go beyond. Mythological schemata, vulgar from now on, have become mere sources of irony. And the conversations that proceed throughout the great "parties" of *The Recognitions* are nothing but noise, in terms of information theory. A depreciated language, phatic at best, parrot-like at worst, issues from the mouths of these "hollow" New York men like the stuffing and straw that bursts from Eliot's scarecrows. But this is not to be seen as an effect of the elitarian and aristocratic conviction that — "the world no longer being what it was" — the masses are unable to communicate and that only Art retains the key. In a more brutal, less idealistic, and doubtless more courageous way, what is expressed here is the post-Nietzschean sentiment that all speech is a counterfeit and pointless concert of language, a repetition, an imitation, more "wasted" than any land, of an original that never really existed. Gaddis goes as far as seeing in the "plot" of the novel itself, in the very presence of the book, just another series of counterfeits. He radically questions any attempt at a return to or a rejuvenation of a well-tempered realism, renounces the relative doubt of a modernism so unsure of its daring that it took recourse *in extremis* to what was then called "psychological" realism. At that time, as is still true today, "psychological" hinted of that which is "little known" or "hidden," and consequently, of that which "retains promise," as though the possibility of other causes, of new origins, the promise of the distant or buried presence of a more secret but nonetheless indisputable "real" might lie hidden there. Hopes such as these have gone missing in *The Recognitions*. The mannequins that gesticulate there are no longer characters and the plot is a game of mirrors that has the convulsiveness of *Citizen Kane* but with no sign of a "Rosebud" to serve as *l'arché*. Since time no longer serves as the instrument of causality, an enormous space of one thousand pages will give monstrous shape to the fiction. Chronology, consecutiveness, simultaneity, the presence or hallucination of character are rendered vague and highly problematic. Transcribing within the writing the problems and the knowledge of the imitator and the forger, Gaddis exploits a complex intertextuality, quotes from here, there, and everywhere, modifies his sources, and alters his references and allusions.

In masterful style, *The Recognitions* explores the hinterland between raw language and narrative, the possibilities offered by a narrative with its seams exposed, its errors identifiable and confessed, the schizoid dialogue of the fake and the invisible, a formal strategy that bears some resemblance to the dangerous "fusion" of contemporary energies, and that even evokes the "all over" of the pictorial realm, hostile to the hierarchies of narrativity and representation. With *JR* (1975), a new step was taken in this direction, a step toward an ever more invasive orality that would end by expelling — all except for the dashes that crowd his text — that which, the year after the publication of *The Recognitions,* Nathalie Sarraute declared no longer to be acceptable:

But even more awkward and hard to defend than indentations, dashes, colons and quotation marks are the monotonous, clumsy: "Said Jeanne," "answered Paul," with which dialogue is usually strewn; for contemporary novelists these are becoming more and more what the laws of perspective had become for painters just before Cubism: no longer a necessity, but a cumbersome convention.[16]

It could be said that, having emerged from and been shaped by modernism, Gaddis and Hawkes are at once its logical and necessary extensions and the instruments of its interrogation. Inheritors of its unstable certainties, they use them thematically to undermine their last formal prop, blazing new trails along the way. If the well from which Gaddis draws is a modernist one, the implications of his stemming of the philosophical stream and its consequences for the form and use of language are no longer modernist at all. Modernists could rely on James Frazer, Jessie Weston, and the mythological vulgate as much as on Art to be assured of a certain Unity as last resort. But *The Recognitions,* marvelously readable in its complexity and so darkly humorous, brings to mind Derrida's *Dissemination,* "Plato's Pharmacy" most of all. Starting from the key metaphor of Art where modernism ultimately took refuge, Gaddis, without denying it, cuts it loose, severs the metaphysical ties that linked it to the Origin and sets it adrift for the reader. "Practice," Derrida would say, "of the *graft* without a body proper, of the *skew* without a straight line, of the *bias* without a front."[17] In the novel, the capital *A* in Art takes on the elusive quality of the letter on Hester Prynne's dress; Wyatt Gwyon's fate also reminds us of another of Hawthorne's works, "The Minister's Black Veil."

To return to the novel's title, we could say, along with Stanley Elkin, that for Gaddis (as well as for Hawkes) imagination has become less a process of invention than of recognition.[18] According to Otto Pivner, when it comes to originality, "the cast" is always there.

John Hawkes: Visionary Realism

. . . So much there in fact that they have become obstacles, according to Hawkes, who would go on to say that he "started to write fiction" on the assumption that "the true enemies of the novel were plot, character, and theme," and that having consequently abandoned these well-known manners of approaching fiction, "totality of vision and structure was all that remained."[19] In fact, this declaration of war preceded the writing of *The Cannibal* (1949) and most of his later work would nuance this provocative statement that stood for his personal poetics. Just like Gaddis, Hawkes initiated in this great novel a rupture of primary importance.

What makes *The Cannibal* a significant work, along with the short works immediately following it ("Death of an Airman," "Charivari" in 1950, "The Owl" and "The Goose on the Grave" in 1954), is their avowed refusal of conventional realism that affects both the form and the texture of the narrative. Flannery O'Connor had already spoken of a "realism of distances"; Hawkes, a great admirer, borrows her gothic tonalities and her effective wedding of the comic to the horrific. He is the practitioner of a visionary realism that breaks with traditional mimesis at the surface level, even as an attempt at a "realism of depths."

On first reading, the narrative could appear to be historical; and it figures in a certain way among "postwar novels" through its evocation of Germany's fate at the beginning of the first world conflict and at the end of the second. But a world of literature separates it from Norman Mailer's *The Naked and the Dead* and from James Jones's *From Here to Eternity*. Hawkes had no more knowledge of Germany when he wrote the novel than he did of England when he used it as a parodic backdrop to his novel *The Lime Twig*, and although he had worked as an ambulance driver during the Second World War, the Germany of the novel is a purely phantasmal product, the field of an imaginary exploration of archaic obsessions, and of images of horror that owe more to the most profound fears of humankind than to any sort of "testimony." The dislocated chronology, with the novel's division into sections lacking temporal sequentiality, assures no continuity whatsoever. As in his work to follow, recurrences, echoes, parallel images, and iconic doubling assure the coherence and solidity of the structure as much as the configuration of the "characters," who often remain nameless and serve only as a geometric network of metaphors and comparisons. Much more than a discursive narrative, what takes shape along the way is a succession of chains, "nucleations," and clouds of images by means of a rhythm and rhetoric striving to create, through systematic use of negation, an ambiguous regime of enunciation, a taut and tense writing that privileges the dual and the compound, precluding all possibility of a "realist" reading. Time, carefully contained within the section titles, is all but dismissed by a narrative relentlessly expressed in the past; space is relegated to one scene — the location of the small town of Spitzen-on-the-Dein is not specified — and to a minimal and symbolic topography. Everything, from the collapse of means of communication to the absurd messages prepared for release by the Nazi narrator Zizendorf, bespeaks entropy, death, and desolation, while Hawkes never authorizes the reader to breach the cold distance that his writing sets up between abomination and himself.

It has been said that Hawkes describes his "landscape of nightmare" (Baumbach) as though through a pane of glass. Suffice it to say that the modes of implication for the reader are not the same as those found in the literature that Julien Gracq qualified as one that "aims for the gut." We could also compare Hawkes's point of view with that of Styron, both fascinated by violence, yet proposing at approximately the same time two entirely different manners of expressing it. While Styron attempts to follow in the footsteps of the modernists by moderating violence through reassuringly mythical terms in *Lie Down in Darkness* (1951), Hawkes breaks with classical generic distinctions between prose and poetry, projecting violence into the realm of the surreal and the hallucinatory in *The Cannibal*. Above all else, Hawkes is a poet in his fiction. Far from analytic psychologism, he channels directly into his prose the monstrous forms produced by psyches assailed by horror. The impossibility of *speaking* this horror, metaphorically translated in the book by diverse figures of impotence, aphasia, and mutilation, as well as by the annihilation of the means of communication, forces a turn toward a type of direct oneiric expression. Composed of displacements and condensations, Hawkes's prose refutes the superficial logic of "realism" and affirms that, following the model of poetry, his fiction is "an exclamation of psychic materials which come to the writer all readily distorted, prefigured in that nightly inner schism between the rational and the absurd."[20]

If, as Wallace Stevens claimed, writing is a form of internal violence that serves as a counterbalance for external violence, then Hawkes's writing is the site of this remarkable equilibrium, recognizable in each line and word of a text that sets up its vague referents only to allow them to be done in by its rhetoric. If language, in Hawkes's eyes, has a potential for representation, then it must — by the sheer force of a style immediately recognizable in its meticulously crafted outpourings — be used to "render concrete the intangible" and not to "render" the real such as it presents itself to the senses. For Hawkes, the novel must "assume a significant shape and objectify the terrifying similarity between the unconscious desires of the solitary man and the disruptive needs of the visible world."[21] The narrative's validity resides in its capacity to respond to the demands of the drives that made it necessary in the first place. The "proof" of the dream, to parody an old English culinary adage (since, after all, our author so masterfully handles oxymorons!), would be then "in its writing." "Imagination is the only thing that matters and one's language is its channel . . . fiction outdoes dreams by its coherence, its power, its ability to *really* represent what we are" (italics mine).[22] But, and this is a vital distinction, "the reality that a writer would discern before he begins to write is of no interest to me. I do not trust those who believe they know what reality is."[23]

Heir to a great number of moderns whom he admires — Nathanael West's sharp surrealism and puppet characters, Djuna Barnes's baroque imaginary, Faulkner's fascinating fluid oneirism — John Hawkes goes further than they, responding in advance to objections formulated by Nathalie Sarraute in 1956:

But how could a novelist free himself from the necessity of having a subject, characters and a plot? For no matter how hard he tried to isolate the fragment of reality that he was striving to grasp, he could not keep it from integrating with some character whose familiar figure presented in simple, precise lines, the practiced eye of the reader would immediately reconstitute and rig out with a "personality," in which he would recognize one of the types he so relishes and which, by virtue of its very true-to-nature, "live" aspect, would absorb most of his attention. In fact, however the author may try to maintain this character in a motionless state, in order to concentrate his own and the reader's attention on the barely perceptible tremors in which it seems to him that the reality he would like to disclose has taken refuge, he will not succeed in keeping it from moving just enough for the reader to see in its movements a plot whose ins and outs he will follow with curiosity, while impatiently awaiting the ending.[24]

In order to reintegrate the parodic dimension he wished to confer upon his novels, Hawkes gradually distanced himself from his iconoclastic declarations in subsequent works. But it remains nonetheless true that in projecting with great poetic flashes interior landscapes born of fascination and disgust onto the page, Hawkes does not allow character, setting, or plot to become disentangled from the imaginary field that makes them equals, hierarchized or framed according to the norms of the real. In *The Lime Twig*, Hawkes feels liberated enough from accepted categories to kill off his narrator by the end of the first chapter. To the extent that "the unaccountable is the only key to inner life, past life, future life," as *The Passion Artist* says,[25] the lime-twig for phantasms that are his sentences, his paragraphs, and his pages always makes the reader return to his dreams and obsessions rather than to a real that cannot be grasped through the usual mode of decoding, constantly hindered by the writing; a real that no longer allows itself to be recounted and that gropingly marks out its path.

Certainly, if it were not for *The Recognitions* there would be no Thomas Pynchon, and if not for Hawkes, there would be no Robert Steiner, nor, possibly, Toby Olson. While the realism of the forties and fifties still predominated, Gaddis and Hawkes, themselves inheritors of an antirealist tradition (Hawthorne's romance and Poe's phantasmagoria for the one;

West, O'Connor, and Barnes for the other), enrich the "tradition of rupture" within American literature. At first they remained unknown, clandestinely putting their mark on a decade dominated by others. With the coming of the sixties, their immense stature imposed itself. With their shadow looming threateningly over other lesser talents, they were made the objects of a cult, but from a distance.

Chapter 3
Revisions

"The poet should prefer probable impossibilities to improbable possibilities."[1] Had he witnessed the 1960s, Aristotle might have been compelled to revise his precepts. What happens, in effect, to the relationship between the possible and the probable, when "reality" starts to teach earlier "fictions" a lesson or two? Or when the "improbable" becomes not merely possible but real, and the omniscient improbabilities of the everyday are substituted for the improbable possibilities of meeting up with the inhabitants of Olympus?

Language and Reality

This relationship was not qualitatively modified in one giant leap, but the times made it difficult to maintain, with events leading far away from earlier notions of the real. Around the middle of the twentieth century, profound social and material transformations altered the landscape, through the rise of industrial empires, the proliferation of technology and media, the demultiplication of social relations, and increased visibility of the structures of control. When even the extinction of the species became possible, the "presence" of "facts" was imposed in a radically different way: through a shower of quotation marks — the new plague of Egypt — raining down upon conventional terms, and with the border between the probable and the improbable starting to blur. "Events" overflowed the sphere traditionally accessible to the senses; they were diluted by the unverifiable and acquired a mode of presence new to consciousness. Like the couple of butchers in Richard Stern's work who have used up their "reality quota," by dint of handling carcasses, we are threatened with reading under "realism" only the "twisted side of things."[2]

The media shape that which they are alone in rendering perceptible. "Speaking" reality becomes more clearly than ever, etymologically, an act of "fiction" (*fingere*: to shape).[3] The Vietnam War and Watergate were full-fledged televisual events, far surpassing any B-series fiction in their violence and Machiavellianism. In order to take the measure of the neutralization and equalization of signs and means of communication as they reached their — do we dare use the term? — "maturity" in the 1960s, one has to have witnessed, from within the Midwestern heartland, the bloody, fire-filled scenes of the taking of Da Nang and Hué interspersed with commercials. The daily "body count" of the victims of Southeast Asia mixed with baseball statistics marked the absolute derealization of "information" and the new interplay of parallel metaphors. Irangate rendered the sideshows of *Dallas* or *Dynasty* somewhat mawkish; not many producers can afford to air the tape of a presidential assassination and broadcast his assassin's own murder live. In the final analysis, how much "reality" do such "events" retain? More precisely, where is the "event" located? Is it not more in the fact of its distance and its evisceration than in its avowed "actuality"? It is tempting to remark of the images and signs making up the world[4] what Einstein once said of mathematical propositions: "To the extent that mathematical propositions relate to reality, they are not certain, and to the extent that they are certain, *they do not relate to reality*." In an "America" whose linguistic creation in the fifteenth century was from the very beginning a fictionalization of the real, and which has been described by Jean Baudrillard as "cinematographic,"[5] the event exists only through mediatization and constrains writers, who gold pan the real, to adapt their art. John Barth's *The Floating Opera* (1956), a moving vaudeville presented to the gawkers sitting along the banks, inaugurated the "spectacular" presentation of the contemporary world. In *Slaughterhouse-Five* (1969), Kurt Vonnegut went so far as to invert a bombing scene, like a film rolling in reverse. Who could be surprised when, in the same novel, it is explained to small extraterrestrials that the "earthling" vision of the world is that of an eye placed at the end of a cardboard cylinder: partial, fragmentary, isolated, artificially framed? After all, don't Americans refer to television as either the "tube" or the "box"?

"Their" War

Of the many novels about Vietnam published around the end of the 1970s, it is remarkable that none met with great success, with the exception of Michael Herr's *Dispatches,* Tim O'Brien's *Going after Cacciato,* and Robert Stone's *Dog Soldiers,* each of which approached their subject indirectly and granted more attention to the war's effects than to the war itself. Realist writing could not measure up to events whose perception had already been derealized and it was ten years before Stephen Wright's *Meditations in Green* (1983) convincingly picked up the gauntlet.[6] The Civil War modified the industrial structure of the United States; the First

World War modified its economic status, changing it from a debtor to a creditor nation, with the effects of artificialization of the economic activity we have come to recognize. The Second World War changed the leadership and gave birth to the notion of the military-industrial complex. Perhaps the Vietnam War changed nothing less than the notion of the real and the possibility of its transcription. Even when observed from the scene of operations, this war called mental categories into question, as Michael Herr has shown:

> pure, manic contradiction, of the abiding reality, in some cases, of that which seemed most real, and of the utter reality, in others, of things so monstrously concrete and immediate that they could only be handled by imaginative conversion into some unreal other.[7]

For David Halberstam, "yes wasn't yes anymore, no wasn't no, and perhaps was more and more certainly perhaps."[8] The language of the battlefield, of Pentagon press conferences, and of press coverage attests to the absence of its own relation to the real.[9]

The balance of nuclear terror can induce one to hedonism and engenders distrust of any system capable of producing such horrors. By an effect of questionable logic, it also inspires a defiant attitude toward technology, science, reason, the powers-that-be in general, and beyond this, it disputes the validity of the real. "The system" becomes the code name for all that causes such exile. Thomas Pynchon's body of work stands as the most general exploration of this theme, Robert Coover's *The Origin of the Brunists* is its most compelling treatment, and Russell Banks's "The Fisherman" (in *Trailerpark*) illustrates it in a local and personalized manner. But the most eloquent title for a novel of the time just might be Joyce Carol Oates's *them,* the anonymous "them" of *"they* really got us this time," of multinational conglomerates, whose lowercase *t* banalizes its nature and universalizes its presence. Distrust is the norm regarding the army, industrial empires, the CIA, bureaucracy, and all established intellectual, moral, and sociophilosophical systems. (And yet the gurus of the sixties, the psychotherapists of the seventies, and the religious demagogues of the eighties gambled on individual salvation and all managed to profit.) Their value can be judged by their results: murderous wars, poverty, exploitation, alienation, existential dis-ease. The themes of scheming, entropy, and exile flourished during the sixties and seventies.[10] But there could no longer be literary "muckrakers," as Theodore Roosevelt had baptized writers like Frank Norris, Jack London, and Upton Sinclair, who stirred up the turn-of-the-century slime. Nor did the political or proletarian novel of the thirties and forties remain a viable form for protest. Nonfiction works and works in other media invaded the domain of ideas. Protest and proposition no longer seemed able to pass through fiction's narrow channel, lacking confidence in the words and the tools they must use, and fearing above all integration to that which they most wanted to denounce. In some ways, the fate of the postwar novel is comparable to that of painting during the rise of photography. The true and profound nature of its activity was revealed by one simple fact: the stealing of its informative function did not rob it of its justifications. At which point, one begins to realize, or at least pretends to realize, that Chardin did not paint hares out of his love for game, and that Melville was only moderately interested in whales. As Carlos Fuentes puts it, "Art is not an imitation of life, but a measure of it." The language of fiction will find its strength, then, in indirectly reflecting the suspicion weighing upon the structure of the real. Novels and short stories can no longer be "cultural documents" to the extent that we increasingly read the environment as a network of signs, signs that are readable in and of themselves, but that would be rendered immediately redundant should they be directly reproduced. Literature can no longer reflect that which remains accessible only as a reflection. Overlooking the irony hidden by Valéry within his remark, we could say along with Monsieur Teste that "the overstimulated brain, overcome by cruel treatment, necessarily produces, of itself and without knowing it, a whole modern literature."[11]

The "era of suspicion" was created as much by a modification of the real as by that of its supposed relation to language. We should not neglect, however, the literary thinking that had been carried out in Europe at an earlier date, and then, following a period of cultural latency, was continued in the United States.

It is hard to imagine novelists permitting themselves to undertake anything that would be comparable to the evasion attempted by painters when, with one blast, they blew up the entire classic system of conventions — which had come to serve less to reveal, as it once did, than to conceal what, to their eyes, was the real object of painting — abolishing subject and perspective, and wresting the spectator from the familiar appearances in which he had been accustomed to find satisfactions that had ceased to have much in common with painting.[12]

Not all American writers since 1960 have been so bold, yet this attempt represents an important characteristic of the years that interest us here. In any case, throughout this period, "transparent" literature ("see-thru" — like those tops in the sixties whose fabric guaranteed their success) gradually gave way to a kind of writing that declared its worth, as Vladimir Mayakovsky intended for "self-apparent" words. Perhaps language's lexical and syntactic ability to comfortably measure up to the world had not survived Saussure and Wittgenstein, but certainly the theoretical writings of the French New Novel tolled its death knell.

Realism had already known for some time that it was doomed by its own principles. In the nineteenth century, Samuel Butler, hardly a utopian in these matters, felt compelled to destroy chronological order in *Erewhon* for the sake of digression, and to forsake the details and the "infinite absurdities" that hindered his narrative. How many full-length portraits in "realist" texts never descend below the waist? But, beyond these earlier realizations and modernism's subsequent engagement with them, the relationship between narrative, characterization, chronology, the reader, the narrator, and the author were profoundly questioned by Ricardou, Robbe-Grillet, Sarraute, and many others, united as they were in their refusal of what Stéphane Mallarmé had termed "the old forms that poets inherit from one another like mistresses."[13] For example, Sarraute tells us that the evolution in methods of characterization "testifies"

on the part of both author and reader, to an unusually sophisticated state of mind. For not only are they both wary of the character, but through him, they are wary of each other. He had been their meeting ground, the solid base from which they could take off in a common effort toward new experiments and new discoveries. He has now become the converging point of their mutual distrust, the devastated ground on which they confront each other. And if we examine his present situation, we are tempted to conclude that it furnishes a perfect illustration of Stendhal's statement that "the genius of suspicion has appeared on the scene." We have now entered upon an age of suspicion.[14]

Valéry's celebrated marquise got angry this time and refused to go out at five o'clock for good.

The French brand of suspicion inspired various reactions in the United States, ranging from restorative attempts, to a broadening of the concept into an entire genre by means of a "So be it" that opens on to the core of our subject here. If the novel must die, fiction can and should be reborn from its ashes. Many American writers would no doubt be quick to say that the novel is quite dead, if by this we mean the literary form historically designated by the term, an inheritance from the schools of realism and naturalism, who had themselves stolen the term from the "fantasists" denounced as irresponsible by both eighteenth-century moralists and by the early Victorians. Protean by nature — as Bakhtin demonstrated — the novel's functions are too diverse for the periodical announcement of its death to prevent it from living on.[15] Its permanent death could even become part of its definition. In the United States, this particular obituary in no way discouraged the inheritors of the "romance," a form relatively unencumbered by the norms in effect elsewhere, nor did it dismay those writers for whom Joyce and Beckett symbolized an innovation that could no longer be ignored. Charles Newman has claimed that this other heritage insists that fiction no longer be considered a machine for producing narratives, but that it be seen as "the multiple voices of thought and of verbal innovation."[16] Just as *Don Quixote* arose from the ashes of the novels of chivalry that had run their course, contemporary American fiction, vigorous as ever, phoenixed out of the novel's ruins. While the form had been challenged by the New Novelists, American writers felt under no obligation to follow the same French itinerary. Strivings toward the universal, toward coherence and the ineluctable linkages of causality could not outlive the overriding sense of precariousness, impotence, unreality, and opaqueness that characterized the period inaugurated by the 1960s. I will group the various creative reactions to this new situation under half a dozen headings.

Moralisms

The first reaction consists of a sharp temptation to analyze the new situation, to attempt to understand and explain it, or else to criticize it and call for a return to a supposedly less polluted era. The detached humor of John Cheever's novels (*The Wapshot Chronicle, Bullet Park*) and short stories (*The World of Apples*) dissimulates their stinging denunciation of the changing times under the gentle tones of the leisured and cultivated New England bourgeoisie. Cheever's new generations live in a world that no longer has much to do with the semirural universe in which the narratives are set. The apple of the American dream is riddled with worms: a dream where droll situations arise from the confrontation of a familiar world on its way out with another, more absurd one, from which good old American-style values are disappearing, and where only a "geometry of love" remains, a golden patina of towns of nostalgia where the light is fading. The delicate lyricism of Cheever's stories, in which eccentricity comes to be replaced by madness and death as the years go by, scans the changes of their time, and attempts to capture without too much bitterness the remains of an existence in which tenderness, love, and good humor reigned among values. As villages were slowly swallowed up by suburbia, Cheever's imaginary grew darker, finding within itself the resources that reality could no longer supply. But this also led to a more somber place, where one could only be redeemed by barely credible epiphanies, such as that experienced by the aged Asa Bascomb in *The World of Apples*. No matter how seductive such moments may be, this lightness tends toward mannerism, and, after a while, superannuated perfumes will give you a headache.

Or we can follow the intermingling of Eros and Thanatos straight to the heart of the suburbs in a less evasive way. For thirty years, John Updike has pursued a talented dissection of the misbegotten lives of suburbanites through his hero's evolution in *Rabbit, Run* (1960), *Rabbit Redux* (1971), *Rabbit Is Rich* (1981), and *Rabbit at Rest* (1990). As a Babbitt for modern times, but one whose sophistication and intelligence spare him the more

cruel traits of Sinclair Lewis's symbolic middle-class hero, Harry Angstrom has a name that serves unkind notice of his smallness, while his
present-day chronicles betray his imprisonment within an immediacy
lacking in perspective. John Updike walks his alter egos, Angstrom and
Bech, through the polite jungle of East Coast suburbia. The vein is humanist, the tone ironic, the sentences sculpted. Beyond the (too?) frequent descriptions of highly eroticized liaisons, the quest is meant to be
quasi-theological, and it attempts to reconstruct some religious sense
from the monotonous horizontalness of secular affairs. Karl Barth and
Paul Tillich are placed in epigraph to these novels of manners, in which
we are constantly shown the unease of the "average sensual man," disori-
ented by the absence of a perspective that his life of material comfort cannot provide. Reading John Updike, one cannot escape the feeling of repetition and reworking that indicates the author's obsessions. For, while
remarkable stylistic work allows Updike somewhat to undercut the vacu-
ous discourse that fills his hollow characters, and while his work is not
entirely lacking in formal aspects that allow him to transcribe, that is, to
resolve aesthetically the imbalance between the desirable and the real,
Updike's work is more truly concerned with morality. His recourse to the
structuring myth, his partial loyalty to an old pastoral vision, his efforts to
transcend aesthetics toward the ethical and the religious (Kierkegaard's
presence can be felt here) practically make of him the archetype of the
modernist writer. But years of collaboration with the *New Yorker* have too
often led him to opt for "catchy" scenes and for a repetitive, trivial set of
topics over the creation of existential propositions that could counterbalance the flat, faded quality of the everyday. In so doing, Updike has
reached a broader public, but his work has lost some of its strength. As a
moralist, he has taken on a moralist's measures, yet, in order to be more
widely heard, he has reduced the potential complexities of his art. Beyond the lovely yet slightly forced stylistic effects of an obviously talented
writer, beyond the attractions of the works' solidly confident narration,
we remain in the aesthetic of "the message." The work-as-message then
becomes part of the surrounding messages that it was meant to oppose,
but it has not been granted the formal means of breaking down their
sophistication. Slickness answers coldness, but coldness does not mind.

One might also see Malamud as a moralist, since he too attempts a
moral righting of affairs in an urban setting. While he arms himself with
formal tools that are sometimes more interesting than those employed by
Updike, he does not manage to untangle his work from an already obsolescent aesthetic. If *Pictures of Fidelman* (1969) takes up the thematic of
The Recognitions in a more accessible mode, *The Natural* (1952) recycles
the American pastoral with reference to the Waste Land, and, as in *The*

Tenants (1971), certain critical analyses of the social evils from which America is perceived to be suffering can be annoyingly didactic. Indeed, didacticism and vituperation are precisely what Saul Bellow appears to have resorted to of late, to the point of publishing diatribes and pamphlets. Once old Sammler's Babylon, "la Reine aux fesses cascadantes,"[17] was no longer favored by the man whose imaginary and language effectively allowed him to smuggle his moral vision into the 1950s, in works like *Dangling Man, The Victim, Henderson the Rain King, The Adventures of Augie March,* Bellow decided to send, via *Herzog,* some threatening letters to people of influence and to philosophers in order to breathe new life into the times. But when Babylon paid no heed, he moved on to the imprecations of *Mr. Sammler's Planet, Humboldt's Gift, The Dean's December,* titles whose genitives suggest some kind of possession of the truth. These novels are the work of a bitter, angry man more than of a novelist who trusts his techniques and his impact. Faced with the crisis of language, Bellow denies it; and his self-confident writing does not seem to allow that the problem may lie elsewhere than in phenomena. This is crisis management through repression.

Holy anger can be an understandable response, but mockery is less pleasant. This is the mode favored by Gore Vidal, whose article "American Plastic: The Matter of Fiction" tried to silence efforts made, in the wake of the New Novel, to ward off or bypass suspicion.[18] Vidal himself only suspects such as espouse suspicion: he berates intellectuals engaged in restoring the "Dark Ages" (*sic*), and, in a demagogic move, he distinguishes between what he terms "Public" versus "University" novels. With great disdain, he places in the latter category writers who have tried to replenish the art of fiction, Barthes's children, all, fallen victim to the "French Pox" from Barth to Barthelme, and Gass to Pynchon. It is not entirely clear what Vidal thinks fiction ought to be, other than that which leads to social success, as demonstrated by the little Washingtonian novels in which the artist appears to believe that by dealing with the "big time" one is able to climb upward to Gotha. The imaginary and technical experimentation found in *Myra Breckenridge* (1968) has long since disappeared from the production of a writer who believes there is a "decent, respectable" way of doing things, and who is evidently quite unable to see just where the problem might lie.

With their various approaches, interests, and qualities, the conservative denunciations of social and linguistic evolution in no way characterize the period. It would be silly to deny that American fiction was *simultaneously* made up of supporters of past traditions alongside those of innovation. But the literary picture of the 1960s, and of the 1970s in particular, mostly consists of two other branches. Our second gathering is double then: on the one hand, it could be defined as that of contestation and derision, on the other as that of absurdist denunciation, although these two aspects often intermingle and intersect.

Derision

Derision may appear under two distinct guises. As descendants of Salinger as well as of Kerouac, the writers most characteristic of the sixties created marginal, slightly lost characters, gentle dreamers, or hardened iconoclasts in search of themselves in a world that is no longer their own, seizing every possible occasion to distinguish themselves from what Flaubert would have been quick to call the "turdiform bourgeois."[19] Aside from Pynchon (*V*), who employs the contemporary mess and historical bric-a-brac toward more intellectual and precise ends, a significant number of fictional characters of our period—and in particular of its first decade—follow in Holden Caulfield's footsteps across the urban crossroads or traverse the landscape in the manner of Sal Paradise. They represent their own variant on walking madness, and defy conventions on principle. From Caulfield, they have inherited a new spoken language and from Neal Cassady—the "secret hero" of *On the Road* and "Howl" — an undeniable case of wanderlust and the jitters. In Richard Fariña's *Been Down So Long, It Looks Like Up to Me,* Gnossos Pappadopoulis spends the time that separates him from his enlistment getting high on mescaline; a failed offspring of Lyndon Johnson's "Great Society," he turns from one pretty girl to another, from the New Left to doubtful gurus. Haight-Ashbury lies in the not so distant future, but North Beach has already come and gone. In Brautigan's *A Confederate General from Big Sur,* Jesse, who also comes from the San Francisco Bay area, hooks up illegally to the city's gas lines in a surprising reprise of the Dostoevskian theme of the underground before going down to Big Sur to fight frogs and to count the commas in Ecclesiastes. Seeing stupid and prevalent pigeons as the comic image of a world off-balance and proud of it, Jonathan distributes plentiful kicks and metaphorically submits the society around him to the same brutal treatment, in David Boyer's *The Sidelong Glances of a Pigeon Kicker.* Shoplifting becomes an art, asking the local watchmaker to weigh a dead ant becomes a necessity, television becomes a kind of background noise representative of the surrounding world, and garbage cans become a source of knowledge. The derision of the sixties happily leans toward a practical surrealism, a kind of neo-Dada that would later be taken up by the characters of Thomas McGuane or those in T. Coraghessan Boyle's *The Descent of Man* and *Budding Prospects,* neo-picaros who, rather than wanting to enter society, dream only of escaping it. Spoken language had definitively won the right to appear in fiction in its most uncontrolled forms, and did just that in Peter Keller's narrative in *The Breaks* (Richard Price), a hilarious novel of initiation in which the allusion to Salinger is explicit. On the one hand, the hero's shock with the outside world causes a number of spiritual bruises. On the other hand, William Fisher's wild hornpipe dance in Todd McEwen's *Fisher's Hornpipe* really does bring him to bang his head against several Bostonian walls, earning him some very real bruises. Among the number of threats weighing on the happiness of humanity within these two books, one should include the foreseeable shortage of doughnuts and plastic toys. A dizzying perspective on values, indeed . . .

Escape can be managed within a more or less livable hedonism, just as one's contacts with the world can be more or less brutal. But the image of society suffers under the onslaught of mad, destructive gazes such as these. Most of the tricks played on their surroundings by these pranksters, these absurd jokers, are as painful as the deadened slaps inflicted by Coco the Clown, blows that cause his white-faced partner more sadness than physical pain. Melville's "Confidence Man" has been succeeded by sympathetic, parasitic rogues, buffoons of a new genre whom the king can no longer tolerate. Escape can also occur through space. In McGuane's *The Bushwhacked Piano,* when Payne pretends to go inspect his assortment of orange bat-traps on his motorcycle, it is merely a pretext for speed and for putting as much distance as possible between himself and the centers of population in which no obvious quests remain. A sign ahead of its time, the sign placed on the front of the bus full of hippies called the Merry Pranksters — a bus driven by none other than Cassady if we are to believe Tom Wolfe's *The Electric Kool-Aid Acid Test* — already read: "Further." An appropriate linguistic and literary equivalent had to be found to express the distance that these individuals sought to put between themselves and society. It comes as no surprise then that these neopicaresque novels are dominated by a spoken language appropriate to the dissidents' world, and by metaphors in which the distance between tenor and vehicle grows larger, until it confers upon the images total autonomy from the real. In William Kotzwinkle's *The Fan Man,* Horse Badorties's speech is constructed "by the mile" as the sole substance of his being. As a systematic explorer of the "parareal," Brautigan writes, "his eyes were like the shoestrings of a harpsichord."[20] In *Even Cowgirls Get the Blues,* Tom Robbins's reigning images proclaim that the only way to translate exile is through similar semantic distances: "On the fifth morning, as the Indian summer sun popped up from behind the hills like a hyperthyroid Boy Scout, burning to do good deeds . . ." or "Amoebae leave no fossils. They haven't any bones. (No teeth, no belt buckles, no wedding rings.)"[21] In *Trout Fishing in America,* Brautigan declares that "language does not leave fossils, at least not until it has become written."[22] The fear of fixity, of enclosure, and of recuperation by the "system" appears in all examples. Once distanced from the demands of the real and of conventional narration, metaphor can become a productive mode in itself. Thus, the verbal picaresque of "athletes of the mouth" joins the traditional picaresque, each in search of the same kind of distance.[23]

Humor, irony, derision. These more or less harmless madnesses are set up to oppose the absolute folly of the world. The absurd, as Nathalie Sarraute has noted, rushes to the rescue of psychological analysis from its failures. In the United States, a literary environment that also tends to bog down in the psychological, *homo absurdus* "therefore, was Noah's dove, the messenger of deliverance."[24] The list of techniques employed must also include our second axis of deviation, that is, caricature, parody, the fantastic, and excess, all elements capable of replacing for language these numerous "surds" whose irrational existence cannot be proven in mathematics. The groping attempt to represent an analyzable real has been replaced by a formal illustration of the apparent absence of all rational law governing society and universe, as well as of the individual's divorce from society. Ken Kesey's *One Flew Over the Cuckoo's Nest* merrily demonstrates that madness does not merely lie within asylum walls. In order to effect a radical substitution of point of view, Philip Roth's defamiliarization techniques in *The Breast* recall the earlier cases of Tolstoy's horse and Gogol's nose. In works by Vonnegut and B. J. Friedman, gallows humor abounds, a more frequent and popular option than parody. Joseph Heller's *Catch-22* is most certainly the cult novel of the time; its title fine-tuned the adjective "Kafkaesque," a modifier that had been rendered banal by a generation in need of defining its own brand of discontent. "Catch-22" is the name for an army rule stipulating that one must be in good mental health to want to avoid combat, but, at the same time, one must also be termed unstable in order to have a shot at being discharged. The literary flights into parody and pure imagination illustrate the fact that the absurd has come to represent reality. The reworking of familiar plots, hijacking of genres, and ironic transcription of mediatic discourses and institutions are just so many strategies wielded to rout the various conspiracies at work (cosmic for Vonnegut, political for Reed, discursive for Barthelme, Brautigan, and Coover, technological for Pynchon), conspiracies whose presence is expressed by an excess of meaning, not as a way of exposing the absurd but of emphasizing the total absence of meaning. Excessive control, conflict, and incoherence are contrasted with the free life of the imagination by these "priests of the possible"[25] who haunt the margins of the real, deforming it in some grotesque manner, or merely playing with its capacities. This is commando literature.

Exhaustion?

However, a third reaction to language's perceived divorce from the real is also apparent. The increase in stylistic research too quickly baptized as "formalist" by critics for whom obedience to conventional forms goes without saying soon found its most convincing practitioners and its most lucid theorists. It was believed that John Barth's famous essay on the "literature of exhaustion" signaled the impossibility of any viable engagement in the writing of fiction.[26] But there was "no need to despair." The sheer abundance of Barth's own literary production would have sufficed as proof of this. As long ago as 1782, Samuel Johnson had complained that with "Pope dead, Swift dead, Gray dead," there was "nothing to look forward to." And in the eighteenth century, André Chénier had written that poetry "laughs when, in his emptiness, an oppressed author / complains that everything has been said and thought."[27] In 1925, José Ortega y Gasset declared that the novel was no longer a mine worth exploiting. Finally, Barth quotes a particular scribe, author of a papyrus preceding the birth of Christ by two thousand years, who despaired of having no new words, no new feelings to express, no unheard sentences to compose.[28]

Nor has our own time lacked Cassandras willing to spread the word that the novel had died sometime around the beginning of the period studied here: proclaiming either that the world's incoherence could no longer be transcribed in such a form, that all of the variants had already been used, or that there was no longer anyone with the creative and imaginative strength needed to evoke a new situation that could not be encompassed by any effort at totalization. The incoherence of the time could no longer be contained within models that dated from more self-assured periods: most means of expression had found their endpoint in *Finnegans Wake*, Beckett's asymptotes, and in the self-devouring fictions of Borges. Nevertheless, a certain idea stolen from André Gide lived on, according to which "incoherence is preferable to an order that deforms," as accompaniment to the Beckettian belief that, since the reality of the individual is in itself incoherent, it should be "expressed incoherently." Beyond suspicion, and beyond the trinity of prohibitions against any recourse to "history," entertainment, or to any reality other than that of consciousness and of language, it remained possible to conceive of a kind of fiction that would be an addition to the real rather than a reflection of reality. In a collection whose title, *The Death of the Novel and Other Stories*, is both provocative and programmatic, Ronald Sukenick argues that "[i]f reality exists, it doesn't do so *a priori*, but only to be put together. Thus one might say reality is an activity, of which literature is part, an important part, but one among many."[29] Such a view extends a formula for novelistic renewal dating back to Cervantes and others, for whom the disintegration and impracticality of existing forms provided compost for new growth. And one could take heart upon rereading the following in H. G. Wells: "The important point which I tried to argue with Henry James was that the novel of completely consistent characterization arranged beautifully in a story and painted deep and round and solid, no more exhausts the possibilities of the novel, than the art of Velázquez exhausts the possibilities of the painted picture."[30] In other words, beyond the flight of the subject in the *Meniñas,* and beyond the modernist vogue for specular narratives, there remained vast territories, those of a fiction that

often ignores old forms, dispenses with plot, characterization, and verisimilitude, slurs the distinction between prose and poetry, between fiction and autobiography or history, makes use of collage, employs new means of narrative order and even redefines the relation of print to page . . . communicates the sense of an exploration to discover new forms that better suit the individual artist.[31]

While it may be that Scheherazade, a character much favored by John Barth, did not really have anything left to say and had finally run out of stories, this did not keep her from talking, nor, as Philip Stevick has noted, did it prevent the king from listening.[32]

One might question the usefulness and validity of the notion of "the postmodern."[33] Perhaps this third reaction to epistemological dislocations, and to social and aesthetic mutations, could be better described by the expression "postrealist." Ronald Sukenick, whose competence as a theorist often exceeds his novelistic skills, develops the implications in this way:

Realist fiction presupposed chronological time as the medium of a plotted narrative, an irreducible individual psyche as the subject of its characterization, and, above all, the ultimate, concrete reality of things as the object and rationale of its description. In the world of post-realism, however, all of these absolutes have become absolutely problematic.[34]

Even after we allow for the provocative radicalism of such declarations, the belief that gave rise to them is, nonetheless, the one most widely shared in the wake of the New Novel. Born into suspicion, Pascal Quignard has a character in *Carus* express it in this way:

I took the liberty of stating — in a fairly general way — that, if language had done us any harm through these words, it had done so only through meaning. That, by itself, it fooled no one. With the exception of boredom. That, in this sense, it dizzied us in a rather lovely way. However, language did become a most dangerous practice as soon as it spoke of a truth in which it somehow partook, or else again, as it fed the illusion of its ability to reveal or transmit something, or by accrediting the idea of an unbelievable reference to an object of some kind or to an event somehow located outside itself.[35]

Convinced of these dangers and determined to renounce novelistic conventions, some tried to adapt to the expectations of the new era by prolonging those of modernist fiction, forsaking either the desire for totalization or the aspiration for transcendence contained therein. "Facts," says one of Grace Paley's characters, "not necessarily the *truth*."[36]

As a result of this realization, fiction becomes a matter of supplementing the world as it is, of the "truth of the page," of discontinuity, fragmentation, and the deconstruction of the real. Each of these elements call for "an erotics of art," to use Susan Sontag's expression in *Against Interpretation*,[37] rather than for games involving formal prescriptions or cognitive demands. "We live in language," Sukenick claims, "and only writers are free."[38] In 1971, in a novel of that title, Gilbert Sorrentino called for the fictional development of something William Carlos Williams had previously termed the "imaginative qualities of actual things."[39] Patterns and internal structuration are constructed as a line of defense against external discursive systems, while imagination and writing are employed to give birth to the form rather than to serve or illustrate pre-established models. Mimesis could no longer be what it used to be. Why use chapters when life itself does away with limits and regularity? Why burden our reading with artificial plots when happenstance persuades us to doubt teleological visions? Why introduce argumentation and dialogue into an absurd environment inhabited by pseudo-subjects who have lost the ability to communicate? Why have recourse to inherited rhetoric when the modes governing discursive organization have been confiscated?

In "The Explanation," Barthelme suggests that "the content of reason is rhetoric" and that "rhetoric is preserved by our elected representatives. In the fat of their head."[40] In the "Silence" section of "Paraguay" he ironically proposes another line of defense:

The softening of language usually lamented as a falling off from former practice is in fact a clear response to the proliferation of surfaces and stimuli. Imprecise sentences lessen the strain of close tolerances.[41]

Beyond the questioning of modernist principles and the demolitions performed by the New Novel in the name of suspicion, American fiction writers gathered together material into significant forms, without, for all that, labeling their enterprise. Similar to the making of jazz and the new styles of painting exploding around them, fiction writers "improvise [their] art as they improvise [their] lives. No hysterical imposition of meaning."[42] In order to combat the surrounding entropy and debris, they launched what Tony Tanner called "Operation Unjunk." Feeling his way along, George Chambers put it thus:

Something about the only kind of novel possible being pieces of real, of the real; language, experience as it happens? Rather than what? Invention? The imposition of some 'order' on the 'material'?[43]

In John Hawkes's words, "Design and debris, I thrive on it."[44] Robert Coover flushes the forms out from beneath the jumble of myths in order to reroute and combat them. The astonishingly different directions that have been taken as part of this search for new suitable forms will be discussed in subsequent chapters.

If by "formalism" we mean the passionate exploration of the means by which fiction can create other modes of understanding the world, remaining faithful to its etymology in actually "giving form," rather than the dry, superficial activity divorced from all preoccupation with the real that the term usually evokes, then "formalism" was the word and it could provide the world with the definition it sought. Jeremy Bentham's "necessary fictions" and Immanuel Kant's "regulative ideas" having been challenged, contemporary American fiction set itself the double task of ordering a "real" that would escape all previous models and of providing a number of pleasures too often forsaken by the New Novel in its dry bareness. The extent to which this endeavor has succeeded will not be known until some time in the future. For now, as stated by Sukenick, one of the founders of the Fiction Collective of Brooklyn, "we write beyond any definition of form"

because we believe that fiction is always in the process of defining itself. Not the form but the imaginative process that creates the form is exemplary. Form is the embodiment, the temporary context of the imagination, an embodiment that is the consequence of the questioning of form by the imagination. For the fiction of the seventies, this point of view resulted in a proliferation and variety of formal options. . . . In a world that pushes constantly in the direction of the impersonal and systematic we need fiction (and criticism) that is subversively personal and unsystematic.[45]

In less careful terms, Ishmael Reed throws the issue wide open:

What's your beef with me Bo Shmo, what if I write circuses? No one says a novel has to be one thing. It can be anything it wants to be, a vaudeville show, the six o'clock news, the mumblings of wild men saddled by demons.[46]

It would be an understatement to say that claims such as these were cause for debate. To give an idea of the polemics they provoked, I will focus on three elements concerning morals, culture, and literature itself.

Fiction as Morals?

Like those who supported the Soviet proletarian novel in the 1930s, some critics were quick to voice their protest against the "unacceptable novel" that seemed to have abandoned all sense of its social and moral responsibilities. Long columns were filled with descriptive terms such as "self-important," "mocking," and "useless." Writers were denounced as either irresponsible narcissists or as buffoons of no interest beyond the temporary and unjustified fads that they generated. Employing Aristotelian principles in their least supple interpretation, John Gardner launched a particularly violent attack on innovative fiction in *On Moral Fiction* (1977), a work that crystallized into sharp cutting blades the reproaches leveled against the new fiction from within the most conservative critical domains. Gardner, himself a novelist, espoused a Manichean view of art that many have deemed unworthy of a cultured intellectual concerned with the honest debate of ideas.[47] For him, as for Bellow—who stands as the book's final reference—fiction must be "moral." It must try to improve reality rather than excoriate it; it must attempt, above all, to ward off the decay of man and society, chaos, death, and entropy. According to Gardner, much of contemporary fiction glorifies the trivial and debases the culture and civilization from which fiction sprang. Content with cynicism and self-satisfaction, it accepts and even wallows in the bleakness of the times. Somewhat unfairly, Gardner contrasts works by writers of the most antirealist fiction with works by Homer, Shakespeare, and Tolstoy. He suggests—as a consistent idealist—that the "bad art" of the period is not engendered by the state of society but that, on the contrary, it in fact causes society's decline. Fascinated by myths, which in turn influence his fiction, he claims that "real art creates myths a society can live instead of die by, and clearly our society is in need of such myths."[48] The product of a somewhat dated humanism and of his puritanical heritage, Gardner's criticism hardly convinces the reader; it banks too heavily on obvious excesses, while very weakly confronting the most convincing contemporary fiction.

At the very least, Gardner's work forced its critics to explain themselves. During a debate with Gardner in Cincinnati, William Gass thus argued that Gardner was nonetheless affirming that a writer is only accountable for the integrity of his works to his own imagination. Pushed to qualify his argument, Gardner amended his jarring declarations over time until his accidental death in 1982. He increasingly referred to a number of exceptions, eventually describing Gass, for example, as a "closet moralist." What might now be considered a dated and uninteresting debate permits us to clarify two major lines of thinking.

The first, whose moral direction Gardner ascribed to Gass, affirms the writer's duties to language and locates art's deepest morality at the heart of the linguistic creativity of which fiction is capable. Such an undertaking calls for: the conquering of new novelistic spaces able to expand our ways of knowing; demystifying overly transparent approaches to the effects of language; arming the reader against the effects of contemporary myths whose ability to alienate decreases as soon as their nature and mode of functioning is revealed. This is the realm in which resides the greatness of writers such as John Barth, Robert Coover, and Robert Steiner. The second line of thinking attempts to bring the novel closer to a "realism" that, as we will see, no longer shares the traits of earlier, obsolete, or dated practices. Until 1988, this tendency was best exemplified by Raymond Carver, a former student of Gardner's who also died before his time.[49]

The Me Cult?

Written from an entirely different perspective, Christopher Lasch's *The Culture of Narcissism* (1979) nonetheless mirrors the reservations of the first line of thinking discussed above. In this work, Lasch constructs a scathing critique of the state of American society, not out of nostalgia, but in the name of the defeated principles of a New Left horrified by the drift of the 1970s. Subtitled "American Life in an Age of Diminishing Expectations," this critique focuses on the secondary narcissism that has taken over his contemporaries.[50] A pervasive "I" empties social relations of their meaning; a "self" reduced to its simplest expression rids individualism of all value;[51] the "cretinization" of the masses has by far surpassed that of previous decades; manipulation reigns; spontaneity has disappeared; collective institutions are rendered meaningless, as personal commitment to public service becomes increasingly rare; the body becomes an unquestioned object of worship. We have entered the age of therapy and of "liberations" that are all the more openly welcomed because they avoid questioning fundamental alienations. We entertain increasingly intense relations with merchandise, and experience the growing commodification of social practices, including sports, education, politics, and sexuality. There is a general loss of depth and of breadth, narcosis, fear of all true intimacy, hypochondria, permanent pseudo-analysis of feelings and relations with others, defiance of natural cycles, vengeful ignorance of the past, disregard for the future, superficial "lifestyles" replace ideas . . .

The panorama is exceedingly dark, and Lasch cannot resist the temptation to identify signs of this new narcissism in certain works of fiction. He even goes so far as to use the metafictions and autoreferentiality of certain texts to prove his point:

As for art, it not only fails to create the illusion of reality but suffers from the same crisis of self-consciousness that afflicts the man in the street. Novelists and playwrights call attention to the artificiality of their own creations and discourage the reader from identifying with the characters. By means of irony and eclecticism, the writer withdraws from his subject but at the same time becomes so conscious of these distancing techniques that he finds it more and more difficult to write about anything except the difficulty of writing.[52]

As an example, Lasch refers to Barthelme, in whose work self-parodying texts discussing the difficulty of writing about the difficulty of writing are frequent. Quoting Morris Dickstein to support his critique of the "emotional retreat" of the "experimental" writer (the terms themselves are marginalizing), Lasch leads the reader to believe that contemporary literature is threatened by catatonia:

Giving up the effort to "master reality," the writer retreats into a superficial self-analysis which blots out not only the external world but the deeper subjectivity "that enables the imagination to take wing. . . . His incursions into the self are as hollow as his excursions into the world."

Lasch's book does provide food for thought. However, upon close examination, it becomes clear that the brilliant historian of ideas did not push the analysis of the implications of his literary criticism as far as he did those pertaining to psychology, sociology, and ideology in general. Consequently, the philosophical idealism which he has managed to defeat in these domains returns to modify his hasty analysis of the effects of language. It is important to keep this critique in mind, however, since it continues to inform debate. Ironically, its very themes had been addressed by sectors of the fiction of the 1970s.

Literature Against Itself?

Published the same year as Lasch's *The Culture of Narcissism* and originating from an adjacent ideological realm, Gerald Graff's *Literature Against Itself* was the most effective volley launched against the new fiction, in that it was written by a literary specialist whose analysis remained closest to the philosophical and epistemological concerns of the discussion. Without calling for a simple "return" to a more reputable realism, Graff tries in the first three chapters[54] of the work to redirect the somewhat unreasoned credos that, as reactions against the dominance of thematic schools and the criticism of ideas, had moved literary criticism and theory away from social, ideological, and moral realities toward an "aestheticism" perceived to be both decadent and reprehensible.

One of Graff's central arguments is that today's world does not need antirealist literature to deconstruct earlier values. For him, this task appears to be on the agenda of the very powers that the new fiction has set out to combat; the true avant-garde of our time is constituted by modern capitalism, which chooses "to destroy all vestiges of tradition, all orthodox ideologies, all continuous and stable forms of reality in order to stimulate higher levels of consumption."[55] Far from playing an "adversarial" role, then, antirealist literature would merely assist in the disintegration of the social for the greater glory of the economy. Like it or not, abandoning the concept of reality by labeling everything "unreal" in order to combat a doubtful reality amounts to combating alienation by rendering it total. In moral terms, the aim of literature would be to distinguish the real from the "unreal," while the confusion between fiction and truth, materially and intellectually, gains by the universalization of the lie. According to Graff, it is quite possibly meaningless for any literary undertaking to systematically tear art away from the efforts of recuperation of the real by cutting the ties that could link them together — and this in the first instance by throwing suspicion on language. All things considered, this attempt would simply provide a new kind of merchandise for an all-devouring environment that thrives on differences by exploiting rather than fearing them. The trap that Graff wants the new literature and art to avoid is the one set by a society that encourages them to undertake the destruction of values by which it feels restrained. First among these values would be then the notion of the real — since a consumer society is interested in derealization the better to sell the signs of a phantasmal real — but in which we also find reason, objective truth, humanism, culture, tradition, and meaning.

Graff has been heavily criticized for his views. His book appeared when the world of criticism was polarized, dominated by enthusiastic observers and proselytes ill-prepared for philosophical reflection, by inspired and deliberately gnostic exalters of "the postmodern" who were not above wanting to become gurus, or by intellects for whom getting clear of earlier critical practices already had proven sufficiently difficult to risk endangering their own "liberations." In total confusion, supposedly fatal epithets such as "Aristotelian," "conservative," and "Marxist," were leveled against Graff's work. At times polemical, but always admirably informed, gifted with a feel for nuance, Graff nonetheless poses fundamental problems to which numerous responses can be found. We will refer readers to his work; his courageous questioning of the "newness" of "postmodernism" ("The Myth of the Postmodern Breakthrough") deserves to be recognized, as does his refusal to throw the baby of reason out with the bath water of its aberrations, along with his refusal to confuse the impossibility of arriving at the truth with the contemptuous or cynical abandonment of its quest. We should also note that Graff's work treats a historical dimension of the problem that contemporary American criticism too often blissfully ignores. In so doing, it also critiques the romanticism that secretly resides in more than one "radical" position. Where Gardner's bellicose moralism overshadowed the complexities and nuances of the literary situation, Graff intelligently modulates his interpretations and forces a revision of the corpus, by distinguishing between varying degrees of self-reflexivity in fictional texts, by establishing links between apparently different tendencies, and by dividing "postmodernism" — particularly where myth and its uses are concerned — into various opposing projects.

An overly facile discourse around the "liberation" of writing is thus brought into perspective. Graff demonstrates that a certain vision of contemporary art is indebted to Kantian thought whenever art is defined as an autonomous expression of the imagination that, rather than passively inheriting the laws of nature, dictates those laws quite freely. In a profoundly altered environment, a dialectic that is potentially dangerous for antirealism is established between the negations of art and between the negation of these negations by an assimilating society that reduces these rebellious efforts to nothing. The all too often neglected analysis of what separates political from aesthetic radicalism is thus made somewhat more precise. Thus also are more clearly drawn the limits that separate innovative literature grounded in a true reflection on the profound ties that link art and society from a type of literature that sometimes too facilely self-qualifies as "experimental," not to be easily considered as just another way of whiling away the time.

Chapter 4
Evolutions

The profusion of contemporary American fiction is such that a final set of clarifications must be made lest we be blinded by the fractured light of what Grace Paley has called the "prism of 'isms."

From the Producer to the Consumer

First we must update, at least partially, the evolution of the conditions of literary production in the United States, from the creation to the reception of literary texts.

In the early sixties, there were, practically speaking, only two writing seminars in the United States: one at Stanford University, the other at the University of Iowa. As spaces entirely devoted to the writing of fiction and poetry in a university setting, creative-writing workshops have become considerably more popular over the last twenty years and now number in the dozens. Certain programs have acquired excellent reputations, as in the case of those at Johns Hopkins and Brown; but all of them, no matter how famous, have had multiple effects upon the writing of fiction. The workshops are usually run by writers (of varying reputation depending on the university's finances) and include a substantial number of students. Since the university functions as the site of culture par excellence in the United States, these workshops contribute to literature's broader influence, particularly through public readings by established writers and newcomers. The writing programs have also provided stable jobs, and therefore incomes, for writers who otherwise might not have been able to pursue their craft. Certainly, many writers have never benefited from this means of survival and have continued to work in relative obscurity and penury, aided from time to time by grants (Guggenheim, National Endowment for the Arts, among others), or by taking different jobs in order to pay the rent. For years, William Gaddis worked in advertising; Raymond Carver held all sorts of jobs over the course of his life, as did Russell Banks, and Richard Brautigan lived for a long time with extremely slender means. But over time, even they have held either temporary or permanent university positions. This osmosis between academia and writing has colored many productions, either thematically (as in Mary McCarthy's novel *The Group,* Alison Lurie's *The War Between the Tates,* and John Barth's *Giles Goat-Boy,* which turns the university into a metaphor for the universe), or indirectly, by favoring certain forms, styles, and narrative strategies.

Since the end of the seventies, this increase in the number of writing seminars has been accompanied by a return to the short story. Is this coincidence, cause, or effect? Often the direct product of writing workshops, short stories are easier to publish, all things being equal: either in magazines to which the form is suited (*The New Yorker,* where short stories are a long-standing tradition, *Playboy, Esquire*); in a growing number of reviews (*Southern Review, Georgia Review*); or in publications created for this purpose (*Antaeus, TriQuarterly, New American Review* until recently, *Grand Street, Between C & D, The Iowa Review, Blatant Artifice, Black Ice, Fiction International, Conjunctions, High Plains Review*). Various reasons have been given for the success of the short story: the abundant production of writing seminars as laboratories of narrativity; a length suited to the rhythm of contemporary existence and to the rapid consumption of a population that no longer has time to read novels; a genre adapted to a "time of short attention spans, broken marriages, and exploded families."[1]

Whatever the reason, publishers quickly adjusted to this situation, and university presses (of Louisiana, Georgia, Illinois) and commercial houses no longer hesitate to market collections of short stories. Consequently, writers who have published a volume of their shorter works without ever having published a novel have become increasingly visible. These include writers such as Bobbie Ann Mason, Jayne Anne Phillips, and Tobias Wolff, all reputed to lie within Raymond Carver's sphere of aesthetic influence. Carver himself, of course, became known through his short stories. Needless to say, there had been earlier masters of the genre as well, as John Cheever, John Updike, Peter Taylor, Bernard Malamud, Tillie Olsen, Eudora Welty, and Flannery O'Connor serve to remind us. On the other hand, Gass was unable to publish the short stories of *In the Heart of the Heart of the Country* until after *Omensetter's Luck* had appeared. The same logic forced Robert Coover to publish the previously written stories of *Pricksongs and Descants* (1969) after *The Origin of the Brunists* (1966). And whereas a publisher was eventually found for Thomas Pynchon's early stories in *Slow Learner,* it would have been unthinkable without the critical success of his novels. On the downside of this development, it may not be overstating the case to say that there has been an increased tendency on the part of writers, as the objects of questionable infatuations, to allow works to be published that they had previously relegated to the back of their desk drawers. If not for the kindly attentions of editors eager to publish a novel in the wake of a successful collection of short stories, even at the risk of straining an author's talent, these works might not have seen the light of day. The diminished tension in the writing, which is clearly evident between the adamantine stories of Jayne Anne Phillips's *Black Tickets* and her novel *Machine Dreams*, Bobbie Ann Mason's *Shiloh* and *In Country*, Tobias Wolff's *In the Garden of the North American Martyrs* and *The Barracks Thief*, should serve to illustrate that writers formed in the hothouses of writing semi-nars should be granted the time to deepen their art before changing genres, or that they should be granted the freedom to work in the genre they had originally chosen.

In the 1980s, the return to what R. M. Albérès would have termed a "tempered" realism may somewhat undercut the apparent ease with which publishers were found for new literature. The publishing world is only wide open to the extent that it is convinced that these new voices will reach a larger public. Regarding the publication of innovative literature, the situation was not good in the sixties and seventies, nor has it become so now. Although editors like James Laughlin, Ted Solotaroff, and Jona-than Williams have always been around to support young writers of chal-lenging works, the changing policies within large publishing houses in no way favor them. Arguing for a necessary turnover of stock, marketing catalogs that contain fewer and fewer entries, many houses have turned their back on innovative fiction and have been purchased by conglomer-ates — Gulf, CBS, Xerox, RCA — whose first concern is less with promot-ing promising writers than with profitable investments and whose general approach often focuses on the audiovisual and leaves only a limited slot for books. This is perhaps the key to several developments. Recently, many new small presses have managed to profit from the relative neglect with which the larger houses treated a lively segment of literary produc-tion. North Point,[2] Sun and Moon, Black Sparrow, Coffee House, Burn-ing Deck, Station Hill, and many others have thus become important points of reference.

Frustrated by the fact that, in the best of cases, a novelist published by a large firm had little chance of seeing his book remain available beyond the six fateful months that would send it off to be pulped and little inclined to tolerate a situation in which the most innovative literature of quality was of almost no interest to commercial editors, a handful of writ-ers, who had all published under such circumstances (Baumbach, Spiel-berg, Sukenick, supported by Coover, Barthelme, and others), founded the Brooklyn Fiction Collective in 1974, a collective publishing enterprise inspired by a Swedish example. From 1974 to 1988, the collective published around fifty modestly priced hardcover and paperback works, whose reprinting until the end of the life of the collective was guaranteed. The profits were in part reinvested in the business, with each author contributing a refundable amount. Decisions concerning the works to be published were made by a rotating committee. While it was a true success, this enterprise was not big enough to compensate for the existing gaps in the market. Since the creation of Fiction Collective 2, the organization has been somewhat altered, but its ambitions remain the same.

In October 1981 there was a meeting of the Congress of American Writers at the Roosevelt Hotel in New York during which protests were lodged against concentration within the publishing industry, cuts in financial support of the arts by the federal government, and the increasingly frequent cases of censorship of literary works in different states of the Union. To claim that the United States is a haven of free speech is to stretch the truth somewhat. Protected by federal law and by state constitutions, this freedom is as gravely endangered by editorial choices as by local school boards with the power to ban or discourage the purchase of works considered offensive or incompatible with the moral limits defined by the intellectual backgrounds of the board members. In addition to the charges made against "Howl" and *Lolita* in the fifties, more recently there have been those brought against far too many others, including Malamud, Roth, Brautigan, and Coover. The dominance of lawyers and judges and the existing regime of systematic litigation can sometimes encourage self-censorship on the part of writers in order to avoid prosecutions their editors are not always prepared to contest.

Finally, it must also be said that the American public hardly favors the diffusion of quality literature. The United States is not a country of heavy readers any more than is France.[3] Reading is often limited to a cultured public centered around institutions of higher learning. What is more, while libraries are many in number, they vary greatly in quality. And the important centers for the distribution of books are few and far between. The American book trade offers all too few examples of bookstores that systematically support serious literature. Bookstores in New York, Chicago, Berkeley, Los Angeles, Boston, and on some campuses are alone in offering prospective readers of contemporary fiction a significant choice. The seemingly insurmountable concern with "turnover" hardly improves the situation.

Did You Say "Post"?

Even if the diffusion of books were better managed, the problem would nonetheless remain considerable and the literary domain difficult to judge, due to its size and to the present state of criticism. An essay by Charles Newman bears the title *The Post-Modern Aura* and the subtitle "The Act of Fiction in an Age of Inflation."[4] In this work, contemporary literature appears to be in a state of rapid flux; it is defined as a permanent search for the new, an experimentation lacking in conviction, an impatient quest for the profound truth of a period that can no longer be grasped. Newman locates the heart of the problem in the notion of the "velocity" of change; he analyzes the "inflation" that reduces the life span of works whose numbers increase while their impact decreases. There are no longer the driving critical consciences such as those incarnated by Edmund Wilson and Lionel Trilling. The disorder and abundance of ideas and intellectual fashions, oversimplified in order to assure mass distribution, do not allow for general overviews or for any intellectual control over change. The cultural bric-a-brac seeks refuge in terminologies whose terrorism masks anxieties; it manifests itself in the rapid profusion of labels that frequently serve only to reveal the most effective show-off, proclaiming particularly ephemeral "ideas" the style of the day, the shortness of their life span is practically announced on the pages describing them; it is expressed by the appearance of what Newman terms a new species of "regionalism": a regionalism of the mind, of petty loyalties, incapable of encompassing entire aesthetic movements and their relations to the real, of proposing a general view of artistic productions, of sorting out works, of supporting the forms most able to express the major lines of thought, of choosing the cultural knots that must be undone, of pointing out dead ends. Understood in an almost intransitive sense, "creativity" becomes a value in and of itself, like "change" and the "new." The notion of crisis is institutionalized to the greater profit of a consumer society or of the critical establishment that lives off it. The "elite," repudiated during the sixties, becomes indiscernible. There is no one to propose "hierarchies," however debatable they might be, hierarchies that are repeatedly denied by blurbs wherein any judgment less than superlative is considered pointless. The most popular drugs in the literary field are neither LSD nor cocaine, but rhubarb and senna, Molière's symbols for flattery. Self-proclaimed avant-garde literary activities in no way affect general aesthetic choices.

According to Newman, the literary and critical tendencies of the time, categorized and locked up in ghettos that they polemically defend, have settled for expressing themselves solely through denunciation, lost in the general din, of whatever troubles them. (Valéry taught us what to think of such "intestine fermentations.") They are content with a kind of division of aesthetic labor between humanists who are behind the times and innovators equally cut off from the contemporary world. This situation appears to Newman to provide the very definition of what has been called "postmodernism" in the United States: "a kind of static double helix, in which the velocity of two rotating aesthetic traditions shorn of historical context simultaneously cancel each other out, testifying to the absence of any experience strong enough to modify habits of mind."[5] Newman's judgments are severe, but not without foundation. The confusion between "postmodernism" and the "postmodern," a confusion to which Newman contributes in this work, demonstrates just how vague a term can remain while being bandied about in contemporary criticism to refer to works that should in no way be lumped together under one heading, works whose very variety illustrates their richness while marking the difficulty of signposting the present. Since Jean-François Lyotard has recently made the postmodern easy enough for children,[6] a few remarks will suffice to show my distaste for these terms and my lack of faith in their usefulness.

It seems, to begin with, deceptive to use in an undifferentiated manner, as is always the case, the compound adjective "postmodern" (referring to a relatively distant break in intellectual history, roughly, at the time of Hegel and the end of the Enlightenment) and the adjective "postmodernist" (referring to an artistic movement whose beginning dates from the early twentieth century and whose end, if we are to believe contemporary works, is not yet in sight). Equally dubious is the validity of a lexical construction founded on a chronological prefix when the supporters of postmodernism and of the postmodern frequently stud their arguments with examples from periods preceding the one(s) under consideration, referring to writers such as Sterne, Rabelais, Cervantes, Melville, and Thomas Browne, thus dangerously blending production and reception. Especially since the interest of these critical theories is to encourage rereadings of earlier works in a new light. What is more, as Guido Almansi has noted with irony, "the danger is not just in believing in postmodernism, but also in its brilliant future."[7] These terms seem to me to be more or less comfortable platforms on which to await the arrival of the saving term that will define the nature of new times. Terminology, no matter how vague, replaces the thought that would be required for us to take the risk of giving up on terms that "work well" but whose staying power is solely due to a kind of incantation. If we confront the choices implicit in our use of "postmodern" with the multiple forms this term prevents us from seeing, we are reminded of Mallarmé, who considered the contemporary moment

an interregnum with which the poet should not be concerned. The current time is at once too obsolete and in a state of preparatory effervescence for the poet to do anything other than work away secretly for the future or for no time in particular, sending the inhabitants calling cards, verses, or sonnets now and again, so as to avoid being stoned by them lest they suspect him of knowing that they don't exist.[8]

Whether masking emptiness or horrors, "postmodern(ism)" cannot account for either the variety or the complexity of the contemporary writings we are concerned with here. Truth be told, the most interesting writers try desperately to avoid being stuck with such labels. Beneath Charles Newman's humor lies more than one clever perception:

> Labels for the ongoing are invariably sloppy, which is one reason most critics sensibly eschew the present entirely. In the efforts to propound a Post-Modernism, there is an air of melodrama which suggests either that something is happening far beyond the establishment's powers to recognize it, or that nothing of moment is occurring — which is all the more terrifying.[9]

This first term of the alternative marks a shortcoming for which no one is directly responsible; but the second is in no way a true reflection of reality. American fiction is without a doubt one of the richest of our time. It is the most powerful literary form in the United States today: theater has moved toward an aesthetics of "performance" in which the text is of secondary importance; and the isolated examples of good poetry are crushed beneath an avalanche of confessionalism that is more lax than unrestrained. Perhaps the failure of "postmodernism" to unify literary production under one descriptive, generative vision is due to the fact that, in a certain way, we have in fact left modernism, since the profound truths of our society can no longer be grasped through the metaphors of art. In the 1940s, R. P. Blackmur sought an access to reality and to culture through the aesthetic experience. It is easy to believe that the changes that have occurred since then have rendered access through that age-old channel obsolete. Unless one demonstrated that science and technology have invaded the literary form other than metaphorically and thematically, this would open onto another debate.

New Directions

Because there may be no need, after all, to call upon nostalgia, since we could not term "postmodernist" in its entirety, nor even in its majority, a literary production that seems to continue to carry on a certain number of formal projects inherited from modernism unless the term "postmodernist" were to be given a chronological sense that would be so vague as to render it descriptively useless. Might we suggest here that "most modernist" or "lost modernism" are often more appropriate than "postmodernism"? The variety of its traits, even within the works themselves, should keep us from using simplistic terms. The changing aspects and the different contrasts attest to a diversity that has been poorly understood or overshadowed by outdated or willful epithets. The evolutions that occurred between 1960 and 1990 testify to this, confirming Newman's opinion that the duration of literary generations, empirically fixed at twenty-five to thirty years by Malcolm Cowley in his time, have been cut down to around ten years or so.

To speak in the most general terms, let us say that the 1960s were principally characterized by a move in theme and tone toward the absurd, contestation, the picaresque, marginalism, and by a certain amount of formal experimentation. The 1970s marked the real birth and generalization of these experiments in form, the rise of parodies, demystifications, the denunciation of systems and caricatures of them, the rise of a powerful wave of experiments slowly changing the accepted novelistic conventions. And that in the 1980s there came the beginnings of a vast synthesis, while a partial reaction against the antirealism that had dominated the seventies was also making itself known. Upon examining each of these decades more closely, we can see the coexistence of all these dominant modes, but general tendencies can be sketched out. Their rapid succession, far from excluding pileups, sedimentation, and osmosis, favored mutual fertilization and enrichment, the hybridization of works begun in a given aesthetic context, continued in another, maturing and modified in yet a third. The taking up of the exploration of the consecrated domains by the cultural tradition of American fiction occurs at each stage — picaresque in the sixties, "romance" in the seventies, mimetic testimony in the eighties — but it is modulated by the advances immediately preceding it. The liberation of tone in the 1960s is carried into the 1970s, whose dominant character is more formal and theoretical; the neomimesis of the 1980s is affected by the coefficient of refraction due to the formal findings of the preceding decade, preventing us from speaking simply of "returns." Concerning the early 1980s, someone wrote:

We are home again. The narrative voice levels with us. Clocks tell time. Characters have returned from vacation. Their behavior is motivated. Fantasy is intact but framed in reality so that it produces recognition rather than vertigo. The reader feels welcome. The reader *feels*. Yet these writers of the beginning of the 80's are not suffering from cultural amnesia. They have borrowed from and react to the fashions of the 70's.[10]

To say this is to forget that the writers who dominated previous decades had in no way forsaken their work and that some writers gained success after having worked for quite some time previously, that for each author there is not only one sort of aesthetics, that innovation by some is sometimes less important than the deepening of a furrow by others, that the effects of maturity are, finally, sometimes more spectacular than sudden irruptions.

All things considered, however, it seems possible to affirm that, in the years between 1960 and 1990, an important qualitative leap was, if not accomplished, at least confirmed: the leap that invites us to speak of American "fiction" rather than of prose or of the American "novel."[11] This is not only the result of a set of circumstances: the invention, in the sixties, of new forms such as the "new journalism" (Truman Capote, Norman Mailer, Hunter Thompson, Gay Talese, Tom Wolfe) and the rise of the short story in the seventies and eighties that were able to destabilize the imperial domination of the novel as a literary form; but also the profound change in the very idea of the novel itself. There is still, more or less, a "slice of life" in the notion of "novel." With the antirealist break of the sixties and seventies and the programmatic demonstration of the constitution of worlds by discourses, the word "fiction" takes back all of its etymological force. An effect of disillusionment occurred, of distrust of the referential illusion. The most "realist" writer of the eighties is fully aware of addressing readers who are not as easily led as before, and the most "transparent" writing has become willy-nilly thickened with signs proclaiming that it is fully aware of the nature of its activities. The omniscient narrator has become scarce, and when "character, plot, and theme" are established, it is rare that these three elements continue to dominate. The act of fiction, even of a "realist" nature, is no longer understood as a mere reflection, even of "unreality," but as a gesture that informs that on which it feeds, giving it, sometimes, existence. The passage from the "American novel" to "American fiction" is not a simple matter of vocabulary. It translates the emergence of a set of new aesthetic values; it indicates that American fiction, having learned the lessons of modernism and made use of later developments without being led down a path not of its own making, has moved beyond suspicion.

Part II
Beyond Suspicion

Chapter 5
"Entire Days Within Texts":
Aspects of Metafiction I

In real Parisian life, everyone is free to take their cat for a walk in the Parc Montsouris, even if a mouse hides in that name. In literature, this is a dangerous, even impossible, act. Impossible, that is, without at least an emphatic wink to encourage us to focus on the game of cats, mice, and words, to accept Jean Rousset's earlier invitation to consider the work as a "verbal being": to detach oneself, in reading, from the spectacle offered by that which, as Henry James would say, is found on the other side of the "window" made of words, to admit that words can be material and opaque, to read the structures and usages of the "referential illusion" as an illustration of our way of relating to the world and of the way in which literature would have us apprehend that world.

Reflexiveness, an axiom of poetry, has remained — until the moderns and with those exceptions already mentioned — an aberrant trait of novels confident in their virtues and their mimetic powers. Such reflexiveness eased the arrival of the "age of suspicion" which the French New Novel, somewhat aridly, at times, exemplified. It seems to me that the question then arose of the means by which one could both use and pass beyond a self-consciousness that ultimately threatened paralysis; over the past quarter-century, American fiction has attempted to answer this question in very diverse ways.

Along with suspicion was born "the same painful sensation that the birds who tried to pilfer Zeuxis' famous grapes must have had":[1] after constantly knocking their beaks against the dry limits and acrid paint of the mimetic novel, some decided that, rather than permanently play the part of fools, they had better accept the "death of the novel" as they knew it. In the 1960s, there ensued a rather lively debate over this "death," not without some shortsightedness (a long view of literary history would have nipped the discussion in the bud), not without some duplicity (the most coherent spokesman for this side, Ronald Sukenick, went so far as to publish *The Death of the Novel and Other Stories,* thus bearing witness to the productivity of the so-called demise), not without sometimes excessive solicitation of theoretical texts.

I say shortsightedness since, if it was still easy to ignore Bakhtin's un-translated essays in which he argued that self-consciousness and self-criticism constituted two of the novel's distinguishing features,[2] it was altogether less legitimate to be unaware of more easily available view-points: whether this was Roman Jakobson's remark that "great works do nothing other than tell of their birth," in which the critic affirmed the necessarily self-reflexive nature of the literary work; or André Gide in *The Immoralist,* for whom "in art, there is no problem for which the work of art is not itself a sufficient solution"; or the ironic remarks of Herman Melville himself on the "literary sin" of "divergence"; or finally, the works of Nathanael West, Djuna Barnes, James Joyce, William Faulkner, and Flann O'Brien. From the farcical dismantling of narrative devices by the first, the highlighting of the play of signifiers by the second and third, to the awareness that the writer goes from abortion to abortion in works by the author of *The Sound and the Fury*: everything announced the presentation of the novel as a *mise en abîme* of themes, situations, and early devices found in the work of the Irishman whose famous *At Swim-Two-Birds* was again becoming available in bookstores in 1960. One could read the following there: "The modern novel should be largely a work of reference. Most authors spend their time saying what has been said before — usually said much better."[3] And the writer-hero, that subversive who peoples the major works to speculate on counterfeiting (from *The Counterfeiters* to *The Recognitions*), was already represented in the grip of his own creation by O'Brien:

You are writing a novel of course? said Byrne.
He is, said Brinsley, and the plot has him well in hand.[4]

Moreover, the tradition of the "specular narrative," historically well-nourished, would have sufficed to relativize a feeling of disorientation experienced periodically over the centuries.[5] In addition to the examples given above, as early as the 1950s, Flannery O'Connor was lamenting that Faulkner, seen under the form of the "Dixie Express," did not encourage the young Southern writer to venture along tracks that he himself had traveled. In "The Literature of Exhaustion," John Barth emphasized that, since the traditional modes of fiction appeared limited, the authors of our time found that they had inherited the difficult task of patching up a genre ripped apart by an awareness of its devices, of renewing literature by gathering its worn tatters within new forms. In other words, of finding new ways to break through the obstacles, to transcend a genre that had been practiced for too long in a referential perspective little adapted to new situations. In a text placed at the very heart of the daisy-structure of *Pricksongs and Descants* (published in 1969, but made up for the most part of texts written before 1966), Robert Coover, an advocate of the new consciousness, proposed that the situation of the contemporary writer resembled that of Cervantes, constrained to a qualitative leap in his writing by the new horizons of the Renaissance. Addressing the master, Coover thus affirmed:

The universe for you, *Maestro,* was opening up; it could no longer be described by magical numbers or be contained in a compact and marvelously designed sphere. Narrative fiction, taking a cue from Lazarillo and the New World adventurers, became a process of discovery, and to this day young authors sally forth in fiction like majestic — indeed, divinely ordained! — *pícaros* to discover, again and again, their manhood.[6]

Sartre, for whom the transformation of novelistic form was not the principal concern, was already calling for a more conscious artist who, by reflecting on his art, would attempt to endow it with his own human condition.

Furthermore, it was less fair to attribute to John Barth, as many commentators have done, something that he did not say: that fiction had no future whatsoever, that other artistic forms were needed to replace it for the short term, that the novel, an outmoded form of expression, was doomed to stutter. Like Pierre Bonnard, who punctuated an evolution by exclaiming that "it's not a matter of painting life, but a matter of making painting lively," Barth called for a change in perspective that did not deprive fiction of a future. Bonnard had also warned against a formal reaction that would misjudge the nature of painterly activity, thereby preventing the desired evolution: "The only solid terrain of the painter is the palette and the tones, but as soon as the colors effect an illusion, we stop judging them, and that's when we get into trouble." Whether this indicated a feeling of disinheritance, or a revolt against what Gilbert Sorrentino calls "the puppeteer school of novelists," Barth and those who understood him deliberately turned toward a "less innocent" practice, one that, to varying degrees and in various forms, seemed able to renew the act of fiction by emphasizing the nature of the act itself.

In the text by Coover mentioned above, there appears a "mutual friend" disguised under the name of "Roberto S." According to him, fiction "must provide us with an imaginative experience which is necessary to our imaginative well-being. . . . We need all the imagination we have, and we need it exercised and in good condition."[7] "Roberto S." is in fact Robert Scholes, professor at Brown University, who launched the term "metafiction" and who, in *Fabulation and Metafiction,* would later set forth a view of contemporary fiction that rejected the mimetic tradition and referred back to fiction's roots in fable and allegory:

A sense of pleasure in form is one characteristic of fabulation. . . . [M]odern fabulation, like the ancient fabling of Aesop, tends away from direct representation of the surface of reality but returns toward actual human life by way of ethically controlled fantasy.[8]

Scholes's formulation insists on the idea that any renewal of an "exhausted" genre must occur through the undoing and the placing in perspective of stylistic devices, approaching them from a distance in order to reflect on their ethical, aesthetic, and ideological functions. In this way, the originary forces of literary creation are, shall we say, *thematized*; the focus is shifted from the content of the texts toward their forms, from a semantics that betrays aesthetic comfort — as "common sense" speaks of intellectual comfort or smugness — toward the open deployment of a rhetoric and a semiotic. Thus, the naturalization of literary devices will give way to their high visibility within texts resembling the Pompidou Centers of writing, with all of their tubes, pipes, and plumbing exposed. Artifice and artifact will anchor a fiction that has become aware that, as Claude Simon so beautifully expressed it,

just as it is not the desire to reproduce nature that makes a painter, but rather a fascination with the museum, so it is the desire to write created by a fascination with the written object that makes a writer, while nature is limited, for its part, as Oscar Wilde so cleverly put it, "to imitating art."[9]

There is an increasingly strong desire to pass from the writing of "transparent" texts, to an exploration of filters and lenses through fiction. Both Coover, in the three short stories of "The Sentient Lens" that make up the nuclear manifesto of *Pricksongs and Descants,* and Annie Dillard, in "Lenses,"[10] will announce this shift in focus.

To the satisfaction of those who like to collect categories, it has become handy to indiscriminately refer to a "group" of "metafictionists," but the lessons they have learned are varied. The contrast between two equally penetrating remarks is striking. Alan Singer argues that "a catachrestic style is in fact the catalyst of formal innovation in the modern novel" where discontinuity would dominate for the greater good of linguistic invention.[11] Singer's analysis of the ways in which metaphor informs narrative situations is of great value. But dealing with the same subject (that the writing of fiction no longer consists in "knowing what you are going to say and then simply pouring these ideas into words" nor in "placing an existing idea in a form yet to be discovered"), Gilbert Sorrentino places the emphasis on fiction's return to metonymy, to the juxtaposition of discrete elements, to the conflict between codes, or: the referential emptiness of most novelistic "signals."[12] Ironic in regard to writers who persist in using codified tics and reflexes, Sorrentino offers the contrasting notion of an "American novel without signals" as illustrated by the "antiheroic, plotless, imageless, and artless" prose of William Carlos Williams.[13]

Once the term "metafiction" was launched, neologisms flourished, stressing the displacement Robert Steiner would later illustrate in a far less dry formulation, privileging opacity, danger, desire, and discovery: "Fiction has never been a window onto anything. It's a door, and behind that door, there's a woman and a tiger."[14] Neologisms provide knee-jerk references for those who want to believe in the novelty of a hypothetical "postmodernism." Within the broader field of what he terms "transfiction," Mas'ud Zavarzadeh distinguishes "metafiction" as such, from "surfiction" and science fiction.[15] Raymond Federman and Ronald Sukenick favor "surfiction," whereas Ishmael Reed speaks of "parafiction," and still others of "superfiction" (Klinkowitz), even of "critifiction," a type of narrative that contains not only its own theory but also its own critique; these variations decline the prefix without fundamentally modifying that which they designate. More seriously, David Lodge establishes a typology of such allegedly "postmodernist" fiction; among its techniques are the discontinuity of narrative and diverse methods of short-circuiting, the display of the conventions being used, and a strategy of excess that overloads the novelistic text with signs of its specificity. Robert Scholes, again and finally, making a somewhat weak term more precise, presents a typology of the "forms of fiction" that invites useful combinations.[16] Alongside a "fiction of essences" (allegories) and a "fiction of existence" (the traditional novel that seeks to imitate not the forms of fiction but the forms of human behavior), there is a "fiction of forms," which imitates other fictions and where Scholes locates the "romance," as well as a "fiction of ideas," by which he does not mean the "novel of ideas," but a fiction driven by the "essential ideas" of fiction, among which myth predominates.

Commenting on Vico's historical views, Joyce concluded: "I would not pay overmuch attention to these theories, beyond using them for all they are worth."[17] I will perform the same pirouette in order to remove myself from this theoretical thicket made up of useful but simplistic outlines. Indeed, there is a wide variety of illustrations and modulations, of this burning desire or obligation to transcend the obstacles of the codified mimetic narrative, to gather energy from such blocks, to use these limits and markers as heuristic springboards. Paradoxically, the writing displays a simultaneous desire to lose its utilitarian function and its innocence by fully declaring itself as fiction, as shaping (*fingere*), scaffolding, as an enrichment of the real, and even as a means of constituting the real.

The Character Actor

Since 1960, American fiction has readily placed its sires on stage. Perhaps, as Robert Steiner has remarked, because contemporary generations are hegemonically constituted by authors who have received a true literary education, their characters tend to bear a family resemblance, to live as though in a novel, and to know writers even when they are not writers themselves. There are degrees to this reflexiveness; furthermore, it had already been initiated by certain moderns — James, Huxley, and Gide — who gladly created characters who were artists or writers. But it remains important that these references have become more precise and more insistent. In "The Aeroplanes at Brescia" (*Tatlin!*), Guy Davenport, as in all of his culture-saturated works, introduces Kafka and Wittgenstein; the figure of a writer dominates Andrée Connors's *Amateur People*; the central character of John Irving's early novels, ancestors of *The World According to Garp* with its conscious mirroring of literary creation, is himself a novelist, and the fetus of a stillborn manuscript is found on the typewriter of a character in *The Cider House Rules,* which takes abortion as its central theme. The list of contemporary works in which the hero writes and the privileged moments dramatize literary discussions would be exhausting but inexhaustible. The parties that make up the purple passages of *The Recognitions* are peopled with the bohemian set, from more or less failed writers to parasitic successes: one takes himself for Melville, while another inscribes his host's volumes by signing Dickens. Even writers who are attached to a more traditional vision of their art have trouble resisting the temptation, witness: Styron's *Sophie's Choice*; Roth's *The Ghostwriter*; the rivals in Malamud's *The Tenants* in which the writer is violently rejected by an envious neighbor, who throws his manuscript in the garbage and his typewriter out the window; and John Gardner himself. Gardner ironically places in perspective the Anglo-Saxon saga of *Beowulf* (narrated by Beowulf's enemy in *Grendel*) and enthusiastically enters into textual games in *Freddy's Book,* whose title alone is revealing. The "city of words," to which Tony Tanner once made himself the guide, is truly inhabited by those who make use of them and by their offspring.[18]

Lampooning Narrative Instances

An awareness of self and of literary activity can lead to ironic narrative gestures and to complicitous winks intended to popularize the distance that it has become almost natural to place between oneself and outdated modes of writing. A turgid, badly constructed, and pretentious sentence opens Jonathan Baumbach's "The Traditional Story Returns," in which the misfortunes of a couple plucked from the naturalist novel are subjected to a devastating irony that constantly displays the artifice involved in creating characters, setting the scene, and in rendering a mediocre plot plausible:

> Too many times you read a story nowadays and it's not a story at all, not in the traditional sense. A traditional story has plot, character and theme, to name three things it traditionally has. The following story, which contains a *soupçon* of mood in addition to the three major considerations named above, is intended as a modest rearguard action in the service of a declining tradition.[19]

Tom Robbins, a popular and reader-friendly writer, owes his notoriety largely to surrealistic images reminiscent of Brautigan. He does not hesitate to parody novelistic structures, introducing *Even Cowgirls Get the Blues* with a "Single Cell Preface" whose connections to the novel itself are clearly tenuous. The title of a chapter of Barth's *The Tidewater Tales* takes up an entire page, whereas a "chapter" of Brautigan's *Willard and His Bowling Trophies* contains only seven words. Little tempted by theory, Stanley Elkin nonetheless entitles a short story in *Criers and Kibitzers, Kibitzers and Criers,* "A Poetics for Bullies."

More recently, in a collection with the significant title *Modern Romances,* Judy Lopatin has the writing of "A Phantasm, a Bird" watch over itself by constantly surprising and commenting on itself; the story is built around its own creation. Manipulating the motivations of narrative ("Anticipation is the sweet pain to know whatever's next — a must for any real writer")[20] or the obsolescence of a model, Richard Ford, a novelist little inclined to take theoretical positions, grounds himself in the story of a sports reporter in order to demonstrate that the novel is less in the process of displacing its emphasis than of undergoing a generic mutation. In Robert Coover's first novel, *The Origin of the Brunists,* a journalist named Miller serves to demonstrate the relative value of his writing as compared to the millennialist discourses of the sect whose inner motivations he has been exploring. Ford's protagonist had once been interested in writing a novel whose outline parodies those of a writer behind whom we can decipher Styron and an entire narrative tradition:

> Mine was to be about a bemused young southerner who joins the Navy but gets discharged with a mysterious disease, goes to New Orleans and loses himself into a hazy world of sex and drugs and rumored gun-running and a futile attempt to reconcile a vertiginous present with the guilty memories of not dying alongside his Navy comrades, all of which is climaxed in a violent tryst with a Methodist minister's wife who seduces him in an abandoned slave-quarters, though other times too, after which his life is shattered and he disappears permanently into the Texas oil fields. It was all told in a series of flashbacks.[21]

Even the tired debate about "postmodernism" is fictionalized in Max Apple's short story "Post-Modernism" (*Free Agents*).

The blatant refusal to play the game can be just as noticeable through the absence of visible "tricks of the trade" as through their caricatured representation. This is the case of the description in Gordon Lish's "Picture," whose title announces a critique by example; the narrator addresses the reader so that he too can participate in sabotaging the conventions: "It is not necessary for you to lend yourself to any further effort to create particularities that I myself was not competent to render."[22] In *Travel Notes*, Stanley Crawford generalizes this technique; in this "travel novel," all of the descriptions essential to the project have either disappeared or have been stylized, banalized to the extreme. Under the guise of "travel notes," Crawford effects a radical critique of description, demonstrating that the requisite conventions proceed, as Annie Dillard would say, through an identifiable series of "trompe-l'esprit" techniques just as any painted work of art functions through "trompe-l'oeil."[23] The reader cannot "see" the scenes described, but everything invites him to furnish them with acquired models. The awareness of similar overdeterminations can be integrated within narrative strategies that distinguish, for example, Robert Steiner's *Bathers*, in which voice and myth occupy all of the space, from his *Passion*, in which ellipsis reigns supreme; in works such as these, the reader is free to cocreate the imaginary environment. The fact that Steiner establishes this difference by manipulating (regrouping or cutting) sentences from original manuscripts demonstrates his desire to keep the stays of convention from choking the creative exchange that should circulate between text and reader. Moreover, he emphasizes at all times the semiotic nature of the elements of novelistic discourse: landscapes, characters, and diegetic knots.

An identical game with the variable distance that can be established between text, character, narrator, and reader is illustrated elsewhere. Mole, the voice and focal point of Harold Jaffe's *Mole's Pity*, torn between a personal spiritual search and his social role (he runs a radio station that answers the calls of rejects and marginals of all kinds, a sort of hybrid of West's "Miss Lonelyhearts" and Elkin's "Dick Gibson"), is alternately referred to by the pronouns "I" and "he" within the same sentences. This programmed oscillation between the first and third persons, at odds with one of the most stable of novelistic conventions, is also finely wrought by Rudolph Wurlitzer in *Flats*. The collective "we" that takes charge of Joan Chase's *During the Reign of the Queen of Persia* serves a feminist project that privileges the collective but results in the same experience; the official diegetic thread is undercut by the new enigma of the true identity of the female narrator, a dilemma reminiscent of the one posed by the sexual indetermination of the voice that narrates Harry Mathews's *Tlooth*.

James Purdy is not generally grouped among the practitioners of meta-fiction. However, in *Malcolm,* the artificiality of setting up the plot is as evident as the cardboard profile of the characters and the dramatization of narrative questions asked of the novelist. As the narrative's basic generator, since he allows the successive and cumulative meeting of the characters, Mr. Cox is just as surprised as we are to note that a programmed plot keeps refusing to start up, that the *machina* no longer obeys a *deus* of any kind:

"I have arranged all the situations," Mr. Cox spoke without his usual optimism. "Why can't *they* act? I have brought the right people together, and the right situations. I'm not such a fool as not to know *right people* and *right situations* when they're together. But nothing happens. Nothing at all."[24]

In this way, without entirely devoting themselves to the difficulties and delights of self-referentiality, many contemporary works display in broad daylight the loss of the presumed innocence of their genre.

Yet the writers most attached to questioning such as this do not limit their telling gestures to simple traces. Susan Sontag entitles her collection of short stories *I, etcetera.* A story by Donald Barthelme entitled "Sentence" makes of its unique and unending sentence the true hero of the text; yet another, "The Dolt," stages the inherent difficulty of beginning a story, as contrasted with the relative ease involved in either continuing or ending it. Similarly, there are many other works by Barthelme and Coover that continually play with the conventions and narrative instances in a creative manner. Coover's "Beginnings" opens with the narrator's suicide; whereas a bullet meant for another suicide provides the narrative trajectory of Stephen Dixon's "Fourteen Stories" in the collection of the same title.[25] A set of questions inserted into Barthelme's *Snow White* hypothetically allows the novel's narrator to verify how much the reader has understood of the plots and themes by a certain stage of the story; this device is taken up by Sorrentino in *Mulligan Stew.* Most of the stories in Barthelme's *City Life, Sadness,* and *Come Back, Dr. Caligari* are made up of realistic tatters, of situations and characters whom we reattach to recognized modes, but whose largely arbitrary formal juxtaposition creates previously unknown possibilities of meaning. In this way, it is shown that fiction founded on artifice can function in spite of (or thanks to) its confessions.

When violated with enthusiasm and a certain guilty energy, the rules of narrative appear in negative all the more clearly (Barthelme's *Guilty Pleasures*). This is the project of "The Glass Mountain" (*City Life*) in which the reader, tempted to organize an uncontrollable narrative and made conscious of the strength of old reflexes, has to decide what is attributable to the text and what is due to his inextinguishable desire for meaning and plot. Thomas Pynchon exploits this desire thematically in his novel *The Crying of Lot 49,* in which the discovery of a coherent perspective regrouping assorted bits of information is designated as vital, thereby extending to the novel as a whole the questions raised by the coherence of discourses on the real; the stakes of this "auction" are meant to be existential, whereas the one that opens William Gass's *Omensetter's Luck* takes inventory of the objects that will be redistributed throughout the novel according to the needs of the plot.

But if programs as ambitious as these demand rereading, they cannot make us forget that the stakes of narrative choices are more modestly but just as frequently examined by writers not usually classed among the most engaged metafictionists. One can observe the almost clinical manner in which Grace Paley poses the question of narrative modes in "A Conversation with My Father," a short story whose title appears to tie it to a tradition of intimate writing.[26] A simple story inserted within a larger scene causes a debate between father and daughter over the ways in which things ought to be narrated. Faith's oral account, with little attention to convention, does not satisfy her father. In this way it is suggested that, in the eyes of most people, a novel is not allowed to be just "anything," as described by Ishmael Reed in *Yellow Back Radio Broke-Down.*

The traditional categories of literary history, as said before, have served their time; this becomes clear when we notice that Reed and another black writer come together in regard to an identical question and in similar terms. In *Reflex and Bone Structure,* a novel by Clarence Major that fragments and reshapes itself before our eyes, the narrator declares as we read:

This novel has to keep changing. Hornbeam trees should stand tall in it. Characters should beat drums. Beloved friends should arrive at airports. Hackberry trees should be used for firewood. Everyone should learn how to defuse a bomb. The chorus line in every theater in New York should be the beginning of a new novel. I want to take a stand. I am like everybody. The gross national product sleeps with the national debt. A novel is everything. Fiction is a stained glass window.[27]

Beneath the humor of the parataxis in this dehierarchized passage appears Barthelme's most favored texture, called to service in an identical cause. If fragments are the "only form" that a character of Barthelme's trusts, Major goes further by suggesting that: "Fragments can be all we have. To make the whole."[28]

Binocular Works

Once the question of genre has been raised in this way, the doors are wide open to a second-degree exploitation. We will discuss parody as a means of renewing forms and themes later, but we must insist here on the general aspects of the parodic attitude in contemporary fiction, a metafictional gesture that is older, more tested, at times more secret, but no less pertinent.

Barth's texts first worked this vein until taking a more personal turn. The existential novel gave a playful base to *The End of the Road* and *The Floating Opera*. But the temptation to unveil the artificiality of the endeavor was already felt there, through the theme of the spectacle as much as through a specular form. The interlocking structure of *The Floating Opera* referred to a reduced manner of representation. Beneath these "floating works," the title encourages us to read the reciprocal and problematic positionings of the narrative and its commentaries, yet it also suggests an evident superposing with the central object of the novel (an "opera floating" alongside the banks of the stream that figured even more strongly the diegetic development). Within the text, Todd Andrews keeps a journal and memoir, creating his own scenes there that are in turn thematized and taken up by the plot. In *The Sot-Weed Factor*, narrative confusion characteristic of a Fielding pastiche is reinforced metaphorically by the farce of a hero desperately attempting to lose his virginity. Whether or not the impressive volume of the novel results from the desire to have the publisher inscribe its title perpendicularly to the spine, the anecdote signals an unusual overdetermination. This was followed by the weighty allegory of *Giles Goat-Boy*, in which the book aspired to be a universe, an ambition that all of Barth's works, in their most extreme involution, would not fail to satisfy. Pynchon's novels want to be their own work-worlds, exemplary attempts at mastery; taken together, Barth's novels constitute a self-referential universe pushed to its ultimate possibility. The structure of *Lost in the Funhouse* figures a desire for permanent, autotelic return, symbolized by the Möbius strip; this astonishing laboratory of contemporary fiction constructs stories that only a hasty reading could see as independent one from the other. This volume was, however, meant to be autonomous. Such is not the case of *LETTERS*, in which Barth's entire *oeuvre* is represented at the conclusion of a truly hallucinatory labor of internal intertextuality: all of the characters from Barth's earlier works reappear there in conversation with one another, and for good measure, so does the figure of the Author himself, engaged in a permanent debate with his past creatures. This kind of book would not seem to authorize a disjointed reading of the rest of the *oeuvre*. In order to describe this work, we would have to coin a term even more barbaric than "metafiction" and speak then of "autometafiction." The twin theme, omnipresent in Barth, finds itself demultiplied here.

But if, in an extreme way, Barth puts to flight the literary work, in a manner similar to the questioning of origins seen in Djuna Barnes's

Nightwood or in Gaddis's *The Recognitions,* he is not alone in having exploited the hermeneutic device of the work within the work. With varying intensity and intentions — it would be awkward and imprecise to suggest that the aims and effects of one technique were necessarily identical — authors as different as Jerome Charyn, David Carkeet, Russell Banks, and Vladimir Nabokov have successfully employed the metafictional *mise en abîme* in their novels.

Pale Fire

The game of mirrors played by the great Nabokov is better known than the work performed by other writers in this area, even though American critics display uncommon scruples in still hesitating to claim him as their own. Let us simply bear in mind that the shadowy narrator named Kinbote succeeds in casting doubt on the very origin of John Shade's poetic text, whose title ("Pale Fire") is granted to the whole novel. The suspicious or shameless claim — since it occurs after the fact — to the poem's inspiration by Kinbote's autobiographical narrative is at the origin of the shuttling between the second and first texts — although their order is not established in an incontestable way — that weaves together the threads of both the novel and its filigreed figures. This is less a matter of a self-reflexive novel than of the production of a fictional text through the possible fictions of the genesis of a text and/or of its reading. The hierarchical indetermination of the relations between the commentaries and the poem, the narratively centrifugal and psychologically centripetal movement of Kinbote's voice, the game of doubles, shadows, and returns, the accidental and provoked coincidences, the speculation on possibilities, and the suggestions of doubt make of this work an absolute reference for triumphant metafiction. Subject, characters, critical insights, and the fundamental problematic, while explicitly literary and reflexive, never block nor prohibit specifically "novelistic" situations — up to and including the adventure story. On the contrary, they favor, to a point previously unequaled, the verbal pyrotechnics, creative flights, and, finally, the magic that we continue to seek in the most traditionally satisfying stories and that makes use of all narrative instances: a character indirectly psychologized by the alterations of his voice, the genius of the portrait, the exoticism of the references, the multilayered plot . . . The greatness of a text that, without ever deluding us, consents, as though beyond the effort required by the reader, to let him return to childhood — a literary childhood, that is, if I can be excused for using a term so heavily charged in Nabokovia with perversity, a word singularly stripped of all wide-eyed innocence.

The Fiction/Magazine

The narrative universe in Jerome Charyn's seventh novel, *The Tar Baby,* is entirely different. While it is perhaps a more accessible book than Nabokov's *Pale Fire,* it is without a doubt more dated since it reads easily today as a symbolic gesture, a friendly doff of the hat addressed in passing to a metafiction once in vogue, by an *oeuvre* not characterized by metafiction on the whole. Not that Jerome Charyn does not resort to such knowing, even learned, winks on frequent occasions, whether by taking up forms inherited from detective novels in early works from his abundant *oeuvre,* such as *Secret Isaac, Marilyn the Wild, Eisenhower, My Eisenhower,* and more recently in *Paradise Man* or *Elsinore,* or by his use of motifs from popular literature in *Darlin' Bill* and *Pinocchio's Nose.* In *Pinocchio's Nose,* we recognize throughout the chapters such famous figures of contemporary literature as William Gass and Stanley Elkin, borrowing for the occasion their pseudonyms from the heroes of their own fiction ("The Pedersen Kid" and "George Mills" respectively). But one only has to leaf lightly through the pages of *The Tar Baby* to notice that the *mise en abîme* rules there: different typographies, insertions of many passages from outside the text; insets, statistics, classified ads, advertisements, readers' letters. This novel presents itself in the form of "a sometimes quarterly review"[29] whose title is *The Tar Baby,* a special issue in honor of a certain Anatole Waxman-Weissman, published in 1972 (the novel dates from 1973). The person in charge of the issue is the journal's editor-in-chief W. W. Korn, whose name easily inspires ridicule. This very amusing parody resorts to all of the headings of a magazine in order to stage an impressive number of characters who comment on each other's manuscripts and their papers, on the activities of inhabitants of the Galápagos Islands,[30] and even on those of a "school of Pragmatic letters and philosophies." The parody deploys all kinds of typographical and typesetting tricks to bring us into contact with the modes of composition of a dazzling variety of genres. The introduction in the form of a program by which Korn presents the object of his efforts stands as an example:

Here, then, are the detractors and the faithful, bitcheries and love notes, critiques by confidants and men who never met him, the gossip and crisp evocations of his teacher, his wife, a rodeo clown, and mother-in-law, comments on his work and illness, in an attempt to celebrate *and* grasp my one-time friend and contributing editor.[31]

Wittgenstein, about whose work the deceased (among others) constantly fantasized and wrote, holds — need it even be said — a preeminent place in this luxuriant novel.[32]

A Writing Course/Novel

Russell Banks claims to have conceived *Hamilton Stark* as a kind of writing course. Following the examples of many of his colleagues, Banks is certainly conscious of the stakes of narrative and of the means of its construction, capable of taking some distance from his creation while elaborating it; yet at the same time he is a marvelous storyteller whose language and talent for creating scenes never allow our attention to be caught solely by the literary devices at work before our eyes. Neither a haughty fan of metafiction nor a naive writer, Banks appears quite accurately to represent the particular synthetic stage at which a certain number of writers have arrived, those who practice what Alan Wilde has termed "midfiction."[33] Whereas *Hamilton Stark* excludes the possibility of any "magical coherence of fiction," it does not begrudge us the joys of narrativity, of portraiture, of description, and of plot. The novel is, however, a reflection on the mysteries of identity and, consequently, a study of the question of character in literature, paired with a meditation on point of view, the function of the hero, and the art of fiction. For the French reader, the novel is reminiscent of Robert Pinget's *The Inquisitory* (1962). It is made of documents having to do with the environment and the tradition within which Hamilton Stark lives, of testimony by his successive wives, recorded on tape and transcribed verbatim, of digressions and of notes permitting the contribution of peripheral information, of certain episodes of the lives of the hero and of the author/narrator, and, finally, of the text of the autobiographical novel (*The Plumber's Apprentice*) written by Stark's daughter Rochelle. Within this novel one finds anecdotes, detachable stories, bundles of memories including entire tales. The entire novel asks what might be the appropriate form to give to a narrative if there is to exist any chance whatsoever of penetrating the mystery of the principal protagonist. The criticism of the book is done, *in fine*, by a friend of the narrator. The structure of the novel is summarized explicitly by a spiral *ouroboros*; it brings to mind other images, those of Russian or Chinese dolls characteristic of the genre, or rather, of those genres rolled into one.

Delirium Clemens

David Carkeet's *I Been There Before* is also an amalgam of genres, combining daring intertextuality with equally audacious *mises en abîme*. It is a kind of dissertation, written by a man named Frederick Dixon who has been frequenting Berkeley's "Mark Twain" archives for years. Properly prefaced, introduced, and annotated, this academic survey makes known at least two important events. The first is that it was Twain's older brother

Orion Clemens who was the author of *Huckleberry Finn*; the second, that Mark Twain, born the year of Halley's comet in 1835, deceased the year of its return in 1910, remains faithful to this pattern by returning to America with the comet in 1985 and carrying out a brief second career, whose major highlights the "novel" attempts to relate. The West, the Mississippi, the East: each of these remains the same the second time around. The chapters are followed by letters written by Twain to his wife and children during his second stay on earth, by manuscripts of stories and travel narratives, by a series of appendixes in which the indispensable chronologies and bibliographies take their rightful place. In addition to these documents compiled with an impeccable knowledge of Twain's production and of his time, Carkeet enlivens Twain's correspondence with letters to Howells, the champion of literary realism at the turn of the century, in which the respective merits of various aesthetics are carefully discussed. In one of these letters to the respected dean of American literature of the time, Twain announces that he is thinking of writing a novel entitled *The Comet Man,* a work similar in many ways to the one we are in the process of reading.

Twain's return also allows him, as in the second part of *Don Quixote,* to remark upon the critical commentaries on his works written during his "absence." The extreme diversity of the discourses and documents, the declension of all genres and subgenres that this (at the very least) tempered realism allows for, the recourse to notebooks, sketches, notes, poems, annotations, unpublished works, tapes, and films would suffice to provide an interesting perspective on the mechanisms of literary history in which this novel itself is caught. Moreover, taken together, this constitutes an abundant and secret commentary on the preface to *Huckleberry Finn* in which the question of the relationship between lying and truth, between morals and morality provides a remarkable examination of the mask in literature. But Carkeet does not stop there; he goes on to double the new Twain-85/86 with a usurper named Oscar Umlauf, who takes his identity in order to throw another twist in the works. Disguised as a woman, just like Huck in his famous novel, Twain even manages to interview his double. We learn that God himself bears all the traits of Samuel Clemens: the literary joker enjoys a relationship with the cosmic prankster that is reminiscent of the one between Ellerbee and God the Father in Stanley Elkin's *The Living End.* It is clear that, on the basis of a comic situation and with lesser ambitions, and by resorting to devices that Nabokov would not have renounced, Carkeet restages the serious questions posed in *The Recognitions*: those of the counterfeit's relation to value, the status of the apocryphal, the connections held by invention, exaggeration, lies, and the double with the truth. Throughout the literary world, Twain sows the same anarchic upheaval that the passage of the

Duke and Dauphin always provokes in his famous work. No one emerges unscathed from this demolition by *delirium clemens*: neither criticism — Dixon's assistant, Olivieri, is presented as certifiably insane toward the end of the book, as he keeps on changing the official versions upon which the work of erudition relies; nor the pious images of literary history, passably worn down by situations in which certain of Twain's traits erode the vulgate; nor literary history itself, with the game of influences and borrowings blithely mocking chronology so that, for example, Twain is able to be influenced by James Thurber; nor, finally, the reader, misled for his greater pleasure by the stunning research work of a writer who is constantly setting traps for him. Listing the writers whom Twain has met, the text keeps checking that the reader is making the necessary leaps between history, fiction, and metafiction that a dizzying literary maelstrom is determined to confuse: "Howells, Kipling, Emerson, Longfellow, Holmes, Whittier, Lowell, Aesop — did that wake you up? — John Hay, Bayard Taylor, James Whitcomb Riley, etc."[34]

Reflexiveness Reigns

Critics tend most frequently to categorize such works under the broadened heading of "metafiction" — although they rarely enough refer to the specific works mentioned above in order to document the notion. Indeed, by attributing these writing techniques to long works, we run the risk of ending up with a kind of systematization that detracts from their effect. The uneven works of Raymond Federman are proof of this. For example, the technique of *Take It or Leave It* or of *Double or Nothing* is so visibly exploited that the novel ends up giving an impression of stylistic gadgetry; on the other hand, *The Twofold Vibration*, which owes part of its references to science fiction, fulfills its contract in a more satisfying way. The same is true for Sukenick; a remarkable theorist of new fiction, his works do not always serve as its most convincing illustration. While there is pleasure to be found in reading a short story as good as "The Birds," an integral part of the no less stimulating collection entitled *The Death of the Novel*, or novels like *Out, 98.6,* and *Long Talking Bad Conditions Blues*, the reader experiences a regrettable sensation of *déjà lu* in exploring *The Endless Short Story* or *Blown Away*. The staging of characters who are always named Ronald Sukenick can become tiring with time, no matter how innovative was their invention with the publication of *Up*, in the context of a "Jewish novel," whose profile and texture were thereby singularly altered. Nonetheless, in their best moments, these representatives of hard-core metafictional practice succeed in sharing their vision of a performative writing that tries, at times, to have literature considered as one of the plastic arts. Thus Clarence Major includes his own painting in *Emergency*

Exit; Steve Katz ranks first among the effects of *The Exagggerations [sic] of Peter Prince* or of *Moving Parts,* the dramatization in situ of the problems raised by the sentence or the plot under construction; Katz's *Weir and Pouce* parodies the conventions of the Tolstoyan novel; Peter Spielberg's *Crash-Landing* deliberately undermines all possibility of suspense by inverting the chronology of the reported facts.

But, in addition to these novels of metafictional structure, there exist many other exploitations of a literary mode that is open to a finite but abundant number of variations; indeed, the variety is so tempting that Robert Scholes has remarked that as many manuscripts of sub-Barth and sub-Vonnegut arrive on editors' desks today as the post office was able to deliver of sub-Fitzgerald or sub-Hemingway in the twenties.

For a long time, one was able to take Kurt Vonnegut's well-intentioned thematic platitudes exclusively for what they seemed to be: talented tales blackened by the experience of the Second World War, decrescendo variations on the beauty of simple values, existential formulations simplified for the soft-at-heart. Yet, the forms themselves and the thematized forms of certain of his novels — *Slaughterhouse-Five* and *Cat's Cradle* in particular — stem directly from our subject here. It is not insignificant that science fiction should underpin certain novels by Vonnegut, since its use authorizes changes in chronology and distortions of the categories of perception suitable for showing that mimesis is no longer de rigueur in a world whose spatiotemporal dimensions have undergone profound alterations. In *Slaughterhouse-Five,* Billy Pilgrim travels through time in order to escape the memory of the unforgettable and the unspeakable (the bombing of Dresden), the Trafalmadorians have such a peculiar conception of time and of the possible ways of seeing things that we can easily read this as a poetics; the adopted form is at once a commentary on the shattered real and on the possibility of prolonging obsolete novelistic forms.

More comically, but with more finesse and seriousness too, the form and the network of images of Brautigan's *Trout Fishing in America* prevent the reader from considering this "writing" — no other official mention of genre appears on the title page — as the mere cult-book of the generation of Woodstock hippies, the fictional equivalent of the best-seller *The Greening of America,* symptomatically parodied by Max Apple against the kitsch background of Howard Johnson restaurants under the title *The Oranging of America.* Beside the fact that the cultural tissue of America is reduced to literary shreds in Brautigan — in an iconic reprise of the rags of literature that covered the tattered hero of *A Confederate General from Big Sur* — all of the images of *Trout Fishing* lead toward a generalized metaphor of the book as object, as a kitchen, or as some sort of "Erector Set" of letters; no plot, no apparent continuity, no characters, strictly speaking, apart from a protean signifier that is at once the title of the book and the description of the activity carried out there principally but not exclusively; but a landscape that can be dismantled, a unity masterly forged by the distribution of images, an arbitrary and deformed ending, a cover whose unchanging illustration over the course of various editions refers to the immobility of an imagery that convinces us that literary speech is a variation on death: "Language does not leave fossils, at least not until it has become written."[35] Library-cemeteries and sentences no more capable of following the slender movement of trouts than of surviving their own completion, fixed statues and references immobilized by literary history, a quill in the shape of a hook caught on the cast of the imagination, a nylon line that unravels to give birth to paragraphs: so many expressions whose metafictional nature leaves no room for the least ambiguity. Book and metaphor of the book, *Trout Fishing in America* belongs to those literary objects about which Barth, adapting Borges, nicely said that even if they knew their algebra, they didn't forget their fire. Such a "writing" illustrates the observation made by LeClair and McCaffery in the introduction to their collection of interviews: "Now, though, we have novelists shifting among different modes, merging traditional forms and experimental energies, redefining the methods we've used to keep them separate."[36]

If, in many respects, this singular product of Brautigan's overflowing imagination proposes metaphors for writing, other masters of the genre integrate them more or less visibly into texts that refer constantly to their own genesis: "I wander the island, inventing it," proclaims the narrative voice in Coover's "The Magic Poker":

I make a sun for it, and trees — pines and birch and dogwood and firs — and cause the water to lap the pebbles of its abandoned shores. . . . I impose a hot midday silence, a profound and heavy stillness. But anything can happen.[37]

Should this movement of writing solidify into a "realism effect" (the sudden "hardness" of a blue kettle), the voice will take offense and be frightened off. Incessant variations on the theme of magic creation, a renewed visit to the museum of literary accessories, the title, "The Magic Poker," refers both to the combinations of a card game in which bluffing plays an important role and to the shape of a banal object, a stick, whose phallic possibilities become the object of amusing exploitations and the gesture of a fiction that always titillates and reignites the dying embers of the imagination. Variations on possible narratives, again, in the exemplary "The Babysitter" — whose structure, incidentally, has Gil Orlovitz's *Ice Never F* as its source — or in "Quenby and Ola, Swede and Carl," fragmentary stories whose kaleidoscopic aspects encourage the reader's hand to rotate the cardboard tube in order to create new configurations of a problematic "real," a real that holds only thanks to the fantasies generated by chosen details. The punning title of *Pricksongs and Descants* announces both an erotic and the structure of a collection faithful to the rules of counterpoint; it abounds in texts that stage, with an admirable variety of devices and means, the fundamental act. Thus, "The Leper's Helix" succeeds, at the completion of a carefully programmed itinerary, in fusing together reader, narrative voice, and character by relying for its development on the opposing forces of desire and repulsion, in a kind of geometric design that engenders and results from the superposition of theme and form.

In *Second Skin*, the fourth novel by John Hawkes, we again encounter the question of inscription upon a surface, yet in a more clandestine, submerged way. Tattoos, marks left on the desert, arabesques of natural forms, each of these complete for the attentive reader the games of ironic narrative distance due to the voice of one of those narrators whose word Hawkes has so often and so subtly encouraged us to doubt—from Zizendorf in *The Cannibal* to the crazy driver in *Travesty* through Cyril of *The Blood Oranges*. Under cover of dreamlike and aestheticizing narratives, Hawkes consistently proposes a meditation on writing that is discreetly caught within a complex web of metafictional practices.[38] An earlier chapter privileged the most provocative elements of Hawkes's first novel in order to establish its historical importance. *The Cannibal* is at least equally spectacular by reason of the parallels made there between text and sex, myth and history, and of the emphasis on the theme of communication, which is delicately tied to the more general question of the constitution of a credible referent, that is, of a second real, through signs. To forget that Zizendorf places his hopes for taking power in the thaw and the remobilization of sign systems would deprive this novel of an important dimension.

With *Willie Masters' Lonesome Wife*, William Gass literally gives body to textual activity. This curiously fashioned work (its covers display the front and back view of the naked wife of a "Will" who could, in the guise of Shakespeare or the author himself, figure all giants impassioned by writing; the paper of the pages changes color and texture according to the intensity of the passion exhibited there) represents a woman-text whose variously talented lovers struggle valiantly to satisfy her; this babbling "Babs" addresses them in erotic/literary terms as though in response to Susan Sontag's suggestion. The meanderings of the imagination and the material aspects of the writing figure there in the form of endless cross-references, textual drifts from one asterisk to another, circles left by the writer's coffee cup, and wrinkles resembling those of tousled bed sheets. The text takes body, becomes a body, while the body puts itself into words and expresses itself in the course of an alibi-narrative in which theme is strictly form(s).

Such is also a design of *Spanking the Maid,* Coover's brief novel whose project is linked to the ironic staging of a sadomasochistic Victorian paradigm in which to read the relationship of the text to its author and its reader, the tensions between referentiality and textuality, the reiterations of a largely intransitive desire. I will later discuss a text (Paul Metcalf's admirable *Genoa*) that, in a comparable manner but with different ends and means, stresses the interpretation of preoccupations with a literature of the past (in this case, the diaries of Columbus and Melville's stories) and the problems of writing experienced by the writer-narrator. In each of these cases, we are in the presence of works that would disprove Barnett Newman's statement, according to which "birds would make bad ornithologists"; furthermore, and inversely, the acute awareness of problems raised by the creation of fictions never blocks the development, dims the attraction, or confirms the potential dryness of the most highly metafictional narratives. If it is at times legitimate to find tiresome their confessions, or to borrow a term from painting, the "forefronting" of the experience of creators overly inclined to a kind of literary exhibitionism, no one can deny that such texts, not content with revealing the skeleton of the work, clothe it in a fictional flesh, where the lover of textures and grains, the hunter of narrative curves will also find what they seek. The humor, irony, and culture of their authors prohibit them from appearing as mere stylistic exercises, slimming plans for the imagination, an excessively systematic exploitation of a new theoretical vulgate.

For all that, some aspects of the grand metafictional gesture, which reached its peak in the seventies but whose traces are clearly felt in today's works, tend to feed on relationships to the real that the new nature — or perception — of the "real" justifies. Certainly, to echo Annie Dillard, the world is no longer the artist's subject, but it "is a warehouse of forms which the writer raids: this is a stick-up."[39] The contemporary reality of America can no longer be grasped monolithically, and, consequently, innovative fiction must reflect and interpret the signs of change in its own way; it is also worth recalling that a "self-aware" and "suspicious" literature can no longer think of itself *directly* as a "cultural document." Everything happens as though a new referential sphere had come to replace an accepted referentiality rendered impossible by the awareness of the diversity of social semioses. Distinct from its predecessor, this new sphere would refer to a world that plays on its own activities in a critical and distantiated manner, a mediated world to which fiction could now only refer in an apparently indirect way — but, in reality, closer to its methods of functioning, to a world of codes and signs, a world itself become fiction. Renewing the perceptions and practices of James, metafiction would in this way be the rediscovery and the "shameless" (in the true sense of the term), Pelagian exploration of the new space offered to a literature with blocked referential horizons. This is how, tangentially, the "new novel of manners" appears; Jerome Klinkowitz stresses that this genre cannot help being situated halfway between "realism" and "metafiction," to the extent that the real is increasingly perceived as a system of signs.[40] Lives lived as stories or as a collection of codes are answered by a fiction that, at the very least, tends to present the life of texts. Beyond the methods of reading the everyday, methods that have become indispensable to contemporary scientific research — in which true fictions are substituted for the more dated notion of hypotheses — encourage us to find again, in the logics of narrative, devices that seem astonished to correspond to the logics of the real. Dillard's "Lenses" recounts the reasons why our perception of the real supplies the frame for metafiction. Whence, perhaps, stems the idea, which Davenport relates to modernism, whereby the constraint of forms is bound to art, which is, strictly speaking, life itself. We shall return to this.

Potluck

Before we leave metafiction, let us briefly turn to the monument supposed to have put an end to it through sheer excess: *Mulligan Stew,* a dish concocted of whatever ingredients are at hand, a kind of potluck. By choosing this title for his novel, Gilbert Sorrentino declares his intention to have done with the sophistication of bourgeois literary cooking. *Mulligan Stew* could be to metafiction what Fielding's *Shamela* was to Richardson's sentimental novel: a form of revenge that "lays it on thick" in order to put an end to things. The heroes (Ned Beaumont), plots, styles, and clichés sprinkled throughout this hefty work are borrowed from the literary tradition. Whether stolen from Fitzgerald or Hammett, lifted from a note in *Finnegans Wake,* or chosen from among the most ridiculous offered by the enormous corpus of sentimental and serial novels, the characters' names program their behavior to a great extent. From Joyce and Flann O'Brien, his favorite prose writers, Sorrentino borrows plot fragments (the revolt of the characters) and literary arrangements that come to roost any which way in a grotesque story. *Mulligan Stew* has as its main protagonist a failed writer named Martin Halpin who is writing a novel in which is sketched the figure of another novelist who is equally unsuccessful. Sorrentino's parodic talents garner for us an amazing collection of "in the manner of . . ." depictions, covering a spectrum that ranges from pornography to the detective novel, by way of esotericism, erudition, and popular literature. His project consists in using the banal and the déjà vu to create something new and original by simple virtue of excess. *Ad unicitatem per trivia,* if you would. Hostile to metaphoric writing and confident in the "imaginative qualities of actual things" that his master Williams wanted to glorify, Sorrentino amasses genres and styles: letters, catalogs, bad poems, diaries, an incomprehensible play, leaflets, notebooks, questionnaires, directions. He inflicts upon us a hodgepodge of intertextual references in which he sees the reign of banality and of literary involution; he composes huge lists of imaginary books and journals, titles of artistic works, popular songs, illustrating on every page the exhaustion and redundancies of a fiction that puts its faith in old recipes. There is no development that does not reek of déjà vu or expose the emptiness of novelistic conventions, no matter how "innovative." By placing rejection letters from various editors at the beginning of the book, Sorrentino attacks critical clichés and mocks the literary circles and their jargon. At the earliest opportunity, the prose blisters, swells with overly rich food, gathers clichés and trivia. Through intertextual saturation, by defamiliarizing the obvious through accumulation, by overcoding the narration and constantly forcing its effects, Sorrentino goes "over the top," as they said in the trenches, and thus escapes a literary field that has already been plowed a thousand times. As soon as he touches it, his material self-destructs; the mediocrity, spinelessness, and vulgarity of his central character condemn the game of a time gone by to be convicted with no chance of appeal. Iconoclast, buffoon, show-off, mocking, and contemptible, the book becomes to literature what Falstaff is to the court.

Two impressions or two surprising effects survive these demolitions made joyful by Sorrentino's rare verve. First, by accumulating heaps of literary debris, mountains of clichés, wobbly metaphors, Sorrentino makes noticeable, as though by default or by the effect of implicit contrast, the possibility of a language other than the devalued one of traditional fiction. He is a remarkable producer of effects comparable to those that result from the "noise" of the intransitive, erring conversations of *The Recognitions*; he makes almost palpable a simple, direct, or dreamed language that routine and overuse have worn out or dismissed. A poetics can be read in the fault lines, like lovely colors seen in mire, vomit, bruises. He then secretly equips his narrative with a game of arbitrary structural doublings, a game based on rhythms, repeated colors, images, and identical segments, constraints foreign to those of narrative logics, all adventure playgrounds with precise rules that constitute, being freely assumed, so many spaces of freedom. Moreover, Sorrentino makes light so marvelously of the conventions he mocks; his voice so easily slips between the interstices of genres; his jubilation is so perceptible when he stuffs himself (and us) with the horrors exposed there, in the manner of an aesthete who contemplates, incredulously, the piles of kitsch souvenirs that line the streets of Lourdes and Mont-Saint-Michel; in short, his position, while infinitely serious, is so playful that the well-disposed reader can hardly resist it. In reading the passionate and highly original work that is *Mulligan Stew*, it is easy to believe that we are playing inside the magic room that Andrée Connors describes for us:

And the room of creative wonders: another strange small room not everyone gets into. But the lucky ones who do — that room pulsates with something eternal, is lit up like a neon slot machine hitting jackpot, delivers the most expensive thrill in existence, gathers together essential and mystical beings and lets you touch them for a minute, grants your soul total relief, allows you to tapdance with past and future races, invites you to probe into hidden recesses for goodies, and suggests you make the most of it all while you're in there, because you can only stay a minute anyway. The only key for that one is an insane trust in a gift of some obscure gods, and slavish work between visits.[41]

And who is not reminded, whether in reading this novel by Sorrentino, *Imaginative Qualities of Actual Things*, or *Aberration of Starlight*, of the unmatched joy of the child who, grown tired of his complicated toys and his picture books, goes quietly out to join his friends, rolls up his pants, gets his boots wet, and, deep in a puddle, kicks old tin cans until sunset?

Chapter 6
The Rule and the Games:
Aspects of Metafiction II

Accident, he would leave to life, which specialized in it.
— Alexander Theroux, *Darconville's Cat*

The "room of creative wonders" is strewn with toys. Each carnival that passes, each escape from childhood into a "room of one's own" proves to us that the ludic is simultaneously a more or less arbitrary, more or less motivated, mode of organization of the life of the imagination and a privileged path of access to new states of awareness. Games have their territories and their rules; to a great extent, metafiction delimits the former and institutes the latter. When the laws governing behavior and days are momentarily abolished or placed *en abîme*, a new space calls forth the games that it allows and the discoveries it makes possible. The fictional gesture authorizes all departures: departures "toward a new horizon and new sounds," as Rimbaud would say, "partings" too — and proudly displayed — of the real and the imaginary. We have seen that, with his monumental *LETTERS*, Barth invents a world exclusively peopled with characters from his earlier works, whom he urges to communicate among themselves. Such total artificiality is advertised without shame, since the author is sure that in this kind of laboratory instructive revelations will emerge, that the shocks of particles will set free a certain "charm" or "beauty," as molecular physicists would put it. In this clinic of the intertext, he pushes Valéry's definition to the extreme: "A work is executed by a multitude of minds and circumstances (ancestors, climates of opinion, chance events, previous writers, etc.) under the Author's supervision."[1] "To the extreme," because it is no longer a question of the ordinary intertextuality that infuses and sustains all works of fiction, but of an internal intertextuality where the relations and rules are determined by the sole arbitrariness of a creative gesture. The "Author" becomes a character, *primus inter pares,* like a circus ringleader in the center of the ring, tempted at times by an affair with one of the acrobats he presents (in this case, Lady Amherst, the only character added to the earlier cast of characters).

But I will not delve further here into the much broader — and much examined — problem of the often unconscious games of intertextuality, nor into that of the parodic exploitation of subgenres.[2] At the most, I will mention the conscious, voluntary, and even mischievous intertextuality of recent works, since the ludic dimension is of such importance there: *Four Roses in Three Acts,* by Franklin Mason, in which Gertrude Stein and Ernest Hemingway are the main topic of burlesque stagings, or Curtis White's *Heretical Songs,* where the "heresy" consists of playing with the imaginary adventures of such respectable characters as Mahler, Rossetti, or Debussy.[3] This is only briefly to indicate another type of border, or qualitative threshold, that allows us, for practical (and thereby artificial) ends, to distinguish "metafiction" from pure play.

Games Are Never for Nothing

Supposing, of course, that the expression "pure play" is not an oxymoron in the context we are concerned with here. In literature, play is not without ethical, political, or heuristic functions. All games imply morals; are there still places where the notion of a "debt of honor" has survived so well? Do rules so totally divorced from notions of power and coercion exist anywhere else? However, beyond this, games are never meaningless no matter how pure they might be, and the "stake" (*enjeu*) tells us just what the essential can owe to the ludic. Can one imagine a more religious place than the playing field, where the Law is transcendent at all times, right up to its status as absolute reference, in order to found, to make possible, the only moment in which it can be applied? There can be no games without the Law, and the cheater pays for his lapses with his plea-sure . . . except when he rediscovers it in the complications of the Rule that his actions create. The only cheater worth his salt is never caught, since, because he does not exist in the eyes of the Law that excludes him, he plays with the game, obeying its most stringent demands. In this way, there is nothing more devoid of existence than a cheater caught in the act. This is the reason for the disdain reserved for him. The touchstone of this moral absolute resides in the gratuitousness of its law.

When it comes to language, however, this law can only be relative: the received meaning of words serves as a measure of value, forces the game onto a field of power, rendering it less pure and gratuitous and, conse-quently, more constrained by the taking of positions that place it on a transitive moral field. Play is anathema to puritans because it sets aside current morals in order to institute its own. It is even more contemptible in that it threatens the established order of things by entering into an ideologically marked perimeter: that of language and its uses. If, as John Ashbery nicely puts it, metaphor is the figure in which "words, act [. . .] happy," we can see that puritanism, about which Mencken commented long ago that it incarnated "the haunting fear that someone, somewhere, might be happy," has only a relative tolerance for poetic language as defined by Jakobson (*pace* Michael Wigglesworth and Anne Bradstreet). One can also understand why Nabokov should have revolted a world that favors utilitarian language with his orgasmic overloads (*horresco referens*) of verbal networks and relations, perceptible, from then on, in literal terms of "obscenity." In truth, his texts are "off-scene" in their defense of a nonreferential moralism for literary art, at a considerable distance from the morality of art upheld by Gardner. As Joseph McElroy tells us, there cannot be

> morality in art unless there's art to begin with, in the sense of some successful passion for the medium, originality, radiance. So the message, for there *is* one, in *Pale Fire* is nothing without the life-giving shock and delight and composition of the pieces forming and reforming like parts of a model.[4]

In response to the "moralists," for whom the notion of literary "play" immediately implies gratuitousness— "art for art's sake" is as absurd an expression as "abstract painting" —narcissism, and uselessness, their opponents present the notions of respect or of the transgression of the rules of a language that governs social values and organization. When accused of self-complacency, they point out the "immorality" of complacent fictions, texts that push their fawning attitude toward their readers to the point of expanding their mimetic conceptions to include an imitation of those very readers' language. In this way, they claim to have too high an opinion of their readers and of the beauties that language brings to resort to such routine writings.

For Wittgenstein,

> there are *countless* kinds: countless different kinds of use of what we call "symbols," "words," "sentences." And this multiplicity is not something fixed, given once for all; but new types of language, new language-games, as we may say, come into existence, and others become obsolete and get forgotten. . . . Here the term "language-*game*" is meant to bring into prominence the fact that the *speaking* of language is part of an activity, or of a form of life.[5]

Linguistic investigations conducted by means of play inherit these formidable stakes, and one pays for the pleasure of the game with anxiety. It is Hind's fate in Joseph McElroy's *Hind's Kidnap*, to fall victim to this, since his existence — like that of the contestant on a TV game show governed by incomprehensible rules that Coover describes in a scene from "The Panel Game" — is doomed to the discovery of a path marked only by word games, synonyms, unknown quotations, vague allusions, tempting connotations, by the "noise" that fills the channels of a communication that is impossible, since it has no framework.[6] Lost in the labyrinth explored by Barth according to a different set of rules, Hind is unable to use this system of plural and contradictory information to carry out his hypothetical research, nor can he use it to chart the map of identities he is attempting to discover for himself.

"The Panel Game" parodies all efforts to discover an absolute truth through language. The unfortunate contestant — and the reader as well — tries to uncover the language that underlies this jungle of words,[7] only in order finally to realize that that upon which meaning "depends" might result in his own death by hanging. A macabre farce, this story has the brutal but scarcely forced realism of the stakes of language. From the possibility of discovering meaning by accident or through discursive changes suggested by the hazards of lexical vicinities, the itinerary of this buffoon-victim is doubtless none other than the one that makes us set out in discovery of meaning and ends, armed only with our own impoverished language. Regarding the latter, Annie Dillard in *Living by Fiction* describes vocabulary and syntax as the "decorated bucket" and "shovel" with which we reconstruct a world that can in no way be achieved with such childish tools. In *Pale Fire*, Shade decides to transform "accidents" into so many "ornaments," to amass the incomprehensible. The excess of uncontrollable information outside of recognized frameworks leads these characters to discover that "systems of perception and value, both inside and outside of fiction, are delimited by arbitrary selection and closure."[8] Perhaps this is the source of the enigmatic marbled page, an icon of the unthinkable and of impotence, that Sterne inserted into *Tristram Shandy*: we could "read" this "ornament" then as a reflection and structure to control "accidents," or the literary chaos pouring forth from both sides of this strange page, a chaos limited by the barely organized chaos of the flyleaf pages; we could judge then the power of the horror that governs the organization of "playful" objects and of the intensity of the terror that can result from it; we would understand the value of the arbitrary gesture that tries to master irresistible drifts.

In *The Postmodern Condition*, Jean-François Lyotard argues that the real is made up of "moves against discourse."[9] A whole range of contemporary American fiction shares this view and sees its own responsibility in a fight against the unacceptable "moves" committed by ideological apparatuses, in the proposal of "countermoves," new or oppositional moves likely to elaborate other frames within which the real can otherwise conceive itself.[10] In literature, play can never be meaningless: it continually presents these new frames for the experiencing of the real.

The ludic is easily subversive in a utility-minded and puritanical environment, even if, ironically, the *New England Primer* resorted, in order to educate the children of the American colonies, to forms of linguistic play that a fastidious orthodoxy should have condemned. America was able to accept the drifts proposed by the imagination as long as it was able to categorize their authors as jesters, to reduce comic subversions to the dimensions of humor. Most often, Americans prefer the buffoon in Twain to the iconoclast. James Thurber's revolting linguistic explorations (in *The Wonderful O* in particular, where the disappearance of one letter throws off an entire vision of the world — "shoe is she and woe is we") have suffered the fate reserved for Carroll's *Alice*: as books considered not safe for everyone, they have been locked in the ghetto of children's literature. In recent years, religious fundamentalisms have even succeeded in purging the body of children's literature of the classic *Wizard of Oz*, a work that is guilty, in their eyes, of offering an unacceptable "frame" for reading the real because it is "secular humanist." Old reflexes the weight of habit had managed to suppress, to repress at the center are now reemerging in monstrous folds on the margins of American society.

A Throw of the Dice, Often, Abolishes Chance . . .

"A man had the habit of drawing lots whenever he had to make a decision. And fared no worse than all those others who weigh the pros and cons."[11] Taking Valéry's scenario at its word, John Barth, Luke Rhinehart, and Robert Coover, each in their own way, explore the possibilities of stochastic existences.

In *The Floating Opera*, Todd Andrews — whose given name suggests that he is haunted by the idea of death, contemplates suicide from the first page of the novel. He does not relegate his choice to survive or die to a throw of the dice, but to the logic of an arbiter more libertarian than free, to a logic that, when pushed to an extreme, reveals the absurdity of the reasoning it makes possible. As the first element in a segment of literature dominated by a distanced and seemingly derisive existentialism (*The End of the Road* takes up this theme but moves toward different conclusions), *The Floating Opera* stresses that, having arrived at the inescapable conclusion that his life has no meaning, Andrews cannot escape a second conclusion: that his death would not make any more sense than his life. Certainly, the arbitrariness that presides over the decision to put an end to one's life is accompanied by a painstaking examination of reasons and ends. For all that, it reveals the gratuitousness of the fundamental act. The study of causes and of their infinite regression in time, of their familial and philosophical genealogy, allows Barth to set to flight, in infinite regress, the production of a discourse that could justify Andrews. With crate upon crate of index cards and notes amassed for the writing of his interminable "Investigation," philosophical research becomes a game in that there can be no hope of its ever being completed. Thus, in his first novel, Barth already affirms that, by throwing the snare of language upon the real and consciousness, one reaps only more language, rather than a siren who might be made to confess the secrets of her song.

By contrast, Luke Rhinehart decides to live "his" life armed with real dice (the protagonist's name is indistinguishable from the author's pseudonym). *The Dice Man* entrusts the making of even the smallest of his decisions to his little ivory cubes: whether or not to go out, whether or not to resort to violence, to leave his wife, to quit his job. The possible combinations transcend this binary structure, opening even wider ranges of chance to the protagonist; but, on the whole, he has no recourse to them. Everyday he makes a wager that lacks the programmed continuity of Pascal's own; he refutes the long term, playing one moment against the next, the minimal option against the maximal, leaving the solution of the black moments of his existence up to the chance arrangement of the little black dots. His days result from a multiplicity of throws whose sequential logic does not differ fundamentally from that which would be imposed by a "logic" for living informed by the life of events, equally aleatory and yet somehow perceived as more legitimately determining. The novel's irony is due not only to the fact that Rhinehart "fares no worse" than "all those others who weigh the pros and cons," but also to the fact that, unhindered by the stays of reasoning, which ordinarily leads to a definition of identity through choices, he finds himself in a privileged position for defining himself, beyond any utilitarian or motivated reaction that might contaminate his notion of a pure identity.

J. Henry Waugh, for his part, does not find his bearings in the world thanks to a pair of dice; he creates his world and makes himself its demigod, as his initials indicate (JHW, Jahweh). With *The Universal Baseball Association, J. Henry Waugh, Prop.*, Robert Coover examines the act of fiction under cover of arbitrary invention. Waugh creates, throw after throw, a detailed history of baseball teams that he places in competition on his dining-room table through the intermediary of a sophisticated system of equivalences: for a certain combination, a certain throw, movement on the field, and score; for a certain sequence of combinations, a certain violation, penalty, or mishap; for a certain series of sequences, a certain succession of oppositions, a certain development of the championship that is taking place in his head. Since, all things considered, this is an assisted exercise of the imagination, a situation in which the dice serve only to set in motion a world created outside of themselves through the sole power of the desire to imagine. So we believe. For *The Universal Baseball Association*—the name given by Waugh to the championship whose archives he meticulously compiles over the course of the "seasons" spent in his pitiful interior, compensating in this way for his no less pitiful existence as a bullied accountant—seizes an unexpected independence one day. When a lethal combination puts an end to Damon Rutherford's days as the league's favorite pitcher, the Association, divided by the myths that quickly attach to the existence of its lost heroes and by the concurrent readings of its history, asserts itself: the creator disappears from the novel, his creatures set themselves free in order to remain alone on stage and play each other. The dice end up throwing chance out of the game, once the time immemorial of their creative function has passed. History and myth step in. The demigod relinquishes its place to other demons. *The Universal Baseball Association* is not the only novel by Coover that is modeled after a game. Hidden beneath the tragic and grotesque detective enigma of *Gerald's Party*, there is another game in which dice play an important part. This story without a past, generated *ex nihilo* by the possibilities of gratuitous propositions, has its obscure source in an old, unpublished play entitled "Murder and Entertainment," which was intended to poke fun at the enigmas of 1950s British taste, with cocktail parties as its setting. Based on the rules of the board game "Clue," in which players must find the murder weapons in various rooms of a house in order to identify the murderer, the play merrily breaks the rules and has all five characters confess to the crime. The dice are loaded this time and they "abolish chance" with a vengeance, since their decision no longer matters.

Ciphers and Letters

Dice allow for an arbitrary organization or even creation of the real. Numerical sequences and alphabetical order allow for others that are just as effective, and whose heuristic power is just as great. A segment of contemporary fiction, while distancing itself from the gauche, hybrid, and poorly defined genre of the "poetic novel," borrows from poetry that aspect that was for a long time considered its most characteristic: the arbitrary constraint, that creator of new meanings. Constricted by intangible forms, the poem makes language bend to them, setting new meanings and unknown pleasures free. The preconstrained and arbitrary structures of Walter Abish, Harry Mathews, or Gilbert Sorrentino lend their fiction an excess of order that makes obvious the extent to which the more familiar order of conventional structures entails equal, and equally meaningful, constraints. Within such demands, these writers find pleasure; preferring ribbons to straps and girdles, they practice an erotic of the fancy corset.

The works of Walter Abish are published by New Directions, where they frequent those by cousins named Queneau, Nabokov, Jarry, David Antin, and Borges. For a good number of them, as is the rule in Oulipo (*Ouvroir de littérature potentielle,* to which Mathews, Georges Perec's translator and friend, belongs), literary language relies on formal constraints, among which absolute freedom appears only as a variant. For Abish, playing with the latent energy of the mechanisms of language means forcing language to confess more than its heedless usage can offer; creating the impression that language plays with the consciousness of the writer, an active partner, master of tactical choices, certainly, but only a partner. Language, in turn, drags him further than he may want, perhaps even to his project's limits. Gaiety, independence, positioning, and ruses of the one toward the other and of the other toward the one, invitation, acceptance, refusal, interference: games. The production of unpledged meaning.

Deciphering a Continent

As indicated by its title, Abish's *Alphabetical Africa* is arranged alphabetically. The first section, which attempts to remain a narrative, can only use words beginning with the letter *A*; its second section allows for words that start with *A* and *B*; its third extends the possibilities to *A,B,* and *C* . . . And so on until the twenty-sixth section, in which "anything goes," before the twenty-seventh section drops the *Z,* the twenty-eighth drops *Z* and *Y,* as it heads back toward the *A,* the second point in a horizontal diamond structure.[12] Regarding first-person narratives, one can imagine the complications: "I" cannot appear before the ninth section, nor can the narrator's presence; "me" and "my" must wait until the thirteenth section. The "I" is a victim of the game: je(u). The problems are considerable; for the French reader, only the inventiveness found in Raymond Roussel or Georges Perec's *La Disparition* (*Disappearance*: how painful the most playful titles become in time!) might serve as an equivalent example. This novel demonstrates that such a radical constraint is not a matter of "pure play"; creativity is needed to an extreme degree; certainly, the exploration inspires us to do some deciphering; it also forces us to clear new and fertile land.

Spelling and Nothingness

In a similar but not identical way, the alphabet structures Sorrentino's *Splendide-Hôtel*. Each section has a letter as its title, in the usual order. But this short "novel" of sixty-four pages has more than just a Rimbaldian title — "The Hotel Splendide was erected in a chaos of ice and polar night."[13] As in the sonnet of vowels and *Illuminations,* the letters of the alphabet function as pretext to verbal meditations resembling those of Rimbaud, certainly, and those of William Carlos Williams and William Gass as well.[14] The text feeds on sensorial and intellectual associations; forms of the letter, contexts of the letter, sound of the letter. Creation feeds on the plastic, acoustic, and semantic evocations of letters taken as the primary material of language, minimal forms/meanings whose incontrovertible reality can even prohibit transcendence: "One wishes simply to say that the writer cannot escape the words of his story, he cannot escape into an idea at all."[15] As Williams said, "No ideas but in things," and everything would seem to indicate that, following his lead, Sorrentino is investigating not the "imaginative qualities" of "actual things," but of letters/forms themselves.[16] *Encyclopaedia* does not have Richard Horn as its "author" but simply as its "editor." From "abortion" to "zoo," just under two hundred entries classify the objects of a world where action and characters live on in the explosion of a borrowed form. *Curricula,* objects and products, quotations, excerpts from diaries find their place there amid an arbitrary structure that is proposed as more "logical" than the disorder of the world.

"Imaginative Qualities of Actual Words"

In *Minds Meet,* Abish focuses his attention and ours on the possibilities of signifiers making sense autonomously, signifiers being used here somewhat as pictures are used in Godard's films. Arranged alphabetically, this is a series of micronarratives, of events engendered by the semimotivated closeness of words ("The Abandoned Message," "Abashed by the Message," "Abashed While Receiving the Message," and so on); the texts produced in this way are at once programmed and unpredictable. On the one hand, the developments that might justify these "legends" are limited; on the other hand, Abish treats signifiers as Terry Fox and Robert Smithson do their sculptures: inert objects at first, they allow their meanings to resonate according to a group of emotive and/or intellectual "keys." The desired aim entails breaking the ordinary associations between words and things, defamiliarizing common usage in order to create new familiarities. *Mutatis mutandis,* Abish manipulates our verbal expectations in the same way as Andy Warhol manipulates the viewer's pictorial expectations. He constructs texts made of signifiers that have been exploded and deformed by the ensemble of refractions produced at the heart of language, the absolute medium of the writer, demonstrating that his material is infinitely divisible. This limited sample of the possibilities of fission and reprocessing inspires greater respect for that which is described as a considerable source of energy and power.

In the Future Perfect contains the seed of *How German Is It*: "The English Garden"; its title and its combinatory recall the setting of Peter Greenaway's film *The Draughtsman's Contract.* "Ardor/Awe/Atrocity" list the imaginative and generative possibilities of a certain number of words taken from the dictionary in alphabetical order, duly numbered and "recycled"; when they reappear in subsequent sections, they bear in superscript the numbered reference to their first occurrence. Thus the entropic list from "ardor" to "zero" never stops returning to the seventy-eight remembered terms. Inspired by computer science, "Read-Only Memory" is structured around speculations on the word "message" that generates the story. This is also the case of the word "barrier" (emotional, absolute, physical, linguistic) in the short story ironically entitled "Access." "In So Many Words" announces the number of words in the paragraph without stating whether this number programs the writing or whether it merely summarizes the verbal energy expended in the narrative unit. America is treated here in somewhat the same fashion as Germany in *How German Is It*: the glistening surfaces of "the real" are barely able to contain the probable eruptions of an enormous repression. But, what is more, a sophisticated iterative model forces alternate paragraphs to be composed only of terms that follow each other alphabetically in the dictionary, whether syntax is respected or not.

A similar creative combinatory that aims to interrogate the possibilities when starting from a finite object inspires certain experimental projects, among which I shall mention "2," the "dodecahedric" story by A. B. Paulson,[17] and the symbolic factorization of the Möbius strip in "Frame-Tale," which "frames" our entry in Barth's *Lost in the Funhouse.* In all of these cases arbitrary formal systems are set in place and in action, intended for the systematic exploration of linguistic possibilities that a strictly referential language would never have occasion to exploit. The determination to signify under constraint is perhaps best illustrated by Sukenick's *98.6,* where the very failure to derive new meaning from arbitrary combinatories generates the text itself. Sukenick (or rather "Ron") wants to compose a "pangram," a "sentence that uses every letter in the alphabet once but only once."[18] His greatest success is "Vex'd nymphs waltz jig fuck borq." Of course, in this sentence only "borq" does not manage to signify according to everyday semantics, even if the balance of the pangram demands some imaginative acrobatics. The pangram collapses, but its failure brings with it variations on the letters that cannot be integrated and that will henceforth circulate in the novel, in search of a meaning. An artificial revenge but one that conforms to the ruling arbitrariness, these variations designate an invented language called "bjorsq" that takes on increasing power as the story continues. The art of cooking up such leftovers calls everything into question, up to and including the idea of waste.

To different ends, Joseph McElroy resorts, in a more utilitarian manner perhaps, to identical alphabetical structures so that he may provide David, the central character of *A Smuggler's Bible*, with the means of constructing the book of multiple compartments that we are reading and makes it possible to smuggle its many possible meanings. Eight "memories" are sequentially tied together by brief narrative sections that go from *A* to *Z* and back from *Z* to *A*, and provide a structure for the assembly of the book itself. The sentence that ends the first page under *Z* shows us David trying to subtract the letters *t, u, v, w, x, y, z* from an old friend's "soup of letters." Thus is organized the memory of a character in search of narrative structure, thus is a familiar form borrowed in order "clandestinely" to set in transit plural and multiform meanings, that were not receivable in their original form.

Learning to Tell

One comes before two. This fact is perhaps considered more "natural" than the fact that *A* comes before *B*. We must have counted before we wrote, with the hand preceding the pen. Yet, to arrange a narrative by numerical order with no relation to chronology raises, no matter the intention, the question of the motivation behind such an order. Some choose to emphasize this very arbitrariness, adopting as the logic of their narrative the skeletal structure of numbers alone. In so doing, they stress that suspicion falls, perhaps above all, on causality, narrative time, narrative links, on what Aristotle will forgive me for naming the "teleo-logic" of stories.

These questions, illustrated in France by the works of "Alamo," of which Jacques Roubaud is the most eminent representative, are formally picked up by Ron Silliman and the stories of Robert Coover. Silliman turns to the Fibonacci series to structure *Tantjing*, in which each paragraph contains the number of sentences equal to the sum of those included in the two previous ones. The deep structure of "The Elevator" in *Pricksongs and Descants* is numerical. Each "level" of the narrative has its number, its numerals, and its secret equations; each section of the story has its "floor." The opening — the nonresolution — desired for the problematic "end" of this series of phantasmal explorations is illustrated by the nonequivalence of the parts and the "floors." Stephen Dixon's collection of *Fourteen Stories* poses an analogous enigma. Thanks to the hesitation between "story" and "stor(e)y" in English, Dixon exploits the "play," in the mechanical and ludic meanings of the term, that exists between the title of the story that gives the volume its title and the number of texts it contains. This book, like Sorrentino's, and Brautigan's *Trout Fishing in America* in part, is a hotel: the metaphor is serious in that it reminds the reader of his/her necessary contribution to those literary Spanish inns and secretly designates the lack from which all novelistic structures suffer (for superstitious reasons, there is never a thirteenth story in old American hotels); the numbering of the parts draws attention to the impossibility of making the real correspond to its linguistic exploitation and emphasizes the gap between the imperious order of numbers and the structural liberties of stories.

With the forty-two fragments of "The Gingerbread House" (*Pricksongs and Descants*) Coover places the possibilities of narrative side by side, telescopes the literary time and sources of a selection of tales into improbable simultaneities, mixes the pronouns into ambiguous and embarrassing confrontations: ever imperturbable, the numerical order of the fragments stresses the ironies by artificially framing what is uncertain and diffuse. This silent irony of numbers, employed by Jonathan Baumbach as well, grows in effectiveness when the gap between their neatness and the necessarily vague and less controllable proliferation of the objects described or the narrative possibilities increases: in "The Hunchback Trout" (*Trout Fishing*), Brautigan compares a creek to a row of 12,845 telephone booths, not one more, not one less; the cat that answers to the name "208" stubbornly refuses to see this name justified by the number of the room where he lives. "The World War I Los Angeles Airplane" (*Revenge of the Lawn*) reduces the mysteries of a life and of a disappearance to thirty-three apparently unrelated propositions in order to illustrate the inevitability of a "story" transcending the logic of language: "Always at the end of the words somebody is dead."[19] Donald Barthelme pours the form of his "Glass Mountain" into the preconceived mold of one hundred largely unrelated propositions, and places numerical splints on the existential disorder that fills the eighteen sections of *City Life*. Rather than one hundred paragraphs, it is one hundred chapters that lend a semblance of controlled form to Alexander Theroux's extravagant novel *Darconville's Cat*, and the fiftieth, not surprisingly, is a "dialogue."

Not only does Harold Jaffe divide his short story "Underbelly" into two seemingly unconnected but numbered parts, but the fragments of each of these stories are themselves numbered in an intentional disorder.[20] At the bottom of a page, a note in the form of instructions indicates the following: "The numerals (41) within parenthesis apply to an alternate way of arranging the 'panels.' Several other arrangements are possible too, since the panels are portable, variable. Try it with dice."[21] Finally, in "Mr. and Mrs. McFeely at Home and Away" (*The Life and Times of Major*

Fiction), Baumbach goes so far as to semanticize the panels of alpha-numerical signals that he uses to organize the various fragments; in using the letters *A* to *N*, he confers an infinite numerical value upon this last letter ("N . . .") in order to point out that this final section is not the last possible one; in this way, the explicit thematics of the double and of "pretending" are reinforced.

Assumed Arbitrariness

Beyond suspicion, contemporary American fiction often chooses to display the arbitrary nature of its formal and thematic choices in numerous other ways. Dismissing the official parameters of the novel, Hawkes followed in the footsteps of Flaubert, who once said to the Goncourt brothers: "I'm not interested in the story, the adventure of a novel. When I write a novel, I want to render a color, a nuance. For example, in my Carthage novel, I want to make something purple."[22] Defining character as the source of linguistic energy on the page, William Gass masks the fictional nature of *On Being Blue* under the ironic subtitle, "A Philosophical Enquiry"; in this surprising text, the color blue occupies the space left vacant by the rejection of character and plot. I want to suggest here that *On Being Blue* is perhaps, in the last analysis, the kind of novel "about nothing" that Flaubert dreamed, whether puce or purple, of writing. In the place of plot, we find a systematic exfoliation of the suggestive possibilities of the color blue, somewhat like Sorrentino's *Blue Pastoral* or *Splendide-Hôtel*.[23] From skies to periwinkles, to the pornographic harmonics of the adjective,[24] blue invites us to consider the halos and auras of meaning that take shape around those objects associated with its shades, like so many stories or secret tales. Gass is a verbologist just as one can be an oenologist, a gourmet of the small sensations of vocabulary and syntax; he can well afford to have only one "official" novel to his name thus far, even though his by now mythical twenty-five-years-in-the-works *The Tunnel* will be out by the time these pages appear in English: his philosophical and critical essays have the flavor of fiction, and they work in an identical way. In concentrating the fires of his immense intelligence and culture on the mysteries of language, Gass denounces the arbitrary nature of the borders between literary genres, relying instead on the arbitrary nature of his personal dictates. An essay on the conjunction "and" makes of it a character, its syntactic insertion makes of it an element of the plot; the sensual waves of phonemes and signifiers often serve as decor. Without doubt, the abrupt aphorism that Purdy attributes to Madame Girard in *Malcolm*: "Texture is everything, substance is nothing,"[25] applies nowhere better than to Gass's work — except perhaps to that of Alexander Theroux, for whom the exoticism of sound and vocabulary contends with the convolutions of rhetoric, a major character, all the better to minimize the themes. A very similar set of choices governs the strategy of Jaimy Gordon's *Shamp of the City-Solo* and many of Guy Davenport's stories.

By shifting the arbitrary, and sliding the Archimedean point of fictional conventions, Gass chooses to give text to his visions of the world. Convinced that language is everything, permitting even the sensorial perception of things, he sets it up as a hero, as an enigma and as the theme of his writings. In this way, he restores their heuristic power to games of language and stresses to what point we are affected by them. There is no experience, he tells us, beyond that of language, and he sheds new light on a number of recent texts by showing that their imitation of old languages or invention of new ones functions as more than banal mimetic representations of a given experience.

When voices as different — and of as unequal interest — as those of Barth (*The Sot-Weed Factor*) and Erica Jong (*Fanny*) rediscover the language of the eighteenth century, when Mary Lee Settle in *Prisons* adopts the speech of Cromwell's time, and Norman Lavers the language of the explorers of the sixteenth century in *The Northwest Passage,* these choices contribute not only to the local color and the historical veracity: beyond obeying certain mimetic determinations, they claim the arbitrariness of a filter. On a more profound level, the linguistic inventions of Russell Hoban (*Riddley Walker*), Georgiana Peacher (*Mary Stuart's Ravishment Descending Time*), and Joseph McElroy (*Plus*) force us to reexamine the unstable relations between language and the real. The invention refers to a new mimetic mode, bends the usual determinations, and emphasizes the almost plastic constraints to which language subjects our world, both inside and outside of ourselves. We might recall that, in a more polemical mode and harsher terms, this was the keystone to William Burroughs's creations. Yet, by identifying language as a virus before subjecting it to prosecution in his tortured texts, attempting to destroy the totalitarianism of discourses through the tempered arbitrariness of his "cut-ups" and "fold-ins," Burroughs chose to do violence to the source of all violence. Gass chooses to make love to words, the origin of all pleasure, to play with language in order to escape the arbitrary oppression of traditional rules. Burroughs fought. Gass fraternizes. Others decide to truly get to know language, that old acquaintance, to study its arcana, to make it reveal under hypnosis, as Georgiana Peacher does, what it wouldn't ordinarily admit, to pull new maps of meaning from its secrets, like Russell Hoban, to push to its extreme the exploration of a vocabulary that "pretended to exhaust elements for which even the reaches of uncommon brutality had no interest, no access and no word,"[26] to make it retrace the steps that lead from first words to memory and desire, like McElroy in *Plus.* Complicity, love at first read, new decks of cards: arbitrariness.

Gutenberg's Revenge

Topographical investigations (these explorations of textures, reliefs, and flows) are only separated by one letter from typographic games: the context makes it our merry duty to change it.

These games are the most visible means of demonstrating that we are no longer fooled, since they dramatize *ex abrupto* the materiality of language whose potentialities preceding games had it as their sole goal to emphasize. The visual concreteness of the page and the "voluminosity of the word itself," as Mikel Dufrenne puts it,[27] motivate a plastic exploitation of words and phrases. The work of Federman feeds—perhaps meagerly—on similar confessions, as though the written, cut to the core by McLuhan's hasty dismissals, wanted to be assured of revenge. With pages organized in double columns for a hypothetically simultaneous reading,[28] typographical chaos miming the conflict of consciousness, mirror-like compositions intended to reinforce the thematics of a problematic identity: *Double or Nothing* and *Take It or Leave It* shift the mimetism of narratives to a material mimetism that can be read from a distance. We have seen the ways in which Gass profited from this materiality of signs in *Willie Masters' Lonesome Wife*. But others make use of it to different effect. This "self-reflexive visual exuberance," this "typographical chuckle"[29] characterize Steve Katz's *The Exagggerations of Peter Prince*, whose doctored title reinforces the semantics of the words that make it up and whose dense pages mix a self-referential story with typographical pirouettes characteristic of this imp of contemporary fiction. *Creamy and Delicious* avows his pleasure (its subtitle is "Eat My Words [In Other Words]"), *Cheyenne River Wild Track* his harassment techniques, *Weir and Pouce* the outrage that spelling can inflict on Tolstoy. Arbitrariness reigns in *Creamy and Delicious*, with the "chapters" appearing in an apparently handset typography not exempt from overloads and deletions, with numbers that are not sequential (the first one is 10), the "three satisfactory stories" at the beginning are "numbered" *H, U,* and *B* (with "hub" designating the nonexistent center), the "mythologies" that make up the essential part of the book are strewn with old photographs bearing no direct link to the story. Moreover, the preface to *Saw* tells us:

The order of these "reports" is arbitrary although their accuracy is strict. They can be read at any hour of the day and there is no time limit. The natural number and order of words in each report has been strictly regulated by universal laws that are presently being studied, and the events accounted for within each individual report are arranged in a sequence and system according to a code that isn't yet deciphered. Each report is numbered and those numbers may be disregarded since they were imposed on the text by myself as an expression of my personal fondness for a certain number.[30]

Word Rain by Madeline Gins declares up front the aspect of the "rain of words" that will fall down upon its pages in a form that owes a bit to the logic of calligrams and much more to a kind of typographical determinism. Subtitled "A Discursive Introduction to the Intimate Philosophical Investigations of G, R, E, T, A, G, A, R, B, O," it is based on the theory of sets, and superimposes its deletions, its volumes, and its returns on the developments of a formula where *G* is gas, *R* is reason, *E* is energy, *T* is time, *A* is attention. The text is contaminated by noises surrounding the scene of writing and the desirable rhythm for reading is indicated by "keys" meant either to control our level of attention or to distract us.

More than as novels, these works are intended as "performances," in the theatrical meaning of the term. Their narratives constantly move away from the linear logic of their progression, preferring spirals, digressions, little leaps over obstacles, angles, ellipses, fading away. Sukenick puts these devices to great use and constantly reminds us that they are no more artificial than the traditional modes of narrative development. To turn to books such as *Long Talking Bad Conditions Blues, The Endless Short Story,* or *Out* is to contemplate a verbal landscape, a possibility-producing machine, rhythmic couplets of a music aiming to fill a space. These "word-spewers" fill what they consider, in an almost Mallarmé-like fashion, "volumes" and usually answer yes to Barthes's question: "Is 'to write' an intransitive verb?" The rejection of traditional narrative forms literally jumps into sight. Although their successes are uneven, these works consciously belong to a radical fraction of contemporary fiction. Borrowing their forms as much from "rap" as from painting and concrete poetry, they are not content to manipulate language in order to reveal the traps it sets for our conception of the real and of history; like printers or musicians, they prefer to compose autotelic objects in which the pleasure of the game plays a large part, and that all place a spectacular emphasis on the devices relied upon to fabricate any fiction.

Paradigms Refound

Arbitrariness can also be displayed through the adoption and systematic declension of apparently unmotivated paradigms that, on the whole, could be read as allegories. Self-reflexiveness, in this case, is located, in a play on themes rather than in a play on forms. While it is often difficult to distinguish between the two manipulations, the stress often falls more on the transformation of finite materials than on an exploratory journey along an axis of infinite possibilities. In "Woman Followed by Blue Lions," David Diefendorf forces the theme of its fragments to develop the narrative promises of a title whose possible sonorities vary along with phonetics: the program changes to "Woman Followed by Blue Lines," then "blue lives," "blue limes," and so on, until reaching "Woman Followed by Beau Linus."[31] But the maieutic potential of paradigms is more spectacularly illustrated in fictions where, significantly, text, sex, and cooking exchange mechanisms, combinatories, and variations.

Within the limits of a closed metaphor governed by a game of "instructions" — from cooking recipes to treatises on sexual hydraulics by Masters and Johnson, the possibilities are staggering. *Creamy and Delicious* is presented as a shopping bag "filled with a nourishing assortment of various fictions."[32] *Country Cooking* by Harry Mathews gives unmakable recipes that in the end provide only the pleasure of savoring the text itself. Coover's *Spanking the Maid* tirelessly reworks the possible variants of a spanking, going so far as to equate the pleasures of this sadomasochistic exercise with those of reading the text itself. One of the more noteworthy passages of Peter Spielberg's *The Hermetic Whore* superimposes a nightmarish culinary vision with erotic dreams. Food, sex, and death decline their metaphors in a more dynamic but equally closed fashion in *Trout Fishing in America*. The book's shape and the logic of its iconography result from recurring images of recipes, fictive or real drunkenness, cravings, orgasmic ascents, their imaginary exploitation and their sad results. The mechanical diagram of composition explodes in "The Cleveland Wrecking Yard": the central elements of its imagery and thematics are sent off to the scrap heap, sold off altogether. The "mayonaise" with which the book ends, produced through mixing and repeated movements, a final concerted effort to leave the last word — misspelled at that . . . — to arbitrariness and to preserve the openness of a narrative that is doomed by its physical dimensions to closure, cannot help but "turn" bad.

Festivities in the Prison of Language

Page after page, chapter after chapter, these fictions decline the possibilities of well-worn thematics. The game gathers momentum in the banality of the themes, springs in the liberties of the imaginary, before it runs more or less violently into the prison bars of language. Substitutions, combinations, permutations, transformations, all of this juggling within the most free and playful narratives demonstrates the unavoidable limitation that is inherent to the medium. The varieties of desire profit from the rules and the limits imposed on them and find their true nature there. This frustration, intensified by language, proves to be both fertile and formidable. Just as desire is never exhausted, due to the barriers imposed on it, so too these fictions, programmed failures, call forth the creation of new fictions, a site for the play between the imaginary and the means at hand. Reworked a thousand times, these privileged paradigms, in their declension, mimic on another level the stakes of all fiction. And therefore of all existence.

Relying on the recognizable series of nodal concepts (Love, Marriage, History, Desire, America, and even Anthropology) that supply the chapter headings for *Why I Don't Write Like Franz Kafka*, William S. Wilson examines the problems inherent to the act of fiction through the linguistic scruples of logical positivism; investigating the most appropriate forms to account for their interferences (Socratic dialogues, correspondences, overheard conversations), he redefines them in a tangential way: each text seems far from its official topic; in fact, it illustrates the impossibility of identifying in it the fixed concept to which common usage tends to refer.

The paradigm can be identified thematically: Stanley Crawford draws the portrait of a paranoiac from the inside by communicating to us the tyrannical structure of maniacal "instructions" that he leaves for his wife, daughter, and son (*Some Instructions to My Wife*). It can also take the form of a recurrent discursive or syntactic model: in *Wrinkles*, Charles Simmons composes forty or so minibiographies that, no doubt, only amount to one. Each section recounts the hopes of the past, the present situation, the horror of disappointments to come. "Then," "now," and the future perfect imperturbably scan the becoming of ideas, of life, and of things. The subject changes with each section. Since the form remains the same, it becomes the subject. As it intersects the official subject (the "wrinkles" of the title), it is more deeply worrying. The paradigm can accentuate the arbitrariness of its choices through borrowed structures (Sorrentino) or objects stripped of their objective value (the number forty-three as generator of Katz's *Moving Parts*, the number seven in Vonnegut's *Slaughterhouse-Five* or the image of the threshold in Clarence Major's *Emergency Exit*). Whatever its nature, in all cases it stresses that the "emergency exit" of fiction often opens onto life, that fictional games are on the order of the pleasures and pains of this world.

Sport as Metaphor

Meaning cannot be mined in its raw form in nature and is no more available "ready to use" from the stores and galleries of culture. Meaning is construction, "rhetoric with a vision" as Henri Meschonnic would say, and its quest, barring one's acceptance of the jails of the absolute, gains worth in its trial and its wanderings, enriches itself from its limits, as from its necessary and liberating failures. Process, therefore, a movement of consciousness, subjected to the active geometry of desires. The real is constituted by the scaffoldings of a narrative, is read behind the grids of tinkered forms. Meaning is not given; it is given shape, given body, given detail; it is given order. *Poiesis*: creation, an ardent modulation of the given aiming at transitory, ephemeral, volatile meanings. The everyday is literary. Human activity feeds on its own story. Sports can thereby become a kind of poetics if, as in the case of Coover, DeLillo, Charyn, Nabokov, and Baumbach, we agree, rather than limiting ourselves to violent or bovine, but always vicarious contemplations of the body, to look at it in the same way as all metaphors, to read in its practices the displacement of earlier battles (war, aging, collaboration, love, or self-transcendence . . .) where for all eternity is projected or translated the difficulty of being, a way of being in life, a manner of recounting the world, of giving it, for a fleeting moment of creative dream torn from the revolting weight of things, a possibility of meaning.

In literature, sport is a "game" that is more motivated than others. It distinguishes itself — through the rigor of its rules — from absolute arbitrariness; but it is only a game among others, like fiction, and so, it lends itself well, in literature, to secondary games. The novels of Don DeLillo often have games as their central notion: sport (football) in the ambiguous *End Zone,* whose title signifies the end of the world as well as the playing surface; mathematical games in *Ratner's Star;* baseball in a novel in progress. At all times, rules are the rule. "Strict rules add dignity to a game," we read in *Ratner's Star.*[33] Carefully structured, games — and sports in particular — satisfy our need for order and, paradoxically, for security. In games, everything is a matter of limits, boundary lines, non-negotiable codes. As DeLillo tells us, games provide a frame within which excellence might be attained: "We can look for perfect moments or perfect structures."[34] Selvy takes part in a kind of game by trying to escape his murderers in *Running Dog.* Southern Texas is so vast as to appear limitless; but its immensity is compensated by the interior rules limiting a game that has no spatial constraints. These "almost metaphysical"[35] rules organize the equally violent games of *Great Jones Street* where they constitute the last refuge of a crumbling identity. In Nabokov (*The Defense*) or Charyn (*Going to Jerusalem*), the game of chess, a traditional metaphor for life, is transformed into a metaphor for artistic strategies. In *The Defense,* it leads the protagonist to suicide on the rebound, when he realizes that this secondary metaphor is the image of his existence. The chance repetition of a move brings about his death, somewhat like the accidental disappearance of Damon Rutherford causes the disappearance of the demiurge in Coover's *The Universal Baseball Association.* William Kennedy's reputation as a mere "realist" cannot survive an analysis of *Billy Phelan's Greatest Game.* The notion of the game is central to this work, borrowed perhaps from Johan Huizinga's *Homo Ludens,* and is illustrated, in any case, by "just about every form of game you can imagine."

This meaning of the game, including "the way people live life as a game," has "always been valuable" to Kennedy, who burdens poker, billiards, and horse racing with the existential stakes of Billy Phelan.[36]

Sporting metaphors allow Coover to probe the structures and attitudes of a nation at certain stages of its development. For this reason, baseball is pertinent to a global consideration of the nineteenth century, whereas football refers to the twentieth century. In *Whatever Happened to Gloomy Gus of the Chicago Bears?*, the narrator explains:

Football is not about violence or atavistic impulses . . . it's about balance. The line of scrimmage is a fulcrum, not a frontier. . . . The struggle is not for property, it's for a sudden burst of freedom. And the beauty of that. In football, as in politics, the goal, ultimately, is not ethical but aesthetic.[37]

The "hero" of this meditation on history and its models loses when he confuses the structures of sporting play with those of erotic play. Respectful of structures, no matter how devoid of intelligence he might be, as soon as he applies the numbers of tactical combinations to sports rather than love, he is an extremely lucky player. Even if blind routine keeps an alienating process from becoming a source of discovery and creativity, the awareness that one is in a metanarrative confers a new freedom and responsibility. Like *The Origin of the Brunists,* both *Gloomy Gus* and *The Universal Baseball Association* tell us that man's need to build fictions to give the world in which he lives an indispensable order and meaning is dual in nature and double-edged. Artificial fictions, whether in the case of sports or mathematical formulas, these allow us to grasp what would otherwise escape our awareness or reduce its ambitions; more subjective, and as discursive effects, they are called myth, religion, and history.[38]

In Jonathan Baumbach's work, the sports that make up the central activity of the dream (*Reruns, The Life and Times of Major Fiction* . . .) are basketball and tennis. Leonard Michaels has explained the metaphoric virtues and stakes of the first;[39] Baumbach has discussed those of the second, used for its fictional productivity by authors as different as Barry Hannah (*The Tennis Handsome*) and J. P. Donleavy (*De Alfonce Tennis*). But he uses both sports in an identical way. His basketball games only involve two people, never a team, as though to emphasize the relations of power. The rules are constantly broken. This breaking of the rules is an unambiguous message that, in his books, dreaming is the foremost rule.

Without a doubt, it is Jerome Charyn who goes the furthest in illustrating the ties between sports and fiction. The "baseball novel" is so plentiful in the United States that it is considered a subgenre, like detective novels, romance novels, and Westerns. Its most illustrious and oldest avatars include Ring Lardner's "You Know Me, Al," or James Thurber's irresistible "You Could Look It Up," which considers the consequences of dwarfism upon the sport. Among its most recent examples, we find Bernard Malamud's *The Natural* and Philip Roth's *The Great American Novel.*[40] From this angle, Malamud reintroduces the American pastoral and a palette of national myths; Roth makes his subject the place for exploring myths with moral ends, from which Jewish ethics and political satire are not absent. But it seems to me that Charyn, like Coover, has set the stakes of *The Seventh Babe* in a higher and more distinct region. Analyzing baseball as a strict metaphor for itself, he succeeds in slipping his conclusions into the writing without resorting to literary metadiscourse. Baseball is such a self-contained activity that it engenders its own history, a history experienced so intensely that it constantly threatens to substitute itself for that of the entire country. In its closed field, which creates rules for the outside world, baseball refers to principles that a large part of contemporary fiction would like to share: namely that the world is only a world thanks to fictive structures inherited from other places. And now, "it is necessary to dream up new approaches to the predictable."[41]

Demolitions

Rather than use characters or plot to present conflicts whose resolutions are usually provided by factual or psychological dynamics, our authors tend to avoid them; instead, they prefer broken forms and oblique presentations. Far from constituting gratuitous and "purely formal" exercises (as if the manipulation of representation could ever be gratuitous), these manipulations of words, signs, sentences, and metaphoric networks attempt to found these texts on a transformational practice, rather than on a linear exploitation of actions confident in their progressive unfoldings.

This presentation would be incomplete if it did not include some brief examples of manipulations, of traditional narrative instances adopted by certain writers when they decide to use them. When they do so, it is in a critical, distanced, subversive manner, by drawing attention to the artificiality of devices naturalized by usage and time. In *Beasts* (Harold Jaffe), *Don Quixote* (Kathy Acker), *The Exagggerations of Peter Prince, Death of the Novel,* and *Pricksongs and Descants,* the broad structures of representation are alternately set in place and broken into pieces, either through irony or through more or less glaring interventions on the part of the author or narrator. The temporal assembly exposes its gaping holes, the notions of a beginning and an end are thrown off by the respective emphasizing of their arbitrariness and their imaginable multiplicity; we now possess an innumerable sum of fictions ending in "or," missing a final period, or with, as in *A Confederate General from Big Sur,* "186,000 endings per second."[42] Along the way, characters lose their integrity, landscapes fall apart and come back together, while integrating descriptive elements that should remain foreign to them.

In a novel identified as "detective" fiction, a character crudely asks a question about plot:

"I really like the way you write . . . but why's there no story?"

"No, seriously, tell me Bobby, don't you read enough stories in the paper every morning? . . . Don't you need a breather once in a while?"[43]

Inspired by similar feelings, Judy Lopatin begins "Murder History" in this way: "Outside Detroit, in a wooded suburb, a killer came to visit a young woman who had a baby — only the baby was not there and the killer did not kill."[44] An opening like this places the reader on the defensive, prohibiting him from following the "clues" that might lead to a solution. The fictive world cannot be ordered according to the anticipated narrative logic, and the reader must either assume responsibility for ordering the given events or refuse to do so. "But can you expect clues when a plot does not exist? You can only expect facts."[45]

Expectations such as these can be deceived or disappointed by describing nonexistent objects or by resorting to empty references. In Lopatin's "The Death of Joe Dassin," the impossibility of communicating is not suggested through psychological notations but through the dislocated nature of strange dialogue: "I said to Michel, 'Look at that waiter. Doesn't he look like somebody from the French Revolution?' But Michel did not understand what I was talking about, and I could not explain, since I knew nothing about the French Revolution."[46] In *Little America,* a description by Rob Swigart makes use of signs with no referents in order to suggest an attitude: "If he had had a pipe, he might have been puffing on it with a philosophical air, nodding perhaps over the tenuousness and evanescence of life, the random violence of the universe."[47]

The catalytic function of these conditional descriptions is similar to that of the images in Brautigan's work (cf. infra): it creates a parallel and almost immaterial narrative in the margins, founds a sort of "pararealism" that relativizes the importance of the facts that are narrated, and encourages us to read within this emptiness, not "between the lines," but in the interstices and the lacks, stories that go much beyond the sum of recounted facts.

When it comes to characters, the breaks operated by Nathanael West in the thirties have gained wide acceptance. His protagonists, far from the full-length portraits and physical and psychological descriptions of the realist novel, are reduced to puppets with mechanical gestures. In contemporary fiction, they are usually limited either to caricatures or to simple functions, cardboard cutouts, and they serve no purpose other than that of their role. Greimassian "actants" rather than actors (or "actors," indeed, if we understand by this term only that they are representative voices lacking psychological substance), they are often made, whether major or minor characters, only of schematic signs. McElroy depicts the lowliest of his minor characters with care (*Lookout Cartridge*), but Joseph Heller (*Catch-22*), Coover (*The Public Burning*), and Vonnegut limit themselves to simple sketches. Gaddis's works, *JR* in particular, are crawling with peripheral characters that figure faceless forces. A significant trait, a tic of language, or a certain grotesque characteristic are enough to signal the presence of characters that might consider themselves lucky — if they had been given the means to do so — to be granted two dimensions. The names of the protagonists of Pynchon, Swigart, Robbins, and Vonnegut owe more to the music hall, radio series, and comic strips than to the symbolism that generates the names of characters in James or Gass. Marionettes, shadow figures, their family names announce that they have been borrowed from popular culture and that they should be treated as signifiers. They maintain practically no connection with their colleagues; only their names communicate. Their dialogues obey the regime of the apostrophe (address) and of the vocative, the relationships they form resemble those "connect-the-dots" drawing games. As spatial coordinates in a field of forces rather than carefully painted portraits — "well-rounded," as we say against the grain of language, to describe such flat, two-dimensional physicality — they are representatives, sent out on a mission, flat figures cut from the paper of the pages; in *Ghosts,* Paul Auster's pseudo–detective novel, the actors are mere color: "White," "Blue," "Black," "Grey," and "Brown"; they are phantom characters, *specters* of characters actually. C. Card is but a farcical generalization of Sam Spade in Brautigan's *Dreaming of Babylon*. The names of their authors are given to the characters — and not necessarily to the narrator — in *The Voice in the Closet* ("Federman"), *City of Glass* ("Paul Auster"), *98.6* ("Ron") . . . One is content with characters whose only name is that of their function: *The Cannibal* by Hawkes with its "Census Taker," its "Colonel," and "Signalman"; Baumbach's fictions with their countless "fathers" and "mothers," a "president"; Coover's "pedestrian," "magician," or "fat lady"; and there is also Pynchon's Pointsman, the true switchman of *Gravity's Rainbow.*

The mystery surrounding the identity of names themselves can provide the narrative thread. Who is "Trout Fishing in America" in Brautigan's work? Who is Pynchon's "V"? Auster's "Fanshawe"? *Who Is Teddy Villanova?* asks the title of Thomas Berger's novel. The functional polysemy of these wandering signifiers (the semantic "play" — manipulation and shimmy at the same time — that equally affects the title of *The Crying of Lot 49,* as well as the "systems" — WASTE or Tristero — that make up its core) is that of Hawthorne's scarlet letter and of the runes in *Narrative of*

Arthur Gordon Pym; it constitutes the inaccessible heart of all hermeneutics. But it also serves to mark out the themes of paranoia and the ungraspable, to provide the narrative with what it retains of "intriguing" power, to reinforce the ways in which these texts are both fabricated and essential; to emphasize, in other words, the impossibility of knowing the real without choosing a narrative, a version, without grasping one handle or another, without resorting to fiction.

Blanks, Gaps, Undersides

Finally, Barth's double-bottomed stories and Brautigan's images invite the reader to play games of "hide-the-thimble." Pleasure is increased upon discovering the narrator's identity in "Night-Sea Journey" or upon finding out the identity of the text that constitutes the secret matrix of "Glossolalia" (*Lost in the Funhouse*). The plot is grammatical in Harry Mathews's *Tlooth*, where the gender of the person who is speaking remains secret until the final pages.[48] To say of a hunchback trout that eating it is like tasting the sweetness of Esmeralda's kisses, to compare a picnic bench to Benjamin Franklin's glasses and to make oneself at home on it "like astigmatism" (*Trout Fishing in America*) amounts to making the reader an accomplice and an actor in these games, forcing him to fill in the blanks, those little syntactical and lexical "Moby-Dicks" in which the fascination of a meaning is hidden. To describe fishing by comparing the creek to a row of telephone booths, a flat white rock to a "fallen" white cat, and the quivering of the "line" when one strikes to the screaming of ambulances that one was able, "logically," to call after the "accident," is to confer superior diegetic powers on description, and to differentiate the way in which the story is assembled from traditional modes. To affirm that an undergrowth is like those phone booths, since the ceiling is invisible and the walls have been torn down, is to create a big hole, an enormous gap in our imaginations that we are only too happy to be able to fill or satisfy with the felicities of a language, no matter how semantically void. Truth, then, is no longer an affirmed value; poetically, and no longer discursively, attained, it is discovered by surprise.

Prodigal Writing

At times, faced with the hollowness of any narrative enterprise that trusts its mimetic powers to communicate a truth, writing becomes not only playful but a thriftless gambler and squanders itself away. Or, if we were to draw on Jerome Klinkowitz's pop reference to "bubblegum fiction," it blows up and "bursts." Its favored territory, then, is the image. The crazy image, gratuitous or overdetermined, anarchic, an image for image's sake, the proliferating image that would like to replace the plot, to become a plot itself, to engender countless divisions, to reconstitute the entire narrative fabric starting from itself. The "Single Cell Preface" to *Even Cowgirls Get the Blues* allows Tom Robbins to establish the reproduction of amoebae through endless division as emblematic of his method. Throughout his texts, from *Another Roadside Attraction* to *Jitterbug Perfume*, images dominate, they engender countless micronarratives whose interest displaces that of his highly fantastic plots, they constitute at once the glue, the framework, and the fragrance (laughing gas) of his novels. Their charm is due less to the delirium of the imagination invested in plot than to the local application of the iconic treatment that leads, precisely, to its unreading (*dé-lire*), to a reconstitution on a different level, to the discovery of the pleasures of pure fiction in the drifts of the imagery.

It is an understatement to say that William Kotzwinkle's plots are of relative rationality—there is even a wink in his name. The volatile and mysterious charm of his books is doubtless owed to their childlike and playful style. *Fata Morgana* is a parody of popular French novels from the end of the nineteenth century, a kind of fairy tale for grown-ups where the exquisite thematic of toys, magic, and automatons—also found in the stories of Steven Millhauser (*In the Penny Arcade*)—dominates a barely pretextual occultism borrowed from Gaston Leroux, but stripped of its macabre harmonics. The stories of *Elephant Bangs Train* (1971) give full rein to Kotzwinkle's taste for strange images and comic language. But in *The Fan Man* (1974), the irresistible logorrhea of a lost hero, a confused hippie whose language is as disheveled as his appearance, reaches the height of prodigal waste. The chaotic flow of this interior monologue gets bogged down and clogged up by the debris of a language intended to encourage empathy, superficial brotherhood, through an excess of what Jakobson would describe as the pure "phatic." Such a flood of what we scarcely dare name "expression" could prompt us to discuss *The Fan Man* only in the chapter dedicated to celebrations of the voice (see Chapter 13, "The Mouth and the Ear"), were it not for the text's propensity to make words proliferate for the simple pleasure of squandering their energy. Here as elsewhere, everything happens as though these fictions of America wanted to fill with words a space that cannot be grasped by consciousness and concepts.

"Orville felt his father's voice as though it were an unripe lemon being squeezed into a series of small lacerations up his spine": Swigart. Who later describes for us "her soft white hands folded in her lap, two meek lambs of the Lord lying down with the lion."[49] In *Little America*, the image proliferates to such a point that there is barely room left to develop a minimal but nonetheless outrageous plot. The reunion of two very ma-

ture and previously frustrated lovers unleashes images that illustrate the
eruption of bridled libidos:

> Flora's hand, which had been smoothing the layer of fat over his ribs as though
> she were straightening the sheets on the imaginary Beauty Rest somewhere in the
> murky motel of her desire, now scurried, a white mouse that had studied for years
> with a metropolitan classical ballet troupe . . . her hand closed around Andre's
> shaft like a bank of thick evening fog around a lighthouse, and her eyes glazed,
> fixed on what she held, even as her legs fell open like a dictionary of dirty words.[50]

Comparison, which is preferred over metaphor by Brautigan, Swigart,
Vonnegut, and Hannah, offers the advantage, when playing with conventions, of making more clearly evident the distance separating the
"comparant" from the "compared," of emphasizing the arbitrariness of
the gesture that creates it, and thereby establishes what we might see as
two texts in parallel columns. Most of the time (as with Brautigan and
Swigart), this dual sequentiality authorizes the setting up of secondary
thematics, that is, the composing of true clandestine narratives in the
column of the "comparants." These narrative doppelgängers constantly
interfere and compete with the primary thematics and narrative line.
The twin sequentiality allows the highlighting of alternatives that undermine the supposedly principal credibility of the official "stories," already
passably manhandled by the absurd, the arbitrary, the improbable. When
Vonnegut assures us that "the gun made a ripping sound like the opening of the zipper on the fly of God Almighty," or that "the gaping trunk
looked like the mouth of a village idiot who was explaining that he didn't
know anything about anything,"[51] we face more than one suggestion to
move away from the principal argument: the Almighty just might go
hand-in-hand with the simpleminded. Is there a better way of expressing
the absurd? The "unspeakability" of the horrors of Dresden is in part
contradicted by these vivid images of distance and stupidity. In Barry
Hannah's *Airships,* French plays the clarinet. Of the friend who is listening, he asks: " 'What do you think?' . . . after he'd hacked a little ditty from
Mozart into a hundred froggish leavings."[52] Ask a stupid question . . .

I read these texts as more than mere whims or joyous and rebellious
irresponsibility and prefer to identify there an active iconoclasm that
preys on what might remain of mimetic stability and confidence. At stake
in all this is the will to show how desire is fixed in language by resorting to
illogic or to an arbitrary, underground logic, to incoherence or to fabricated coherences, to radical nonsense. The goal would be to avoid the
programmed effects of language, to fight the discursive prestructurations
that enslave the individual to their law; a "new look" manifestation, perhaps, of an old American antinomianism that, while it illustrates itself

more clearly in the *themes* of contemporary fiction, does not affect the *forms* that it takes any less.[53] One reflection on play and its function would lead directly to another, on the media and history. But henceforth, play has an influence on contemporary science (game theory, catastrophe theory, the slippage from "hypothesis" to "fiction" in astrophysics); "Quantum physics has taught us that the universe is a balance between irrevocable laws and random playfulness."[54] Therefore, we will examine some of the connections between the fiction and epistemology of our time, deepening in this way what Henri Bergson would have termed our "intellectual auscultation."

Chapter 7
The "Connoisseurs of Chaos"

Mit dem Wissen wächst der Zweifel.
(With knowledge, doubt increases.)
— Goethe

Computer processing, biological and genetic engineering, atomic physics, information and catastrophe theories: "Science is now an international language, like love used to be."[1] The books of Carl Sagan and Hubert Reeves on astronomy, those of Stephen Jay Gould on natural history, which challenge the metaphors of evolution and progress, take their place on the best-seller list alongside Douglas R. Hofstadter's work on Bach, Escher, and Gödel, and Fritjof Capra's book on the *Tao of Physics*; the number of popularizations of the "quantism" of our time grows from one week to the next. On the other hand, "pop science" and "pop epistemology" sell well. Together with this popularization of scientific and technological discourses, fiction increasingly reflects upon the complex elements of contemporary epistemology. Even those writers who seem the least preoccupied by such questions join in the chorus, as in the case of John Updike's *Roger's Version*, where Updike contrasts the views of the theologian Roger Lambert with those of the fundamentalist Dale Kohler, convinced that physics and computer science are in a position to discover the hand of God in phenomena.

Against the reflexive tendency in fiction — but we should beware opposing two modes that turn out to be quite compatible — the fiction under consideration here finds in epistemology, more or less explicitly, the novelty of a triple field: thematic, formal, and linguistic. Going beyond literature in order to investigate their time and to provide fiction with new food for thought, our authors use contemporary science to replace the imaginary prosthetics that the novel borrowed from nineteenth-century science (psychology, sociology) and whose analytical methods had become naturalized from overuse within the novel form. Cybernetics, anthropology, linguistics, physics, and mathematics lend their models to a fiction that finds enough systems there to substitute for narratives, enough force fields to substitute for plots, and enough specialized vocabulary to replace artistic and literary discourses — that is, common language — to profit from their heuristic powers. The paths taken by this new "realism" are quite clear, yet it is somewhat puzzling that critics persist in seeing these new forms as nothing more than a means of distancing oneself from conventional representations of the real. Ironically, Nathalie Sarraute inverted the semantics of the epithets employed in contemporary polemics, when she treated supporters of the old forms as "formalists" and identified as "realists" those whose innovative forms and style had as their aim a faithful and more credible presentation of the transfigured real.[2] Today, Coover proposes to rest certain of his effects upon a deep awareness of intervening changes. In *A Political Fable*, he writes: "As for the magic, well, an age of wild scientific leaps is well-conditioned to accept amazements."[3]

Uncertainties

A revealing sign, when it comes to culture and ideology, the term "uncertainty" has enjoyed great success. If, as Meininger explained, words do not travel well from one country to another, they also tend to have their semantic baggage altered in moving from one discipline to another. Today, to invoke the name of Werner Heisenberg is to boil down a complex theory to the simpleness of the popular (or populist?) conviction that "we're no longer sure of anything." Bandied about in order to short-circuit the difficulties of analysis, the term nonetheless reflects a major preoccupation, even if, in literature as elsewhere, comparisons are odious. For Heisenberg, its meaning does not extend beyond the troubling observation that it is impossible for a particle's velocity and position both to be known, a modern-day subatomic avatar of Zeno's paradox. Rendered trite, either badly or not at all contextualized in numerous hasty analyses of contemporary fiction — following the example of "entropy," "cybernetics," and "relativity," terms too often used as conceptual shorthand — it has become a mere metaphor, referring now only to the sense of alarm, the difficulty of knowing experienced here and there: "we cannot know," nothing is determining in the establishment of truth. But "Heisenberg's principle of uncertainty," as Georges Devereux tells us in a more sober and useful manner, is neither "as is often mistakenly believed, a statement about physical reality thought to be 'unobserved' or to occur 'without interference,' nor is it a rejection of causality, but a theoretical formulation and a creative exploitation of the limits of experimentation."[4]

Whether fleshed out, made-up, trafficked, or reduced, according to one's needs, the notion of "uncertainty" does serve some purpose: It refers to an unease that is often more existential than epistemological as illustrated by numerous contemporary fictions. These fictions reintegrate the possibility of formulating questions into the generalized absence of answers that dominated, a few decades ago, the idea of the "absurd":

Questions, questions, I have cancer of the questionmark, but what the devil is a questionmark but a bend and a poke, what the devil is anything but a bend and a poke, what the devil is that child sitting there but a friend and a hope for reprieve? But then again, what bending devil is that child, poking at my hope with his beginner's age and easy wisdom? What's a child anyway, but an amateur person? I'm old and I've lost my answers.[5]

As here, certain fictions are characterized by an accumulation, interesting in itself, of questions without answers or of vast problems that the text does not give itself the means to resolve. This is the regime most characteristic of Vonnegut's novels, close in tone to the horrific squadron gaieties of Heller's *Catch-22*. Try as these novels might to give themselves themes of monumental complexity and moral depth (the war in *Mother Night* or, more ambitious still, the evolution of Earth in *Galapagos,* relations with other planets in *The Sirens of Titan* or *Cat's Cradle*), their treatment of these themes generally remains light, dilettantish, and evasive. Hardly at all before *Slaughterhouse-Five*— and not much afterwards — does Vonnegut allow himself the manipulations of language, inspired in part by cybernetics, that enable him to play with the structures of control of communication, to sketch a fictional answer.[6] Elsewhere, he contents himself with the "as if" tactics suitable to a science fiction that would not fundamentally call into question the mimetic strategy of fictions made possible by this axiomatic gap.

In literature, the "uncertainty principle" is often no more than a handy allusion, since rare are the writers who, like Pynchon, McElroy or DeLillo, possess the scientific background needed for its motivated use. Annie Dillard surveys the metaphoric drift that led to the principle's application to fiction in this way:

This is the fiction of quantum mechanics; a particle's velocity and position cannot both be known. Similarly, it may happen that in the works of some few writers, the narrative itself cannot be located. Events occur without discernable meaning; "mere anarchy is loosed upon the world." What if the world's history itself, and the events of our own lives in it, were as jerked, arbitrary, and fundamentally incoherent as is the sequence of episodes in some contemporary fictions. It is, these writers may say; they are.[7]

Dillard's own works, *Pilgrim at Tinker Creek* and *Holy the Firm,* seize upon questions considered by the sciences of the living. Solidly documented, her texts do not offer an answer, contenting themselves — an enormous task — with resonating the mystical paeans that humility imposes upon her in the face of the mysterious complexities of the natural universe. An impeccable stylist, Dillard extracts pages of a troubling and moving beauty from rigorous scientific observations.

At the opposite end, no doubt, from Dillard's speculations, colored by her Christian beliefs, but in the same framework, the mood and texture of numerous fictions owe much to Beckett's works, with their flat landscapes, dialogues that never seem to take off, their deserted feeling, stylistic bareness, ontological etchings, and stagings of voices and silences that appear able to progress only by "dragging" laboriously through a universe without a paraclete. Certainly, Barthelme's stories still rely on the resources of irony, and the narratives of Coover's "The Sentient Lens" attempt to trace upon the ground of deserts of snow, dust, or sand forms in which the ambiguities of a surviving desire assure a design of positively valorized aesthetics. But both write on a page cleansed by Beckett's great asceticisms; death and bursts of creativity are tied together there in dialogic lines woven for Godot, Malone and Molloy. And what are we to make of the novels of Rudolph Wurlitzer (*Nog, Flats,* or *Quake*) where this influence takes the extreme form of quotation? When Joseph McElroy writes an occasional review, he chooses to focus on *The Lost Ones.*[8]

Yeats was afraid of this; others will rejoice: the center did not hold. The "masters of suspicion" and contemporary science have done their job, and the epistemological debates that occur within fiction are tainted by the "nihilism" of the generation of Foucault and Derrida, in the sense, of course, in which we understand Nietzsche when he announces the rout of positivism: "No facts, just interpretation." While it appears that everything is to be redone, that the impossibility of any certainty leads us to seek new means of reconstruction, or so we might hope, it is important to discover more reliable routes than the reconstitution of faulty dikes with the debris of culture dear to Eliot. Even if this hermeneutic tropism of contemporary fiction enters into conflict with others, its presence at the center of literary creativity appears incontrovertible.

Apocalypses Now. Or Later. Or Past.

Our universe is threatening. The pollution of minds and of the atmosphere, with its "airborne toxic events," provides the central theme of

DeLillo's *White Noise*; the fear of plane crashes is central to Peter Spielberg's *Crash-Landing*. But, beyond these fears, catastrophes, cataclysms, and apocalypses serve as both frame and resource for many works of fictions. If novelists are also, like poets according to Ezra Pound, "antennae of the race," the world as we know it is going to die. In Swigart's *Little America,* the presence of the bomb is integrated in farcical manner into a pseudo-Freudian hoax where it represents the Father. The humorous and absurd tonality remained the same as that of *Catch-22* or the books of Vonnegut. Swigart goes further in *The Book of Revelations,* recalling a way of reacting to catastrophes comparable to that analyzed in *The Origin of the Brunists* (Coover): the sectarian thought at work there or that their perspective engenders. Swigart's "bibbles," like the Brunists, protect themselves from a disturbing universe by withdrawing into reassuring fictions. All of them announce the end of the world in a religious environment informed by the millenarian perspectives of Puritanism. Religious sects relay for farther reaches the self-identification of secular groups (hippies or yuppies, punks or dinks). The latter seek existential crutches in a hedonistic exploitation of the present in order to fight off fear and the absurd. Messianic or narcissistic, they proclaim the necessity of such crutches.

Although they decrease when it comes to computer science or soft technologies, the fears inspired by new technologies lead us to envisage planetary self-destruction or, as in Peter Matthiessen's *Far Tortuga*, nostalgically to deplore the passage from one world to another. Perhaps not without ideological slyness, representations of science as antihuman authorize the use of postapocalyptic settings from which history has been de facto and conveniently exiled and to which metaphysics return in force. Walker Percy subtitles *Love in the Ruins* "The Adventures of a Bad Catholic at a Time Near the End of the World," as prelude to a more generalized *Thanatos Syndrome.*[9] No doubt, the end-of-the-world atmosphere in *Amateur People* (Connors) and *Quake* (Wurlitzer) has more Beckettian foundations, but the general frame of *Birthplace* (William S. Wilson) or of Georgiana Peacher's unpublished *Mephistolily,* refers to a- or protohistoric speculations against an eternal backdrop. Steve Erickson's novels (*Days Between Stations* or *Rubicon Beach*) plunge the megalopolis into fog and sand storms caused by an apocalypse of some kind. The world decomposes, becomes blocked by garbage, dries out, and dies. The scenes that conclude *Fiskadoro* (Denis Johnson) and punctuate the journey in *The Birth of the People's Republic of Antarctica* (John Calvin Batchelor), the atmosphere of Mark Richard's *Fishboy* recall the flight into the enigmatic great white expanses of *Arthur Gordon Pym.* Explorations of the night, within the furthest withdrawn human consciousness, or advances toward the wide openings of dazzling day, they choose or combine ways of exiting time. Finally, many titles serve to remind us of the omnipresent dread: *Searching for Survivors* (Russell Banks), *The Nuclear Age* (Tim O'Brien), *Nuclear Love* (Eugene Wildman). Technological themes that are more or less explicit—from genetic engineering in *Vector* (Rob Swigart) to the shock of molecules in "Our Golf Balls"[10] (Jerry Bumpus, a large fraction of whose work is obsessed by nuclear holocaust) —are increasingly substituted for the mysteries of an earlier age.

Neuromancy

William Gibson's *Neuromancer* (1984) no doubt represents the summit of this type of fiction. In this work, the titanic confrontation between two artificial intelligences is remarkable not only because it subjects language to distortions comparable to those of spatiotemporal categories, with distance in this cyberspace being only a matter of nanoseconds; it is also remarkable for the surprising fact that this novel, a bit ahead of its time, does not present its readers with the elsewhere of ordinary science fictions. In this totally computerized world, the real is dissolved, manipulated, and reconstituted by means of sensorial devices that are biologically implanted and capable of any kind of transmission and any simultaneity; it is not so distant from the high-tech universe in which we are already deeply immersed. As one may have gathered, "Neuromancer" is a loaded term that combines more than just neurons and necromancy: when pronounced "new romancer," it hints of the conversion of the old but always effective "romance." An opening onto the irrational, sensitivity to the suggestions of a world that does not always speak clearly to logical or discursive thought, exploration through image and language of the edges of consciousness and the limits of the conceivable, programming of the marvelous, systematic expansion from the methods of knowing to poetics, to the diffuse, toward everything not yet embodied by language: Gibson applies the lessons of Hawthorne to the digitalized universe opening dizzily before our eyes.

Hallucinations and fantasies materialize under the pen of a modern-day Jules Verne in whose work landscapes and the color of skies are recorded, the hardness of the world is changed into holograms, and the variety of synthetic materials emphasizes the passage from one world to another. To read *Neuromancer* is to see *A Clockwork Orange* or *Alphaville* as mere diversions; to write this sentence on an IBM PC is to enter into a revealing hall of mirrors. The vocabulary of computer science, cybernetics, and genetics lends its cold and angular flatness to a world whose lexical bewitchment, all surfaces and deformations, becomes irresistible. Horrified and conquered, fascinated, we recognize this world in which memories are grafted, flesh is fabricated, semiotics are studied at the age of twelve, "landscape" has become "datascape," "memoscape," and "cyberscape," and where multidimensional screens radically alter the most longstanding means of perceiving and reconstructing the world.

When a computer pirate, a cowboy in an era where dead and living memories invent and project worlds, suggests to him that he is capable of reading minds, Finn replies:

"Minds aren't *read*. See, you've still got the paradigms print gave you, and you're barely print-literate. I can *access* your memory, but that's not the same as your mind." He reached into the exposed chassis of an ancient television and withdrew a silver-black vacuum tube. "See this? Part of my DNA, sort of. . . . You're always building models. Stone circles. Cathedrals. Pipe-organs. Adding machines."[11]

Power is conquered at the level of neurons, the most powerful weapons are programs, eroticism is governed by machines more concubine than celibate, and true desire is found in the only moments when "the meat" (the equivalent of the "savage" in Huxley's *Brave New World*) takes back its rights in order to allow an analysis like the following:

[Desire] was a vast thing, beyond knowing, a sea of information coded in spiral and pheromone, infinite intricacy that only the body, in its strong blind way, could ever read.[12]

New Paradigms

"Now . . . writing is produced which is by, and for, and mostly about survivors — persons living on after the decisive things have happened — as if no one could remember any other condition of being."[13] Warner Berthoff goes on to cite Orwell's remarks on Henry Miller: "He believes in the impending ruin of Western Civilization much more firmly than the majority of 'revolutionary' writers; only he does not feel called upon to do anything about it."[14]

The remark is accurate if we believe that fictions are "only words" and that writing is not already a form of "doing something about it." In an occasionally unconscious way, those writers preoccupied by the molds in which our consciousness flows do not appear any the less as "revolutionaries" if we compare their function to that of the "upholders of traditional literature," about whom Sarraute tells us that they are, even without knowing, "as it were, the privileged classes before revolutions, the agents of future upheavals."[15] Without being the administrators of a past they do not necessarily disown for all that, they are perhaps, we were saying, what Pound named poets, the "antennae of the race"; since fideist or positivist certainties have given way to "necessary fictions" that their inventor would not have recognized, they feel responsible for the form that will be given to consciousness, they become lab engineers of the large frames that are to organize it. In this way, they confirm the desire of authors of "novels," the game of the genre being, always according to Sarraute, "a deeper, more complex, more lucid, more exact awareness than that which they could have by themselves of what they are, and of what their condition and their lives are" (102). We shall see further on the relations held by history and myth with these "frames," the coming to consciousness and participation in the setting in place of these processes, of these "abstract realities as sure and as invisible as DNA."[16]

The mutation represented by the works assembled here is clear, as it is made more or less visible by their recourse to a thematic that is still relatively exotic for most readers. Whereas in the sixties and seventies the traditional novel had us contemplate beings (Bellow's Sammler, Styron's Turner, or Malamud's Fidelman), Pynchon, McElroy, and DeLillo conceive and present processes, models of consciousness by which to apprehend conditions of existence that have not yet taken shape. For McElroy, "models are . . . not just hypothetical systems to predict weather or nuclear attack . . . but maybe also . . . condensed anatomies and paradigms, an escape into concentration which itself becomes a model of what might be true."[17] In *Lookout Cartridge,* the consciousnesses are in fact barely conscious of what they know, constrained to deciphering the details. The mind functions like an alarm system, like a self-reflexive information mechanism that corrects the reactions of an organism immersed in an almost incomprehensible world. Cybernetic models are used to exploit, without apparent recourse to the spectacle of the emotions, the fear that haunts McElroy's characters: the fear of seeing or feeling the world escape beyond all grasp. The heuristic dynamic of these fictions is altered. The (re)discovery, step-by-step or by epiphanies, of "human truths" equally useful to the reader as to the characters caught under surveillance by the text becomes radically problematic. Certainly, it is taken for granted that "truth, if it exists, is not a matter of presence and possession, but rather one of difference and of path, it is one with the long journey that we must make in order to grasp it — without ever reaching it, without ever losing hope."[18] But we have even traveled beyond this relatively old suspicion. What is more, it is considered probable that these paths follow maps rigged by language and by a biased application of available "data." And, it is sometimes considered that it would be more helpful to tear down the labyrinth in order to rebuild it on a more solid foundation.

Scientific Fictions

In his book, Gérard Cordesse analyzes the stakes and practices of American science fiction.[19] Larry McCaffery lists contemporary works that resort to the techniques of science fiction in order to make themselves radically other.[20] I will only discuss here fictions that, while being scientific, do not belong to this genre. I consider these works more valuable to the extent that they remain with us on the near edge of change to guide our steps, rather than behaving as though the problems of the passage itself had already been resolved. Science fiction usually starts from an invitation to move one step aside by means of the imagination in order to locate ourselves in a universe different from the one we know, but at the heart of which, *mutatis mutandis,* the rules of classical mimesis still hold true. On the contrary, Pynchon, William S. Wilson, and McElroy examine modifications that are taking place in a consciousness faced with a universe transformed by contemporary epistemology. It is no longer a matter of thematizing the new or supposed consciousness, previously assumed to be external to the problems posed by language or to those it poses to language, but of interrogating the possibility and the effects of scientific knowledge itself *through* the states of language, its logic, constraints, and limits.

Between V and V-2

V. V-2. Change. Changes. The enigmatic letter that provides Pynchon's first novel with its title refers, *nolens volens,* to the lethal ballistic arc of the missiles in *Gravity's Rainbow.* There figures here — in these two books as in *The Crying of Lot 49* — the permanent fluctuation of the mind between two temptations, when confronted with an oceanic universe of information. The first temptation is called nonsense. This is the world of Profane (*V*), the world of the Zone (*Gravity's Rainbow*), a world where nothing can come together to make sense. The second is the "system," the world of Stencil (*V*), who suffers from an excess of "connections" and, consequently, of sense. By its sheer mass, information prohibits mastery. In *Fiskadoro,* Denis Johnson speaks of "the sabotage of knowledge by a wealth of facts."[21] The systems, proliferating, obliterate or stifle any possibility of relation that is external to them. Between these two schematized poles, a gulf, ironic and destructive, which cannot — a perfect illustration of the questions raised — be filled by the mountains of glosses poured into it by Pynchon's commentators, victims of the mass of information that *Gravity's Rainbow* places at their disposal. Whether attention is drawn to a certain scientific theory (thermodynamics, information theory . . .) or in a certain thematic direction (history, communication . . .), the discourse will become lost in the labyrinth of specialized treatises that can be consulted without having read Pynchon. When efforts are made to rationalize and unify these proliferations of elements, the texts themselves denounce such abrasions in return. As Bruce Herzberg emphasizes, "[t]he metaphorical imposition of structure upon variety is just the sort of informational control that the novel opposes."[22]

One cannot glance at this enormous book without at once renewing the problems it raises. To outline it is to choose, to cut into sectors and arcs the semicircle between sky and earth where the novel is held. To describe the possible readings of *V* would be as absurd as adding to the list of concepts to which the letter *A* sewn in scarlet on Hester Prynne's dress might refer. In Pynchon, the objects of the quest remain largely pretexts; that is to say, they are less important than the ways of knowing that they strain to set in motion and to contemplate. The profitable traps his novels set for us are decoys led along the paths of our hermeneutic strolls. Their themes are the form of our thought, which becomes stuck there.[23] On the whole, readings of Pynchon are performed in the gaps of the ideas, in the furrow — V without top or bottom — traced between the strategic structural devices and the question of language. Pynchon's novels can be taken from "on top" or grasped from "the inside." But no one can — except by devoting a multiple of the years invested in their conception — lay siege to them or program their intellectual occupation.

The Crying of Lot 49 is like a summary of Pynchon's entire *oeuvre*. Oedipa Maas, whose name unites, among other suggestions, those of an enigmatic heritage and a rhizomatic identity (*maas* means "net" to the Dutch), plays detective in order to penetrate the secret of a hypothetical clandestine postal network. The four possibilities offered to her for "reading" this strange world in which she moves are outlined in the following passage:

> Either way, they'll call it paranoia. They. Either you have stumbled indeed, without the aid of LSD or other indole alkaloids, onto a secret richness and concealed density of dream, onto a network by which X number of Americans are truly communicating whilst reserving their lies, recitations of routine, arid betrayals of spiritual poverty, for the official government delivery system; maybe even onto a real alternative to the exitlessness, to the absence of surprise to life, that harrows the head of everybody American you know, and you too, sweetie. Or you are hallucinating it. Or a plot has been mounted against you, so expensive and elaborate . . . financed . . . in a way either too secret or too involved for your non-legal mind to know about even though you are co-executor, so labyrinthine that it must have meaning beyond just a practical joke. Or you are fantasying some such plot, in which case you are a nut, Oedipa, out of your skull.[24]

Language imitates the involutions of the organization of the real by the designs of thought and, until now, there has been too little made of the mimetic dimensions of Pynchon's syntax;[25] too little attention paid to what the name of the presumed author of the apocryphal play "The Courier's Tragedy" (Wharfinger) might owe to the linguist Benjamin Whorf, whose *Language, Thought, and Reality* (1956)[26] attempts to establish the necessary links between syntax and forms of thought; too little time spent reflecting upon the impossible sentences sprinkled throughout Pynchon's paragraphs. Could it be that these sentences often appear outside of those episodes cherished by the least literary critic for their appetizing thematic content? This trivial scene, for example, in which Oedipa's husband is shaving:

Mucho shaved his upper lip every morning three times with, three times against the grain to remove any remotest breath of a moustache, new blades he drew blood invariably but kept at it . . .[27]

Impossible to read, this strange sentence is built on the necessity of using the preposition "with" again in the third clause, as it had been used in the construction of the first; in the first few pages, this sentence figures the transfers of mental diagrams indispensable to the heroine in order to confer or force some meaning from the real. The available words (the nickname "Oed," as her friends call Oedipa Maas, may refer to the *Oxford English Dictionary*) do not suffice to say the world, and this woman-lexicon implores any system to lend her the necessary articulations. The "forced connections," the logical reinforcements of paranoia as a way of knowing, as emergency syntax, are built or installed at the level of words at least as much as at the level of theme.

As we know, there is nothing very new about the latter. Concerning its dramatic developments, in "Raise High the Roof Beam, Carpenters," published by Salinger in 1955, Buddy was already saying ironically: "It was a day, God knows, not only of rampant signs and symbols but of wildly extensive communication via the written word."[28] As for the justification of its use, in Nathanael West—as is required in a period dominated by Freud—hysteria occupied the same strategic position as paranoia in Pynchon:

He knew now that this thing was—hysteria, a snake whose scales are tiny mirrors in which the dead world takes on a semblance of life. And how dead the world is . . . a world of doorknobs. He wondered if hysteria were really too steep a price to pay for bringing it to life.[29]

Paranoia performs indispensable services; calm, "normal" in our daily resorting to it in order to comprehend, acute and pathological in its stampedes toward misunderstanding, it offers, in varying degrees, systems that permit an organization of the perceived, without which, however minimal these systems might be, there can be no meaning. To reflect upon its usages extends such reflection to the language of knowing. Paranoia also allows Pynchon to place himself—or to be placed—in an antinomian tradition that might be the key to his relative popularity in American culture, which has never failed to provide the "them" necessary for defining a collective identity as "us."

In DeLillo (*Running Dog*), paranoia engenders a story around an object that does not exist, making the meeting of the protagonists the real fruit of an unreal idea. The feelings of his characters turn out to be products of the text alone. A conspiracy, more surely "intransitive" than those of Pynchon, serves as a metaphor for the establishment of networks of meaning. Conversely, Pynchon's novels repeatedly emphasize, in the unitarian and transcendentalist tradition more than the strictly puritanical tradition of deciphering signs, the possibility of brutal revelations of meaning by hierophancy or epiphany. The apocalypse has its advantages. The regime of openness, of unending expectation is its structural figuration. Language, then, would have no efficacy, other than that of "extravagating" (Thoreau); for all knowledge, we would have to rely upon the sudden appearances of an irrational that exceeds its possibilities of expression, sacrificing, as epileptics do, memory to the brief abolition of the night.[30]

Language cannot hope to channel a meaning outside of itself. Copy, sign, countermark against idealist conceptions of the real (as in the versions of Plato or Diogenes), it becomes devalued, following the example of currency. In Gaddis — and in Pound — currency is presented (in *JR* and in *The Recognitions*) as a destructive mediation between technology and art, between the cartel and the artist.[31] Understanding that one only grasps the real from the angle of empires of devalued paper can foster imperial as well as empirical fictions. The theme of entropy hunted down by numerous Pynchon readers via the second law of thermodynamics and information theory can be found more literally and immediately in a suspicious conception of the book, that "parallelepiped" whose proliferation, as Queneau said, had been made possible by the industrial age and had produced only two kinds of reactions: pyromania or the supplementary creation of illusory guides. Certainly, entropy occupies a place of choice in Pynchon, but as a theme it carries a largely divided vision of the "machinery of the cosmos"; Purdy expresses it in the following way:

> It will go on being autumn, go on being cool, but slowly, slowly everything will begin to fall piece by piece, the walls will slip down ever so little, the strange pictures will warp, the mythological animals will move their eyes slightly for the last time as they fade into indistinction, the strings of the bass will loosen and fall, the piano keys wrinkle and disappear into the wood of the instrument, and the beautiful alto sax shrivel into foil.[32]

Thus "entropology" replaces "anthropology" in Harold Jaffe (*Mourning Crazy Horse*), who borrows his fertile pun from Lévi-Strauss. Thus, contemporary epistemology plays on the same term by analyzing the more or less "anthropic" principles governing our interpretations of the universe.[33]

From Opposition to Collaboration

A priori, the questions raised by McElroy are those that Pynchon also asks. *Lookout Cartridge* looks back to the preoccupations of *Gravity's Rainbow*, about which McElroy has said that it "tries to show forth the process of which human life is an instance."[34] But the main themes that give the two texts their personality are quite distinct and suggest that even though the initial questions are shared, the methods — that is, the possibilities — of responding to them are not. In an interview, McElroy outlines his project in this way:

My books, up through *Lookout Cartridge* anyway, tried in a sane more than a paranoid way to create a collaborative network which human experience is. We can never know enough in order totally to understand it but it is there as some kind of mysterious network. . . . In the process of understanding the network, one sees innumerable correspondences, and these yield what we may call metaphor. . . . Also fear that I might be outside the network — therefore it exists.[35]

"Collaboration" is part of McElroy's vocabulary. In *A Smuggler's Bible*, David defines himself as a kind of "epistemological reuniac." "Paranoia" is part of Pynchon's vocabulary. Thematically and technically, Pynchon is a "plot" man; McElroy is a "field" man. Their definitions and their uses of metaphor differ. For Pynchon, metaphor is an "unfurrowing of the mind's plowshare,"[36] it is a kind of *tremens* that inspires us toward reading (*lire*) rather than toward unreading or delirium (*dé-lire*), a brutal, sudden, and encompassing manner of shaping that which is scattered. In McElroy, we participate in the analysis and the progressive, patient, and attentive installation of the constitutive elements of metaphor that ends, finally, by transcending it, by removing its totalizing and partially reductive character. To the frenzied binarism of thought that Pynchon emphasizes in order to, in my view, condemn it by the force of his paralyzing examples, McElroy prefers the shadings of a gradual reflection, with no solution of continuity. As McElroy explains, the Austrian biologist Paul Kammerer argues that

there is a force in the universe parallel to — not excluding, but parallel to — causality which is like what we might call coincidence or convergence. The events of *Lookout Cartridge* are not only linear but also a collection of dispersions toward what you might call disorder or provisional transition and magnetic nodes or points at which everything comes together. . . . What I have wanted to do is transcend metaphor and work toward homology.[37]

For all that, this new and fittingly unrecognizable form of "naturalism" does not repudiate — far from it — the passion for language. It is significant that a writer as concerned with the possibilities of form can express himself in this way; this is because it has become impossible to separate the most "realistic" approaches in the world and the consciousness it is possible to have of them, from the problems raised by the language that allows such approaches.

As Frederick Karl judiciously writes:

that stress on verbal constructs is not withdrawal from statement, but statement itself. Fiction has become an intensification of a verbal universe. Gaddis and Pynchon, in particular [and I would add McElroy to these names without hesitation — M.C.], do not use language to enter an interior world where all is self, narcissism, or indulgence; but as a way of exploring the outer reaches of language where it blurs into disorder. Their verbal construct is not a hiding behind words as a shield, but the forcing of words outward, where language and things merge into each other.[38]

McElroy and Pynchon share this ambition. In the final analysis, perhaps what distinguishes them further is the question of the "religious" in its broadest sense. Turning his gaze toward the possibility of revelations after having left face-to-face two modes of consciousness condemned by the doubtful becoming of his substanceless representatives, Pynchon seems eternally tempted, even beyond his deconstructions, by a simple move into meaning. In his work, everything happens as though, things having been seen for what they are and any archaeological inquiry at the point of divergence in the fork having been deemed overly ambitious, Pynchon left the reader free to perform the famous "leap of faith," to place himself in the hands of the numinous accessible, perhaps, at the "interface" of the System and the Zone. Save for accepting the equally condemnable modes of connection and of disconnection that it indicates, his *religere* leads back toward metaphysics. Setting aside the paranoia that makes horizontal links proliferate, "branch to branch," it suggests that there is no exit except on high. McElroy's *religere* brings us back down from these heights. The task is perhaps more complex, and less pleasant for the reader, to the extent that he does not have the familiarities with the world, the language, and the popular culture, and the pleasures of farce to make his journey more enjoyable. However, all things considered, McElroy carries this out with greater warmth. His affectionate attention to things recalls a remark of Guy Davenport's, who sees in this attention a weapon against "narcosis." For McElroy, " 'attention' is a rather cold word I use to suggest that the ways in which we embrace the world and embrace other people can be more precise and clear than we sometimes think."[39]

Neural Language

Like Pynchon, McElroy possesses formidable scientific knowledge and a sharp awareness of the large epistemological questions, of the necessity of searching for new models (*paradeigmata*), and of the need to proceed in an analytical and rigorous manner. He declares he wants to "turn microscopic seeing into meditation," and confesses: "I like books that try to push the reader into a strange state of mind in which everything has to be relearned."[40] To my mind, McElroy is the only contemporary writer who tries to bridge the gap reputed to separate the "two cultures" of C. P. Snow. His method does not borrow simple metaphors, but analytical tools:

Science and technology offer forms by which we can see some things clearly; their experimental and measuring methods, their patterns larger than life or smaller than sight, beckon us out of ourselves. If you assume your assumptions are only one of many possible views, maybe one day you find a way to drop, say, the reassuring habit of scale models and conceive distorted models, a model you can visualize only in fragments that the mind must leap to unite.[41]

Plus represents the best of McElroy's efforts. In this work, he studies the very origin of the logic of language and of the forms this logic allows us to give to the real. I will describe this novel — his shortest but not the easiest — as an epic theatricalization of language, the only fictional illustration, perhaps, of what Jean-Pierre Changeux has called "neuronal man."[42] Tony Tanner has described this work as a "continuous synaptic drama," and McElroy himself sees it as "a space idyll in which the body and the mind are reintegrated into a whole, organic substance."[43] To say that this is the story of an engineer's brain, covered with electrodes and placed in orbit 22,300 miles above the earth, might suggest that this is science fiction. Not so: it is language-fiction and simply fiction, a "cosmitragic" work, if Italo Calvino's stories are "cosmicomic." The revolutions of "IMP Plus" (Interplanetary Monitoring Platform) sketch a Chirico design in space, progressively reanimated by desire and reheated little by little by the work of memory (the "Dim Echo"). It is the analysis of the functioning, of progressive regeneration, starting from a point close to "zero," of language (vocabulary and syntax), of consciousness, time, thought, logic, identity, and finally, of will, that leads IMP Plus to self-destruction. Bit by bit, the vocabulary of physical materialism ("A change of charge. And the cause was the jolt which was a thought.")[44] allows accession to the domain of language as such: "Words remembering other words, but new words for what he had become" (142). One moves imperceptibly from raw perception to the notion of pain, to desire, to a project, one is made witness to the progressive identification of remembered images. One recognizes in the past two women, a child, a beggar, a beach, a car, a bird. Language acts as a lattice, a window, a blind.

McElroy brings to light and into action all the poetry of which scientific English is revealed to be capable; he makes us sensitive, beyond this, to the moving beauty of a language evolving between the organic, the analogical, and the digital, that is discovering itself in its diverse powers; and he makes us spectators to ballets of light, synapses, sounds, geometry, chemistry, physics. Assembly and dispersion of this emerging consciousness operate in dialectical relation, differently from Pynchon, where irreconcilable binarities make themselves felt. "He knew *memory*, but saw that it was not the same as *remember*. . . And then he saw what a question was. And did so by seeing he hadn't known before. And by finding these specimen questions. A question was what an answer was to" (167).

Coordination, the only concession, for a time, to a painful parataxis is moved to find the paths of subordination, to discover the order of discourse. Gifted with language, by the end, and capable of thought and decision-making, but not wanting to rebound toward the infinitudes of space or to reintegrate an old world, IMP Plus chooses to crash against the atmosphere and burn, the space of a lightning-flash. He has then pierced the secret nature of all strength and all power, of all struggle for power and strength, in terms of physics:

The combat for power which was the fight to find, beyond perfectly imperfect semi-conductors or beyond an element out of which to make wasteless black bodies for solar receivers, the clue to Reactive Reversibility by which to bend spent Energy through the interface of its own use and thence refract it rewound rebound. (189)

Programmatically — and paradoxically — the implication of the reader occurs in the absence of any theory. McElroy had wanted to introduce the discordances of chaos into *A Smuggler's Bible, Hind's Kidnap,* and *Lookout Cartridge*; from the sentences and the information they bear, the feeling is created here of an overload intended to give the reader the impression of constantly being on the edge of incomprehension, while knowing that all of the available information is there, in front of him, ready to be applied, if only he knew how. Perhaps the closeness of McElroy and Pynchon appears here; one declaration of McElroy's sums it up, when he describes the project of producing "a feeling of in-betweenness, of being caught between what we know too well and what we know too little."[45]

Physics of Emotions

The gap between the two thoughts changes along with the readings. In *Lookout Cartridge,* Cartwright formulates a law: "You will not have both power and the understanding of it," and tries to communicate to us the idea of an "oceanic conspiracy of refractions."[46] In the novel, the systems of power that inhabit and surround him swirl endlessly around at different angles and speeds. And yet, "they have the look of subsystems waiting for a supersystem to subsume them."[47] "No such thing as randomness," Cartwright informs us.[48] The only certainty exists in God and paranoia. McElroy emphasizes the analogies, the homologies liable to lead to one or the other, and stresses, simultaneously, the lack of clear links and the threatening resemblances between the systems of power that our consciousness identifies (one of the "lookout cartridges" of the title). Caught between what lives inside us and the world we live in, our consciousness projects as much as it records. The shock of these two sources of morals and religion can only be negotiated in language.

In *Why I Don't Write Like Franz Kafka,* William S. Wilson's study of the problems of language around essential lexical poles (Love, Men, Motherhood, Desire, America . . .) recalls the work of McElroy. Admittedly, Wilson's tools are most often borrowed from the analytical philosophy of Wittgenstein, Whitehead, and Davidson rather than from the "hard" sciences, but his essential and recurrent metaphor is that of the *operation* (linguistic, logical, surgical) and it refers to an identical question: "Every problem of medicine is a problem of language, and this operation was a malapropism."[49] This ironic sentence expresses his permanent attempt to link body, language, and experience. Although he is an art critic, Wilson is also acutely aware of scientific questions. If McElroy can propose approaching psychology through physics, Wilson argues that "matter and energy may yet be understood as successive asymmetries of primal symmetric space."[50] He therefore tirelessly correlates the physical, nature, culture, and the parallel modifications that all may undergo in their relations owing to the act or inhabitual desire — usually violent — that begins each short story. McElroy, for his part, founds his project of a "physics of the emotions" on the fact that "energies measured by physics are the patterns felt in life," and on the fact that it is possible to establish a link between the movement of bodies and the movements of the soul.

We are far from outdated realist notions. But a new one is appearing on the horizon, one that is more in accordance with the recent teachings of science that affect forms as much as subjects:

Then what do the stories mirror? Nothing. They are neither mirrors held up to nature, nor mirrors moving along a roadway, nor mirrors that reflect an infinite unity and then when smashed continue in each smallest fragment to reflect the same infinite unity. They are like shards of glass in a glazier's bin, the scraps that fall when a sheet of glass is cut to specifications. That's why I don't write like Franz Kafka.[51]

Trivial Pursuit

DeLillo's most explicit integration of epistemological reflection into his work appears in *Ratner's Star;* he explains that his use of themes and forms borrowed from the exact sciences was dictated by a desire for new frameworks:

I started reading mathematics because I wanted a fresh view of the world. I wanted to immerse myself in something as remote as possible from my own interests and my own work. . . . Pure mathematics is a kind of secret knowledge.[52]

The novel's characters shift constantly between science and superstition, according to the central model of Coover's *The Origin of the Brunists* and Swigart's *The Book of Revelations*; the novel owes its political and social pertinence to the proliferation of, or rather, the obsession within contemporary American society with analogical debates (evolution, religions, millenarian fears, the fascination with and mistrust of scientific and technological developments and of their impact on the *épistémè*). But for DeLillo, the perspective is different. He is especially interested in the heuristic value of discourses and scientific logic, in what they teach us about the powers of the work of fiction, and in what they reveal to us of thought patterns, the conditions of discovery, the constraining modes and grids of reflection. *Ratner's Star* deals openly with scientific thought; it is also a metafiction with a vengeance, in which the novel does everything possible to demonstrate that forms are always dictated by the ideas developed within them, that the narrative can only function according to the laws of its themes.

I wanted the book to become what it was about. Abstract structures and connective patterns. A piece of mathematics, in short . . . Connections led to other connections. I began to find things I didn't know I was looking for. Mathematics led to science fiction. Logic led to babbling. Language led to games. Games led to mathematics.[53]

White Noise seems to be connected to this universe only by the emphasis laid there on the perils of technology (pollution, dehumanization . . .); nonetheless, the novel raises questions related to the broader problem of knowledge in a world saturated by data, a world that seems to swear by information and communication alone, even as they become increasingly problematic.[54] DeLillo does not contrast the "background noise" of a blindly technological commercial society with what might be considered the real information and knowledge of the characters in the "foreground"; he points out the banalization and trivialization of consciousness on what is not a "ground" of death, but which literally becomes confused with it. "White noise" is that undifferentiated noise about which information theory tells us that it is the opposite of the recognizable reliefs of true information traveling through the used channels. Beyond this, DeLillo cruelly shows that this "information" is itself reduced to a "noise" that, far from surrounding information and, by contrast, making it recognizable, identifies itself with it.

In his poem, Wallace Stevens showed "thirteen ways of looking at a blackbird"; Richard Yates gives a collection of dark stories the title *Eleven Kinds of Loneliness*; in *White Noise,* Don DeLillo studies several ways of being dead to the world by refusing to dissociate them. In this novel, one finds death, the real kind, physical death, of which Babette Gladney is so frightened that she participates in questionable scientific experiments intended to relieve her paralyzing fear (she serves as a guinea pig for a new drug reputed to rid people of all fear of death). There is also the chemical death that prowls around the small town; and, the death to which, symbolically, Jack Gladney, a particular kind of academic, devotes his career by running the "Department of Hitler Studies" that he founded at the "College-on-the-Hill." But there is especially — not "above" all but "in" all, dictating the other forms and their perception — the death of all significant consciousness.

The Gladneys both undergo tests of knowledge, but the elements they possess simply float without any connecting links, rendering any understanding of the world impossible. Only Heinrich, the oldest son, the epistemologist in residence, questions the foundations of such knowledge. Murray Jay Siskind, a specialist of "popular culture," collects the most trivial data on American society, contenting himself with surfaces. Not far from the university, there is a barn everyone comes to photograph because it is "the most photographed barn in America."[55] Trademarks, fragments of advertisements interrupt the story, limit it; radio and television become full-fledged partners in dialogue. Data abound, but all meaning has vanished. The American world appears stripped of any force field, like a demagnetized plaque on the surface of which information no longer gives shape, for lack of current, to any spectrum, reducing the cultural filings to an incoherent sum of discrete units, devoid of the patterns Takis manages to give it in his work. A few decades ago, during a time of economic development and veneration of capital, the country's most popular board game was "Monopoly." Today it is fitting that the most popular game in the United States should be "Trivial Pursuit," a strange place where one exchanges discontinuous pieces of information that come together to form no coherent cultural discourse. The frequency and pessimism of studies documenting the ignorance of the majority of the American population find in response only propositions that are the academic equivalent of "Trivial Pursuit," as the works of E. D. Hirsch on "cultural literacy" attest. Knowledge is defined as an information puzzle, as a batch of data without value or direction outside of received and worn-out cultural discourses. Bakhtin's "official monotone" finds there its most stunning illustration: no dialogic activity can any longer inform a culture made of meaningless fragments, while no set of information proves itself capable any longer of crystallizing into an antagonistic discourse. The death that hovers over *White Noise* is not the "cloud" people think it is.

In social terms, it is perhaps the consequence of a practice that privileges the sacrosanct individual "experience," a narcissistic and solipsistic mode of relating to the real that betrays day after day the impoverished muddle that passes, in the most various places, for thought and language. Kotzwinkle's *The Fan Man* satirizes all of this. *Nog*, the "head-venture" of Rudolph Wurlitzer, provides the psychic causes. *Olt*, by Kenneth Gangemi, theorizes its seeming ineluctability: in this text, existence in the world becomes the simple flow of experience, devalued from an aesthetic and moral point of view. If paranoia appears threatening by its excess of meaning, the absolute negation of all systems, of all structure and hierarchy is a way of defending oneself by refusing to mount a defense. By no longer demanding that a structured vision of the whole, feared for its perverse and "totalitarian" effects, give meaning to the event, one exempts information of all need for relation or congruence. Only an incantatory resorting to a "holism" can ward off the dreaded harmonics of the "totality" for the ecobeliever, thus "freeing" him from the "tyranny" of rational analysis. The nonsense — too realistic in *Olt* and *White Noise* not to be disturbing — becomes figurative. Facts are facts, what is, is, and it is to be grasped as is in the immediacy of perception; to accept to organize any system of thought would be to run too great an intellectual and existential risk. It would mean committing oneself, compromising oneself. Thus, we have libertarians celebrating madness: Pyrrhic victories of a consciousness without object over knowledge and the necessary fictions, idealistic abdication of the hermeneutic, abandonment of definition of order to semiopolitics, who dictate what they have in the "fat of their head" (Barthelme). Better soft totalitarianism than self-censorship?

Novels of Mastery

In this perspective, one can pose the question of the connections that exist between this epistemological situation and the relative abundance of heavyweight fictions.[56] *The Public Burning, Gravity's Rainbow, JR, Ratner's Star, LETTERS*, William Gass's enormous *The Tunnel*, Gil Orlovitz's *Milk-bottle H*, and the novels of McElroy — with the exception of *Plus* and crowned by the immense 1,192 pages of *Women and Men* — raise, by dint of their sheer mass, the very epistemological problems that they discuss. While Poe believed that a historical tendency was carrying fiction toward "the curt, the condensed, the pointed,"[57] it appears as though these enormous works reflect the state of our consciousness, and, in so doing, they ask us to consider whether it is possible to turn the situation to our advantage. These works seem to try to reunite in one unique and relatively manipulable place what escapes us in the variety and incomprehensible abundance of things and ideas, attempting to shape some impressive but fragile architectures. It was possible to describe *Gravity's Rainbow* by stating that Pynchon seemed to hope that this architecture would "survive to 'sing' its tenuousness through the entropic, mutable growth it contains, rather than the world it shadows."[58]

Less "encyclopedic" than concerned with providing proportional space for the breadth of the questions raised, these novels are the sign of a mutation. It is no longer a matter of *romans-fleuves*, if we understand by this the vast mimetic frescoes that, like *The Human Comedy* or *The Rougon-Macquart* or *Men of Good Will* attempted to contain a world, to give of that world as complete an image as possible. As Coover pointed out in *The Water-Pourer,* a rejected chapter of *The Origin of the Brunists,* "the universe is all we have. All narratives, like the universe are explosive. . . . The eye is jittery, distractable,"[59] and it is easier to focus one's gaze on one or another representative vector or fragment of a mass that can no longer be taken in. Accepting the challenge, these lengthy novels choose, however, to *figure* complexity. Tom LeClair offers another explanation: by their excessive size, they compel the attention of those readers who might remain unaware of the importance of the questions raised if such questions were to appear in more concise or almost banal fashion.

> Not many readers choose to be "stunned" as Coleridge describes the Mariner's listener, so novelists seeking powerful effects practice the art of excess. They solicit traditional interests, draw the reader in, then exceed conventions, build up bulk, changing the work — and the reader — in mid-work.[60]

Something happens in long novels that cannot occur in shorter works. Whereas, in shorter texts, it remains possible simultaneously to observe structure and texture interpenetrate, in the "big work," for the reader simply to survey the surface in order to measure, appreciate, and estimate the structure prevents one's access to the finely grained immensity of the work's texture. Inversely, attention to detail becomes problematic: it is difficult to avoid getting lost in the fine threads of the texture, to keep in mind the structure that underpins such density. The excesses of form bear witness to the problems of consciousness in a world that defies global understanding and represent the difficulty of focusing on the minuscule without losing sight of the large structures without which it would be devoid of meaning.

At the same time, the related question of the *difficulty* of certain works is raised. This question also has "neomimetic" or indirectly figurative virtues, reflecting an aspect of our condition. It also attempts to renounce the false relations between writers considered as simple producers and readers who "consume" book-commodities. Sketching the reflections he would later include in his work *On Difficulty*, George Steiner writes:

Above all, the "unreadable" book will humiliate, confound, and rout the reader. This is the essential aim of "ultimate unreadability" (*l'illisibilité finale*). For has there ever been a lazier, more patronizing, more exploitative relation than that of reader to writer?[61]

Fictions of profound intelligence, these novels refuse the facile or trivializing consumption of a literature threatened by the expansion of the media and new art forms (video, virtual reality, television clips . . .). They refuse to simplify a world that can only be understood by accepting to penetrate its real complexities. Difficult works, they are "avant-garde," perhaps, if, by ridding the term of its worldly rags and forgetting what it denotes today of vanities and self-promotion, we return to it the courage of "scouts" and the skeptical honesty of their reports on what they have seen lying ahead. For, this "avant-garde" is marked by its humility. McElroy, Pynchon, DeLillo, and Coover do not desperately chase after honors, and there are certain "recognitions" Gaddis does not seek. Most of these writers hide themselves, as became philosophers before they declared themselves "new." As Frederick Karl observes: "The writers who either reject the limelight outright, or shun it because celebrity insists on assimilation, are frequently the experimenters."[62]

Chapter 8
The Constrained Nightmare

History is a constrained dream.
— Georges Duby

For Durtal history was, then, the most pretentious as it was the most infantile of deceptions. Old Clio ought to be represented with a sphinx's head, mutton-chop whiskers, and one of those padded bonnets which babies wore.
—Joris-Karl Huysmans, *Down There*

Fiction and History

The profound changes undergone by historical theory over the last decades have of course affected American fiction, even if—and perhaps because—the relations entertained by America with history have always differed from their European models: any thaw will make for drifts. Oscar Wilde, lamenting that "lying [should] have fallen into disrepute," already considered Herodotus as "the father of lies" and believed that our duty toward history was to rewrite it. The works of Michel Foucault have provided the final push, shifting the status of history from positivistic science to "Western myth." These new perspectives of European historical thought have been relayed in the United States by Hayden White and Dominick LaCapra.[1] Vincent Descombes, reviewing them in *Modern French Philosophy*, prudently concludes: "Nobody seeks to 'deny history.' Our only concern is to ascertain whether a sober conception of it may be reached after the twilight of the Hegelian idol."[2] Such questions may be superfetate here, as the "Hegelian idol" never had many American worshipers; one might as well briefly indicate the reasons for which a discourse of suspicion should have fallen, in the United States, into particularly receptive ears.

America, as we know (I resort to this imperial designation on purpose),

always had difficult and complex relations with history. Henry Ford's
exclamation is their emblem: "History is bunk." The founding acts of the
country (from emigration to the colonies to the Constitution, via the
Declaration of Independence) indeed consisted in removing the stains
of Old World pollution, in "denying history," or at least running away
from it, in leaving it behind, inventing an elsewhere, entering — according to the Puritan or lay versions of a fundamentally identical vision — the
canopied antechamber of eternity or a new, inaugural phase of time.
Hegel has no hold on a vision hostile to dialectics where a double evasion,
spatial and temporal, originates; in leaving the Old World, one also leaves
behind what Althusser termed "le continent Histoire." However "sober"
the conception of history may have become, it remains a fundamental
axis of European thought where myth and fiction straightaway removed
it, as soon as the first foot was set on New English shores, to a reputedly
lustral time-space. Decreed "new," history, in the United States, has consistently haunted the mind, but in a different way, one that provides an
ideal hold for contemporary fictions. Thus, Robert Scholes explains:

The North Americans in particular are obsessed with their own history — perhaps
because they live in a country which was itself a fabulous fiction that grew in the
minds of men like Columbus, Hudson, and John Smith before they found it and
founded it — and in the minds of other men like Paine, Jefferson and Franklin,
who invented its political and social structures out of their ideals and hopes, and
then sought as actors on the stage of history to make a real nation out of their
fabulous dreams.
    In America myth has always been stronger than reality, romanticism stronger
than realism. What Barth, Pynchon and Coover have tried to give us in these
books is nothing less than the kind of realism this culture deserves. . . . *The Sot-
Weed Factor, Gravity's Rainbow* and *The Public Burning* are offered as atonement for
the guilt of having created a fabulation and pretended it was real.[3]

American history has always shared its ground with fiction. In the first
half of this century, the bumpy ride that made a most Jeffersonian Dos
Passos traverse Marxism, Faulkner's idiosyncratic historical vision, the
resounding failure of political fiction in the thirties, all underline in
their own way this constitutive unease. Fitzgerald's celebrated "crack-up"
is in part due to the divorce occurring between a mythical vision of
American history illustrated in the sumptuous last pages of *The Great
Gatsby* (where Dutch sailors are imagined casting their enchanted eyes
upon the "fresh, green breast of the new world," illuminated now by "the
green light at the end of Daisy's dock") and a life/work tossed by great
historical storms (from World War I to the Great Depression). In *The
Armies of the Night,* Norman Mailer—who knows about such things—
wonders:

Yes, how much of Fitzgerald's long dark night might have come from that fine winnowing sense in the very fine hair of his nose that the two halves of America were not coming together, and when they failed to touch, all of history might be lost in the divide.[4]

The antinomian temptation remains quite strong. A classic position, this act of faith reduces all official systems of reading to the hell of conspiracies working toward the destruction of the nation's soul. It is the secret source of such ideologies to proclaim "the end of ideologies," of the drive to immerse oneself in the stream of experience, wherever it may flow: it shall always be far away, at any rate, from historical abysses. In Harold Jaffe's *Mole's Pity*, the protagonist sees himself "tugged out of the white holes of nature into the black hole of history—untransfigured. The way it's always been"; further on he sees "shards of history pricking the devastation."[5] A permanent thrusting forth of events, immediately buried, that cannot interpose themselves between the past and the advent of an idea, history is mysterious and soughing with narratives. It gives itself up to writing and visionary enthusiasm, unable or unwilling to drive them away. "History will always remain a mystery," says Ishmael Reed, a reputedly "political" writer.[6] And Alice Walker raises the ante: "mystory, just that, a mystery."

Everything can therefore happen as if, instead of traditional definitions of history, a new meaning of the word was conjured up, one derived from the name of the muse who, from time immemorial, always confessed to the etymologist the fictional nature of her empire: Clio, in the United States more than anywhere else, is Kleio, from "kleien," to celebrate, or "Kleios," glory and fame at the same time. History, as it is perceived in the country as a whole, can only be the occasion—unless one rejects it completely—for incantatory discourse, a paean to Manifest Destiny or a threnody for a glorious past. Hagiography retains its part within it, and the reductive distortions exist side by side with blown-up religious imagery in official speeches: the litany as argumentation. American history, in its ideological uses, is a landscape populated by giants, a catalog of exploits reminiscent of the tall tale, an epic, a Mount Rushmore of the imagination.

One understands why this great narrative should invite a number of writers to rewrite or deconstruct it. Joseph McElroy admires Kleist because in his works history appears as a kind of "physics in a fictional mode," and a novel by Günter Grass because in it history appears as "the obsessed, uninhibited voice flowing out of broken memory."[7] For others, since civilization revealed itself to be a liar, one should analyze its treacherous tactics, break down its clichés, rummage among its ruins, criticize the discourses that make it possible for its smoke screens to remain operational. Once in a while, a murderous formula signals such a consciousness, or power: "The world remembers only what power and money tell it," Monsieur Girard says in James Purdy's *Malcolm*. And he adds: "There is a limit to time and fortune. . . . You are now—history."[8]

I shall not deal with the "historical novel," an expression designating a kind of hermeneutical eunuch that contemporary thought has practically made redundant, in all senses of the term. William Dean Howells, at the beginning of our century, and without subversive intentions, spoke of "this aoristic freak, the historical novelist." Even though dated formulas go on, in Europe as in the United States, pandering to the needs of temporal exoticists by providing a structure for well-crafted and sometimes talented books, the suspicion that weighs upon history generates works generally more interesting than those that are untouched by it. Unlike the novels of Gore Vidal, William Styron, or Mary Lee Settle, all of which indulge in ideological criticism operating, so to speak, from the inside, or the enormous frescoes that, from Clavell's *Shōgun* to Michener's *Chesapeake,* take us on guided tours of remote periods, many recent works of fiction address themselves critically and creatively to the very foundations of the genre.

Because they endeavor to speak of the horror of more recent historical events, one tends not to label works dealing with the Vietnam War "historical novels." This being said, with the exception of writers such as Tim O'Brien and Robert Stone, their authors have often written only one novel, as if to exorcise their experience. Reading John Briley, James Webb, Charles Durden, Gustav Hasford, John C. Pratt, and John M. Del Vecchio (*The Thirteenth Valley*) is tantamount to hearing these men whisper to themselves, deep in the jungle or in some trench near Dak To: "Should I ever get out of this, I'll write a novel about it." Repertorial (as in Michael Herr's *Dispatches*) or intimately cathartic rather than fictionally exploratory, these at times beautiful novels belong less to the "fictions" I mean to discuss here than to the ancient and respectable genre of the "war novel." Their makeup rarely constitutes a significant advance compared with the writings of James Jones or Herman Wouk, even though the sense they convey of the "derealizing powers" of the war situation matters to our concern.

Derision

"When the historical discourse is falsified as a language, all referential coherence becomes irrelevant and even laughable," writes Raymond Federman, with no excessive concern for nuances and evolutions.[9] He thereby justifies his own practice and that of the most radical antirealist writers.

"As soon as you introduce a narrative thread in the novel, you immediately become a prisoner of the plot," he says elsewhere, and denounces the nicely wrapped up narratives that provide their chains of satisfactions, from predictable openings to proclaimed endings.[10] Which does not prevent him from prolonging his initial roughshod remark with the explanation of a break no less than . . . historical: "It is this idea which sets off the first wave of self-reflexiveness (between 1960 and 1968) in the American novel when it begins to question but also mock and parody the official discourse, and even more so the historical discourse of America."[11]

The mode in which World War II is dealt with in *Mother Night* and *Catch-22*, with their chronological distortions of déjà-vu, does not encourage us to take official discourses seriously. An analogous effect is born of farcical digressions integrated into the historical themes or backdrops of Pynchon's novels; it reinforces the impression of dubious reality that constitutes their real preoccupations. Having a professor who doesn't read German teach "Hitler studies" helps DeLillo make us understand that Jack (J. A. K.) Gladney—who, living only on the superficial meaning he takes from the juxtaposition of signs, removes a letter from his name in order to increase his status—only consumes "history" toward perverted ends; but such an exploitation of history, reduced to a salmagundi of anecdotes, can hardly serve the characters of *White Noise* as a whole, with the obvious lack of referential frame favoring the pollution of the cultural air by clouds of discrete information, making knowledge well-nigh impossible. Relativized by the ironical glance of the Trafalmadorians, the events related in Vonnegut's *Slaughterhouse-Five* also invite skepticism: for these extraterrestrials who have walked straight out of a comic strip, the troubles of the world stem from the fact that humans tend to stick to chronology and causality. Following their advice, the film of history backtracks. This is one way of unmaking history, of pulling it out of time, of making it, at least, stop its erratic and disordered gesticulations. This is what the first scene of Brautigan's *A Confederate General from Big Sur* tries to do, immobilizing in marble the march of Confederate troops against imaginary Indian positions (the civil war "between the states" as the North called it or "of the Northern aggression" according to the South never affected California in this way); the images neutralize the very idea of war, deny its dramatic and culturally traumatic impact by means of the almost comic freeze technique.

In Bobbie Ann Mason's *Shiloh* this same war no longer takes place between enemy troops but opposes an estranged couple on a Tennessee battlefield transformed into a picnic ground. Barry Hannah was born in Mississippi; several of the stories in *Airships* have the Civil War as their theme: he has been classified as a Southern writer. In spite of this, the specificity of his work owes much to the hilarious debunking and derision that govern his thematic use of hackneyed nostalgias. As it stands, his work often mixes the Civil War and that in Vietnam — in *Ray* (1980), in particular — blurring such artificial borders. Furthermore, in order to escape an inexorable temporality and the possibility of any history (which is definitely not in the Southern tradition . . .), Ray, the medic and protagonist of the novel, has recourse to spectacular forms of protest. History, whose waves and tides threaten the individual, causes him to scream stridently: "Oh, help me! I am losing myself in two centuries and two wars."[12] Between two wars, two structurally delimited historical seas, is also where the victims of Germanic mythology get devoured in Hawkes's *The Cannibal*. In Vonnegut's *Slaughterhouse-Five*, reconciled with an arbitrarily defeated time and about to address the Ilium community (at the time, forever known, when he is about to become the victim of a murderer he has forever seen coming out of an ever-present past), Billy Pilgrim explains that "all moments always have existed, always will exist";[13] so Trafalmadorian philosophy would have it, for which time is but a string of synchronous moments caught in amber. Ray, in a painful echo, proclaims: "I live in so many centuries. Everybody is still alive."[14]

A comparably inspired reversal underpins John Barth's 1960 *The Sot-Weed Factor*. Barth's "historical" novel reverses and stems the history of the colony of Maryland: the picaresque adventures in this work are no longer the traditional mishaps confronting the European immigrant come to seek his fortune in this Eldorado, but those of an American who goes back whence his fathers came only to lose it. Slothrop, in Pynchon's *Gravity's Rainbow*, will himself reverse the historical itinerary of his ancestors. Such a vectorial inversion, the total confusion presiding over Ebenezer Cooke's quest for his origins, obviously damages the American historical vulgate as well as the discourses deployed to lend it credibility. The values illustrated by Cooke's peregrinations are not easy to integrate into the American tradition; derision is further accentuated by the fact that this particular character poses as an approximative reproduction of the most historical "poet laureate" of John Barth's native state, the title of the novel having been lifted from the poem to which Cooke owed his glory. A fabulous novel, in the most rigorous sense of the word, *The Sot-Weed Factor* indulges in the invention and interweaving of secondary plots that have no clear relations with the main thread of the narrative, the total invention of fantastic documents engineered to plug the most conspicuous gaps in the chronicle. This is the first rape of history Barth invites us to witness, even before the succulent gymnastics shared by "the Author" with Lady Amherst in *LETTERS* against the very official background of the War of 1812. Imagination necessarily provides the intereventual tissue; novels of such caustic ink want to persuade us that their difference from official narratives is a matter of quantity as well as of quality. We shall see that this temptation to stage the raping of history by myth will take on literal configurations in Coover's *The Public Burning*.

Continuing the cycle of his merry debunkings, Barth undertook with *Giles Goat-Boy* (1966), under the cover of scientific discourse, that of the ruling myths of the Cold War. On the same historical phase, and with the same purpose in mind, Richard Condon had published *The Manchurian Candidate* (1959) a few years earlier. In a more classical form than Barth's top-heavy allegory, this novel preceded, in a manner just as convincing and terrifying, the fictions later conceived to ward off the shutdowns of history. Or rather its internments: more parodic than allegorical, it presented the America of McCarthy and the House Committee on Un-American Activities as an insane asylum; the image was tempting and, in a novel of no historical appearance (*One Flew Over the Cuckoo's Nest*), Ken Kesey adopted it in order to denounce what Ginsberg had earlier called "the syndrome of shutdown" that seemed, in the eyes of more numerous marginal citizens, to threaten anew the individual in the United States of the sixties. For Condon, history is this "abandoned woman" (*The Abandoned Woman*, 1977), reclining naked on her sofa, holding out her arms to whomever would embrace her, a noble whore that the novel presents under the imaginary traits of Caroline of Brunswick. The princess's ornaments and the disguises of history are reflected in the ironically precious stylistic and lexical ornaments; her laughter comes in "star-bursting shapes: sagital, bicorne, infundibular";[15] the *mise en abîme* of the rococo mirrors in which she contemplates herself refers us back thematically to the mirror palaces of the various historical versions in which her personality, her acts, and the motivations of her husband George IV are presented.

Robert Alter thus sums up the dominant feeling of such specialists of derision:

Real history is above all a field of constant, nuanced but always delicate differentiation; but with Vonnegut and other American novelists of the 60s and 70s, we find the following simple chain of equations: all history is blindly destructive; all destructivity is the product of the same forces with underlying motifs and can be reduced to the same basic formula; therefore all commitments to a particular historical cause are equally futile and senseless.[16]

History can transmit its germs from generation to generation, as witness the proletarian heritage of *George Mills* (Stanley Elkin), the complicities of generations of women in Joan Chase's *During the Reign of the Queen of Persia*, Toni Morrison's novels, and Joyce Carol Oates's romantic sagas (*Bellefleur, The Bloodsmoor Romance*); the amplitude of the temporal frame and the continuum of a descendance then constitute an essential dimension of time, providing a mythical hold that frees the imagination from the dictations of history (however obsessive it might be, as in T. Coraghessan Boyle's *World's End,* for example). Such a conception of the heritage refers us to other legacies: those of Faulkner and García Márquez.

Protest

Protest against received readings of history finds its most lively manifestations in the work of writers whose social origins allow them to measure their properly political stakes. It constitutes the dominant form of the treatments "minority" writers reserve for historical narratives. Ishmael Reed's satirical verve and freedom of imagination rank him first among those, men or women, for whom all liberation has to begin with radical revisionism. In *The Free-Lance Pallbearers* (1967), but above all in *Mumbo Jumbo* (1972) and *Flight to Canada* (1976), he rewrites in uncommon terms the history of slavery in the United States. Everything happens as if official narratives, but also such a respectable classic as *Uncle Tom's Cabin,* were made to stand on their head, steamrolled by a devastating irony, scraped clean by an imagination that borrows its images from popular culture and its voice from contemporary black speech. Justifying his recourse to most personal imaginary landscapes in order to protest not only official history but also the novelistic forms that relayed it, Reed declares abruptly: "Poe is my favorite historian."[17]

Less flamboyant, but in pursuit of similar goals, some representatives of ethnic minorities take on official history. Native Americans and Chinese Americans appear more attracted by myth than history for reasons I do not have space to discuss here; it is, however, a choice that gainsays prevalent epistemological hierarchies. To propose practicing "mythic realism" for the reason that the very reality and communal feelings of such populations are underpinned by ancestral mythologies equals opposing one vision of the real to another. The attraction of Latin American "magical realism" for such a famous and popular writer as Toni Morrison has the same causes. But James Welch (*Fools Crow*) and Maxine Hong Kingston (*The Woman Warrior*) appear to be among the rare authors who consider taking on American history from the inside.

It is a particular reading of history that women protest (Alice Walker and Grace Paley, especially, whose writings are not, properly speaking "historical") by proposing a distinct viewpoint that draws attention to thematic concerns long submerged by the male domination of institutions and daily life. Alice Walker may suggest going against the grain of etymology, lexicon, and grammar and propose to substitute "herstory" for "history." It is history itself that tends to vanish from *The Color Purple,* if not from *Meridian.* But if it is remarkable that the events of recent history during which Morrison's *The Bluest Eye* or Walker's *The Color Purple* take place never appear in these novels, as soon as one makes it clear that the Other's wars are of no interest, one indeed passes judgment on a certain conception of history. The forms of fiction are however very seldom altered in this case, even if the "quilted" structure of *The Color Purple* is combined with ancient linearities; but the contents of the master narrative are enriched and complicated by elements that have remained exceptional in an American literature long dominated by white male viewpoints, as demonstrated by Leslie Fiedler in *Love and Death in the American Novel.*

According to the same logic, but with lesser aesthetic success, other novels deal with the becoming of the working class, faithful in this to the tradition of the 1930s proletarian novel. Possibly a sign of the times, what we read are no longer celebrations of heroic destinies but chronicles of decline, as evidenced by *Rivington Street* (Meredith Tax, 1982), *Dogs of March* (Ernest Hebert, 1979), *God's Pocket* (Pete Dexter, 1984) and *Red Baker* (Robert Ward, 1985). If convincing working-class voices are raised, they generally convince for reasons other than the themes they exploit, thanks to the new forms found for these fictions of "the other half" (Michael Harrington). Thus, William Kennedy rediscovers the realistic manner of James T. Farrell and Nelson Algren in order to make the industrial city throb in his Albany Trilogy (*Legs*, 1975; *Billy Phelan's Greatest Game*, 1978; *Ironweed*, 1983), after having triumphed over it by excess (*The Ink Truck*, 1969, took him indeed well beyond realistic conventions). Bobbie Ann Mason leavens the insipid quality of daily lives etiolated by poverty thanks to historical myth (*Shiloh*, 1982) or retraces the impact of the Vietnam War on Kentucky families (*In Country*, 1985); Jayne Anne Phillips either has recourse to the dark lyricism of her shorter forms (*Black Tickets*, 1979; *Fast Lanes*, 1987) or to the novelistic montage (*Machine Dreams*, 1984), the working-class scenes of West Virginia alternating with painful memories of Vietnam.

Finally, Mason's and Phillips' master, Raymond Carver, dressed with ever threatening forms, in spite of their apparent simplicity, real narrative wounds; his stories frame the ungainly speech of the unfortunate and the disinherited, suggest the smothered violence of the voiceless.

Debunkings

Rob Swigart wrote *Little America* during the Bicentennial frenzy. All the moments of glory of American history find themselves sabotaged in his novel by the concentrated, but by no means exaggerated account of the "kitsch" use to which they have been put by the world of commerce. In the restaurant of the service station named "Little America," in the heart of Wyoming, menu specials and ice-cream dishes have been given the names of men and places of the Revolution, of famous battles ("Custard's Last Stand"). From Custer to Crazy Horse and Sitting Bull, there is only so far as an arrow can fly. Harold Jaffe crosses the distance by entitling a rather disrespectful collection of stories *Mourning Crazy Horse*. Everywhere, examples of mocking demystification abound. A very few will suffice to illustrate the point, consisting in the strange relationships entertained by Mussolini and Pinocchio in Jerome Charyn's *Pinocchio's Nose,* in the grotesque scenes that take place in Charyn's earlier *American Scrapbook*, in which a paternalistic senator visiting a Japanese detention camp during World War II gets bombarded with vegetables by "suspects," and finally in the free-for-all madness of a rather extraordinary convention in Robert Coover's *A Political Fable.* If "history only repeats itself as farce," as the recent recourse to the once tragic Maoist formula of the "politically correct" amply demonstrates, a number of its fictional illustrations thus have legitimate recourse to the art of "slapstick" so dear to Kurt Vonnegut's art.

In a definitely graver mode, history is presented from a defamiliarized point of view in Jerzy Kosinski's *The Painted Bird,* one very close indeed to Agota Kristof's *The Notebook*, in which two young twins become totally amoral witnesses of their time.[18] The "painted bird" is a child abandoned to the bloody maelstroms of history and designated by his speechless singularity to the cruelty of his fellows. His gaze, unfiltered by any set of moral values whatsoever, framed only by his will to survive, efficaciously dents the possibility of a heroic vision, illustrating in its own way the "creepy minuet History and the inner psychic history must dance together" in Hawkes's *The Cannibal.*[19] History opens its maw wide in this novel whose form crushes its characters between two symbolic dates: 1914 and 1945, only to get devoured itself by a Germanic mythology of enormous appetites. Unreliable — "the Merchant" dies in two different sections of the narrative; cyclical — Ernst takes the place of Gavrilo Princip during a temporally misplaced assassination attempt; unpredictable in its ironies — Stella's mother dies when she is run through by a piece of the only plane to have crashed on their little town, history cannot be considered as the major force to activate men. Rather, as William Gaddis suggests in *The Recognitions,* it appears as the desire of historians, who anxiously try to salvage the appearance of some system from the chaos of the past. There is quite a distance between historical narratives and the way in which, as a child, the narrator of Joseph McElroy's *novel* learned of "ancient history" at the same time as he was constituting a parallel one for himself. When he has become an adult, there is no longer any rivalry between the two versions, even though they continue coexisting in his memory: "I know the two histories, one verbatim in the graceful English of Herodotus [*sic*], the other poly-vectored in my doomed memory."[20]

In *The Franklin Scare,* Charyn revisits the great paranoid fears that punctuate American history, from Salem to Joseph McCarthy via the Palmer Raids and the Red Scare, mixing history and fiction in a way that practically founded a subgenre in the seventies. The Rosenberg affair is at the center of *The Public Burning* (Coover) and of E. L. Doctorow's *The Book of Daniel.* In both cases, the reexamination of the historical dossier is not so much the result of a minute staging of the documents as that of internally listening to the protagonists of the drama and laying out on the page the prevalent discourses about to solidify themselves into "history." In *The Book of Daniel,* one of the Rosenberg sons, hidden under the pseudonym of Isaacson, reconstitutes in a library the argumentative logic that destroyed his parents.

The metaphor of the circus governs *The Public Burning.* Nixon, the main narrator, is not its ringmaster, however. This particular part is played by the mythical figure of Uncle Sam. A parade passes, tickets are hard to come by, each in their turn, beasts, clowns, political tightrope walkers, and jugglers troop by. The highlight of the show consists in the execution of the accused in Times Square, and Nixon never stops meditating on the details of its organization and publicity. Responsible for the latter is the "Poet Laureate" of the United States, Henry ("Mother") Luce, founder of *Time.* Rather than present his show on the triple ring of Barnum and Bailey, Coover prefers distinct places and genres: Nixon's monologue as he goes from meeting to meeting, the theatrical drama of his encounters with Ethel Rosenberg or Dwight Eisenhower, "poetical inserts" transforming the media (*Time* or *The New York Times,* heralds of "historical time" both) into bards who sing an epic that Bakhtin previously proved impossible because of the abolition of distance by the actuality of point of view.

Nixon seems to be the politician who most interested contemporary novelists; of all presidents of the period, he is the one most conscious of historical processes. It is perhaps because Coover — following Mailer (*St. George and the Godfather*) and Philip Roth (*Our Gang*), but after having observed for twenty years a character who fascinates him — vigorously highlights this particular acumen that he managed to avoid the legal suits that threatened the publication of the book and delayed it for so long; in the end Nixon certainly does not emerge from the novel unscathed, but he is endowed with the only worthy historical consciousness, the knowledge of the reading grids imposed upon the real by the power of myths (the "Phantom" of International Communism, the Crockett- or Sam Slick–like figure of Uncle Sam). He thus towers above his first avatar in Coover's work: "Gloomy Gus," a conscientious student of football, women, and history, totally incapable of transcending or even of adapting his models from one activity to the other. Historical consciousness may well end up literally and literarily sodomized by myth at the end of the novel; but the immense fresco thus composed by Robert Coover is such that Nixon can only be condemned by the reader for having accepted a part he knows to be phony; he still has the merit of having understood and of not being duped by historical mechanisms. In *Gloomy Gus*, an explicitly historical narrative, the narrator, working on a bust of Gorky, cannot achieve the rendition of the writer's eyes he has in mind. History, however, Coover tells us, is directly predicated on that glance.

Ironical Visions

"The irony of history," Frederic Tuten announces in the first pages of *The Adventures of Mao During the Long March* (1971), "knows no limit." "In cauda venenum": following the long dissertation on the great irresistible forces of history triggered by a theme he handles somewhat in the manner of Andy Warhol's serial Mao Tse Tungs, he adds: "Each soldier knew that the outcome at the Tatu Bridge might well decide the future of the entire Communist movement in China."[21] As for Gloomy Gus, these "adventures" draw their lessons from the rules of montage. In both cases, a comparable discourse on sculpture prompts a comparable meditation. One's glance interacts with history: angles and perspectives, cultural a prioris, status of the subject. The savory questions concerning contemporary aesthetics that Mao answers in the final interview take up in another discursive order the political and military strategies broached in a distanced and would-be documentary fashion in the body of the novel.

It is also to the manipulation of scales that Russell Banks's *Continental Drift* (1985) owes its ironies. From the beginning, history is contemplated from an elevated vantage point, measured in terms of geological times and climactic variations; individual destinies, intimately mixed with the political peripeteia of the Caribbean world, appear only as local illustrations of wider evolutions from which history is thus, tongue in cheek, commodiously removed. The reader is periodically made witness, at the hinges of personal tragedies, to sudden elevations of tone that, by referring to the indifferent accidents of the planet's behavior, efficiently relativize what is then perceived as anecdotal in the miseries undergone by the characters.

In *Giles Goat-Boy*, the irony consists in the fact that Barth seems willing to reconcile artifice and reality, refusing for a time to unravel the logic of politics and history from that of myth. The result of which tactics is immediate: he seems, immediately, to be the one history dreams up. His project temporarily undone, he makes a new attempt with *LETTERS*, plotting revenge. Someone proposes, in perfect psychoanalytical logic: "If history is a trauma, maybe the thing to do is redream it."[22] Answering that challenge, Barth proceeds, in this epistolary novel, to creatively recapitulate every one of his previous works; he invites them to dialogue, in order to discover and correct his previous positions vis-à-vis the history of the world "as it is." The internecine quarrels of this literary family, laundering its dirty pages, want to be the reflection of combats attested by history. The "goat-boy" goes back to the fold: abandoning the wide metaphor of the nameless university that contains and represents the world, *LETTERS* refers us back to factual history in order to show that the process of history is to be read in the world, not in the ghetto of an allegory devised for private use.

At any rate, the historical myth might well be but the result of a monstrous imaginary collage of events. Such, at least, is Tuten's suggestion:

The Long March is already a myth . . . imagine all these events concentrated into one year, under one leader: Washington and his tattered men crossing the Delaware and the agonizing encampment of the foot-bleeding, frostbitten troops at Valley Forge; Columbus's voyage to America; Napoleon's cracked winter retreat from Russia; the flight of the Armenians from the Turks; the Seminole Indian Florida swamp resistance; the Lewis and Clark expedition; Hannibal's passage over the Alps; the Watts uprising; the Oklahoma migration of the 1930s; the partisan activities throughout Europe in World War II; Che's flight in Bolivia; the Confederate General Mosby's guerrilla war in Virginia, 1863; Moses and his followers fleeing the Egyptians; Castro's eighty-man invasion of Cuba, his stay in the Sierra Maestra and the subsequent military struggles; the parade of the Barnum and Bailey circus through the main street of Chicago, 1903.[23]

Let history appear in these fictions and it is under the form of a problematic theme. In *The Adventures of Mao*, a whole series of historical narrative lines (the Long March itself, of course, but also a workers' strike in San Francisco and the Civil War) are paralleled with speculations on art and poetry that make it possible to accentuate idealistic conceptions of history: "As these busts in the block of marble, thought Miriam, so does our individual fate exist in the limestone of time. We fancy that we carve it out; but its ultimate shape is prior to all our action."[24] There appears under these lines the entelechial mode of Puritan conceptions of history that underpins Pynchon's narratives. It is because of them, of the immoderate lust for ends that hides in them, of their profound understanding and of the faithfulness of their representation, at least as much as because of the illustration of the impossibility of an objective historical knowledge illustrated by *V,* that Pynchon has been accused by some of irresponsible Pilatism:

From the very title of *Gravity's Rainbow,* this lust makes him imaginatively guarantee the divorce of historical actions from any commonly accessible sphere of judgment and responsibility. He carries out this operation just as efficiently as he reduces individual behavior to mechanical programming, all intelligent reflection to the stencilling of pre-determined reflexes.[25]

History/Fiction/Politics

Historical. Hysterical. Such lexical vicinities are too tempting for some writers not to exploit them. In them lies the hermeneutic formula for the domination of the world that haunts American fiction from Nathanael West to Thomas Pynchon. David Bradley, whose *The Chaneysville Incident* takes place against the backdrop of slavery and the Civil War, adds to the irony of words when he claims that "history is hysterical reconstruction."[26] His title ironizes the merely factual; novelists like him have clearly integrated their theoretical consciousness into their creations; "reconstruction" says clearly that the stakes of such fictions have shifted their nature toward ideological counterattacks but that they do not necessarily, for all that, crudely or directly thematize their ideas in order to turn into pamphlets.

The techniques are just as sophisticated in the works of the most innovative authors (Coover or the Walter Abish of *How German Is It*) as in the more popular novels with a more conservative project (Vidal's *Burr*), or a more subversive one (Doctorow's *Ragtime*). The fabulous is mixed with what is verifiable. One uses in equal doses and, by means of juxtapositions more brutal than those of Balzac, Dumas, Hugo, or Vigny, characters created from scratch and historical figures; free rein is given to secondary comments that interrupt the narrative; the event is embroidered to make visible the twists of historical and/or political discourse, to discern the share it owes to language and imagination, bringing water to the theoretical mill of Hayden White for whom all history is always, to a certain extent, metahistory.[27] Eternally reshaped and remodeled, the fiction of history weighs as much as events themselves on whomever adopts it indiscriminately as an authentic reflection of undisputable events. Quite naturally, whoever disputes them will have to answer too easily accepted official fictions by means of private, freely invented historical fictions. Such is the essence of Robert Coover's endeavors.[28]

The techniques arming such "historical" fictions in their incorporation of recent critiques of history are many. First, one might highlight the new balance reached in the particular use of real characters alongside fictitious ones; nowadays, the latter jeopardize the credibility of the former, whereas the former, in historical novels, used to lend some of theirs to their invented neighbors. Several illustrations can be found in the works of Doctorow (Houdini, Morgan, or Ford in *Ragtime*, for example) and Guy Davenport. *Tatlin!* and *Da Vinci's Bicycle* incorporate them in their titles but they make suspicious encounters everywhere. Thus Wittgenstein and Kafka, Gertrude Stein and Fourier can live side by side; a theory of Greek philosophers troops by, punctuated here and there by a dialogue between Heraclitus and some imaginary disciple. The fortuitous and totally hypothetical encounters of historical characters prepare the field for the fabrication of the imaginary Dutch philosopher who narrates "The Dawn in Erewhon" (*Tatlin!*). "Ernst Machs Max Ernst" is an essay from *The Geography of the Imagination,* but it functions as an analogue to Davenport's stories; it borrows from Ernst the collage technique favored by Frederic Tuten when he makes Mao stop in front of a tank from which Greta Garbo then emerges.[29] Franklin Mason (*Four Roses in Three Acts*) and Judy Lopatin (*Modern Romances*) fictionalize the lives of artists and creators to nourish their own creations ("The Death of Joe Dassin" features Cocteau, Radiguet, Brancusi, Picasso . . .). Marx appears as a character in *Oxherding Tale* (Charles Johnson), as well as in Max Apple's *Zip,* where he lives side by side with Castro, Sartre, and J. Edgar Hoover. In *Free Agents* and *The Oranging of America,* Apple makes the Disney Brothers and Howard Johnson lead the dance; Stanley Elkin founds his *Franchiser* on the destiny of Krok (the founder of McDonald's restaurants). Such "factions" shorten the imaginary distance separating history from fiction and invite superpositions of the legendary and the historical.

The methods of historical research, not separated from subjectivity and the options that accompany it, are the real heroes of Bradley's *The Chaneysville Incident.* Should one speak here — or concerning Mailer's *The Armies of the Night*— of metafiction or of metahistory? Probably of both at the same time since the novel feeds on speculations concerning the modalities of historical research and writing while not neglecting characters, plot, and decor, a series of notions whose very historical nature is thereby itself demonstrated and exposed.

Mixing the fabulous and the historical is one of the foundations of mythical thought, a theme to which we shall return. But Coover, starting from a reflection on history, claims that even an "innocent" history, a collection of facts, events and deeds, may itself participate in myth, and that this particular myth has lost, in our days, its capacity to convince. The metaphor of baseball is therefore of great use to him: "Quite simply," he says, "baseball is among the most precisely historical activities known to humanity, and one of the most structured. Every single meaningless twitch . . . is recorded in some way. And every sequence of events is subject to some kind of regulation."[30] Thanks to this metaphor, Coover shows it is easy to get lost in the forest of facts constituting a waterproof autonomous world that does not include the means of its own questioning. What fascinates J. Henry Waugh in baseball are "the records, the statistics, the peculiar balances between individual and team, offense and defense, strategy and luck, accident and pattern, power and intelligence."[31] One is tempted, of course, to watch for clusters, coincidences, echoes, and harmonics, to try to derive some immanent sense from signs all the more redundant as the limits of their movement have been precisely drawn. Outside of the regulative discourse that constitutes it, what can history be? "Of course, we share a certain quantity of information, let's say that . . . but it's not enough to call it 'History.' What do we have in fact? Births, debts, deaths, and the weather."[32] In *The Universal Baseball Association,* the past of the "Association" is questioned to the point where history can step down in favor of myth: "Can't even agree on facts. . . . History; in the end you can't prove a thing."[33] The fear of no longer having a discourse that could unify the signs of history is a source of anguish, of an anxiety easily alleviated by the first unifying mythical discourse that passes by. More than anything, man fears the absence of meaning and constitutes it at all cost, even should this price be paid by the unconsciousness of his gesture: to become conscious of it would compel him to recognize the nature of his needs and the artificiality of the fodder he is fed. In Coover's work, the gesture of "fabulation" is not, as one might think, something that intervenes after the events have been gathered, thus diminishing their credibility; it is presented as an activity of the mind preceding all historical construction and influencing events themselves as much as their ulterior shaping.

This idea accounts for part of Mailer's work. In *The Armies of the Night*— subtitled "History as a Novel, the Novel as History" — the narrative of the march on the Pentagon dissolves the borders between reputedly distinct types of writing; but beyond this, one should notice that Mailer is not represented in it as a historical witness, but as an actor. A highly colorful figure, he is going to attend this demonstration — or the launching of the Apollo flight, or Muhammad Ali's fight — with a view to making of it simultaneously an event, a book, history, and a myth. The event of *The Executioner's Song* and of his other "journalistic" works is that Mailer should give them shape. An analyst of society, a high priest, Mailer does not only write novels that say and are history. Conscious of the processes of its elaboration, he aspires to make and be history. McElroy dedicates to him several paragraphs of an article in which he ponders the interface between interiority and exteriority, continuity and discontinuity, and sketches an author

who is not quite the risk-taker he'd like to think — particularly in the work itself — but who begs the century to entertain him, who asks to be ambushed by experience, and whose celebrity performance is not only an embarrassment of greed but also an open assault on his own privacy, so that, through some freak frequency in the urine-sparkling night of missed connections, inside Norman might come to equal America.[34]

History and Writing

"It takes me so long to write a novel that it always turns out to be historical." David Bradley's pleasantry is indeed pleasing but it is not, in fact, a mere pleasantry.[35] It only efficiently reverses another remark: "To date means to caption a time, built and cut out of another time which cannot bear apprehension either, nor, a fortiori, meaning. It means telling a story. Time is legendary stuff, it is telling!"[36] Which of course does not mean that the duration necessary for writing a novel comes anywhere close to a "real time" representation; but the generative processes, the recourse to the laws of causality and relative determination of what comes after by what comes before, of the right side of the text by its left, the various pointers, allow rough comparisons that justify such a belief in the "history" of a text. That the form of a work depends on the historical a prioris of an author as soon as the latter becomes conscious of them and accords them great importance, one will ascertain merely by thinking of the revealing cubism of Gertrude Stein's *The Making of Americans* or of John Dos Passos's *U.S.A.* trilogy. Thus it seems to me erroneous to distinguish, in Coover's work for example, novels with a strongly thematic and historical structure from the stories of *Pricksongs and Descants* or of *In Bed One Night* in which history doesn't appear as such. In effect, since the former conclude on the impossibility to seize the real without a point of view prestructured by former fabulations, it would be astonishing that their author should accept the use of linear forms for the latter.[37]

By the same token, if Walter Abish's most historical novel is indeed *How German Is It*, it is not because he deals with the German military heritage there, with terrorism or with concentration camps, but more subtly because this text, which explores the relationships between surface effects and unconscious depths, insists on psychological rather than social repression. It stages the lying-in of a narrative by means of questions directly borrowed from psychoanalysis that punctuate it at regular intervals ("Answer. Answer immediately." "What else?" "Could everything be different?"). The narrative that confesses itself under our eyes, with its ruses and evasive answers, its drifts and its obsessive recurrences, is the result of an interrogation during which the very engine of German history is progressively revealed in its deeper structures. The cannibalistic powers of myth were at work in John Hawkes's novel.[38] Those, no less subterraneous and frightening, of the collective psyche dictate Walter Abish's. The absence of a question mark at the end of the title provides latitude for us to fill such an absence with an interrogation or an exclamation, letting recognition measure up with inquiry; it also makes it possible to leave it as is, the stress then falling on an "it" close to the status of the id, more strongly suggestive than a discourse on history of what, dynamically, the latter owes to the internal fictions that animate us. When Georgiana Peacher uses on-the-spot self-hypnosis to compose the "historical" fiction of *Mary Stuart's Ravishment Descending Time* in a Scottish castle, she makes possible the osmosis of the underlying patterns of history and the desires of a present voice at the same time as she makes it perceptible by means of the strange Joycean text that gives it shape.

Such indirection explains why in Mailer's *Why Are We in Vietnam?* (1967) one searches in vain for a mere mention of the war in question, except if one infers it from the presence of a helicopter. The book takes place in Alaska and the bear-hunting party reveals motivations of which politics is only a different manifestation. A violent type of writing substitutes itself for the violences writing could transcribe, and the permanent surfacing of mental structures with obvious political implications stands for historical speculation. The voice we hear is that of a disc jockey; it might as well present — and probably comments, more accurately — the scratched record of American history. The expressionism of "new journalists" thus contains pertinent historical aspects. Tom Wolfe — and Hunter Thompson in *Fear and Loathing in Las Vegas* or *Hell's Angels* — may well try hard not to be historical, either through his choice of subjects or through the viewpoint he adopts, yet two hard facts remain: from *Electric Kool-Aid Acid Test* to *The Right Stuff* via *The Kandy-Kolored Tangerine-Flake Streamline Baby* and *Radical Chic and Mau-Mauing the Flak Catchers,* he crystallizes discourses on the times, transforms them into landmarks of consciousness. Beyond this he creates, in spite of himself, historical material for further reference. And this in two ways: first, because he chooses to weave together his unforgettable vignettes around scenes supposedly representative of a period (he was responsible for baptizing "the me generation," anticipating Christopher Lasch's *The Culture of Narcissism*);[39] second, because his writing foregrounds the debt of events to language, far more efficiently than the more openly documentary chronicle of *The Bonfire Of the Vanities.* Hunter Thompson, in *Fear and Loathing on the Campaign Trail,* seems to be writing an objective reportage because he writes about the presidential campaign of 1972. But his language frames the event in such a way that it is the reactions of one segment of public opinion to this campaign that are effectually and directly illustrated in his pages.

At any rate, the fusion of history with mediatic activity need no longer be demonstrated. History, myths, and the media are now so inextricably linked in the American imagination that one should be forgiven for not dealing with them together. What fiction would not be altered by the fact that Oswald was murdered live after having killed John F. Kennedy just barely off the air? DeLillo's *Libra* (1988) suggests that the Warren Report to follow could be the "megaton novel James Joyce would have written if he'd moved to Iowa City and lived to be a hundred."[40] In Harold Jaffe's *Mole's Pity,* Mole trains on the roof of a building to assassinate "Dix," a combination of Nixon and Kennedy; his "Tyrannus Dix" brings to mind Ferlinghetti's *Tyrannus Nix,* whereas the murder refers to Nixon's triumphant ex-adversary of 1960. So does history at times abandon particularities to make room for the generic. It is hard not to think of Reagan when one reads Jonathan Baumbach's "From the Life of the President" (in *The Life and Times of Major Fiction*), but the signs of the novels might apply equally well to others. "If the content of history can be manipulated by mass media," Raymond Federman writes, "if television and newspapers can falsify or justify historical facts, then the unequivocal relation between the real and the imaginary disappears. . . . Consequently, history must be reviewed, re-examined, especially recent historical events as presented or rather RE-presented to us by mass-media and fiction."[41]

There is indeed novelty in these forms of epistemological suspicion. But let us not forget the long-standing presence of less theoretically buttressed ones. Two hundred years ago, in *Modern Chivalry*, the enormous novel he published in 1792, Hugh Brackenridge staged the following dialogue:

You are a man of books —
A little so.
What books have you read?
History, Divinity, Belles-letters.
What is the characteristic of history?
Fiction.
Of Novels?
Truth.[42]

Chapter 9
Myth and Suspicion

Any tale untellable is believed as untellable
and becomes legend. Leg-end is where toes
and tails begin.
— William Wharton, *Scumbler*

The imposition of an order — at the very least, of a shape — upon the
disorder of the world conditions both its reading and its use; this is also,
in part, the definition of fiction, and more generally, of art. Forms and
discourses can also reveal the perception, or rather, the acceptance of an
irreducible disorder; myths of disorder are just as effective as those of
order. But, on the whole, whether one seeks the meaning of history or
contributes to a vision of the world, everything stems from a desire for
coherence.

These master narratives are fleeting. At more or less regular intervals,
stories and *Weltanschauungen* join the old narratives that strew the abundant but ever fertile fields of myth. After Homer, at least, *mythos* was
legend and fable, as opposed to *logos,* historical narrative. An avowed
fictional narrative often including supernatural elements, it belonged to
the real by informing our vision of it. With time, its meaning became
somewhat diluted, and for our purposes here we will use the term in its
most watered-down meaning in order to include the lesser "myths" of
modern life. Myths, classical and universal or modern, popular, and local
legends, shape our existence. Certainly, Oedipus is no Snow White, but
king and queen arise from the same shorthand of the imaginary. The
overlaps are clear when Hugh Nissenson recreates the journal of Johnny
Appleseed under an ambiguous title (*The Tree of Life*), when Coover
gives Joseph's point of view on Mary's apparent infringements of the
bounds of marital fidelity ("J's Marriage"), when he provides Noah's
brother's point of view on Noah's "madness" ("The Brother"), or when

he stirs some Freud into Andersen and the Brothers Grimm ("The Door," "The Gingerbread House").[1] The functional equivalent is emphasized by Rachel Ingalls in "Blessed Art Thou" (*I See a Long Journey*) in which Brother Anselm, made pregnant by the angel Gabriel, meditates on particular structures that are revealed to be "political" in the rest of the text:

Once upon a time, he said to himself, *there were three bears: a mama bear, a papa bear, and a baby bear.* There was a king who had three daughters, a woodcutter with three sons. *Once upon a time there were three little pigs and they all lived in the forest, where there was a big, bad wolf.* Everything went in threes and everything was told as if it had happened only that week, or it could just as easily have been centuries ago. *Once upon a time,* he thought, *there was the Father, the Son and the Holy Ghost.*[2]

The highest hours of modernism, marked out over a contemporary history at drift in which Eliot perceived an "immense panorama of futility and anarchy," had resorted to the method of myth to confer an aesthetic order upon a world plunged deep in uncertainty. One hoped that the wanderings of the modern period would thus be contained by the solid grids inherited from the depths of the ages. After all, no one could banish the Fisher King, Tiresias, or Phlebas by force or by decree. Classical myth, transcending all and incarnated by art, would erect its barrier against the unfolding of disorder and of the hordes of the deceased, who, in *The Waste Land,* cross a Thames reeking of the Styx. In idealist terms, a vision of art as the source of order such as this can only disappear if one calls into question the very notion of art. But the time no longer holds with this sole modernist conception of art as archmyth and one has grounds in discerning the opening of a new aesthetic period inaugurated, once again, by Hawkes and Gaddis.

In *The Recognitions,* there is a return to *The Waste Land* as well as to its subtext, Frazer's *The Golden Bough,* while the myth of Faust is omnipresent. Mythical parallels abound in characterizing the players (Agnes Deigh/Agnus Dei), a fly bothering Otto becomes a goddess, the "parts" suggest Dionysius and the Walpurgis Nights, Mithra and a thousand mythological arcana underpin Wyatt Gwyon's sermons. At all times, Gaddis sketches mythological grids that encourage a redemptive reading of lives that are doomed, unsound, or neurotic; but he does this the better to invert them, to leave them unfinished, to refuse that the novel's meaning could be reduced to the unifying decoding of such figures, that the cultural fissures could be so easily and conveniently sealed over. In 1942, Santayana observed "mythology was accordingly placed in a sad dilemma, with either horn fatal to its life; it must either be impoverished to remain sincere, or become artificial to remain adequate."[3] From this point on, irony dominates the turn toward myth, denouncing the "modernist heresy" that an idealist reading would recognize as a dominant value. Through the stuttering and unsure voice of Stanley, the musician whose work, when performed on the organ of the old church of Fenestrula, causes his own death, Gaddis states a position: "When art tries to be a religion in itself . . . a religion of perfect form and beauty, but then there it is all alone, not uniting people, not . . . like the Church does but, look at the gulf between people and modern art."[4] As for *The Cannibal*, it showed that the mental structures governed by myth devoured both beings and time. Regarding literature, Annie Dillard argues that nothing has really changed since all narrative must obey laws similar to those of the great mythical narratives:

> The writer makes real artistic meaning of meaninglessness the usual way, the old way, by creating a self-relevant artistic whole. He produces a work whose parts cohere. He imposes a strict order upon chaos. . . . The work of art may, like a magician's act, pretend to any degree of spontaneity, randomality, or whimsy, as long as the effect of the whole is calculated and unified. . . . In this structural unity lies integrity, and it is integrity which separates art from nonart.[5]

But this structural unity, should it solidify into myth, is not necessarily, for all that, its dupe. Its relationship to modernism and to its aesthetic or pancalist belief is critical and reduced. Sukenick, a militant "postmodernist," admits he agrees that "the Modern period is dead, but in the same sense that Symbolism is dead or Surrealism is dead — dead but not dead-end. It is the Moderns now to whom we can look back and it is the problem they raised that we have to contend with."[6] And he goes on to quote Joyce, Stein, Beckett, and Genet, to reject the divorce of myth and reality, to demand a synthesis of symbolism and the real. Moreover, on American ground, myth — which embraces both causes and ends, prospers in paradox and contradiction, for which Lévi-Strauss tells us it is the "imaginary solution," and warps or abolishes time — has always been a powerful means of organizing the real. In a country that distrusts the forces of history, mythical narratives supplant other modes of reading. "American writers struggling with the nightmare of their own history," writes Craig Hansen, "a history which now includes Joyce, frequently accept his emphasis on myth and stylistic variety."[7] For Robert Scholes, the even stronger awareness that myth constitutes a device of literary structuration has the increasing effect of giving birth to "allegorical" productions that stress the gap between artifice and reality. Each in turn, the New Jerusalem, the Frontier, and the American dream have focused the gaze and raised hopes. By contrast, the most glaring protests have ironically denounced their failings. Whether they favor or combat them, American literature's greatest works at once confirm and contribute to these myths. Even today, Hunter Thompson gives the subtitle "A Savage Journey to the Heart of the American Dream" to *Fear and Loathing in Las Vegas,* and DeLillo claims, in *Americana,* that the fragmentation of contemporary forms results from the "settling of a myth into the realism of its component parts."[8] The keystone has failed. Yet some interesting rubble still remains.

American history is conceived in a manner somewhat like that described by Praxiteles regarding the emergence of forms: they were hidden beneath their layers of rock, and it sufficed for the chisel to eliminate that which they were not; in the United States, politics, religion, and literature could and should be the tools used in unveiling the constitutive myth as it really is. This is one of the foundations of the *romance* that, from Hawthorne to Jim Harrison (at the end of *Warlock,* Lundgren perceives the rustling of Pan's reeds), calls for a reading of the ideal beneath the real. This porous form that blurs the borders between reality and the imaginary can be permeated by the sudden appearance of myth; it continues to provide the foundation for contemporary works whose authors use myth as such, whereas — as with history — it is the *mechanisms* and the *stakes* of myth that engage the attention of others. Recent events and intellectual history have taken their toll and, to use the language of Wall Street, myth, in contemporary fiction, "seems bearish." At least it is often used in a conscious, distanced manner. While many may make use of it, few are blindly confident of its powers; it can be used to different tactical ends, can be made into a tight ideological analysis, and can be turned against itself. Everyone — or almost everyone — recognizes its dangers, but its heuristic value remains, provided one keeps one's distance. The recent uses of myth bear witness most often to the difficulties inherent in its prima facie usage, to the necessity of stripping, by means of myth itself, forms of thought that are seen to be alienating.

Relative Confidence in Myth

The legend of the Holy Grail lends its structure and themes to Malamud's *The Natural* (1952). Hobbs's given name of Roy connects him to the royal Fisher King and, when anachronistically superimposed on the world of baseball, this new kind of pastoral claims to be a reflection of the fortunes and misfortunes of Percival. Yet when Thomas Berger gives the title *Arthur Rex* to a text he describes as an "homage to Sir Thomas Mallory," the purpose is entirely different. This "salute to the Age of Chivalry" by an author "enmired [. . .] in the Time of the cad" recreates the Arthurian legend. Berger confesses his "sincere craving for chivalric bravura and his passion for panache," but this does not prevent him from demonstrating that our age is no longer one for the simplicities of Good and Evil. The world has become so complex that Arthur is overcome. When Arthur claims that "the most difficult thing in life is to maintain the faith one has in one's own hoaxes," it is clear that, beneath this last word, myth lies hidden.[9]

The romantic imagination still has its followers. Although the mythical works of Joyce Carol Oates aim only to give a particular form (the genres she uses are as varied as her writings are numerous) to the violences that haunt her, the explicitly mythical frame of *Cybele* topples the story of the life of Edwin Locke beyond the grotesque and the horrible, beyond sexual obsession and impotence, in order to end with the traditional themes of fertility and its rites. In *Bellefleur,* the gothic characterizes the presentation of a disappeared world (even though this familial saga has been read as an allegory for the fate of the Kennedy clan), in which the supernatural figures strongly, makes the strange and the normal coincide, authorizes metamorphoses and apparitions, and allows Oates to unify a narrative that spans six generations from which all historical notation has nonetheless disappeared, leaving room for mystery. *A contrario,* when the mythical frame disappears from comparable narratives, we witness the collapse of *A Bloodsmoor Romance,* in which only the title suggests the coherence, solidity, and imaginative efficiency of an eminently American genre. By borrowing too much from various forms, Oates runs the risk of not always being able to feed them with an imagination that cannot lend itself with equal success to each form. Relying on mere abundance, this novelist, who has literally written her weight in books, apparently counts on the enormous volume of her production in order to bequeath us, eventually, a lesser anthology.

The stakes of Updike's *The Centaur* are more clear. The myth of the wounded centaur Chiron and his son Prometheus (George and Peter Caldwell in the novel) serves as backdrop to a largely realist narrative. The text feeds off the struggle between these two levels, with the mythical presences providing dignity and a universal dimension to scenes rendered sordid by the ugliness of the times. But it remains unclear — and the ambiguity demonstrates the difficulty henceforth apparent when these materials are used in an insufficiently "suspicious" manner — which of the two levels of discourse, mythical or human, Updike is proposing as dominant. Emphasizing the connections that link them, he appears to be following Joyce's lead by forcing himself to create an intermediary space. Only the emphasis has been displaced:

It seemed to me that there was something mythical about the events. It's an experiment very unlike that of *Ulysses,* where the myth lurks beneath the surface of the natural events. In a way, the natural events in my book are meant to be a kind of mask for the myth.[10]

It is remarkable that space, and intermediary spaces in particular, form the thematic center of several of Updike's novels. The hesitation at the borders between city and countryside, the displacements from one to the other emphasize the mythical quest for a meaningful space. *Rabbit Run, Rabbit Redux,* and *Rabbit Is Rich, Bech: A Book,* and *Bech Is Back* are at least in part dramatizations of an American space in which the temptations of the pastoral and those of a problematic conviviality alternately dominate. Forever mythified in American literature, space brings, moreover, a renewal of mythification at the same time as it displaces its questions toward new spaces of writing (Sukenick, *Out*): largely rid of the thematic of the Frontier unable to defend itself against creeping urbanization and commercialization, as seen in "Camping Craze" and "The Surgeon" (*Trout Fishing in America*), American space remains in Jim Harrison (*Farmer, Legends of the Fall*), Thomas McGuane (*The Bushwhacked Piano, Panama*), Carol Sturm Smith (*Fat People*), and Toby Olson (*Seaview*) the refuge of romantic flights in an environment that stifles them. The rebirth of a certain regionalism (William Kittredge's Northwest, McGuane's or William Eastlake's West, Carolyn Chute's, Howard Mosher's, or Thomas Glynn's New England, Harrison's or Michael Martone's Midwest) plays a part in this; but the traditional mythical ascendancy of American space undergoes some interesting resurgences in these writer's works.

Coover suggests that, in the United States, space is masculine and time is feminine. Perhaps, on this ground, certain mythical confrontations are played out that social tensions cannot express. In this case, we might better understand then that history fares as badly as women in a male literary tradition illustrated within the "macho" fictions of Harrison and McGuane (in *Panama*, Jesse James dominates a cursed landscape where men are "real men"). And perhaps one might also understand why historical time, although it does not appear more clearly in Alice Walker or Toni Morrison than in Joyce Carol Oates or Joan Chase, seeks refuge in "our mothers' gardens" through the evocation of multiple generations.

Nevertheless, spatial and temporal myths are experiencing some reversals; in *Seaview* by Toby Olson, the movement no longer proceeds from East to West but in the opposite direction, even if the encounter with the Indian occurs at a comparable stage of the story. Beginning in California, this fiction has its hero and his companion cross the Midwest and end up in New England. Whereas the myth's direction is reversed, the struggle with which the novel concludes perpetuates an attachment to its constitutive forces. While it may be enacted on a golf course rather than in wider open spaces, myth — although certainly shot through with holes — has not lost its vigor. However, Olson, like his true contemporaries, develops an equation between mythical work and textual work that places him beyond obsolete uses of myth. Whereas Mark Helprin is happy to lend an

Emersonian ambience to "The Schreuderspitze" (*Ellis Island and Other Stories*), and subjects Herr Wallich to a purification ritual comparable to that undergone by Marshall Pearl in *Refiner's Fire,* a revealing title, and whereas *Winter's Tale* employs the stuff of legend (with its flying horse, Athansor, formerly a milkman's nag) that permits him wildly extravagant chronological upheavals, Olson, for his part, in *The Woman Who Escaped from Shame,* develops *in parallel* the mythology that explains the existence of his marvelous palominos, tiny, clever horses the size of a dog. The entire novel is grounded in the exploitation of narratives — and of stories within stories — whose ritual reiteration becomes the key to the mythological trials structuring the novel.

If myth becomes flesh in his novel, it is because narration is revealed to be at the origin of myths and not different from them. At no time does the mythical material attain autonomy, constantly bridled by the spectacle and analysis of the birth of narratives. The fiction that we read has no other origin than the myths that haunt it. The new stories integrate old elements, justifications and causes are born and discover themselves in such a way that the mythical narratives reveal themselves to be subordinated to the activity of fiction. *The Woman Who Escaped from Shame* illustrates a device whose function is ironically noted by Barth in "Menelaiad" (*Lost in the Funhouse*) by the infinite multiplication of pairs of quotation marks: quotation within quotation within quotation; in this way, the mythical narrative hardens at the heart of the texts and of the reality figured there until it takes up all of the space and is substituted for reality itself. We will see by what other device Olson attacks myth by putting it to use.

Branches of contemporary fiction remain, nonetheless, confident in myth and rely on it to accomplish their strategic projects. Some women novelists find there, as we have seen, the means of expressing a time that goes beyond that of history; but one must nuance somewhat Larry McCaffery's overly generalized remark that they have turned "toward popular genres to find plots and myths more appropriate to female life than those of conventional realism."[11] I am unsure whether vampirism and wild kisses are especially inspiring to women, even if Anne Rice turns insistently (*Interview with the Vampire, The Vampire Lestat*) to this particular myth; on the other hand, I do know that the vampire myth holds a privileged place in Baumbach (*Reruns*) and that he has stolen it from the movies. I do not know whether Rachel Ingalls finds particular advantages in her use of horror films (even if the hero of *Mrs. Caliban* is a monster of a lovely green hue); but I am sure that Sukenick places Frankenstein at the center of *98.6*; I doubt, having read John Gardner, that Gail Godwin, following the example of Joyce Carol Oates, differs from her male colleagues when she resorts to the gothic tonalities of *Violet Clay,* nor, having read Carson McCullers and Flannery O'Connor, that she is being particularly innovative. I do not feel that a particular sexual propensity dictates the threatening mysteries of *The Shadow Knows* (Diane Johnson), since the mode is so fashionable among male authors—a number of whom have parodied it; and, however biased and excessive my views on her work might be, it is my contention that Kathy Acker (*Don Quixote, Great Expectations*) does not deliver on the promises of her shameless appropriations of the great novelistic myths any more fully than on those of the provocative and slipshod program of her "punk" fictions. Androgyny for androgyny and Tiresias for Tiresias, we are permitted to prefer to her confused fictions the clear and poignant song of William Goyen's *Arcadio,* where myth truly does come to life, the original form that Ursule Molinaro gives to *Encores for a Dilettante,* or the strange poetic fruits of Alan Friedman's *Hermaphrodeity.* Both gratuitously aggressive and ferociously mythological, Kathy Acker's novels are fashionable, modish attacks; they are equivalent to what, in his time, Tom Wolfe might have christened "mau-mauing" or "radical chic." To hound the mythical past in so unrelenting and unconvincing a manner is to declare oneself a "punk" indeed: No Future. Literary, that is.

Briefly stated, if myth still holds a certain charm for some mainstream authors who reached maturity and celebrity before the rise of suspicion, a majority of the period's most representative writers are less complicit and more rebellious where myth is concerned.

On the other hand, myth dominates the writing of authors currently and paternalistically identified as "ethnic." As argued elsewhere, myth can offer a positive response to questions raised by the fragmentation of the real and their identity crisis. As in earlier stages of the tradition these writers represent with talent, myth can often bring a form of healing: reconciliation, regeneration, and uniting of collective identity. Native American writers, dear to Toby Olson, naturally turn to myth. The most important among them, N. Scott Momaday, Kiowa by birth, brings his tribe's mythology to life in his fiction (*House Made of Dawn*). For Leslie Marmon Silko, writing is a way of relating the myths in which the reality of experience resides. For Silko and her people, technological evolutions and their consequences on the daily life of non–Native Americans have a lesser impact on the reality of life and the relations to the world than the tribal myths that need to be revived, or than the traditional stories, the images and memories that cradled her youth and from which she creates a convincing collage in *Storyteller* or *Ceremony.* For the Native Americans of our time, myth is more than a refuge; it arms a threatened identity; it is a "natural" and fundamental mode of expression. The spatiotemporal categories of mainstream fiction do not appear there, nor do the dominant preoccupations.

Concerning myth, and with an eye to relativizing its uses, we might recall that in ancient India no event was considered important if it lasted less than thirteen minutes, the time needed to cook rice. In fiction by American Indians, events of the white / European world are measured on a similar scale, even if engaged and militant writings bear witness to these works' insertion in the twentieth century. In a certain way, to bear witness means to struggle, and in the autobiographical narrative by Chinese American author Maxine Hong Kingston, *The Woman Warrior,* with its procession of traditional stories and of ghosts raised from a cultural past distinct from that of the United States, similar forces are at work. The political engagement of a good part of Chicano literature depends on the affirmation of the existential validity of traditional myths. By editing his multiethnic literary journal, *The Yardbird Reader,* where all national minorities come together, Ishmael Reed consciously carries out politically engaged work.

We should not neglect to mention that a reliance upon the myths and values of the country's first inhabitants — a relatively popular tactic over the past few decades — entails certain risks for members of the dominant culture who are tempted by such a move. In *At Play in the Fields of the Lord,* Peter Matthiessen takes a gibe at harmful intellectual confusions. Under cover of understanding indigenous values, the religious debate ends up — after having got off to a bad start by missionaries whose ardor is more impressive than their thought — with Jesus being presented to the Indians of Amazonia as the obvious equivalent of their god Kisu. The fact that Kisu is but the first among an entire pantheon of evil spirits does not unduly trouble the Reverend, who is not terribly sensitive to the dramatic ironies of language.

For Nathan Scott, the use of myth proposes a "radical sacramental vision" in the work of a black author like William Demby (*The Catacombs*). But Ishmael Reed's work warns us of the potential dangers of mythical radicalism: his novels, so seductive and beautiful in their flamboyance and excess, so innovative in their skillful mix of everyday speech and popular images, at times only invert the excess of totalizing mythical readings, rather than critically examining the questions raised by the fundamentalism of the myth itself. It is understandable that, having seized the enemy's weapons, Reed should be tempted to use nonwhite and nontraditional myths in American culture in order to resist the discursive domination of the culture in which he lives. In a civilization perceived as oppressive, any means may seem viable. Yet, taking only one example, this does not prevent Reed's use of voodoo from leading him to the edge of perilous ideological positions. That voodoo is an expression of black culture irrecuperable within white culture has been established. Yet, from there to considering Duvalier as a liberator is to make quite a debatable leap, even from his point of view. The adverse and polemical use of myth as buttress prevents it from encountering any opposition from the ways in which myth itself can be alienating.

Toni Morrison's strategy contrasts with that of Reed. Less head-on, she is more conciliatory, even if she relies on similar analyses. Certainly, in speaking of *Tar Baby,* whose title comes from a black legend, she explains unambiguously that she wanted to "take myth and boldly push it to the front." But whereas Reed, in *The Last Days of Louisiana Red* or *Mumbo Jumbo,* takes black myths as given, Morrison reveals them, making their genesis and their importance understood, and subtly downplays the dominant Euro-American myths in order to substitute a more African mythology. Her aim appears to be threefold: first to show that the use of Euro-American myths is but a veneer for African American culture; second, to seek a synthesis between the two mythological systems; and finally, to cast out blind or innocent uses of myth in order to make of it a more positive force. Like Coover, Morrison recognizes that people live through myths and that when they know what they are doing, they can triumph over them.

On first reading, *Song of Solomon* proves that African Americans have adopted white mythologies: the characters' names come from the Bible and Christian references abound. Circe makes an appearance. Upon closer reading, their use is ironic and defensive: the name of Pilate was chosen for its graphic attraction, Solomon is less the biblical king than Shalimar or Chaleemone, a flying character from African mythology. The authority of white myths is eroded as the work progresses, allowing the repressed myth to rise to the surface and then take over. Lest this meaning escape us, Morrison, following the example of the "magical realists" of Latin America, crystallizes dream images around her realist passages: the characters dream the world around them but, for that, they do not confront the real to any lesser degree. Follies, considered stuff and nonsense by the dominant culture, the myths of *Song of Solomon* are revealed to be vital to the protagonists' existential balance.

Certainly, the "color purple" of her prose, to borrow the title of Alice Walker's novel for stylistic purposes, moves Morrison dangerously close to sentimentalism or otherworldliness, sins of which Reed could not be accused. But Morrison's more "gentle" approach permits some useful comparisons. For example, the myth of the man who flies implicates Daedalus and Icarus as well as Shalimar. A similar synthesis allows Morrison to anchor more solidly her use of myth and distinct folklores. What her work seeks, metaphorically, asymptotically, is "to write the passage from ground to air,"[12] but what this writing allows thematically is a meeting of the magic and the real. In Morrison's work, the "Icarus complex" does not take on narcissistic and complacent aspects as in works by Erica Jong; it is not a personal complex but a form of collective pride, somewhat like that of the Indian who, at the end of Thomas Glynn's novel *Temporary Sanity,* takes flight from the roof of a barn. With characters like these, the reader better understands fictions that perform leaps away from the real the better to return to it. Regarding *Beloved,* without doubt her most powerful novel to date,[13] Morrison says that "myth must be anchored, in order to lift." Whereas Updike resorts to an allegorical style in which the writing of myth and descriptions of the real are melded together, Morrison, somewhat like Coover and yet as different from him as she might be, constantly makes tangible and insists on the interdependence of dream and the real; yet she does not allow, and this tendency is denounced in her characters, the temptation to confuse the two levels. In Morrison's work, myth cannot be read in the real. It allows individuals to find their place in it.

Reversals and Criticisms

We might argue that a similar project propels *Ancient Evenings,* to the extent that this huge novel, which retraces the four lives of Pharaoh Menenhetet, entrusts myth with this phase of Norman Mailer's permanent existential quest. Anxious to create both Myth and History, and on his way to becoming as mythical as the "great American novel" he believes he alone is capable of writing, Mailer, in a novel that may have received more negative criticism than it deserves, concentrates on the creative virtues of magic. In so doing, Mailer proves that he belongs to an earlier age of American fiction, so uncritical is his usage of myth. Truth be told, one can only attempt to clear him of the accusations of obscurantism by having him reject a certain primitivism in which he has always delighted. To affirm the superiority of magic over science, to erect the basic drives as the guides of consciousness, and to glorify a true metaphysics of experience pushed to its furthest limits — physical, sexual, mystical: the alternately courageous, sympathetic, and exasperating image of an extremely talented Mailer, the very caricature of machismo, the ruddy speechifier and anti-intellectual does not seem to be in much need of modification here.

Mailer recognizes only the thematic angle of suspicion, and his contribution to the revision of myth in contemporary fiction does not stem from a critical use but from his drive to create new ones. However, his novel does allow a comparison that, apart from helping to dissipate any monolithic vision of "Jewish American literature," has the merit of showing how the use of comparable material allows those more clever than he to explore the workings and dangers of mythical thought.

Indeed, in "The Bailbondsman" (*Searches and Seizures*), Stanley Elkin criticizes the "mythic method" by sardonically reevaluating its grounds and by demonstrating the ways in which it offers an inadequate response to our times. The dream of Alexander Main, who claims to be "Phoenician," transports us to the heart of an Egyptian tomb to be pillaged by Oyp and Glyp—former criminals released on bail by Main, who have since disappeared and reappeared in the guise of two antique thieves. Elkin deliberately blurs the connection he has created between these Luxor toughs and the great universal enigmas by resorting to anachronisms of the language used and of the institutions in question. This "mythical drama," integrated into a contemporary story, proves how tortured and fallacious such superposition can be, and explains that it is now merely an unsuccessful artifice since values and the conditions of existence have so drastically changed. "How," Main asks himself, "can I cross-examine the universe when it jumps my bond?"[14] Similarly, Elkin ironically hounds the myths of creation, eternal love, and of "nature" as accomplice in "The Making of Ashenden" (*Searches and Seizures*), and when he borrows the structures of *The Divine Comedy* from Dante for *The Living End,* he does so not in order to give form to chaos but in order to expose the chaos of the world to the light.

We move then, from an "innocent" use of myth to an ironic relativization of its truth and to sophisticated studies of its pernicious effects. By deforming accepted narratives, by narrating these traditional myths from an unconventional point of view, wide fissures are formed therein. From his first collection of short stories to the most recent, Coover has consistently performed such sabotage. After the myths of Noah and Joseph, a lesser myth is damaged, but in a more vivid way. In "Shootout at Gentry's Junction" (*A Night at the Movies*), far from having the last word, the classic Western sheriff is killed by a bullet shot between his eyes by the abominable farting Mexican bandit. It is then the bandit who pins on the badge and rides off into the legendary sunset: "Red gleams the little five-pointed star in the ultimate light of the western sun."[15]

Donald Barthelme's *The King* effectively manhandles the Arthurian cycle. An identical device governs Joseph Heller's *God Knows*, since King David is allowed to tell his own story there; in John Gardner's *Grendel*, another legendary "bad guy" is given the opportunity to express a point of view not presented in the Beowulf saga. In this novel, however, and in accordance with the "moral" vision of fiction Gardner always upheld, the eternal truths are indirectly reinstated by the structure. However iconoclastic this revisionism, however myth-shattering it might appear for the monster to speak rather than the conquering hero, the circularity of the novel's forms, its use of the signs of the zodiac in the structural organization of the different parts, the links established between the number of chapters and numerology are each allied with an allegorical medieval iconography in order to reintroduce myth in a positive light into a book where its reversal is the principal source of comedy.

Inversely, if, in *Seaview,* Toby Olson appears attached to the positive values of American mythology, and if *The Woman Who Escaped from Shame* highlights the natural ties between myth and fiction, in Olson's *The Life of Jesus* (1976), an entirely different strategy is at work. Contrary to what the title may indicate, this is not a revisionist biography of Our Lord. The "Jesus" of the novel was raised in Catholic schools, and the *rhetoric* inherited from the Gospels lends its form to his autobiography. Similar to the life of Jesus in Max Apple's *Zip,* this life can also be read in terms of the life of an Other. And, if a "rational" explanation of the most miraculous events seems to be provided, it is because the story describes different situations that provoke "Jesus" to react in identical words, yet in a changed context. The transfer of the story suggests that we are perhaps postulating the wrong questions by giving the classic explanations as answers. This brilliant manipulation of the pragmatics of language does not necessarily repudiate the Christian myth, but it does allow us to see it in a different light. The plastic force of narratives, in this work subtitled "An Apocryphal Novel," is stressed even in the final lines:

And then Jesus begins to speak to his father. . . . Occasional walnuts, fall with faint thuds, in the grasses around them. And his father listens to him, attentively, as Jesus tells him, the story of his Journey, in another world.[16]

The compulsion to tell stories can be tied, in an intensified manner, to the myth of the great storytellers, as in the case of *Darlin' Bill,* where Charyn calls upon the American tradition of the tall tale. This compulsion can also provide, as in *Pinocchio's Nose,* a true method and a kind of poetics. The hero is alternately the author ("Jerome Copernic Charyn" in this case) and one of his avatars, the wooden puppet whose features are, as we know, affected whenever he utters untruths. The image is tempting for Charyn who encourages us to read an almost sexual excitement under the swelling of truth and the expansion of an appendage that Pinocchio, for all that, uses often to ends similar to the usage of a certain other. This verbal priapism is called "mythopsychosis," and Charyn defines it as "the terrifying need to mythologize one's existence at the expense of all other things. The sufferer of mythopsychosis seeks narratives everywhere, inside and outside of himself. He cannot take a move and not narratize it."[17] Charyn's own form of "magical realism" is linked to these permanent metamorphoses of the real into stories. At times punctual (Stefan Wilde becomes a "tzarevitch" in *Panna Maria*; Pinocchio's father goes by the name "Bruny the Rag") or tactical (Admiral Farkus of *Going to Jerusalem* twists a game of chess in order to turn it into a myth that imaginarily prolongs the Second World War), metamorphoses like these declare themselves to be programmatic in a title such as *Once Upon a Droshky*, which refers to a legendary mode of diction. The majority of Charyn's works systematically mythologize his personal life and particularly his Bronx childhood. Its heuristic potential takes over from the relativization of surrounding myths. Lost in what he likes to call the "dream of the text," Charyn draws forth the worlds in which he is suffocating. Popular myths provide him with *personae* and masks; in addition, they allow him to conjure up the strange by way of the familiar, to give back to a real that has been scaled down within our culture perspectives that make it open out before our eyes.

The turn to popular mythology is quite frequent. Aside from Charyn, writers such as Coover (*Pinocchio in Venice*), Baumbach, Donald Barthelme, T. Coraghessan Boyle, Apple, Elkin, and Sukenick question the images of what Alan Wilde has called "ordinary myths," from King Kong to Howard Johnson, by way of Walt Disney and the Three Little Pigs.

Dreams played an important role in Baumbach's first novels and still do. Peter Becker (in *A Man to Conjure With*) managed without too much difficulty to distinguish dreams from the real. But, with *What Comes Next*, the dream life of Christopher Steiner dramatically overlapped with the world. Since *Reruns*, private dreams have become mixed with more public ones, which, as popular myths, often took over for them. The return to dreams, memory, and imagination provided the basis for more solid identities. Popular myths, which reinforce social and personal identity, must still be examined with a critical eye. This is the aim of *The Return of Service* and *The Life and Times of Major Fiction*. Baumbach sees popular culture as an attic full of myths; his stories renew, revitalize, and relativize them. He seeks within these myths the archetypes and models that respond to our most profound needs and desires, or so their success would have us believe. By twisting or deforming the original model in order to study its potential effects, he examines the ways in which people try to put into practice the drives contained within their most preferred motifs. This is what happens to "Blue Beard" in *Seven Wives*. These modifications free new energies at the same time as they build up the energies of primitive images. They allow us to question the value of our fictive constructions, and to consider the extent to which our relationship to the world is a product of our imagination and our lives are determined by the icons of popular culture.

As for Sukenick, he constructs *98.6* around the myth of Frankenstein in order to explore the limits of our abilities to create new forms. At once a creature and a classic myth for cinematic misadventures, Frankenstein's monster is in three ways useful for a reflection on creation. A scientific and Promethean object to some, he is but a familiar monster to others.

The ambiguity of his status and his diverse modes of apprehension establish the tension Sukenick wants to introduce between creator and created object while they nurture his reflection on a gap emphasized by the
becoming of Frankenstein, a scientist in Mary Shelley's novel, an invention of this scientist in other works.

Critical strategies such as these do not exclude summary executions.
We should remember, the exercise is so entertaining, that, in *Little America,* Swigart demolishes all of the cultural kitsch and atrophied mythologies in the country. His blows are formidable and, while lacking the more
somber tones of West's *A Cool Million, Miss Lonelyhearts,* or *The Day of the
Locust,* his "staggering vision of the American cross section"[18] is no more
subtle than Brautigan's antigenre novels, similar in this to the stereotyped and idiotic killers of *The Hawkline Monster,* who "didn't put any lace
on their killings."[19]

In works from the midpoint of Barth's career, myth becomes the object
of fascinating dissections (*Chimera* and *Lost in the Funhouse*). Like Coover,
Barth understands our absolute need for stories; what is more, he perceives both the beauties and dangers of this, and, consequently, advocates
an affected awareness. His central myth is that of Scheherazade; he finds
there, beyond his usual ironies (The first example ever of the academic's
plight, he says: "Publish or perish with a vengeance."),[20] the model of the
novelist as storyteller, with the vital stakes, mortal dangers, pleasures and
luxuries of such constrained freedoms. Scheherazade is also the first to
have discovered, by telling her thousand and one tales to Shahryar, that
in literature "the key to the treasure *is* the treasure."[21] "Sherry's" sister
provides the title for the "Dunyazadiad" that opens *Chimera,* the first part
of this equivalent to the three-bodied mythic monster that is complemented by the "Bellerophoniad" and the "Perseid." This triple narrative,
weaving its theoretical tangles into the threads of plots, rigorously analyzes the nature and function of myths. The wife of Bellerophon is interested in mythology . . . Summing up her discoveries, she declares:

I quite understand . . . that the very concept of objective truth, especially as
regards the historical past, is problematical; also that narrative art, particularly of
the mythopoeic or at least mythographic variety, has structures and rhythms,
values and demands, not the same as those of reportage or historiography. Finally,
as between variants among the myths themselves, it's in their contradictions that
one may seek their sense.[22]

"A Hall of Mirrors," the maze of *Lost in the Funhouse,* is above all a
Palace of Discourse where the distance between myth and reality is permanent and is served by the most garish metafictional devices. The stories literally talk about themselves, even giving their own "Autobiography," and the biography of Ambrose outlines the paths that lead from life

to myth ("Ambrose His Mark"). "Menelaiad" and "Anonymiad" dissect the rhetoric of myth with the sharpest of scalpels. The tales of the Trojan War are so invasive that Menelaus, who unwillingly finds himself at the center of the action, gets lost in the maze of quotations to talk about himself. Section "I½" of the "Anonymiad" confesses:

Once upon a time I told tales straight out, alternating summary and dramatization, developing characters and relationships, laying on bright detail and rhetorical flourish, et cetera. . . . But I fear that we're too far gone now for such luxury, Helen and I; I must get to where I am; the real drama, for yours truly, is whether he can trick this tale out at all — not the breath-batingest plot in the world, but there we are. It's an old story anyhow, this part of it; the corpus bloats with its like; I'll throw you the bones, to flesh out or pick at as you will.[23]

In this part of his work, Barth continues the mythical parallels of *Ulysses*, but by rejecting the "synthetic" approach to myth and the real favored by Joyce. Commenting on the work of Updike and Malamud, he explains why they "have got hold of the wrong end of the mythopoeic stick":

The myths themselves are produced by the collective narrative imagination (or whatever) partly to point down at our daily reality; and so to write about our daily experiences in order to point up to the myths seems to me mythopoeically retrograde. I think it's a more interesting thing to do, if you find yourself preoccupied with mythic archetypes . . . to address them directly.[24]

For this reason, perhaps, it has been argued that "as long as it focuses (as in *Giles Goat-Boy*) on mythological or philosophical histories, Barth's style succeeds," but when "it treats national and political history, Barth's style collapses."[25] In any case, it is worth noting that Barth's verve is better suited to ironic lyricism and grandiloquence, characteristics of his false Huron journeys in mythical country, than to analyses of the relations between the activity of writing, the design of history, and questions about his identity. At his most effective, Barth makes his heroes into truly "mythical" characters by mythifying myth itself, by guaranteeing that his stories will not work for those who would "suspend their disbelief"; he brilliantly manages to make us question the nature of a reality that myth is supposed to explain. In *Sabbatical* and *LETTERS*, myth retains a role in the presentations of the real, but it no longer dominates them, except in witnessing the rebirth of a "myth of the book," which is nothing less than "orphic" from then on.

In *End Zone* and *Great Jones Street*, Don DeLillo stages various stars who are struggling, each one in his own domain (football in the first case, the world of rock music in the second), to free themselves from mythologies within which their talent has trapped them. Without absolutely repudiating it, the athlete and the musician attempt to forge a space for themselves at the heart of the mythical and oppressive world responsible for their glory.[26] This ambivalence explains the reason behind Russell Banks's simultaneous praise and rejection of the romantic tradition. As shown by the stories in *The New World,* myth continues to function for better or for worse, but Banks is obliged to remark that "the democratized consciousness" of our time is "so heightened or 'expanded' by information as to be unable any longer to suspend disbelief."[27] Torn between exploring the residual effects of mythical thought and ironic metafictions, Banks's *oeuvre* places him with writers who are fascinated by myth and who, paradoxically, cautiously accept its dangers in the name of a certain realism. Its vigorous denunciation is accompanied by an heightened awareness of our appetite for myth, of the relative necessity of its use in shaping experience. As a homeopathic cure for evil through evil, the contemporary use of myth suggests that it remains possible to have recourse to it even after suspicion and history have alerted us to its perils.

Hostility Toward Myth

Diametrically opposed to the positive use of myth proposed by certain "ethnic" writers, the denunciations of myth are therefore no less strong. In an excellent short work on Barthelme, Charles Molesworth writes:

Any artist today, who accepts the demystified sense of a humanist vision that turns away from the comfort of a transcendent system of beliefs and values, must acknowledge the irrational and fragmented social structures that dominate our lives. But such acknowledgment need not turn into a maelstrom of existential *angst.* In fact, we can take some comfort — albeit limited — in knowing that humans have at least conceived transcendent schemes as part of their cultural legacy. The problem now is to create an art that disentangles those past visionary schemes from their elements of self-delusion and self-aggrandizement . . . man is most human when he neither ceases to dream, nor takes his dreams at their own valuation.[28]

In this regard, Robert Coover's greatness is doubtless due to its unique combination of lucidity and generosity. In *The Universal Baseball Association,* historical skepticism could be a source of worry:

Or maybe it just happened. Weirdly, independently, meaninglessly. . . . Invention [. . .] implies a need and need implies purpose; accident implies nothing, nothing at all, and nothing is the one thing that scares Hardy Ingram.[29]

In the absence of a historical discourse able to unify signs, such anguish is enthusiastically relieved and satisfied by a discourse that offers a semblance of unity. Set free by the death of their creator, J. Henry Waugh's players, Coover's characters, God's creatures — baseball players, office workers, we — continue to perform the same gestures to which the aleatory determinism of their creation seemed to have limited them. Religious symbolism, the birth of legendary tales, odes composed by the bards in honor of a past that did not occur, of a Golden Age that, as always, never was, the rituals and ceremonies that perpetuate the ideal union of teammates terrified by the possibility of being alone on the cold edge of a horizon without cause or finality: all of this becomes the subject of the last chapter, replaying the events imagined by Waugh. Whereas, in Henry's imagination, the public conformed to the rites of cheers and impassioned elans toward the great sporting myth, to the communions of hot dogs and victory, in future times, the players repeatedly assume their ancestors' same gestures; whereas drunken chants assured team spirit and togetherness, threnodies later perpetuate this memory; whereas Coover invented Waugh's world in order to drive him mad, certain players, the minority, conclude that "God exists and he is a nut" (233). As creatures of a discourse, they cannot transcend their fondness for it, most of them are alienated, doomed to drone this heritage of hermetic truths. Thus Coover, by their spectacle, as by that of the Brunists, and of the crazed who publicly burn "spies" who have betrayed the discourse, leads us toward the courageous freedom of the skeptic, to the contemplation of fictive arabesques traced in the air of a mute world by the trapeze artist who, refusing all false security, knows that our gestures constitute our only net, and who owes the nobility of his art to this same knowledge.

According to a song in his honor, a player in Henry Waugh's little world had given the following instructions for his funeral:

Oh, when I die, jist bury me
With my bat and a coupla balls,
And jist tell 'em Verne struck out, boys,
If anybody calls . . . (215)

Beyond the motives they have either inherited or constructed for themselves, everyone has taken the same path, without knowing whether, to quote one of them, they should trust in "well, legend, I mean the pattern of it, the long history, it seems somehow, you know, a folk truth, a radical truth, all these passed-down mythological — " (233). This man's hesitations, as violently as he is snubbed by a tipsy companion, prove for Coover that, in spite of the meaninglessness of "patchwork" discourse, "the heretic dream of a meaningful life lives on."[30]

In *The Origin of the Brunists* and *The Universal Baseball Association*, Coover saw myth as engendered to a great extent by the individual imagination. In *Pricksongs and Descants* and especially in *The Public Burning*, he attacks all areas of thought in which myth aims at oppression; by enclosing ourselves within borrowed orders (of the real and of thought), we become easy targets for all belief systems, for therapists for the maladjusted, repairmen of the self, salesmen of the absolute, peddlers of the "ready-to-believe": gurus, demagogues, sectarianists, proselytes, charlatans, one and all. But Coover is never lacking in understanding or sympathy for those who succumb to their powers. Coover is interested in myth because it "mediates paradox" and "celebrates it." A synthesis as successful as *The Public Burning* accepts the ambiguities and the dialectical complexities that prevent the American writer from escaping contradictions. It is true, Coover informs us, somewhat like Hawthorne and yet so different from him, that "the tradition of past generations weighs like a nightmare on the brains of the living."[31] Yet, by analyzing and manipulating the myth of Uncle Sam, he makes clear the origins and the logic of the contradictions of American culture and detaches myth from the real in order that they might transform each other. Certainly, he prefers the revelations of a kind of dialogue between creator, reader, and social context to any speculation on transcendence; but, in the voice of Nixon, who is pondering the columns of *The New York Times,* he attests to a lucid understanding of the ways in which myth affects the real:

And perhaps that was why—the tenacious faith in the residual magic of language—this monument was erected in the first place: that effort to reconstruct with words and iconography each fleeting day in the hope of discovering some pattern, some coherence, some meaningful dialogue with time. But so enormous a shrine is it, so prodigious a task just to keep the translation of gesture into language flowing, that all consciousness of any intended search for transcendence must long ago have disappeared and been forgotten, leaving all visionary speculations to the passing pilgrim.[32]

By adapting the Uncle Sam myth and superimposing it onto the "historical truth" of the Rosenberg affair, Coover demonstrates that the American tradition might be responsible for apparent political delirium. If he agrees to make use of myth, it is so as to subject it to aesthetic contortions and symbolic manipulations that will produce a different image of the reality it has made possible. Such distortions merely mime the devices by which politicians profited from the case under cover of objectivity. "Objectivity," moreover, is subject to the same forces as those that give birth to myth: " 'objectivity' is in spite of itself a willful program for the stacking of perceptions; facts emerge not from life but from revelations, gnarled as always by ancient disharmonies and charged with libidinous energy."[33]

In *Structural Anthropology,* Lévi-Strauss states that "nothing resembles mythological thought more than political ideology."[34] With myth serving as an ontological signifier without being able to be substituted for the signified of the being from which it is irremediably divorced, Coover, in "The Dead Queen," treats the mythical model as a body that is foreign to experience and dangerous to use: "She has poisoned us all with pattern."[35] Behind this particular myth lies the notion of a pattern, an adopted grid, or foreign model. An entirely different strategy exposes its effects in Richard Condon's works (*The Manchurian Candidate, Some Angry Angel, Winter Kills*), where a number of true facts are subjected to the arbitrariness of absurd arrangements and then prove to hasten convincing narratives by the sole virtue of rumors, myths, and half-truths likely to constitute the only "reality" that counts. The grids for reading are provided outside of the real; but the real finds its substance there. If it is true that "myths are thought within men, and without their knowing" (Lévi-Strauss), it is best to attack the circuits of their imagination directly.

This is Robert Steiner's belief, for whom myth is essentially fascistic because it robs people of their dreams — a point of view as all-encompassing and as debatable as Barthes's on language in his inaugural lecture at the Collège de France. With the only absolute method of control consisting in explaining the world, Steiner defines his area of work as a place in which to explore, not the "imagination of disaster" dear to Henry James, but the "disaster of the imagination"; he readily refers to the beginning of *The Fall*, where Camus explains that such a fall is the fate of those who have either too much or too little imagination. The only possible defense is found in the creation of narrative gaps and disjunctions, in everything that can bore holes in the myths that never fail to appear and blossom every time a story is born, in order to render them inoperative. We have seen that the writing of *Bathers* and of *Passion* is conceived in such a way that the coherence of an imperial vision cannot resist it. Steiner's approach is essentially linguistic. Whereas, according to him, Coover psychologizes myth in order to subvert it — which is to make too little of numerous short stories — Steiner wants to dislocate our perception of language as primarily a "channel for messages," so to speak, and by using it in his particular way, to prevent us from seeing it as such a neutral channel.

All fictional relation to myth is eminently ideological, no matter how it is established. If by " 'ideology' is meant a particular or relative discourse, seeking to pass itself off as universal or absolute,"[36] Steiner aims to destroy all pretention discursively to unify the real. The grammarian in *Carus* is just as hostile, when he says: "There are those who *repair.* Bandits, thinkers, propaganda ministers, dreamers, prophets, lovers, priests. Detestable tinkerers, all."[37]

In Andrée Connors's *Amateur People,* a character speaks of the "hoax of the Final Solemn Answer":

It has a thousand disguises and as many names, it's the watergod illusion of the thirsty, it will shimmer at you relentlessly. And the tarnished miniature dogmas that you'll stumble across here and there on the road, darling — don't bother even picking them up.[38]

Nietzsche resented Kant for reintegrating into the *Critique of Practical Reason* the prison whose bars he had succeeded in sawing through in the *Critique of Pure Reason*. For, it is indeed dangerous to venture beyond the grids of "regulative ideas." They are never horizontal, never content to mark out a field; rather, they possess the verticality of those that protect or enclose. It remains to us then — save for managing to rid ourselves of them at all times — to bend them, to forge their steel, to make them into trapdoors and air vents, to learn to see them as tools or as toys, rather than as so many prisons or weapons. For William Gass, "beliefs are our pestilence. Skepticism, these days, is the only intelligence."[39]

Chapter 10
Images/Noises

America overstimulates her youth and overdrugs her middle-aged.
This is her crime.

— Vachel Lindsay, *Notebooks*

Movies are made from books. Books are "good" — even if "bad" in other regards — to the extent that their subject, characters, plot, tone, and structure facilitate their adaptation to the screen. Similarly, "historical novels" are made from "good stories." Forsaking their initial surroundings, these narratives undergo a change, and it would be a mistake to treat the media in fiction in the same manner in which "historical novels" treat history. Therefore, there shall be no question here of examining what happens to cinema and television in fiction, a simple inversion of the logic of "adapting" books for the screen, from the simple point of view of the thematic infection of a referent by mediatized forms that have become more and more "naturalized"; but rather of placing this infection under observation, watching its effects on fictional themes and beings, certainly, but also on the forms and the economy of literary works. In concluding an article on McElroy, Barth, DeLillo, and Pynchon, a critic has stated:

[These writers] catalog the realities other novelists leave out. When everybody knows everything by reading *Time* or watching TV news, these writers deform conventions to break through the film of familiarity the media exude. . . . In embracing the age's information, these writers resist its values.[1]

Such is the desired end. However, the tactics abound.

Cinema

. . . [T]he modern painter — and in this connection it might be said that, since Impressionism, all pictures have been painted in the first person — wrests the object from the universe of the spectator and deforms it in order to isolate its pictorial content. Thus, in a movement analogous to that of painting, the novel, which only a stubborn adherence to obsolete techniques places in the position of a minor art, pursues with means that are uniquely its own a path which can only be its own; it leaves to the other arts — and, in particular, to cinema — everything that does not actually belong to it. In the same way that photography occupies and fructifies the fields abandoned by painting, the cinema garners and perfects what is left by the novel.[2]

   Techniques have evolved so rapidly that one might easily believe that Nathalie Sarraute had written these lines quite some time ago: in a time when cinema was still considered a form of adolescent language by Claude-Edmonde Magny, who, in 1948, fascinated by the subject, completed her study of the modernist "American novel" as transformed by the seventh art "at the peak of its progress," so to speak.[3] Come the age of American fiction, it was time to rewrite this same book, revisited by Godard and Peckinpah, to reinterpret the same art, presenting its characteristics, dimensions, and new influences. Indeed, these parameters have changed considerably.[4] Film does not only "garner and perfect what is left by the novel." In certain ways, film does much more than the novel was able to do and can even show it a few things about the sophistication of narrative techniques. What writer has never dreamed of double exposures? Has not the flashback figured among literary temptations for quite some time? And then there is Faulkner who lost the fight with his editor when he asked that the ink of *The Sound and the Fury* be printed in several different colors on the page . . . It is understandable that Sarraute was unable to predict both the increased importance of the influence of film and television on novelistic forms, and the interdependence, brought to light by DeLillo, of cinema (and more generally of the means of mass communication) and of a fiction from beyond suspicion.

   Besides, more than a decade later, Susan Sontag did not yet have at hand the theoretical apparatus necessary for the parallel she was calling for in *Against Interpretation*:

What we don't have yet is a poetics of the novel, any clear notion of the forms of narration. Perhaps film criticism will be the occasion of a breakthrough here, since films are primarily a visual form, yet they are also a subdivision of literature.[5]

Today, not only Gérard Genette, Tzvetan Todorov, Roland Barthes, Christian Metz, and others have passed this way, but what is more, following the example of Nathanael West, John Fante, F. Scott Fitzgerald, and William Faulkner, a growing number of contemporary writers have done their time, eased by the proximity to gold mines, in the "salt mines" of Hollywood.[6] The comings and goings between one world and the other are too numerous to be counted. Thomas McGuane directed the film version of

Ninety-two in the Shade himself; he also wrote the screenplays for *Rancho Deluxe* (1975), *Missouri Breaks* (1976), and *Tom Horn* (1980). He has confessed to Larry McCaffery the lessons this experience brought to his writing.[7] Jerzy Kosinski, whose *Being There* was adapted for the screen, played a part in *Reds*. Fascinated by the movies, he wanted to produce them himself. These are among the better known examples, but those of Richard Yates, Dan Wakefield, and Rudolph Wurlitzer, as well as, more recently, that of John Irving for *The World According to Garp*, of E. L. Doctorow for *Ragtime*, and of Russell Banks for *Continental Drift* would lengthen an already long list. Even Jerome Charyn, who does not find the writing of screenplays at all satisfying, is now working on what — protector of the writer's soul — is still called a "script." Paul Auster's *The Music of Chance* was made into a movie by others but he wrote the script of *Smoke* expressly for the "seventh art."

What is more, as Kosinski's *oeuvre* serves to demonstrate, there is a danger to be avoided in the temptation to write with the movies in mind. In an interview, Don DeLillo has succinctly summed up a real interdependence: "It's movies in part that seduced people into thinking the novel was dead. . . . If the novel dies, movies will die with it."[8] To which McGuane has added, "Contrary to what people think, the cinema has enormously to do with language."[9] On the whole, writers' increased fascination with celluloid rather than with paper has had less formidable effects on a literature that, envious of certain techniques, has often opted to adapt them.

"Rolling"

Film is "rolling" everywhere in contemporary American fiction, not only to pick up where the Hollywood dream factory leaves off for readers of popular literature, but by infiltrating down to the heart of novels as difficult as *Gravity's Rainbow* or *LETTERS*, whose title is so distant from the notion of the image. In accordance with the metafictional logic of the latter superproduction, the title of the movie directed by Reg Prinz is *Frames*, and Pynchon constantly creates a *mise en abîme* between story and film in order to bring out their complicity as narratives. Cinema can alternately be used in its capacity to evoke news reporting (Joan Didion), coverage of big news stories (Paul Theroux), or to provide a recognizable setting for adventures not characteristic of realism by pastiching pornographic films (*Candy* by Terry Southern and Mason Hoffenberg and *Blue Movie* by Southern). It allows Andrée Connors to gather a spectacular cast (Harpo Marx, W. C. Fields, Humphrey Bogart) for *Amateur People*; Brautigan to hire Deanna Durbin and Mack Sennett in *Trout Fishing in America*; Coover to recruit Charlie Chaplin for a "comic" number more daring than those he had already performed, one that tosses us from slapstick to horror ("Charlie in the House of Rue," *A Night at the Movies*); Kenneth Gangemi to provide us with the raw tape of the evolutions of an airplane (*The Interceptor Pilot*); Rudolph Wurlitzer to give us his novelistic — or "metacinematographic" — version of Truffaut's *Day for Night* in *Slow Fade* by filming the life of a director going about his professional activities. Finally, Douglas Woolf's *Fade Out* is composed according to a similar logic.

Mirrors, Screens, and Lenses

With MacDonald Harris's *Screenplay*, Barry Maltzberg's *Screen* — whose hero multiplies the distant liaisons with the actresses from his favorite films — and Walker Percy's *The Moviegoer*, we shift from the departments of personnel and accessories to reflexive thematic use. Cameras and subjects, projectors and screens substitute themselves along the row of fictional mirrors emblematic of *Lost in the Funhouse*. Beyond these self-reflexive games and the exploration/violation of the borders between film and the real that the theme permits MacDonald Harris — approached in the same lighthearted manner found in Woody Allen's *The Purple Rose of Cairo* — the cinema becomes a prop in the search for an identity. In De-Lillo's *Americana*, David Bell, a producer of made-for-television movies, leads an existence dominated by an ever-present sixteen-millimeter camera. In speaking of the film he is directing and with which his life is confused once he stops taking himself for the actors in other people's movies (Burt Lancaster in particular), Bell explains:

> What I'm doing is kind of hard to talk about. It's a sort of first-person thing but without me in it in any philosophical sense, except fleetingly, not exactly in the Hitchcock manner but a brief personal appearance nonetheless, my mirror image at any rate. Also my voice when I start using sound. It's a reaching back for certain things. But not just that. It's also an attempt to explain, to consolidate. . . . It'll be part dream, part fiction, part movies. An attempt to explore parts of my consciousness.[10]

"Binx" Bolling, the cinephile in *The Moviegoer*, lives a veritable exile from himself.[11] Surrounded by a society stripped of integrity and shorn of authenticity by history, Binx Bolling takes refuge in the autonomous world of movies, seeking those values there. Cinema takes on a reality superior to that of the world; blessing of a romantic temperament, film can fulfill the expectations that life can hardly satisfy. But every movie must end, fueled by its time limitations, tracing new limits between itself and the real. Bolling inhabits the borderline between the consolations of film and his surrounding existential emptiness; staring up at the screen, he takes comfort in those privileged slices of time when the real suspends its threats. The "extra-ordinary" images that parade past his eyes offer an alternative to a dailiness that does not suit him.[12] As one of Baumbach's characters puts it: "real life, I realized, never moved me as much as a book or a movie."[13] In this way, the film becomes a screen for real: it protects him. One is reminded of the feeling that a projection creates in Moll in DeLillo's *Running Dog*:

> That special kind of anticipation she'd enjoyed since childhood—a life in the movies. It was an expectation of pleasure like no other. Simple mysteries are the deepest. What did it mean, this wholly secure escape, this credence in her heart? And how was it possible that bad, awful, god-awful movies never seemed to betray the elation and trust she felt in the seconds before the screen went bright? The anticipation was apart from what followed. It was permanently renewable, a sense of freedom from all the duties and conditions of the nonmovie world.[14]

Cinema takes on the thematics of the double explored by Coover, Gaddis, and DeLillo. In *Americana,* Bell films actors who speak or narrate episodes from his true life. His choices and his framing explicitly and deliberately shape a life whose outlines he can otherwise barely trace, without requiring him to take direct responsibility for that life.

Another "schizogram," the "sentient lens" that films three of Coover's narratives (in *Pricksongs and Descants*) would seem a contradiction in terms. Several subjectivities disturb or filter the "objectivity" of the "objective": that—which is personal—of he who, in holding the camera, choosing the angles and the shots, models and sculpts the shapes of the image; that—which is collective—of earlier narratives that tend to colonize the possible meanings of objective perception and form a kind of screen against unmediated apprehension of the image. As McElroy stresses in *Lookout Cartridge,* the circuits that have been previously installed in the consciousness make all images possible. The young and comely milkmaid whom we think we "see" arrive before she truly appears in "The Milkmaid of Samaniego" imposes the characteristics—introduces in our mind the imaginary cassette—already attributed to her in the fables of Samaniego and La Fontaine (Perrette) before Coover endeavored to wrestle with her image. Several figures of desire and repulsion invade a pre-programmed landscape and by their interference they place in jeopardy the simple "recording" of an always already-known story. The sounds that invade the soundtrack of "Scene for 'Winter'" contradict what the lens tells us of whiteness and silence. The lens is not only "sentient" there: it proves to be stubborn and invasive. Finally, in "The Leper's Helix," the survey of the observer, around the repulsive dying man who fascinates him, is perfectly constrained; the camera can only record geometrical movements determined elsewhere, and the last words of the text deliberately create a confusion between spectator, reader, and actors. The problems of narration are thus literally staged and the relative oxymoron that serves as title for the series of three stories ("The Sentient Lens") reverberates its contradictions back onto questions that are more literary than cinematographic. The lens of the camera picks up the filters of intertext and of ideology, their grids and their screens; "transparency" is always that of a model.

In this way, cinema is a dream, since it "invents" only that which desire tells it to see. Without going into great detail, it is remarkable that the contemporary writers who most often refer to the cinema are also those in whose work dreams play a significant thematic part. This proposition cannot be inverted: John Hawkes and his "lunar landscapes" and James Purdy's nightmares lack explicit reference to film in spite of techniques that owe much to cinema. But Mimi Albert, Fanny Howe, Susan Sontag (*The Benefactor*), and especially Jonathan Baumbach are happy to maintain the confusion between pure dream and cinematographic dream. The French version of *Reruns* is dedicated to Jean-Luc Godard, and De-Lillo, for his part, confesses: "Probably the movies of Jean-Luc Godard had a more immediate effect on my early work than anything I'd ever read."[15] This influence is evident in *Americana* and *The Names*—down to the very aesthetic of Bell's film.

As a film critic and a writer of fiction, Baumbach, for his part, channels the fantasies of his protagonists through the angle of their more or less wakening dreams, through their integration, intensification, and coexistence in the great text of world cinema. Filmic quotation plays an identical role in his fiction and in the works of Godard. *Reruns* emphasizes the dual affiliation of fictions that constantly proclaim that the works and the days always take place on some other stage, a stage on which—whether imaginary set or phantasmal universe—Baumbach's indecisive heroes, rattled and knocked about by an oppressive social, familial, and professional environment, succeed in finding, for the space of a few pages, a fragile balance by constantly "replaying" their own life or the fictive life of suitable models. Like so many judokas, when assaulted by strange images, they manage to deflect the huge iconographic mass intended to dictate their behavior and reduce them to roles, by warding off the violence of these images and integrating them into their most intimate dreams, thereby confirming their fragile personalities as victims. In a world that is often incomprehensible and derealized, the arbitrariness and artifice of filmic memories can provide grids for reading and viable forms of defense. "Triumphant scenarios embrace the imagination unbidden."[16] Baumbach's characters combat the social nightmare with their dreams and images; they displace and recombine the icons of the "nightmarish landscape" into spaces of freedom. The osmosis of dream and cinema allows for the transitions and necessary continuities between public and private spheres, reestablishing the possibility of a minimal communication.

Inversely, the impact on consciousness and the identities of predetermined images can be interpreted as a threat. In the work of Richard Yates and Dan Wakefield, more than behavior is modified by imitating screen models. We might remember that, during key scenes in *The Catcher in the Rye*, Caulfield played out scenes in which he was a more or less willing actor, twisting around in his chair and holding his stomach as though, like a famous gangster, he had just been plugged full of lead by the police or a rival gang. While he claims to despise cinematographic fiction, he nonetheless seeks the refuge of a role therein. In Yates, we might say that, to a certain extent, it is the very being of the "glutton" ("A Glutton for Punishment," *Eleven Kinds of Loneliness*), of Walter Henderson or Robert Prentice (*A Special Providence*) that is stolen from them by the media, to the extent that the behavior of these characters can be predicted even before they adopt it. Conditioned by the cinema, their relations to the world are — as the novels of Fitzgerald and West announced in their own fashion — so warped that they are incapable of escaping the clichés of behavior borrowed from war movies if they are soldiers or from romantic movies if they are in love. This kind of occurrence is not unduly grave when such behavior shapes the dreams of a little boy during the Second World War, as in Wakefield's *Under the Apple Tree*. It becomes more serious when adult characters show themselves incapable of ridding themselves of acquired roles.[17] In *A Mother's Kisses* by Bruce Jay Friedman, Joseph wonders "why he can only react to tragedy by doing stand-up comedy."[18] In its most extreme form, the entire world of cinema parades under the helmet of Bell in *Americana*. David is twenty-eight years old. To someone who asks about his experience in the field, he replies: "I've spent twenty-eight years in the movies."[19] Or is this how long the movies have spent in him?

Cinematic Technique and Its Stakes

Cinematic technique has invaded, in a routine and seemingly natural fashion, entire sections of literature. Don DeLillo has stated: "Movies in general may be the not-so-hidden influence on a lot of modern writing, although the attraction has waned, I think. The strong image, the short ambiguous scene, the dream sense of some movies, the artificiality, the arbitrary choices of some directors, the cutting and editing. The power of images."[20] In *Seeking Air*, Barbara Guest comments upon "life's cinema aspect" and records from her window the comings and goings that appear within the steady shot of her vision:

A car turns left onto a street. Cars wait for lights. A bus stops. A yellow cab cruises. . . . A person crosses at a diagonal. A bench is empty. Someone sits on a bench. A person moves quickly. A person stops. Except for a parked car there suddenly is an empty street. I ask if this is a French, Spanish, Algerian, English film. The subtitles will give me the answer.[21]

Without compiling an inventory of works marked by the seal of the seventh art, we shall simply note, by way of radical examples, that at least two novels, not to mention a great number of short stories, borrow their technique from screenplays either with some modifications or none at all. With regard to the writing, it would seem impossible to distinguish Kenneth Gangemi's *The Interceptor Pilot* from the screenplay of the film one might make from it. This narrative mode tends to make novel writing sag under the formal demands of cinema rather than accommodating the literary form, which is sent packing as soon as it threatens to reclaim its rights. Even when it might do so, this fiction ends with the words: "The film-within-a-film begins."[22] The renegade American pilot who is fighting for North Vietnam betrays more than his government: his story constitutes a double defection from mimesis. A new alliance is contracted between mediatic form and the real, beyond the "natural" ties of literary language and of narrative. In particular, the temporal system of the narrative is unified with a pronominal system that dislocates discourse. In *Slow Fade,* Wurlitzer not only takes as his theme the filmed life of a director, but this *mise en abîme* also affects the story's language and its structure. The director A. D. feels himself "disappear, or fade away, slowly."[23] Conversations wither away, relations become difficult, situations decay, words go missing.

The jargon and conventions of cinema invade fiction. In Andrée Connors, as in Baumbach, dream and film combine; but *Amateur People* is more obviously influenced by the technique of cinema. In this work, as in many others, terms like "dissolve," "blend in," "cut," "fade in," and "fade out" are substituted for the usual punctuation and transitions and scan the progress of the narratives. In an internal and nongeneralized way, although no less revealing, we recall that Vonnegut used the "rewind" effect in *Slaughterhouse-Five.* Ursule Molinaro in *Encores for a Dilettante,* Pynchon in *Gravity's Rainbow,* and Brautigan in *So the Wind Won't Blow It All Away* employed an identical technique, by means of which Brautigan sustains a novel of nostalgia and of remorse and Pynchon illustrates his thematic of moving "backwards into the future." Finally, in *Movies* by Stephen Dixon, cinematographic technique serves as the omnipresent reinforcement for the themes of stories that arise from the same world.

What are the functions, the benefits, and the stakes of these forms? What are the consequences for fiction of such influences? In *Movies,* as in

Coover's *A Night at the Movies,* the entire structure of the collection is affected. The succession of "projections" found in Dixon's collection is transformed in Coover's work into a full "program" that includes documentaries, trailers, intermission, cartoons for the kids, and various film genres. In other words, beyond thematic unity, the borrowing from cinema dictates the work's formal arrangement and provides frames for reading. It also allows for internal comic improvisations within the stories themselves. From the changes in perspective caused by the wearing of special 3-D glasses by the anonymous character who, in *The Public Burning,* forgets to remove them in the street, to the mixing of reels that intervenes in a work on which Coover has been working for years (*Lucky Pierre*): space and time are subject to manipulations that the customary linearity of narrative would not allow. More profoundly, the "comical" drifts, in the most violent, Bakhtinian meaning of the term, that Coover effects upon the familiar images of "Charlie in the House of Rue" at once emphasize the formal logic of film and the superior means available to literary language for destabilizing the image and unsettling the reader who might too easily assume that he is merely watching a remake of a silent-movie masterpiece. *Spanking the Maid* steals from the cinema the full circles of its retakes and of its declensions of paradigms. This novel makes no less palpable — if the term fits . . . — and viable the use of conventional and hackneyed images in order to renegotiate the contract that ties the reader to the text.

For DeLillo as for McElroy, the camera and its magazine reorganize a confused memory and allow for the reordering of the slides and patterns of troubled existences. "I'm only a fluid projection . . . ," says Cartwright in *Lookout Cartridge.*[24] Bell's film not only confers existence upon its director, but also upon several of its subjects:

[The women] seemed supremely happy. Maybe they sensed that they were waving at themselves, waving in the hope that someday if evidence is demanded of their passage through time, demanded by their own doubts, a moment might be recalled when they stood in a dazzling plaza in the sun and were registered on the transparent plastic ribbon; and thirty years away, on that day when proof is needed, it could be hoped that their film is being projected on a screen somewhere, and there they stand, verified, in chemical reincarnation, waving at their own old age, smiling their reassurance to the decades, a race of eternal pilgrims in a marketplace in the dusty sunlight, seven arms extended in a fabulous salute to the forgetfulness of being.[25]

In this way, film can stand as proof of the truth of a story in the eyes of those in search of "subtle confirmation": "Perhaps they regarded the lens as history. What the machine accepts is verifiably existent; all else is unborn or worse."[26] Yet, on the other hand, the real is thereby subject to criticism; or, as we read in *Running Dog,* "All of it was verifiable, none of it true."[27]

The form given to two novels whose theme is the search for stolen films allows us to speculate on the reconstitution of the images of memory and the circuits of thought, and, consequently, of what leads us to the "real." Unless he finds the film of *Lookout Cartridge* or the log of the shoot that could take its place, Cartwright has access to his identity and to his activity only through memory fragments of which an extremely complex, shaky, and jumpy writing provides the texture. Like the example of the magazine in film inserted into a camera or projector, the importance of the information at his disposal can only be revealed by illuminations, by the light that suddenly passes through it; the search itself, as in *Hind's Kidnap,* is organized and takes shape only around and through his fragmented discoveries. In a certain way, the logic of information systems is inverted: the active memory of his characters is "dead" and only recorded cassettes and cartridges, dead information, make it "live" again.

In *Running Dog,* the plot hinges on the discovery in Manhattan of the corpse of a man who sold the only existing copy of a decadent film made in Hitler's bunker during the final days of the Third Reich. The regime's paranoia is matched by a narrative that constantly reminds us that "the whole world is on film" and that "the camera is everywhere." As in Pynchon, who devotes much space to the threatening channels of "immachination," these quest novels are also novels of paranoia, of the fear of hidden systems and powers. However, film's inherent movement seems to serve as a way of escaping from a paralyzing fixedness, from a real of perpetual "takes"; it is as though the aesthetic of film, which leaves only fleeting impressions, and, quite differently from literature, does not allow one to link the episodes elsewhere than in memory, were a means of escaping controls. "[Moll] recalled what Lightborne had said about old and new forms. The modern sensibility had been instructed by a different kind of code. Movement. The image had to move."[28] At times the narrative is generated, activated by an object that might not exist at all. It may only exist in the mind of the protagonists, a metaphor for the processes of establishing/reading the real. When McElroy says, "I'm encircled by a wall of film; I'm audience and projector,"[29] or when Oedipa Maas, in *The Crying of Lot 49,* comparing herself to a planetarium, wonders: "Should I project a world?" they display an identical lucidity concerning the mental processes by which the world can be unified for consciousness. "Sentient lens," projector or screen, consciousness, having no other real recourse, "always reruns its own movie."

Radio

When it comes to "voices,"[30] we will look closely at certain revealing uses of radio, a means of communication suddenly outdated by the invasion of television some forty-five years ago. Let us say that radio serves to transmit a certain nostalgia, as evidenced by Woody Allen's *Radio Days*. This is also the case for Brautigan's *So the Wind Won't Blow It All Away* and *Dreaming of Babylon*. In these works, radio becomes the source of references to the popular culture of a lost era, the mysterious heroes of the most famous serials (from *The Shadow* to *The Lone Ranger*) blending with childhood memories or warping the imaginary identities of the protagonists. What is more, we cannot overemphasize the importance of this medium for the writers of a recent generation whose first flights of imagination and first desires to write "stories" occurred while listening to the "wireless." Along with the illustrated books from the thirties and forties and popular litera-ture, from Jules Verne to Dickens, radio has played for Charyn, for exam-ple, the role held by almanacs and chromos for an earlier generation. The voice of the "set" was mysterious and fascinating before it became overwhelming, laden with indoctrination, with advertising "massages," musical assaults, long-distance therapies, and propaganda as is now the case most of the time in the United States. Witness *Americana,* where David Bell describes, pouring out of a sophisticated set, "A never-ending squall of disc-jockey baby talk, commercials for death, and upstate blue-grass Jesus." Language breaks itself up, loses all referential power, be-comes undifferentiated matter. Driving through "cloverland bedlams" and "past the morbid grey towns" he is scarcely surprised to perceive between sound and image a certain "harmony," "the stunned land feed-ing the convulsive radio, every acre of the night bursting with a kinetic unity, the logic beyond delirium."[31] But, for some, radio still maintains sepia tones for the ears. And, if it is a channel of exchange, a place of dialogue and of power struggles that Jaffe (*Mole's Pity*) and Elkin (*The Dick Gibson Show*) borrow from the medium, if Mailer finds a rhetoric or the violence of a delivery there (that of the disc-jockey in *Why Are We in Vietnam?*) and Roth locates in radio a schema allowing the staging of hallucinatory human relations ("On the Air"),[32] for many (Wakefield, McMurtry . . .), radio serves only to date or to furnish a setting, to moti-vate nostalgia and to justify the return of lost radiophonic heroes.

This is not to say that radio's function is always distinct from that of other media in the shaping of the real. In *White Noise,* Heinrich refuses to believe his father, Jack Gladney, when he tells him that it has stopped raining because the radio just announced the opposite; its credibility is so superior that the Gladney daughters each recognize in themselves symp-toms of poisoning described by a journalist as the description evolves of the unhealthy effects of the toxic cloud that is threatening the city. *Amer-icana* also demonstrates that, for DeLillo, radio's power of suggestion is equal to that of television. The fragmented and crazy flow of voices that assail Bell from all sides and fade just as rapidly as the car in which he is riding moves down the road prevent him from discovering any unity, any message, and end up delivering no meaning at all; it covers the physical and mental landscape in thick layers of a soup of words and sounds, stifles the lyrical murmurs of the American myth and dream, homogenizes space, banalizes and derealizes the world, removes, by contiguity, by violent and forced cohabitation, all meaning from the exploded messages that feed it. All things considered, DeLillo explains that which Hunter Thompson was content to describe as equivalence and horror in *Fear and Loathing in Las Vegas*: "Soon drugs are scheduled to supplant the media."[33]

Television

It is no longer possible to exhaust the examples of a medium so integrated into the contemporary real that its effects now pass as natural.[34] Yet we should highlight the conclusions reached by fiction when it comes to television.

On the positive side, there is the awareness that pure narrativity has been taken over by the small screen, thereby freeing fiction of this particular task. As Grace Paley observes:

> You're taught about transitions, but you don't need them. People's imagination has been changed a lot by television. You sit and look at some TV shows, some of the worst, some of the cheapest, and you'll see them do technical tricks with time that Don [Barthelme], Coover, Barth, and everybody rolled into one would be terrified to do. Kids say that something they read is too hard for them; yet watching TV they are making jumps and assumptions and understanding things that none of these so called post-modernists could *dare* to do.[35]

The elliptical composition of the stories in Paley's *Enormous Changes at the Last Minute* turns remarks such as these to its own advantage. Television, down to the detail of advertisements for which it serves as a kind of prop, has introduced a new and sophisticated mode of narration henceforth accessible to the youngest and the least informed. This veritable revolution of the eye and of narrative makes possible new manipulations of narrative forms in fiction. Dos Passos saw Picasso as an artist who had "revolutionized the eye" along with painting; today, a comparable effect has unquestionably been had by television and the media in general.

Perverse and creative effects overlap and reveal themselves to be indissociable. Six long pages of *Americana* provide an analysis of this point (281–86). A similar inquiry is led by Wakefield in *All Her Children,* where he tries to understand the functioning of the soap opera *All My Children.* In *Requiem for a Dream,* Hubert Selby gives his characters the impoverished language of TV game shows and sets their love lives in the sentimental mode of the stereotyped dialogues of the soaps. Barthelme parodies all of the media in *Guilty Pleasures*; nothing escapes his wit, from the letters addressed to magazine editors to the *Ed Sullivan Show* that introduced the Beatles to America. In all of his work, he ferociously attacks, through anemic or conventional dialogues, the manifestations of a new "consciousness" shaped by the media. One is reminded of Michel Deguy inveighing against the "leukaemia of information."[36] Everything is presented — and this is Barthelme's target — as though his characters had internalized the images, signs, language, attitudes, and surfaces of the modes of information that dominate mass society. Not that Barthelme appears to want in any way to construct himself as a moralist or a censor. Like many others, he seems, certainly, at once outraged and fascinated by the power of the media, and alone, in his stories, his art of irony succeeds in channeling and tempering this revulsion.

But — and more than this simple theme, it is the strategy that draws our attention here — remarking the abrasions that the media perform upon critical sense and a sense of the ridiculous, Barthelme shows that, in having taken over narrativity — and having allowed literature to free itself perhaps — the media have now rendered any literary usage of narrativity dangerous. Corrupted by all of the compromises, narrativity has fallen victim, like language for Burroughs and myth for Steiner, to its shady uses. But, whereas Burroughs denounces all language as viral and infectious and commits himself to destroying it so as not to be contaminated, and Steiner dissects myth in order to destroy the assassin, Barthelme continually oscillates between two methods of defense: on the one hand, the recuperation of manifestly popular narrative devices (no harm in it once) in order to ward off their effects and to create an equal chance of delivering an opposing message; on the other hand, the patient and patent destruction of these devices, the undoing of all narrative logic. The aim becomes then to "demonstrate that narrative imagination, in today's world, is no longer a power of coherence or of transformation." Perhaps this is why Barthelme has one of his characters say that "fragments are the only form [he trusts]."[37] Moreover, it is not certain that Barthelme despairs of his powers so entirely: his mastery is truly at its peak in *Overnight to Many Distant Cities* and *Paradise*. But this dual strategy allows us to roughly classify the forms of the stories: from those in which a diegesis still dominates to those in which new forms (interviews, unmarked dialogues, imaginary conversations, combinations of writing and drawing) demonstrate the inevitable third dimension of this type of surface: the hollow into which the counterfeit, the masks, the hypocrisy, the appearances, the signs, the roles, the pretention, the futility fall and collapse.

Elsewhere, the relations of fiction to television cover a large spectrum of thematic or formal sophistication, from the obvious integration of television into settings and activities to the most solid epistemological reflection. In sociological terms, it has been clearly demonstrated that, with the arrival of the 1960s, at the moment when Kennedy became president at the end of a campaign in which the televisual image played a determining role, America was ready to let its consciousness be shaped by the electroshocks of the media. A sublime, rarefied, and schematized image of itself then structures the personality of a people. Metonymically, Barth shows that WESCAC, the powerful computer of *Giles Goat-Boy*, which modulates the relationships between images and desires, is only picking up on the mediatic disturbance of the existing links between the real and the imaginary.

More generally, it is the status of information that fiction calls into question. Aside from *White Noise*, in which DeLillo suggests that the overabundance of facts and of raw data inhibits the understanding of the world that electronivores might have, the works of Bruce Jay Friedman treat information as "alienation" in all meanings of the term. The familiar, unflinching, and darkly hilarious prose of Friedman's novels echoes a vision of the world where beings lacking in roots and friendly ties pillage the mediatized images in search of a way of being. For Friedman, there exists "an increasingly fluid border between the fantastic and reality, a very fuzzy border, a border, goddammit, that's practically invisible."[38] His characters, in any case, are unable to locate this border. The reigning madness is such that, in his eyes, *The New York Times* easily becomes "the source, the fountain and the Bible" of the "black humor" of which, from *Stern* to *Black Angels* to *A Mother's Kisses,* he is the undisputed master. In televised news coverage, he discerns the birth of "mutant modes of behavior that one can only deal with in a new fictional mode, along a one foot in the looney bin model."[39] Coover transforms *Time* and *The New York Times* into modern-day poets in *The Public Burning*, in order to stress that news is created or made rather than reported.

At the center of *Americana*, a perverse exploration of the American myth, there is a television station for which David Bell works as a producer, whose manipulative techniques as well as their effects on the protagonists are shown to us from the inside. The paranoia, depression, and madness in a more or less mild form that haunt the television executives illustrate both their function and their nature, similarly to the way in which Heller approaches the business world in *Something Happened*. Metaphorically, in describing a suicide committed by bolting a shotgun to the top of a television set and rigging a remote control to pull the trigger in *The Sportswriter,* Richard Ford means to suggest that television "kills" for real.[40] In *Being There,* Chance, whose life is confused with his cathode tube — a veritable uterus that takes the place of his mother and father —

has such confidence in his remote control that he points it at people who are aggressive toward him or who annoy him in an attempt to change the program of his days.

The "white noise" that provides DeLillo's novel with its title is made up of subliminal messages — trademarks borrowed from advertisements or decontextualized television news — that slowly invade the characters' consciousness. This white noise formally becomes "background noise" to the extent that discrete messages and "information," equally as gratuitous as unusable, come to reside at the heart of paragraphs and dialogues. Whether one is in deepest Kentucky in a kitchen bathed in the indistinct murmurings of useless TV game shows (*Shiloh*, Bobbie Ann Mason) or in a Las Vegas motel, one cannot fall asleep without turning the television to a channel that has signed off for the night in order to drug oneself with snowy hissing (*Fear and Loathing in Las Vegas*, Hunter Thompson), a cushion of sound comes between the real and consciousness. The phantasmal kaleidoscope of "The Babysitter" (*Pricksongs and Descants*, Coover) switches with the button of the channel changer, arranging its colored fragments within narrative frames determined by the nature of the program: the scene becomes violent along with the Western in progress, mysterious with the adventures of a detective, sentimental or erotic with the affairs of the heart, all of which the set blends together for the viewer. The television is the electronic lead player, the "coryphaeus" of imaginary tragedies; it becomes the generator of narratives as of attitudes, emblem of a scopic drive that declines into voyeurism, narcissism, images of desire. The reflection of images overrides any personal reflection. Kosinski insists on this by taking caricature to the extreme in *Being There*, where he does nothing less than substitute the television for any ontology. A new kind of dead soul, white page, a satisfied and rather sympathetic catatonic, Chance possesses a "cinematic self":[41]

> The figure on the TV screen looked like his own reflection in a mirror. . . . Their voices were alike. He sank into the screen. Like sunlight and fresh air and mild rain, the world from outside the garden entered Chance, and Chance, like a TV image, floated into the world, buoyed up by a force he did not see and could not name.[42]

The irony is increased by the fact that Chance himself becomes "televisual" when he appears on a program that will lead him to a position as adviser to those in power: television provides an explanatory frame within which the formulation of an opinion on the questions of international politics with the help of the only language he knows, that of the gardener he is, suffices to constitute a message. Chance shares the medium's flatness of tone, its lack of color and definition, its two-dimensionality. Artificially unified by a discourse (gardening) and a form (the image), his consciousness is nonetheless deeply fragmented. It is this fragmentation that is figured by the writing of *The Devil Tree,* and that, equally elliptic, of *Steps.* In *The Art of the Self,* Kosinski claims that "the cinematic image has become the key to modern perception." In *The Devil Tree,* Whalen reflects on this complex mode of alienation:

> It is as if the world were very sharply defined, but at the same time remote. Objects vibrate and quiver against me, but I cannot touch them. It's like coming into bright sunlight from a photographer's darkroom. I fear that this sensation will last forever, that I will never be able to explain it and that I'm the only one who feels it.[43]

The Fixed Image

Photography

One uses "film" for photography as well as cinema. One might also speak of a "film" of varying thickness that gradually covers the real and constitutes it as a surface, a protection, a screen. Even identity and the tangible proofs of experience find refuge there. In McGuane's *The Bushwhacked Piano,* the protagonist's girlfriend, Ann Fitzgerald, considers the photographs she is forever taking to be the only tangible proof of her existence. It is in the darkroom where he develops his photographs and prepares his great manipulations that the hero of Kosinski's *Cockpit* feels most truly himself. In *White Noise,* as we have seen, the "most photographed barn in America" is precisely . . . the most photographed barn in America. This is the sole reason behind its attraction for tourists, the constitutive fact for them and in itself. These empty doublings "found" the being, and create, like the animated images of cinema or television, a closed game of mirrors in which, if one is unable to recognize oneself, at least one can momentarily believe in one's presence in the world. Any photo-image tends to take on the strange status of David Hockney's exploded and fragmented photographs, whose exaggerated cubism calls into question and into doubt both space and time. Characters who recognize themselves there or who allow them to act as substitutes for their personality signal in so doing their own incapacity to blend in with a society and a story, emphasize their isolation, the superficial nature of their being, their estrangement from themselves, and confess their satisfaction with, for lack of depth, the shimmering of the empty shell they present to the world.

But what is more, and more pertinent to our discussion here, the uses of photography in contemporary fiction refer to modes of perception, as do the references to cinema for Coover. Paul Theroux does not employ particularly innovative novelistic forms. But *Picture Palace,* a novel that centers on a seventy-year-old photographer named Maude Coffin Pratt, takes up the ideas governing the aesthetic of *Pricksongs and Descants* and of *The Water-Pourer.* The angle of observation is everything and the contemplated object covers multiple realities that do not cancel each other out. The photographer whom Maude Pratt meets is Stieglitz rather than Hockney, but in both cases and in both eras, it is a matter of innovators in whose work point of view is pushed to an extreme. The immediacy of the representation, that in Stieglitz one might link to William Carlos Williams, has been overtaken, in Hockney and Coover, by plural and reduced representations, in defiance of the totalitarianism of unifying ideological systems. Autonomous images have gone the way of master narratives. The narrative break, somewhat like a moat protecting against outside invasions by the occupier, is erected as a defense; dispersal is substituted for narrative. In addition, the "picture palace" in question can also be said to refer to the iconographic storehouse that constitutes our thought and our memory. Certainly, the mind is inhabited by representations of the external world; it projects itself there as well. The photographic apparatus Theroux mentions brings to mind the magazine, the "lookout cartridge" in which McElroy locates consciousness. The "shots" of Cynthia Ozick (in *Levitation*) become all the more disturbing, and the photographer in Hawkes's *Whistlejacket* finds both a refuge and a reflection of his troubled voyeur's soul in his instrument of work. This was already the case for Hugh in *The Blood Oranges.*

Cartoons and Strips

Like television, comic strips go along with the representation of a universe increasingly perceived as a poorly defined image, two-toned and two-dimensional. In an earlier decade also troubled by a crisis in the economy and in representation, Nathanael West claimed he wanted to write a novel in the form of a comic strip. Today, the diverse resources of comic strip aesthetics have been put into action. After having shaped the expressionist style of *The Kandy-Kolored Tangerine-Flake Streamline Baby,* caricature leads Tom Wolfe to depict the USSR under the characteristics of the "Integral," the press under those of the "Animal" or of "Mister" in *The Right Stuff.* In *The Public Burning,* Coover creates general paranoia through a similar device, baptizing under the name of "Phantom" the international communism so feared by Nixon and Uncle Sam, a name directly descended from the comic strips, and "Poet Laureate" the national magazine that lays out in squares the information in its columns. The characters and the action of Vonnegut's novels, the "agents" of Pynchon's novels frequently parody and caricature elements of traditional narrative. The names of Pynchon's characters in particular — but also those of Vonnegut or Gaddis from "Deadeye Dick" to Agnes Deigh — step right out from the comic strips to which they seem destined to return. The function of these names seems to be to demystify the very notion of a realistic character, to make them seem as inaccessible to credibility as to moral judgment. With barely plausible names, the characters declare themselves to be fiction. Mucho Maas, Stanley Kotex, Feel, Bloat, Stencil, and V are thereby programmatically deprived of any depth. Nabokov had previously reinforced the meaning of his title *Transparent Things* by naming his hero "Person." With *The Names*, DeLillo exaggerates this concept and generalizes it for all name-giving.

The actions of such characters obey the logic of their original medium. Coover exploits the nature of paper beings in the cartoon of *A Night at the Movies*; the improbable aspects of "A Pedestrian Accident" (*Pricksongs and Descants*) owed them their minimal credibility. By the same logic, Mark Leyner can describe a car that explodes ten times and then finally have the driver take it to a mechanic who diagnoses an obvious "bomb problem" (*My Cousin, My Gastroenterologist*). The ease with which the wild men of *Fear and Loathing in Las Vegas* recover from their various escapades and their drug use owes much to the "suspension of disbelief" encouraged by the likes of Tex Avery. In Jaffe's "Old Man/Bag-Lady," following a terrible accident, we read: "Nor is the old man dead. As in the subsequent frame of a cinema cartoon all is intact once again."[44] The diegesis is subjected in Brautigan's works to an aesthetics of discontinuity typical of comic strips. The characters of *Willard and His Bowling Trophies* express themselves in the form of what phylacteries might contain, and, as in *The Abortion*, the dialogue is redundant in order to render the superimposing of text and image proper to this medium. These plots convey the logic of the "transmissions" in which the father of the three Logans, a mechanic, specializes. If the comic strip only imperfectly describes the aesthetic of William Kotzwinkle, the illustrated plates from children's tales might also serve as an example.

The comic strip — and in particular the "Classic Comics" of the forties, from which Brautigan gleans more than one image himself — has so influenced Charyn's views ("All my novels are comic strips")[45] that he has expanded his novelistic *oeuvre* by becoming the coauthor of *The Magician's Wife*.[46] For Charyn, the comic strip represents a popular genre that has enriched his imagination as powerfully as serial literature of the late nineteenth century. He inherited from these two genres his taste for "magic," the "marvelous" tone that colors his novels, from *The Catfish Man* to *Pinocchio's Nose*. The shadow of "Little Nemo" lurks around this man, for whom writing is like "sleepwalking."

We can observe the crosscultural impact of illustration by recalling the role it plays in the work of two well-known black writers. Toni Morrison makes use of the drawings of the adventures of *Dick and Jane,* thanks to which several generations of Americans learned to read, in order to contrast the two cultures in *The Bluest Eye,* a novel in which this contrast is the dominant theme. Given West's strong influence (*The Dream Life of Balso Snell* in particular) on Ishmael Reed, it comes as no great surprise that *Yellow Back Radio Broke-Down* and *The Free-Lance Pallbearers* owe much to the tone of comic strips, a popular medium among others featuring in Reed's work, and employed for this reason on ideological grounds, by virtue of its "class" aesthetic.

Pynchon and McElroy warn of the dangers of binary, digitalized thought. Others, like Steiner and Coover, through the combined use of cinema, history, and of a real divided into grids for reading in *Passion* or *Gloomy Gus* warn us of the perils of mythical thought. A certain use of the media in contemporary fiction averts us against what I will call "tabloid thought." In a world whose complexity regularly escapes us, the media industry too often chooses to simplify its contours, toning down in this way some part of an unknown where fruitful contradictions might be hidden and partial answers might be discovered. Under the influence of the media, being and substance becomes images. In the United States today, one no longer finds references to a "way of living," "culture," or "habits," concepts that are either too complex or too contradictory. The shallow notion of "life-style" has come to replace them, all surface and window dressing, a faint outline traced freehand to enclose a space drowned in hedonistic pastels. Friendships and passions are "relationships"; "I feel" expresses the opinions that "I think" can no longer handle. These phrases reveal that, within the empire of images, surfaces threaten to become the only ontology that counts. They admit that the social community is crumbling the sections of more or less slick and luxurious catalogs and magazines; existence, despite individualistic protestations and obscenely narcissistic fashions that promote bodies and health as images of an asepsis generalizable to thought, is no longer defined by the desire to realize oneself and relations with others, but by a gregarious and egocentric obedience to iconic models promulgated within the media. Truth be told, "popular culture" wrongfully assumes its name: produced elsewhere than among the people, by the head semioticians who know that there is always profit to be found in the periodic creation of artificial differences, it is produced only in the guise of a soothing or exciting fodder. Harold Jaffe is saying nothing other than this in *Mole's Pity* when he denounces "this glib bohemianism legislated by an Industry that sapiently modifies the requisites (trappings), so that the current crop of arty weekenders must always commence with (buy) a new variation of the old 'image.' "[47]

To denounce discursively a similar situation is merely to pose as an "intellectual," the ultimate insult. Fiction tries to make us aware of this by other means, just as art has always done. A dialogue forever begun again: "Slow fade," as in the movies. "Fado," say the inspired blues. "Flatness," demands bland mass culture. We can now move on to the reactions and answers offered by a fiction that refuses to resign itself to such "cultural entropology."

Chapter 11

Cultural Tradition and the Present I: Intellectual Culture

The year 1984 has come and gone, just as Halley's comet, in 1985, brought David Carkeet's Mark Twain with it and then took him away again. The demonstrations that marked that date (cursed since Orwell) were for the most part demonstrations of relief: Big Brother, after all, had not taken over, the promised totalitarian leveling and brainwashing had not happened. But perhaps it might not be excessively paranoid if one were to give a less optimistic report on the present situation. The influence of the dreaded *newspeak* is more diffuse, more underhanded, less easily defined, but no less real: from clichés to supreme contempt for language and from dry, wooden language to cosmetic and hackneyed speech, the flattening out of all consciousness by the media and the mass-scaling of information separated from real knowledge and reflection are at the root of the problems of our time. Pynchon, McElroy, and Barthelme, in their own way, testify to this. If the fear of catastrophes that haunts a large segment of contemporary American literature has not yet found its justification in the dreaded "bang," then the end of the world becomes more widely accepted under the form of the *whimper* predicted by T. S. Eliot. Milan Kundera's cynically sketched development makes us hear a "wail" as much as a "moan." In *The Book of Laughter and Forgetting*, the narrator, under the obvious cliché used by one of the characters (while addressing children, the latter claims that "they are the future"), exposes the more profound regression that hides under the growing infantilization of the masses: "The reason children are the future is not that they will one day be grownups. No, the reason is that mankind is moving more and more in the direction of infancy, and childhood is thus the image of the future."[1]

Culture undoubtedly consists in the progressive refinement of the relationship of a given community to the world, in the reading of its spiraled history, in the maturing of the internal relationships that govern its exis-

tence, in the transcendence of raw information, the thought-out tension
of its diverse fields of information toward a knowledge whose order testifies to the establishment of values that have been chosen and shared after
a process of unrestricted and critical examination; but if such is really the
case, clearly, then, contemporary Western culture is in crisis. The cultural
and political failure of the show window humanism that has come to sink
with modernism on the reefs of our century's great conflicts is currently
taken over (especially in the United States but not exclusively, since Europe seems flatly and unquestioningly to adopt the model) by the shred-
ding of culture at the hands of economic priorities, by the auction where
Western civilization converts its heritage to cash. Of course, the critical
revisions of history, epistemology, and the master narratives can be seen
as an effort to free culture from its various paralyses. But they are now
commercially exploited in a way that no modernist from before the information age could have foreseen. The oxymoron contained in comical
allusions to "best cultural bargains" or "cultural industry"; the quantitative evaluation of the cultural state of nations ("More Mozart for the
Masses," "The Growth of Tourism," "Boom in the Museums"); the easy
confusion that makes it possible to assimilate any kind of difficulty and
quality to a condemnable "elitism" that no one would think of blaming in
the worlds of sports, business, entertainment, and the media but that
seems suspect in the world of thought, of the arts, and of literature; the
takeover by financial empires of all means of communication; careerism
and intellectual conformism; the extension of fashionable exploitative
complicity to the world of ideas: all that cannot dissimulate — or rather,
it reveals the disintegration of any coherent vision of culture, and its
submission to the iron rule of commodity, its replacement by the mere
consumption of trinkets, as transient and trivial as they are decorative;
and no amount of colloquiums or cultural events can really alter such a
situation.

Intellectuals are called upon to sell themselves or not be read at all,
thought becomes a matter of marketing, roles become substitutes for
functions, oversimplification makes everything incomprehensible. "Philosophy" makes itself "new" to get on the top-ten list, academics inquire
what is the next "thing," the "coming thing," the ideas that sell, and
there is toothpaste and detergent between the lines of treatises hastily
written to satisfy the "cult of the new." The economic becomes the only
ontology and profit treats itself to kept dancers, books of the week, writers of the month. Since culture is only being consumed as "shows," all
attempts to judge, assess, or distinguish fairly are reputed "hierarchical," — and therefore condemnable — in a world where difference is only
interesting when artificially created in order to generate surplus value.
The "postmodern," even "postcontemporary," vulgate (Wake up, Hegel,

they've gone crazy!) flaunts drifting, uncertainty, indecision, nondifferentiation, and simulacrum as values worth fighting for since it no longer has the courage to oppose them. One has to make a living. Or at least give oneself the impression of living.

Cultural confusion has reached such a level and feels so uneasy that contemporary American fiction makes it its theme, itself "beyond suspicion." Irony, the quest for authenticity, mimicry, or attempts to mine garbage for gold: illusions are dead if hope is not. Resorting to the cultural theme will never again be a reason to celebrate. It wanders between threnody and manipulations, hesitates between binging and purging. Even as the cultural sees itself absorbed by the economic, a fiction said to be too easily detached from its critical functions for the benefit of a condemnable aestheticism makes itself—as much as it can be—ideological commentary, through its raw material as much as through its forms.

The undifferentiated stream of the means of mass communication is in itself an ideological product and conduct—the smoothing over of the real that it invites or provokes can only admit the creation of fake and ephemeral feelings of a "newness" better to comfort the durability of the establishment. So that both the forms and the themes of a fiction that feeds on a reflection on culture constitute the valuable indicators of reactions to such "cultural entropology."

For the sake of convenience—since, no one, indeed, can remain innocent of a lethal simplicity—I will distinguish two major tendencies and detail them as best I can. I shall first point to the reactive temptations that have recourse to cultural tradition, to the "intellectual" culture; then I shall examine the reactions resulting from the various treatments invited by mass culture.

Fortunes and Misfortunes of Philosophy

Anybody who gets lost will at some point turn around or look over his shoulder, hoping that the path will be shown by trail markers or beacons that were left behind, and correct by a few side steps, if at all possible, the faulty itinerary that was followed for lending an overconfident ear to unreliable guides. In the surrounding cultural jumble, brutally emphasized by Gaddis and Pynchon, it is very tempting to follow the main avenues, among which the philosophical tradition must be counted. It has been indulged in with varying success, the exercise being fraught with danger; the pitfalls of the "novel of ideas," an insufferable hybrid that transforms fictions into pure medium, constantly threaten. One thinks—*mutatis mutandis*—of Valéry when he argued that "[to] philosophize in verse was, and still is, to try to play a game of chess according to the rules of checkers," before suggesting that "the 'subject' of a work is what a bad one finally boils down to."[2] From *Herzog* to *The Dean's December,* Saul Bellow transformed the astonishing voice that had made his first novels masterpieces into didactic and moralizing tones; not until *More Die of Heartbreak* did he regain the distance and the ironic games that gave him back his bite and his force. In truth, the gangster's irony toward Citrine's acquaintances in *Humboldt's Gift* remains the trace of Bellow's most efficacious tactics. The ironist — "Him with His Tongue in His Cheek," let us say — is more convincing than the polemicist — *Him with His Foot in His Mouth.* Entirely dedicated to the "moral" stakes of his fiction, Gardner did not quite manage to integrate the philosophical preoccupations of a character/professional philosopher to his *Mickelson's Ghosts:* letting a poorly justified "empiricism" progressively substitute itself for Mickelsson's idealist and militant program, he can only offer the barest possibilities of one kind of individualism as a solution to the evils of another; philosophy clutters his novel more than it clarifies it without even allowing him to resolve his dilemmas.

There are any number of incontinent novelists of the "me" generation in American culture and it is not only the dominant poetical mode of the last thirty years that took pleasure in the "confessional." All the more reason to admire such an unfairly disregarded novelist as Lynne Sharon Schwartz who, in *Disturbances in the Field,* is able to activate rather than petrify the mimetic form by using cultural and philosophical discourse to undergird it. By borrowing Alfred North Whitehead's metaphor for her title in order to describe the tragic perturbations in Lydia's field of existence and the relationship of the subject to the world, Schwartz fills her text with meditations on the pre-Socratics and the Stoics, from Heraclitus to Epictetus. However, she never permits either the meditations begun by her heroine (even while she was studying Greek philosophy) to sterilize fictional movements, or the weight of artificially applied doctrines to extinguish the fire, the vigor, the emotion, the irony, and the charm of her narrative. It is cruel then, without a doubt, even if the sad contemporary rules of reception must thereby be illuminated, to compare this intellectually solid and aesthetically well-tempered, modest novel to the questionable success of Robert M. Pirsig who, in *Zen and the Art of Motorcycle Maintenance,* energetically belabors an impressive series of obvious points. In the 1960s and 1970s, the vogue of misty-mysticism and Californian pop philosophy (from Carlos Castaneda to Charles Reich) undoubtedly played a role in the bookstores' triumphant sale of this naive, ready-to-wear version of Aristotle and Plato. Presented with admirable simplicity as a how-to manual by an eclectic mind obsessed with "disharmony," but quite unable to see where objections to the forced cohabitation of Buddha and the Greeks could come from, this "novel" hammers

Poincaré and Euclid into its readers with such energy that it leaves little chance for the proverbial hairsplitter to ply its trade.

Of course, placed next to such uncritical enthusiasm, many works of fiction with a solid philosophical base have little trouble making the most basic methodological doubt appear as thematic suspicion. Let irony, and even more so culture, become a part of them, and the texts of Guy Davenport, John Calvin Batchelor, William S. Wilson, Chaim Potok, and Frederic Tuten — as different as they may be one from the other — return its viability and usefulness to philosophical discourse in fiction. Even though Potok, in *The Chosen* or *The Book of Lights*, dutifully conformed himself to rules that hardly smacked of "suspicion" and remained within the orthodoxy of traditional Judaism, his will to push back the limits of his model and artfully to open its potential for variation gives his books a more innovative perspective on philosophy and theology than the one promised by Charles Johnson's project, for example: making Marx a character in *Oxherding Tale* does not allow for the integration of an often anachronistic philosophical discourse that tends to stick out all too visibly throughout the story. With Potok, the tension rises from the interference among ideas that are never exposed for their own sake: Biblical criticism, Freudianism, Marxism, and aesthetics, independently developed, collide with each other and the text is constructed not around a thesis but around questions. Though hostile to the "pyrotechnics of language," he still successfully distances his voice from his subject. In Johnson's novel, the constant intervention of the author, in the name of a rather lame metafictional practice, does not generate any energy: the return to the mimetics of the narrative content becomes even more conspicuous, thereby less convincing.

For Frederic Tuten, however, this same combination works well. *The Adventures of Mao on the Long March* is the pretext for confrontations on philosophy and aesthetics in the manner of fictitious interviews. In claiming the arbitrariness of its integration, the philosophical discourse blisters with self-denunciation, and irony makes itself felt both in the form and in the tone. It is to more classical novelistic forms, though in a narrative framework freed from mimetic constraints, that John Calvin Batchelor entrusts the philosophical burden of *The Birth of the People's Republic of Antarctica*. The utilitarianism of Jeremy Bentham and John Stuart Mill constitutes its center, relayed by Charity Bentham whose name itself combines these preoccupations that could be only allegorical, were it not for the character's substance and what must be called her environment's fantastic realism, inasmuch as the pragmatism of the characters makes them follow even the accidents of history, makes them voluntary actors in the extreme situations demanded by a prophesied apocalypse:

which means that their discourse is not devoid of irony, in spite of its superficial "competence." Batchelor's characters, immersed in philosophy, do not show what they are capable of by artificially peppering here and there their ideas with it, but by fulfilling a destiny that owes nothing to their realist or utilitarian discourse and everything to a vision that departs from the real while remaining immediately recognizable.

Guy Davenport is equally fascinated by Fourier and Wittgenstein whom he sees as two great "naives," and whose paths one never ceases to cross in his work. Without ever claiming the status of a storywriter, he modestly designates his "constructivist" writings under the name of "assemblages." Nurtured by Greek philosophy, a well-known Hellenist, translator, and critic, he defines himself as "conservative, democratic and Baptist," a definition that one might be tempted to complete with its opposite: "innovator, elitist, pagan"; it is however Heraclitus's thought that haunts his texts from *Tatlin!* to *Apples and Pears,* by way of *Eclogues, Trois Caprices,* and *Da Vinci's Bicycle.* The Heraclitean logos is the unifying principle of his books. The interplay of opposites, the relativizing perspective offered by the unified categories of time and space are the foundation of his great cultural syntheses where the archaic extends its hand to the modern, nature to art, the machine to the organic, the body to technology and to the universe. The most ancient is the most innovative and every *archaios* keeps engendering a new *archē.* The essential material unifying all things is the Heraclitean fire, the "phoenix-time of Antiquity." The many constants in the cobbled together stories of this high modernist, disciple and friend of Ezra Pound, include the inversion of life and death, the themes of passage and of circularity, and a cyclical vision of human activity where history is reversed and aesthetics proclaims periodical correspondences. In his work, philosophy is the warp and weave of a fragmented style whose economy and efficiency evoke the "tortoises" of the Roman legions; his calibrated paragraphs are hinged, connected and mobile, straight and linked together but not rigid, and overlap like tiles. Every potentially awkward turn of phrase is averted by the elegance of a pliant thought, saturated with cultural and philosophical references that constantly establish innumerable links, constituting as many small, local sutures and overcast stitches; where such a texture could become disjointed and discontinuous, it is in fact from the start unified by a lofty writing style that plays on clever connections and subtle relationships. It owes its unity of effect to the flexibility of an immense culture, and to the complicitous and continual invitations extended by the humor of motifs, the lightness of irony, and an uncompromising intelligence. In Davenport's hands, all of philosophy's truly fictional, shaping power is placed in the service of an aesthetic sensuality that, without ever dulling the sharp edges of the concept, refuses to clutter up with it texts that attach little importance to the conventional markers of narration.

In *Tatlin!*, Wittgenstein barely misses meeting Kafka at the Brescia airport. William S. Wilson chooses, instead, to explain why he "doesn't write like Franz Kafka," even though the short stories in *Why I Don't Write Like Franz Kafka* and especially "Love" are based on the principles of the analytical philosophy of Wittgenstein and Whitehead. He borrows, as does Lynne Sharon Schwartz, from Whitehead's notion of the field in "Motherhood." Frequently dominated by information theory and linguistic pragmatism, his texts, organized around the fundamental concepts that they explore tangentially, constitute a continuous effort to link language to the body and to experience. The notion of "operation" dominates his texts, whether surgical, logical, linguistic, or most often a combination of the three. "Every problem of medicine," declares a voice in "Fatherhood, "is a problem of language, and this operation was a malapropism."[3] The philosophical thinking that comes out of "biology lectures," in notes on the relationships of taste to light, in dialogues between "fire and frost" or "text and context" is never tackled head on; and Wilson's unusual style shows its use is more a springboard than a refuge. In Wilson's works there are few characters in the strict sense, never any scenery and the diegesis accommodates the constant digressions; yet everything happens as if the narrative instances, far from being destroyed by lack of confidence in their powers, were only displaced.

In "Anthropology: What Is Lost in Rotation," a continuous play of correlations is set in motion between the physical, nature, culture, and the parallel modifications in their relationships that all can be subjected to by completing an unusual act. These *rapport*-like relationships are indebted to Cézanne. Thus, the events turn into characters even in their development, the character becomes a cause, the dramatic tensions establish themselves from concept to concept and from field to field. In "Men: The Man Who Ends His Story," preoccupations with reality are distant: the central character projects his own physical dismantlement and carefully examines the modalities of it during the course of five dreams called "rehearsals." Philosophy appears at every moment not as weighty intellectual baggage, the occasional use of which might shed some light on the events taking place, but more as the *deus ex machina* of a new fictional mode. Reading, far from being hindered by the documentary, the cosmetic, the prosthetic, enthuses about the adventures of thinking; and philosophy appears as a privileged means of scraping clean a reality that had all but disappeared under the cracked varnish of habit. It is understandable that in a different philosophical frame, Davenport should also accord an extreme importance to signs and the manner in which they are organized into systems; it is also understandable that he should renew the notion of "defamiliarization" by proposing "attention" more than invention as the source of all art. By renouncing a paralyzing suspicion vis-à-vis mimesis, both Davenport and Wilson prefer, each in his own way, to highlight the fact that "any mimesis is not only imitative: it is organized by the imitator" (Davenport). Philosophy intervenes in their work as a power through which to exhume and reorient signs and not as more or less critical but direct commentary on a real that has been sterilized by received ideas.

Without lingering overmuch on their examples, several contemporary fictions will be looked at where philosophy serves as the foil in which humor feeds on the lofty pretensions of philosophical thought. It has been shown that Swigart in *Little America* plays with Freudianism and mechanistic psychoanalysis with a fine iconoclastic energy. But its parodies do not end there. His novel is dedicated to "Karl & Charles & Sigmund & Albert & most of all Werner Heisenberg, whose Uncertainty Principle is a metaphor with punch . . ."[4] Whereas his story will feature seedy-looking truck drivers obsessed with tires and trailers' shock-absorbers, the first lines are elevated to a "cosmicomic" vision that has the grandiloquence of a three-penny Panglossian tirade.

Even Cowgirls Get the Blues, by Tom Robbins, could prolong this light note. The nostalgia for Haight-Ashbury's orientalist eclecticisms has sometimes made people read literally the pompous predictions of "The Chink" in the novel; it seems to me, on the contrary, that his charm has its source in his tearing apart of pop philosophy by means of merry juxtapositions, next to its exposition, of diegetically abrupt changes of subjects and an insane runaway iconography. The little priapic man who, between sexual bouts, preaches the bona fide anarchy that constitutes the founding principles of the "Clock People" for whom he is the speaker hardly convinces anybody. Rather, he joins the comic effects of his presence to a variety of descriptions, of portraits, and of silly events among which the uninhibited personality of Sissy Hankshaw stands out, along with the enormous size of her thumb, which makes her the best hitchhiker in the world, and this ranch of cowgirls with lovely thighs and sharp tongues who are devoted to undermining an environment set up against the beauties of nature: "One of those sponge words so soaked with meanings that you can squeeze out interpretations by the bucketful."[5]

Robbins's philosophical digressions relay the anarchistic nature of their contents through the structure of the discourse; they are accompanied by too many winks for us even to imagine he is trying to convince us of anything. The playful generative mode of the text, which progresses from the uncontrollable to the perfectly insane metaphor, contaminates *nolens volens* the series of the reputedly serious propositions that come to nest among them only often enough to comfort the pervading lunacy.

The "clockwork" of the "Clock People" works like a time-delayed bomb purchased in the practical jokes department. Throughout the irresistible comicality of a story based on a mode that it would be practically impossible to define except as a sort of "existentialist Gestalt," the categories of philosophical speculation do not escape the happy and general ridiculing of novelistic instances: "The taxi, having no free will, rolled downtown."

Time and space fell in on her like a set of encyclopedias falling off a missionary's shelf onto a pygmy. And time brought along its secretary, memory, and space brought its brat, loneliness.[6]

Following the example of the novelists who happily welcomed the liberating tone brought by Salinger (Brautigan, Fariña, or Boyer previously, and Heller, Boyle, or Price today), Robbins only refers in a quasi-humdrum manner to fashionable philosophical discourses or to the clichés of metaphysical anxiety in order to throw on their pathetic nudity the brilliant colors of a verbal overcoat whose embroideries are so dense that their sturdiness becomes superior to that of the fabric itself. In his work and in the works of his colleagues of more "serious" intentions, the success of the philosophical grafting depends on the extreme diffusion, either formal or thematic, of philosophical borrowings. The aforementioned failures are always due to their rejection by an organic novelistic universe that experiences — and the reader with it — such massive, out of balance, or clumsy implants as intolerable intrusions.

Tradition as Elsewhere

The uncomfortable feeling of working in a cultural world in disarray moves many to look for their starting points in a past that presents the double advantage of stepping back from the Babelization of contemporary discourse and offering solid support, whether one wants to ward it off or to use it as a springboard. The literary or artistic tradition becomes in turn escape route, playing field, or a place of rediscoveries. But the fact that one should resort to it cannot merely signify — for the authors that matter to us here, that is, and contrary to what others may do under similar circumstances, indulging in servile, weak, and uninteresting remakes — a step backward for a new and naive departure, a candid extension: turning toward certain aspects of the heritage, they remain conscious of its being worn out and exhausted and do not forget the most recent lessons of experience. The interest of contemporary American fiction lies largely in this capacity not to get paralyzed by the necessity of some "progress" or of a "new" aesthetics — notions that are close to absurd in literature. It also lies in its energy, its vigorous and complex-free will to pull itself out of dead-ends in order to gather renewed momentum; both save it from the narcissistic, disillusioned, and wan despair of too great a slice of European fiction — and particularly French — since the novels of suspicion, as well as from the regressions, the refusals, and the "petty Realist," as one says, "petty bourgeois" embalmings, particularly British. The audacity and the originality of these refoundations, just as in South American and Italian literatures, often have their causes in creative revisitings of the past.

Not that this exercise always goes without the "anxiety of influence" familiar to the readers of Harold Bloom, but it essentially transcends it. There certainly exists, on the one hand, a considerable mistrust toward the literary heritage. In truth the whole thematics of the father, spreading Hawthorne's remarks in *The Marble Faun* over a diversified spectrum, speaks more or less explicitly of its polyvalence. Largely due to personal factors, in the works of Yates, McGuane, William Wharton (*Dad*), or Baumbach (*My Father More or Less*), its presence is explicitly linked to questions of authority and identity, and even of language itself in *The Floating Opera* (Barth), *Omensetter's Luck* (Gass), or the novels of Purdy, and the motif of the absent father itself becomes insistent in these latter works; but this presence clearly details its cultural implications in Pynchon's *The Crying of Lot 49*, Gaddis's *The Recognitions*, and *The Dead Father*, Barthelme's second novel.

Yet, for all of this, on the other hand, the obsession and the reaction are not so strong that they allow the profile of a generation as Fitzgerald defined it to be traced:

> By a generation I mean that reaction against the fathers which seems to occur about three times in a century. It is distinguished by a set of ideas, inherited in moderated form from the madmen and the outlaws of the generation before; if it is a real generation it has its own leaders and spokesmen, and it draws into its orbit those born just before it and just after, whose ideas are less clear-cut and defiant.[7]

So much so that Roger Sale believed he was able to discern the difference separating the modernists from our contemporaries in the latter's choice not to fight tradition, but simply to ignore it altogether.[8] Whatever the case, the variety of contemporary fictional modes is such that any general definition would require substantial and immediate corrections, since even the temptation offered by the label "postmodernist" never outlasts the study of its minimal content, one that posits a fundamental eclecticism. But even the superficial examination of contemporary productions amply demonstrates the point where Sale goes astray: the creators of the past are everywhere, whether a form can be borrowed from them, or they be taken as objects of reference or concrete allusions, whether the montages favor their appearance in groups for the purposes of analysis and of cultural thinking or they are the object of manipulations and of recontextualizations for various ends.

It is useless to insist on the importance that Cervantes can have for Coover, or Homer for Barth, or the fascination that Stevens and Kerouac have for Sukenick, Thomas Browne or Gertrude Stein for Gass, Faulkner and West for Hawkes. No narrow conception of "influence" could account for that which, for some authors, is no less than a common vision of the means and goals of literature. We might be better inspired to examine the twists and modulations caused by references to past works. Perhaps these — more than the solidity of traditions that the present cannot break from nor chip away at — manifest the need felt by so many to engage in a new dialogue with them. We are far, in this case, from the larger questions raised by intertextuality, which would be the subject of other analyses, since, in order to be able to work as a recourse, all borrowings must be as conscious as possible.

We will see further on that the genres and subgenres have undergone severe treatments that destabilize them and, with them, a somewhat aged notion of literary history. This is a dominant trait of contemporary fiction. But, more simply, and for different stakes, we will observe the more or less ironic but briefly claimed will to extend the canonical modes of national literature; a few examples will suffice: "modern romances" is the title of Judy Lopatin's short stories, "familiar pastorals" is the subtitle of McElroy's novel, *Hind's Kidnap*. Then, a whole formal and traditional plan can become the object of official borrowing: *Oxherding Tale* (C. Johnson) as well as *The Chaneysville Incident* (Bradley) owe part of their form to slave narratives; an identical but more cautious reference, can be found in Alice Walker's *The Color Purple*. It is noteworthy that such publications coincide with a renewal in interest for these models (including Frederick Douglass) as it does with the marginal sentimental works that they have engendered (*Uncle Tom's Cabin* is the best known example). Exploiting the most epic dimensions of the traditional "Western," Larry McMurtry, in *Lonesome Dove*, does not miss the chance to "quote" implicitly the tradition of the "captivity story" by handing over a while his obligatory big-hearted whore to the Kiowas. And finally we know that Russell Banks claims, even in his title, *A Relation of My Imprisonment*, his debt to an older genre: the confessions of imprisoned Puritan divines who in the seventeenth century, while in prison or upon their release, made their religious brothers witnesses of the trials to which their faith had been subjected. Especially in this case, Banks not only shows that the emotive and imaginative power of these texts remains strong; he also proves that it is possible, in spite of the historical distance and opacity that separates us from them and thanks to a sophisticated exploitation of these ancient narrative modes, to propel a pre-realist aesthetic simultaneously beyond realism and beyond any suspicion that might have befallen it. Such is the happiness found in sincere affections, in deliberate and knowing attachments, in the game of differences allowing for the simultaneous attention paid to the truths of the past and the filters of our own gaze.

To limit ourselves to the nineteenth century, which only serves as punctual or occasional recourse for certain authors (Whitman for Jaffe, Darwin for Boyle's *Descent of Man*, Thoreau in the first chapter of *Fisher's Hornpipe* by Todd McEwen), tradition colors entire individual productions. The Puritan and the Hawthornian traditions are implicitly part of the works of Pynchon and Gaddis, and explicitly of Banks's in *The New World* and *Trailerpark*. Banks borrows heavily from the indeterminations and open-endedness of Melville's *Moby-Dick*, Poe's *Arthur Gordon Pym*, and Twain's *Huckleberry Finn* for his own *Hamilton Stark*, as do Batchelor in *The Birth of the People's Republic of Antarctica*, Denis Johnson in *Fiskadoro*, Steve Erickson in *Rubicon Beach*, Brautigan in *A Confederate General from Big Sur* and *Trout Fishing*, and Toby Olson in *Seaview*.

Yet, two bodies of work in particular deserve a closer look: those of Annie Dillard and Paul Metcalf. The latter's motivations are made clearer by his being the great-grandson of Herman Melville. He carries this ascendance like a "monkey on his back," in the same way that the "giant of the past" weighed down on Hawthorne's shoulders. Metcalf's *Genoa* is the prodigious montage that aims at getting rid of it. Metcalf speaks of it as "a mosaic, an abstract painting, a Paracas textile," "the various elements serving to ballast one another."[9] Convinced that one "chooses his own ancestors," Metcalf has the characters of Michael and Carl Mills make the claim for his own, while he makes them assume the legacy of Columbus and of a previous odyssey. Both a historical and a mythical analysis (Metcalf says "genealogical" or "genoalogical"), this text is of interest here in that it deliberately sets a new course — to borrow a nautical term — for the fiction that takes place in the present toward a historical tradition linking Homer to a diary read by the narrator and where Columbus and Melville function as relays. The least of the paradoxes is not, on the surface, that the setting should be Indianapolis and Saint Louis, or as Gass would say "the heart of the heart of the country." It is that the maritime "tradition" that Michael Mills is speculating on permits, suggests, and invites the integration of the unknown to the known.

Genoa endeavors to make the continent that Columbus discovered and that Melville was not able to "digest" familiar to them and to us, to render it accessible by prolonging the logic of their quests. The mystery remains, in the personality of Carl (Michael's brother), caught in the execution of a trivial act that owes more to Truman Capote's *In Cold Blood* than to Columbus's diary. Identity is explored by means of tradition, one type of insanity is echoed in others, Columbus's doubts and Melville's anxieties punctuate this inquiry into the mystery of a criminal personality. The textual obsessions and the remanences mix with daily life, every word, every expression has its own genealogy. The world, now as before, remains a text to decipher. The fragmented palimpsest that Metcalf gives us, with all of its lacunae and leaps in time and logic, refers us back to the gaps, the blanks, the unsolvable discontinuities of identities, lives, and destinies. A brilliant and disturbing montage, *Genoa* mixes into pertinent agglomerations fictitious characters and historical figures, quotes and personal thoughts, learned culture, metaphysics, and the quotidian. Forever escaping the prows of the *Pequod* and the *Santa Maria,* and the pen that is writing the *Journal, Billy Budd, Pierre,* and *Genoa*: the mystery of man, that of the real, that of writing; the whiteness of distance, of the whale, and of the page. By formally transcribing the principles of Melville, according to whom "all human affairs are subject to organic disorder, [. . .] he who in great things seeks success must [. . .], with what straggling method he can, dash with all his derangements at his object,"[10] this "Telling of Wonders" tells of the marvels, the worries, and the questioning combined in its subtitle by means of puzzle pieces, throws the Harlequin suit of its textual assemblages over the truth of a perpetually elusive reality to reveal/dissimulate the author's obsessions with inheritance.

Annie Dillard does not have such personal links to great authors of the past. But she shares an experience with Thoreau and another with Melville. *Pilgrim at Tinker Creek,* a diary composed of a "mystical excursion in the natural world,"[11] calls explicitly on Thoreau's *Walden*; and "Life of the Rocks" (*Teaching a Stone to Talk*) extends and brings up to date the sketches written by Melville on the mysterious Galápagos Islands in "The Encantadas." After a year in the midst of a marvelous little valley in Virginia and a visit on the islands of tortoises, she takes a doubly informed look at these two places: through her knowledge of previous and comparable experiences by the two giants of the past century and of their literary transcriptions, on the one hand, and, on the other, through a contemporary woman's competence and intellectual tools as regards botany, entomology, chemistry, and epistemology. In other words, her stories attempt strange exercises of which both the conclusions and methods can hold our interest. It matters in fact very little that her observation of the Galápagos concludes in a way that is diametrically opposed to Melville's, that the militant transcendentalism of Thoreau is humbly echoed by a Christian faith stripped of proselytism, as well as of specific denomination. For, in the end, what light Dillard manages to shed on the contemporary world has little to do with thematic preoccupations that, as passionate as they may be, are mere surface shimmers compared with the relationships that are subtly established between writing, reading, and the real. Chance or convention are no more responsible for the textual framing of her own texts than whimsy was in Thoreau's and Melville's choice of the quotations that line their discourse; coincidence has nothing to do with her choice of the questions she asks, nor with the answers she gives. The necessary philosophical differences do not prevent a common passion for the *deciphering* of nature. Melville read his runes from the turtle's shell as well as from the head of the whale, while Thoreau, following the example of Goethe, read leaves. Everything *means* in nature and Dillard is no more loath than they to establish bridges ("to pontificate" as Kenneth Burke would say) between the semiotics of *physics* and the necessary paths of her writing.

Just as Thoreau wanted to "[make] the earth say beans instead of grass,"[12] Dillard recognizes on a rock "the lazy sinuosity that can only *mean* snake."[13] Beyond this, the compositional affinities become structural and allow her to move past limitations of reportorial realism with no delusions about the necessary resistance of the limits of language. The "haphazard piecing" of Melville's sketches, reused by Thoreau under the English form of tinkering, has more than a euphonic relationship to the title of Dillard's book; incapable of "covering the real," language must make itself "extravagant" (Thoreau), as nature does itself. Discourse has to spill over its margins if it wants to take into account the overflow of an excess of reality in nature. This, Dillard chooses to see as a divine harmonic of Saint Luke's "good measure, pressed down, shaken together and running over."[14] She finds the paths of an uncommon modernity, despite the constraints of her choice of older models, by devoting herself to a "natural theology" unofficially banished from our world since Galileo. Dillard takes responsibility for a parasitic literary style that she also metaphorizes, through the fascinating entomological description of a "stylops," a word full of inscriptional echoes. Of course, the paradigms are borrowed, but the secret of life looks for its identity nowadays in the DNA; nature's mysteries, its gaps, and its refusal to make sense are displaced and located anew in astrophysics, black holes, and quantum theory. Such movements enable the individual to find his/her place and to interrogate the future.

More generally speaking, "visits" to past cultural traditions give way to new and fecund contextualizations, to instructive relativizations. Edmund White, himself a musical prose-writer, remarked that "the mixture of places and epochs operated by Nabokov, his sense of a compound history, totally invented in *Ada,* have pointed the way to other works based on a cultural synthesis."[15] He gives as examples the "fantasies of Thomas Berger," *Trust* by Cynthia Ozick — specifically referring to her image of a "cannibal galaxy" — and the texts of Davenport, which White strangely sees as "tales." The term is quite suggestive, but Davenport's own term "assemblages" seems preferable. Davenport uses learned culture in order to relativize it; but he does it differently from, say, Doctorow, whose cultural collages, owing more to Dos Passos's modernism than to Pound's, come as illustrations of a history that sees its texture but not the nature of its strengths or directions questioned. The questioning of culture, with Davenport, is achieved through the juxtaposition of apparently disparate units in order to emphasize the Heraclitean logos — that omnipresent "light" in his texts — that allows us better to know the world, whereas the cultural subjects only present its shimmering reflection. Artists (Da Vinci, Tatlin, Monet, Gaudier-Brzeska, Picasso, or Max Ernst), thinkers (Heraclitus, Montaigne, Agassiz, or Ernst Mach), creators (Basho, Virgil, Poe, Butler, or Stein) are the prisms that help him to determine the answer to the central question of his work: is matter living or dead, is there a world outside the signs that constitute it?

By accumulating and superimposing the transcriptions and the intellectual and aesthetic translations of our universe, a "reserve" is drawn up little by little, a mysterious "remainder" that can only be its essential and irreducible truth: "The real world is what is left unsaid when we have said everything. What we have said is language and the world is not language. A rock is not a word"; "signs persist in a coherence just outside the recognized dance of things."[16] This is one reason — another being his amiably iconoclastic humor — for the juxtapositions of strange situations and meetings — whether anachronistic or improbable — that are produced in his collections of stories. In the cyclical and mysterious flux of the world, the "as if" of fiction can only help inevitable parallels along, since every activity of the mind reaches out for the same fundamental questions. In a text or in a culture, all the figures of the past, speak to each other de facto. Against chaos, the dissonances, the creative spontaneity, the organicism, the classical wit of Davenport incessantly propose order, harmony, a grid, structure, geometry, an "attic" kind of cultural ecology. The masterpieces of the mind are such writings, forms, creative organizations of matter, of thought, and of language as, by bringing back to life the primitive authenticity of the archaic depths (a state of mind and not a historical moment, a place of primary principles and of fresh perceptions), grant a sort of attention to the world that saves modernity from a lethal "narcosis"; remythologizing experience gives back its numinous meaning to history.

According to Davenport, "there is nothing gained by displacing the authentic," and noninvention for him is the principle of composition. While reading his work we might think of the "logothetes" that Barthes recognizes in *Sade, Fourier and Loyola*: isolation in language combinations, resuming and reordering of signs of the real, theatricality of writing. The dialects of the logos are multiple, but it can be discovered again through the superimposition and compression of its variants. We are far from the heterogeneous, plural, centrifugal, and splintered vision that Bakhtin proposed of classical culture and especially of Antiquity and the Renaissance. The rigor of a diction devoted to high style will rid our vision of the real of the clinkers that clutter the vernacular. Davenport thus inverts the modernist logic of Williams for whom, since "bad writing is an offence against the State inasmuch as all government must be government through the word" and since "crime" blossoms as the "distortions of language" increase, it is necessary to define art as that which is "in the permanent service of the cleansing of language of all fixations on dead end stinking usages of the past."[17] On the contrary, for him, such "hygienic sanitation" means reconstructing an impoverished language by resorting to the rare word in phrasings so simple they become nearly precious. Davenport's love of the right, special, arcane word—like Alexander Theroux (*Darconville's Cat*) or like his master, Nabokov—is such that one might describe it as cataglottism, both an erotic and a linguistic term that would then simultaneously designate the particulars of a kiss and a type of linguistic sensuousness. The proof might be that the powerful eroticism of "The Dawn in Erewhon" lies especially in the rich and trembling lexical vein with which he covers and reveals the frolicking of the trio of which Adriaan van Hovendaal is the center. Without a doubt the vast culture of Davenport ironically made his ear buzz with Edward Gibbon's modest protest: "My English text is chaste and all licentious passages have been left in the obscurity of a learned tongue."[18]

Even though the language and the philosophical perspectives are dissimilar, the treatment of the life of "George Grosz" (Jaffe, *Mourning Crazy Horse*) is not without connections to Davenport's texts. The "stereoscopic" disposition in parallel fragments (at first alternating and vertical, and then in the last third, in horizontal layers) of the biographical elements and of the philosophical and critical speculations on the work and its influences translates the difficulty that is presented in linking the internal contradictions of the German painter at the same time that it illustrates the movement from cubism to expressionism, forms that were adopted by him. It is the same vast cultural meshing, but according to the writing logic of a poet who temporarily resorts to fiction to shed light on the tumultuous relations between writing and desire, that Barbara Guest puts into place in *Seeking Air* in order to make her narrator pass from the "Dark" of memory, of the unconscious, of the imagination, and of madness to the feminine "whiteness" of an appeased style, free of such weighty subjects. A language, in turns lyrical and reserved, feeds the references of fragments taken from Hölderlin or Werther, of others composed in honor of Ingres, Velázquez, or O'Keeffe, while Guest stages the progressive victory of a speech whose rights triumph after "climbing over the areas of symbolic codifying of Dark . . . jointures with the putrefying heaps of collective thought."[19]

But according to Nabokov's suggestions, others more readily highlight in their cultural kaleidoscopes the game-playing, and the exotic fabric of their references to tradition is shredded by irony. Right away, the title of *Heretical Songs* (Curtis White) speaks to the deep-seated aversion that the author feels for historical and biographical authenticity within the five short stories that make up the collection. The official tradition gets complicated by rumors about the private life of Mahler in "Mahler's Last Symphony" or of Wordsworth in "The Poet's Sister." Here, the author is worried about having "created a hateful thing: a palimpsest, perhaps, which holds beneath its thin outer tissue a mirror [. . .] reflecting whatever extravagance, whatever shameless conceit critics are capable of." "It might be that whatever there is of truth in my observations is the direct result of private passions I have nowhere mentioned."[20] Here, it is suggested that the work of Mahler be considered in the light of his relationship with Krisper, much like the relationship that brought Salieri and Mozart together. The great images of the tradition are used for disintegrating ends, but their treatment naturally refers the reader back to a reading of the present. A softer irony colors the confessions of Rossetti in "Rossetti's Blessed Lady," and in "Claude" listening to Debussy against the background of a "hullabaloo" in Montmartre (guided by White, and where La Goulue and Le Désossé appear at the sides of Béranger, Swinburne, and Satie) introduces, of course, musical dissonance, but also reveals hidden aesthetic harmony and secret personal agitations. "I have tried," says the narrator, "to do for Claude what he was never able to do for himself, to see the bottom of desire." From then on digression is the logical mode of the inquiry, "confusion [being] the very concentrated center of this story," and shakes the stability of the cultural monuments.[21] Finally, it is the very obscurity of Pietro Carnesecchi that allows White his most "heretically" audacious synthesis by making the victim, Duke Cosimo of Florence, a mix of Giordano Bruno, Savonarola, and Campanella.

Everything happens, in this type of return to the cultural tradition, as if the distich of Thomas More that Franklin Mason used as an epigraph in *Four Roses in Three Acts* served as a program for these revelatory demolitions: "You may break, you may shatter the vase, if you will. / But the scent of the roses will hang round it still."[22] Parody and pastiche are here allied to a bashing of biographical facts. Hemingway had four wives. Here, he will have them all at the same time; short respites will allow him to walk Stein's dog. The parties of Great Neck will lend their form to the receptions held by the Murphys in Paris. The entire literary and artistic personnel of the 1920s files past in this comical play, a contemporary and varied crowd exchanges impressions and introduces its friends at the moment of intermission, no one speaks unless borrowing from the style of Gertrude or of Ernest, the man whom she secretly loves. Act 2 begins: "Ladies and Gentlemen: F. Scott Fitzgerald. You certainly all know Scott. Ernest knew Scott et Scott knew Ernest. Gertrude knew Scott too. Zelda knew Scott. You are safe in saying everyone knew Scott."[23] In place of the " 'Great Scot!' Gatsby said," the reader expected comes an obvious " 'Great Gatsby!' Scott said." Should Hemingway, in his grave, think that he created the definitive parody of the world of the "party" in *The Torrents of Spring*, he had better take a second look . . .

Elsewhere as Tradition

Let us note finally that it is even a genre of the highest tradition, from Homer to Diderot and Chateaubriand via the diaries of Renaissance travelers, that is carried beyond suspicion by today's fictions which profoundly renovate its forms. The travel or adventure novel, often doubled by a spiritual quest, lends in effect its grids and framework to numerous contemporaries. The tradition of travel and adventure journalism had already spilled over into fiction with John Hoagland's *Cat Man* (1955), inaugurating an interesting game of interferences of which the best representatives are without a doubt Paul Bowles, Peter Matthiessen, and John McPhee. One might be surprised to find the names of these writers in a context of formal renovations if one did not bear in mind that the works that brought them notoriety go back to the 1950s; but the study of *At Play in the Fields of the Lord*, *Far Tortuga*, or *The Snow Leopard* by Matthiessen, or Bowles's ever barer and more limpid prose (*Up Above the World*) manifests that the geographical framework, whether primitive or exotic, of these stories is the place of existential and philosophical explorations where the nihilistic rationalism of Western culture is critiqued. The same pessimism, rendered more bitter by his most recent adventures, underlies Paul Theroux's travel novels. In truth, the tradition of going to faraway places seems to sustain its motifs today: the challenge of the American way of life and its values, the attempt to find elsewhere an authenticity that has disappeared from one's native environment. Like Bowles, John Hopkins emigrated to Morocco, and he situates *Tangier's Buzzless Flies* there; in *The Attempt*, he sends his protagonists, significantly obsessed by archaeology, to Peru. In this, these examples of quest beyond a thematics of suspicion tangentially accrue to my thesis. Borrowing from the tradition of a genre and more specific borrowing are brought together for example in *Far Tortuga* where, as in *Genoa*, both detail and the global structure refer to the Melvillian tradition, while prolonging this heritage with traces of short stories by Stephen Crane ("The Open Boat") and of *Arthur Gordon Pym.*

These departures toward the elsewhere, clearly motivated by cultural preoccupations, remain essentially classical constructions.[24] They are however complemented by recent works that make somewhat radical attempts at altering forms in order to save the possibilities of the genre from suspicion.

Supposedly retracing the path of Mungo Park toward the source of the Niger River, *Water Music* by T. Coraghessan Boyle is constructed around aesthetic rather than erudite preoccupations. The facts belong to the history of exploration, but the structure of the novel is musical just as each detail of *American Falls* (Batchelor) belongs to the Civil War without substantially hindering the contrapuntal progression of the story of the battle between the secret services of the Confederate and the Union armies. Boyle alters this verifiable historical setting according to the demands of fiction and deliberately plates it with an anachronistic language and terminology. Symmetrical structures and artificial geometries grid jungles of frenzied facts while the proliferation of the writing becomes tropical (with a wealth of parenthetical statements, digressions, narrative outgrowths, and with the luxuriance of the lexicon and of dialogues); the narrative winks ("At this juncture in the history of manners, it was considered *de rigueur* for a heroine to faint dead away when confronted with so sudden and devastating a turn of events."[25]), a shaky focalization (in turns internal and external, often flirting with metafiction), forbid the emotional investment of the reader. The diegesis extracts its vitality from an anecdotal bedrock that is alien to its progress more than from the unfolding of a quest whose results are already known. It is toward the secret source of the tale rather than toward the source of a magic river that the expedition is traveling on.

The Book of Jamaica gives Russell Banks the opportunity to dismantle the anthropological tradition of the travelogue. First by inverting the expected points of view (Johnny, come to make an inventory of the habits and the customs of the Maroons, becomes an object of interest for the population that he observes) and above all by adopting for his own narration not the causality dear to the culture of his narrator but an analogical mode that belongs to the observed culture. Circularity, symbols, returns, masks, and mirrors model the perception of a real otherwise unattainable to an alien consciousness. The ethnological story escapes the suspicion that might have been cast over it by the development of contemporary knowledge.

In Norman Lavers's *The Northwest Passage,* the technique of distancing is further refined by means of a triply layered discourse. The layering in question is visible from the very first pages on which are stacked nine successive paragraphs written in an impoverished language, evoking the signs used on computer screens, three pages of critical language, and the first pages of an eighteenth-century travel diary. Conversely, the novel is made up of a report, written down by Captain Montague in the ship's log, about the adventures of sailors who became stuck in the ice while trying to discover the "Northwest Passage"; the editorial and personal commentaries by George Herbert, a twentieth-century academic looking for work, who hopes that this study will increase his credibility; and finally the notes of a critic from the future who, discovering this attempted volume after a nuclear accident, tries to explain its contents. The three discourses, in spite of different grammars, compositional rules, and contexts, keep intersecting. They converge into a reflection on meaning and the whole can only identify the nature of the strange pleasure due to these surface variations: it is the poetic pleasure one finds in the unfolding of different textures, resulting from a concerted attention to the modulation of the forms attached to an identical subject. The cultural references are seen as programmed by a syntax, the thickness and the richness of existence are direct functions of the possibilities — variety or sameness, flexibility or stiffness — of a linguistic channel. From one text to another, it is not the language that changes, but in truth, it is nature itself, for, devoid of essence, it is only a function of the discourse that speaks it. The *mise en abîme* of the gazes and of the words that hold them is visibly laden with an impoverishment of being.

The epigraph to *A Long Desire* (Evan S. Connell): "The soul has many motions, / many gods come and go,"[26] borrowed from D. H. Lawrence, translates identically powerful reversals of consciousness. And the "Northwest Passage" is also in this book ("The Sea Must Have an Endynge") the touchstone of the "longest" of "desires": the imagination. Paracelsus, the last of the dreamers to people the pages of this uncommon work, writes ("Philippus Theophrastus Aureolus Baombastus ab Hohenheim & Co."): "The imagination produces the effect . . . [it] is like the sun, whose light cannot be touched and yet may set a house on fire. It guides man's life." "As we desire things in our hearts . . . so they appear to us in dreams" (267). Anywhere out of this world; in order to remain in it and to learn to know it. In the eleven stories that will not fail to evoke Calvino's *Invisible Cities,* Connell hesitates between erudition and fiction, just as his subject invites him to do, and takes us in the wake of those who most fervently abandoned themselves to the creative discoveries of the imaginary. Occidental and oriental "tourists" of Antiquity, explorers of the Aztec ruins, spiritual lovers wooing Atlantis, Eldorado, the Seven Cities of Cíbola, or the Indies, the "Innocents" of the celebrated "Children's Crusade," Prester John: deep in their eyes, informing the real, the never-extinguished gleam of a desire to know, or rather (even though Connell favors such an equivalence) to make the reality of the world and of interior dreams coincide. At the heart of fiction are these stories of people who tell tales and try to relive them. Coming back from his great voyage, Pytheas was ridiculed; "which does happen to storytellers" (12). Notwithstanding, their credibility is not essential and the heavily documented texts of Connell accommodate themselves to the bending of rules. Imagination invents worlds and consequently languages and it is crucial that they not be allowed to perish: "We might all have spoken a superior language in the past," Connell writes; such is his conviction and each of his works struggles to rediscover its secrets (62). The challenge of *A Long Desire* looks a little like the choice suggested by Roau d'Arundel, an Anglo-Norman translator of a crucial letter from Prester John: it offered an instructive vision of Eastern miracles; he was free to accept it as the truth or to read it for amusement; but its dreamlike quality became contagious in any case. The charm of this book, and its sumptuous writing style, could easily be analyzed; but perhaps the best way to suggest its fragrance would be to borrow from the sigh that Connell breathes at the first mention of Columbus's mother's name: "Susanna Fontanarossa. She must have been lovely, with such a name" (107).

Finally, in *The Volcanoes from Puebla* (Kenneth Gangemi), it is the very constituent linearity of the travelogue that finds itself compromised.[27] The alphabetical structure of this story about a visit to Mexico does away with the narrative in order to favor the descriptive. From "Acapulco" to "Zocalo," this memoir abandons its superficial sequentialities in order to focus memory on the vignettes that, even though they echo from place to place, remain for all that discrete. The "village" where the narrator will stay remains undefined to the end; its unelucidated mystery replaces all narrative springs. Direct, down-to-earth, objective, or steeped in personal feeling, the style of these fragments taken separately does not seem a priori to favor a critique of the genre, even though the lists that often fill them make fun of the great pirating of images. But the alphabet in its silent ineluctability favors the ironical proximities and the delightful equalization of references, icons, and themes. *Goats* are placed side by side with girls, tequila follows Tehuantepec, eggs scoff at education, and cattle at cathedrals. As for the rest, arbitrariness has its limits; it only needs to modify a subtitle to bring about the most disturbing parallels. Each one of these isolated vignettes corresponds in a quasi-metafictional fashion to an instruction guide for the reader, one judiciously suggested in the last sentence of the book that concludes the fragment (after the one dedicated to Zapata and to zapote) where the square, the Zocalo, in Mexico, is described: "It is a good place for the traveler to sit and rest."[28]

Therefore, a brief pause . . .

Chapter 12
Cultural Tradition and the Present II: The Everyday and Mass Culture

> Shams and delusions are esteemed for soundest truths, while reality is fabulous. If men would steadily observe realities only, and not allow themselves to be deluded, life, to compare it with such things we know, would be like a fairy tale and the Arabian Nights Entertainments.
> — Thoreau, *Walden*

. . . interrupted by the need to return to the images and noises of the everyday and the ordinary.

The work of Evan S. Connell invites such shuttling: profoundly marked by high culture (in *Notes from a Bottle Found on the Beach at Carmel*), in the reflections on art (in *The Connoisseur*), and his attempt to reorient cultural fragments (in *Points for a Compass Rose*), it also questions the deadly routines of the everyday in *Mrs. Bridge* and *Mr. Bridge*. In these two novels, 117 and 142 maliciously titled fragments lend the irony of formal realism to the explosion of the mediocre lives of two respectable Midwestern citizens. The unity of these fragments depends solely on the fact that the events reported there happen to the same people, almost as though by accident. Conventions, conformism, Puritanism, self-repression; ennui, unease, solitude: something there recalls Grant Wood and Sinclair Lewis. A form that owes them nothing nonetheless adds to highly personal ironies: these dry reports on *habits,* adopted by the Bridges as a chosen way of life in order to paper over their dissatisfaction and difficulty in living, reveal, through the fragmentation of the paragraphs, the horrible cracks in these two lives.

Questionable Morals

We approach here a sharp dividing line between the novels of manners by authors who found their style in the forties and fifties, whose work is

little suited to aesthetic suspicion, and those modes of literary exploitation of an existential unease more characteristic of the period under
study. For this reason, we shall not consider works by novelists of manners
such as Updike, except to point out that the chronological spacing (*Rabbit, Run,* 1960; *Rabbit Redux,* 1971; *Rabbit Is Rich,* 1981; *Rabbit at Rest,* 1990)
of the regular updates of Updike's anthologies of ideas enables us to
perceive more and more clearly but less and less convincingly the personal fate of the author, his doubts (*Bech: A Book,* 1970), and his satisfactions (*Bech Is Back,* 1982). The work is now little more than an existential
barometer calibrated in accordance with the times; it withers into the
testimonies of a talented Cartesian imp which one awaits without surprise, with the regularity of a moral health report. After a while, such
everydayness, feebly transmuted by the banal fantasies of the American
male, his uneasily enthusiastic hedonism and rehashed religious scruples, ends up boring the reader (*Couples, The Witches of Eastwick*).

Bellow makes use of the everyday in the mode of *contemptus mundi* (*Mr.
Sammler's Planet*); his aim is not to identify the buds of promise to be
found in the changes undergone by a world in labor, but rather to denounce, in the name of traditional humanism, the disintegration of the
urban social fabric that is familiar to him. This is indicative, as is the
case for Roth, Mailer, and others, of a moralist conception of the novel
of manners that postulates that morals are signs of energies buried
within the psyche, a kind of "emotional lava," as has been said by Mark
Schechner, or symptoms, at the very least. Yet, one is quite free, conversely, to consider this genre as a privileged site for exploring a "depsy-
chologization of signs," or indeed an inversion of the connections between individual and collective psychology and social semiotics. Seen in
this light, the distraction of pathetic, laughable, repulsive, or lost characters would thus be due to the message/massage of signs lacking both
substance and coherence, with cultural and social drift no longer being
read as the sum of individual failings but as the effect of the disconcerting
inflation of signs, at best manipulated, at worst meaningless. Fiction's
more or less great attraction to the social scene, and the pluralism of
forms engaged in studying it, would then be a direct function of the
various modes of perceiving its functioning.

One Never Dips Twice in the Same Ink

Nabokov could already claim that the word "reality" had no meaning
when stripped of the quotation marks that always qualify it, whether
implicit or not. For having been read outside of its own logic, the fiction
of the sixties and seventies was too quickly judged to be evasive, divorced
from reality. Moreover, there has never been a lack of writers tempted by

the "resocialization" of fiction — whether they subscribe to Bellow's condemnations or, more generously, try to point out glimpsed possibilities. But such a move or refocusing of the gaze onto the everyday world beyond the page should not be likened to a "return" to some sort of neorealism: because reality has changed, it can no longer offer comparable points of attack. In addition, works build up traces, erecting their previous paths into insurmountable barriers for those who might dream of such hypothetical "returns."

After several decades during which the "everyday world" was above all presented as an ambiguous artifact, as the moving and enigmatic flux of information, stimuli, words, and images, whose meaning was suspect or uncertain, pushed to the edge of the unknowable and for which fiction's task was to provide temporary forms (cf. McElroy's *A Smuggler's Bible*), no distancing from "fabulation" can ignore the debt owed to it. As the years went by, the various distances traveled away from the dominant mode of "serious" fiction were, partially and in various modes, informed by this.

Certainly, in works by minority writers, in the stories of Grace Paley, or in the works of artists who depict the margins, social critique no longer takes the same textual forms to which we had become accustomed between the 1930s and the 1950s; nor does the presentation of everyday experiences as influenced by race, sex, and geographical environment. The most daring formal advances, including the treatment of conventional themes, are apparently irreducible. In a word, if the marginality of the sixties denounces the dominant culture with a virulence that reminds us of Flaubert's vituperation against the "turd-shaped" bourgeois (see Chapter 3); if the fascination with place informs regionalist writings as strongly as it could inform the writings of a time in which "sectionalism" still marked American literature, if feminism and the struggle for ethnic equality prolong the analyses set forth in the past, we should not conclude for all this that nothing has really changed. The observations and denunciations of the real usually make the most of all the new weapons; only a peculiar formal myopia could make one read Reed and Baldwin, William Kennedy and James T. Farrell, Grace Paley and Dorothy Parker, Michael Martone and Sherwood Anderson, or Jim Harrison and Hemingway with the simple transparency of reproductions. Perhaps, for economy's sake, certain modulations could be suggested by means of several quotations. For tone, we have Paley's comment in "Dreamer in a Dead Language": "Had she been born ten, fifteen years later, she might have done so, screamed and screamed. Instead, tears made their usual protective lenses for the safe observation of misery."[1] For the situation of the writer facing the everyday, we have Vonnegut's remark in *Mother Night*: "The part of me that wanted to tell the truth got turned into an expert liar! The lover in me got turned into a pornographer! The artist in me got turned into ugliness such as the world has rarely seen before."[2] For the basic differences in writing, finally, we have the strange sensation that once seized the traveler in Samuel Butler's *Erewhon*: "He brought a book with him, and pens and paper — all very English; and yet, neither paper, nor printing, nor binding, nor pen, nor ink, were quite the same as ours."[3]

Let us read, in an instructive disorder, the abrasive pages of John Rechy (*City of Night, Numbers*) and Hubert Selby (*Last Exit to Brooklyn*) on the jungle of cities, William Kittredge's dreamlike visions on the rural Northwest (*The Van Gogh Field*), the sudden appearances of the inconceivable at the heart of the everyday in Rachel Ingalls's *Mrs. Caliban*, the renewed picaresque of the transcontinental journey of Carol Sturm Smith (*Fat People*), the harrowing (Raymond Carver), grotesque (*Fat Woman*, Leon Rooke), or naive intimacy (*The Beans of Egypt, Maine*, Carolyn Chute) of fictions dealing with the underprivileged classes while awaiting a naturalism that has become unusable: let us read, and we shall see that strangeness has penetrated surface realism, as we assess formal evolutions; and we shall understand that such recourses to the familiar consistently privilege the obscure and fantastic hidden within the everyday, avoid immediate and closed representations, call into question language's capacity to ensnare the most banal of subjects. In the field of the thematics of the everyday, this repeats a break observed by Valéry in his own time:

Much modern literature sets out to communicate, not the final state of impressions, the state when the author has grasped, sorted out and tidied up his data, but the preliminary state, in which he still needs to understand and has failed to catch up with the initial stimulus; the state in which everything is problematic, confused, sentimental, and sensorial. Instead of writing formulas these authors record data in terms of what the mathematician calls "virtual functions," somewhat as modern definitions are couched in the form of independent postulates and no longer in a single sentence. (Much as in music).[4]

We shall turn now to detailing the polarities between which these fictions of the everyday fan out, fictions in which the essential hides at the heart of the trivial.

Minimalisms?

If one adhered to a vision of literary history that integrates the notion of the avant-garde and worships the "new" at all cost, the label of "minimalists" affixed on a new generation of writers would surely designate the "state-of-the-art" of our period. The most striking "evolutive" contrast could be read by shuttling between the pages of three anthologies published by the Brooklyn Fiction Collective (*Statements I*, 1975; *Statements II*, 1977; and *American Made*, 1986) and those of *Matters of Life and Death* as chosen by Tobias Wolff.[5] Not that a certain amount of overlapping is entirely absent there. Barry Hannah and Stanley Elkin figure in the summary of the latter, and all the short stories of the other three do not demonstrate as great a concern for formal innovation. Still, in their introductions, Sukenick, Coover, and Larry McCaffery, in the name of the Fiction Collective, advance assertions that are clearly influenced by suspicion, whereas Wolff, who even dismisses irony, presents authors who for the most part rethematize their fiction quite classically and take very seriously their mimetic exploration of these "matters of life and death." In the case of innovative literature, such questions were tied to the dangers of a writing at the limits of the expressible; for this new wave, they are tied to everyday existence and the difficulty of being.

Since literature always lags one war behind the plastic arts, the fiction invited for criticism the transfer of a name reserved in the 1970s for the artists seen as heirs to a part of the modernist tradition: that of Malevich and his "white square," of course, that of Gropius, Mies van der Rohe, Giacometti, and Brancusi, all thought to be at the origin of the famous line "Less is more." The fact that Robert Browning is its real author — as Barth has pointed out[6] — does not alter the idea in any way. "Minimalism" would do the trick for a literary journalism in need of categories. Nevertheless, as one might expect, nothing is as simple as that which a generic label tries to designate globally. The confusion, the careless groupings, and the misunderstandings engendered by such shorthand deserve some clarification.

Raymond Carver is the writer whose impact is most felt here. Pulled from the oblivion to which a difficult existence, devoted mostly to poetry, had confined him for years, he was brought to light by *Will You Please Be Quiet, Please?*; he is considered the leader of a spectacular taking of distance with regard to the "experimental" — an unappealing and marginalizing term — fiction of the sixties and seventies. However, it can also be said of his body of work, closed henceforth, that it illustrates a proven tradition of direct economy of writing (diversely illustrated from William Carlos Williams and Hemingway to Brautigan, Bukowski, and Paley), that it modifies this tradition by means of a personal element from which innovation is not absent, that it manages to crystallize a tendency that bears only slight resemblance to it, that it stresses finally — and once again — that one should not judge an entire genre, but the quality of its individual exploitation. Why is Carver dressed as a "minimalist"? He distrusts, in fact, "tricks" of the pen, or what he calls literary "gadgets," embellishments, or "useless" games. This man, who admitted plainly that he had confined himself to the short poem and the short story because life — fierce almost to the end where he was concerned — had never granted him enough time to write anything longer, gets straight to the point. If literature, to take up recognizable pairs, can be divided into "putter-inners" and "leaver-outers," Carver surely belonged to the second group. His short stories are the site of absences, hollow presentations, kingdoms of ellipsis. Unease, the ominous, and a diffuse sense of threat define the morality of these works. His stories tend to be organized around an initial hole, an absence of explicit cause, an ambiguous, undeveloped fact. Waves radiate from a point of impact that their concentricity allows the reader roughly to situate, but we never see the stone hit the water. Carver builds on these territories of the indefinite, full of "its" and "things," with the simplest of materials. Metaphor has been driven out; dialogues are impoverished, such is the precision with which Carver reproduces the voice of these men and women whose language has been stolen, the characters are barely sketched physically, descriptions are limited. As is the case for Grace Paley, who despises them, transitions are often absent, leaving only the juxtaposition of scenes and remarks to suggest the changes and the logic of the developments. Carver summed up his sense of economy — that he claimed came from Chekhov and Pound as much as from Hemingway — in a striking formula: "Get in. Get out. Don't linger. Go on."[7] Clearly, the switches from which the term "minimalist" was woven can easily be found in his work: they have been used to castigate it or, by contrast, to ward off its detractors.

It would be a mistake, however, to see in this master of the art of "reserve"[8] someone who, *a minima,* merely stages the little disturbances of trivial surfaces. It is, as he said,[9] "things that are left out" that give the sense of menace or of nascent communication to the stories of his first collection, those of *What We Talk About When We Talk About Love,* or those, gentler and as though moving toward reconciliation, of *Cathedral.* But, just as Stevens's "The Snow Man" shows us "nothing that is not there and the nothing that is," broad disturbing spaces are subtly revealed here. The art of the unsaid, of the implicit paints "the landscape just under the smooth (but sometimes broken or unsettled) surface of things." Carver does not allow his gaze to slide over these glazes; he penetrates them and performs, like the best fiction in his opinion, "a bringing of the news from one world into another."[10] From this point of view, the delicate balance created by Carver between the spoken and the unspoken suggests that, if "minimalism" is to mean something for contemporary fiction, it can only mean to his ever more numerous epigones that one runs enormous risks in doing *less well* than one's master.

More difficult to imitate, one might think that Carver were to escape if not the tragedy of a foreshortened life, at least the artistic tragedy suffered by his master Hemingway, one so well analyzed by Cyril Connolly as lacking: "the diversifying resources necessary to a quick distantiation from his imitators." For Carver's followers have mostly retained from his work the surface effects, the work on reflection, the absence of explicit commentary and the apparent absence of narrative engagement in order to make of him their flag bearer. Much could be said about the ideological and material environment that has sustained and welcomed these epigones[11] and has caused so many pseudo-Carvers to appear on publishers' desks, just as the 1920s brought pseudo-Fitzgeralds and pseudo-Hemingways, and the 1960s delivered pseudo-Barths and pseudo-Barthelmes. Under the pretext that Carver managed to do so much with so little, those who are wrongly lumped under the term "minimalists" have channeled into their prose certain reluctances of which Barth has made a list: reluctance to confront openly the traumas of recent national memory (Vietnam . . .), reluctance toward "expenditure," socially demonstrated by the "conservationism" born of the energy crisis, reluctance to force a public increasingly unwilling to read to undertake long and difficult investments, and, finally, reluctance toward intellectual and critical distance, irony, and the density of the masters of metafiction. The term merely manages to ease the lives of census-takers who are little inclined to consider the works for their respective merits. But a whole gamut of expressions has sought to account for this collective withdrawal into the nearby, the immediate, and the daily: "dirty realism," "brand-name fiction," "pop realism," "coke" (or "diet pepsi") fiction, "high-tech fiction" . . .

Briefly stated, the works of Tobias Wolff, Ann Beattie, John L'Heureux, Jayne Anne Philipps, Bobbie Ann Mason, Alice Adams, Elizabeth Tallent, Mary Robison, and Frederick Barthelme share a common trait in that they are characterized by a certain surface sameness, by "subjects" chosen from everyday life, narrators little inclined to commit themselves, plots lacking major complications and handled in a smooth tone, and by characters whose personal reflections are but rarely revealed to the reader. With "minimalist" art, they most certainly share a refusal of commentary, of investment, of complicity. The difference becomes glaring as soon as they are compared to the unapologetic narrators/commentators of Barth, Sorrentino, or Coover, to their taste for digression and irony, to the stress they place on linguistic effects, and their generalized reflexiveness. No closer to mass culture than to intellectual culture, these novels and short stories insist on the *communication* that fiction allows (even by means of the implicit and the unspoken), they are little concerned with causes, are loathe to comment, and *present* the real as it reaches them with a certain passivity: is this the effect or the reflection of the heightened privatization of perceptions of the world, and of the reluctance to integrate a reflection on the state of the public sphere, sometimes described as typical of the Reagan era? There would be no point in choosing between these possibilities. Let us merely note, with sympathy, a falsely candid remark made by Robert Coover, who, when asked to give his opinion on this tendency, declared quite plainly that he did not have any firm opinion, but that "if any aspect of his work had been described in the terms [this tendency] had been, [he would] be ashamed."[12] We shall make his prudence ours, for it would be absurd to dismiss an important segment of these literary creations under the pretext that they have been oversimplified and qualified to excess, reduced to a set of interchangeable parameters.

Frederick Barthelme has managed to make a first name for himself, just as Steve, Donald's other brother, is in the process of doing. It is not insignificant that he has been involved with "conceptual" art, nor that he has worked in advertising. The characters in his novels (*Second Marriage, Tracer, Two Against One*) and of his short stories (*Moon Deluxe*), following the example of their creator, take pleasure and consolation in the artifacts of consumer society. At their most convincing, his pages make palpable the threatening strangeness of the banal, make emerge from beneath the greasy, plastic surfaces of fast-food restaurants or from beneath the steel, copper, and smoked glass surfaces of offices and deluxe hotels a deep uneasiness, indeed, an anguish, that are, in turn, projected onto the characters and reflected back by what befalls the environment and the minimal "relations" that remain possible there. "The Nile," which is the condominium in *Second Marriage,* somewhat like the one depicted by Elkin in *Searches and Seizures,* is no more than the architectural representation of the kitschy, superficial souls that inhabit it. But, whereas Elkin transmutes the horror by means of sumptuous metaphorical writing, Frederick Barthelme's writing offers surfaces that are just as mediocre as the ones it reflects. The very title of *Chroma* declares their quality. Reading it, we are reminded, in spite of ourselves, of the remark made by the narrator of Richard Ford's *The Sportswriter:* "Her nature is to put her faith in objects more than essences. And in most ways that makes her the perfect companion."[13]

Carver's texts evoke Hopper or the canvases of Neil Welliver, which, although apparently realist and figurative, borrow their technique and their gestures from the abstract expressionists; they also bring to mind the strategies of certain hyperrealists (Richard Estes or Alfred Leslie) that hold our attention by means of their framing technique and make the spectator wonder about what might be hovering around a center that has systematically defused its surprises. However "accidental" the circumstances that led Ann Beattie to devote a book to the painter Alex Katz (1987), the relationship between their bodies of work is nonetheless a suggestive one: scenes from the lives of comfortable urbanites in their suburban homes, tinged with a diffuse feeling of uneasiness, flat even tints, thin watery colors, a distribution upon the canvas that results in innuendo and focuses on essential trivialities, a frequent recourse to reserve that simultaneously signals the osmosis of meager settings and futile characters, and confesses an awareness of devices that make it impossible to acquiesce to an absolute mimetism. The protagonists of the talented Ann Beattie are not only hippies who cleaned up their act in the seventies, chilly refugees from the counterculture (*Chilly Scenes of Winter*), nor the unconfident yuppies of the eighties (*Falling in Place*), but, it has been said, "nummies" (not-so-young-urban-malcontents), or "dinks" (double income, no kids), stockholders in what has been called "Irony and Pity, Inc." From *The New Yorker*, where she first published the stories collected in *Distortions, Secrets and Surprises* and *Where You'll Find Me*, Beattie has borrowed the slightly cold, sophisticated writing, the knowing and often disillusioned humor, the display of luxury products for which ads haunt the margins and determine the layout of the texts. She thus prolongs John Updike's study of middle-class milieus and adopts his eddy-free prose.

Perhaps the best way to consider the profound transformation suggested by "minimalism" appears within a cutting opposition proposed by Kim Herzinger: "Where the traditional 'realists' had a world and used a complex of ideas and emotions . . . to describe it, the 'minimalists' have a complex of ideas and emotions . . . which they use the world to describe."[14] The difference is due to the legacy left by earlier innovative attempts: in works by the best writers, language has lost its naive transparency, and Phillips or Mason testify to its opaque use in the service of a disturbing baroque (*Black Tickets*) or of discrete evocations of the past by means of play on the texture of voices (*Shiloh*); these techniques are revealed to be convincing but they strongly resist longer applications. Neither Phillips nor Mason has fully succeeded in the detour into novels, de facto imposed upon them by the deserved success of their short stories. The short format seems generally — and logically — better suited for this group of authors. Tobias Wolff's *In The Garden of the North American Martyrs* is more convincing than *The Barracks Thief*; the stories of *Back in the World*, whose title could serve as Wolff's manifesto, testify to the best qualities of a writer tuned in to the secrets lurking beneath appearances.

We find here unexpected signs of the journey beyond suspicion: once the time of sustained efforts to dismantle referential illusions and to demystify writing and reading has passed, everything seems to become possible again, including a return to familiar loci of the novel: plot, characters, setting, and conventions of representation. Since no one remains the dupe of such devices, the invitation to earlier complicities can be made in terms that have become new while remaining identical. As Herzinger argues: "We *know* what stories and characters are made of, and, knowing that, 'ordinary' things-in-the-world could again be talked of with as much assurance as anything else."[15] Such a position would nonetheless demand that such transitions occur within the mind of an up-to-date public that has followed the stages step by step. Should this not be the case, it might not only appear that nothing has changed at all but also that certain texts seem to have learned nothing from fictional developments that preceded more recent adventures in writing. This is what renders an increasing segment of fashionable novel production rather suspect from an aesthetic and, strictly speaking, a fictional point of view. One unquestionably drops in qualitative level when turning to the seemingly indistinguishable works of David Leavitt, Jay McInerney, Brett Easton Ellis, Emily Prager, or Tama Janowitz; all of these authors represent, to a greater or lesser extent, a prose in which linguistic work has been forsaken in favor of the doubtful pleasures of a reputedly "immediate" presentation; the desire to reshape the perception of facts and causes now gives way to the various surrenders of a politics of form based on reflection and effect; the high-tech gloss of an "artistic" world has seen the studios that produce it move from Greenwich Village down to Soho, as if to demonstrate the strength of Wall Street's attraction. In every meaning of the word, these works evoke a world of "show."

It is not only that we pass, as far as atmosphere is concerned, from the antiestablishment era of the hippies of the sixties and seventies to the acceptance of the world as it is by yuppies worried about social success and enmeshed in their cynical certainties. The problem is not only that the ephemeral brilliance of mediatic welcomes has replaced the distrust and invective with which works of literary experimentation were received, that book parties for artists lost in the noise of discotheques — where, fortunately, one can no longer hear oneself think — have replaced openings and receptions where at least some spirited discussion of the works hanging on the walls floated over the cocktails. It is, more precisely, that these unangry young authors seem to worry no more about writing than they would about their first computer, that, instead of the easy rides of the sixties, they propose their easy reads for the end of our century. On the whole, what we have is a set of vaguely anorexic stories that do not take any risk, that, to take up Adorno's critique, offer themselves as "distractions" from both boredom and everyday toil. In that way, they themselves become the "slaves of New York," whose puny adventures Tama Janowitz describes for us: indentured to a counterfeit flashy reality, whose powers they either no longer choose or are able to call into question imaginatively, slaves to the same demand as that which makes for the success of good designers and trendy nightclubs. Reading them, one is reminded of the "caterpillar pluckers" and "echo tinkerers" reviled by René Char.

Not so long ago, Alfred Appell could explain that, in *Lolita*, Nabokov succeeded better than any other American novel in showing the many ways in which songs, ads, magazines and the movies manage to create and control their consumers. May Appell forgive me, but since that time many a dollar has flowed down Madison Avenue, and for the "chic," "with it" fiction of these last years, the order of the day involves fighting over the places closest to the trough. Nabokov brilliantly manipulated the dross; the admirable James Purdy condemns the vulgarities of a culture shaped by advertising; Brautigan, Swigart, and Stanley Crawford make us laugh with their inflatable landscapes (*Trout Fishing in America*) and their hollow signs that have replaced beings and objects (*Little America, Gascoyne*); DeLillo, who practices an art that we could call martial in order to underline its techniques, rechannels the energy and power of the media and their massage; as for the writers whom Jo Bellamy calls our "literary Republicans," they offer the artificiality of their world for strict consumption rather than proposing to critical intelligence the artifices of all real creation. Even Tom Wolfe, the ex-"new journalist" from whom they borrow their taste for an ontology of the "life-style," once defamiliarized the banalities of the everyday by means of his linguistic inventions. The "orchestration of platitudes" dear to Thornton Wilder managed to make a certain music heard; "yuppie fiction" no longer makes us hear anything other than the sighs of the affluent.

"Conservative chic" echoes the "radical chic" of earlier times. It is a matter, as Charles Newman tells us, of "the classic response of conservatives to the phenomenon of inflation, underuse of potentials, stock reduction, verbal unemployment."[16] People always argue less with photographers than with painters, and Warhol at least *dared*. With "yuppie" prose, the question no longer obtains of the eventual moves from modernism to another phase. In their case, "postmodernism" is understood in its flattest ornamental meaning: a commodified "postmodern" of shopping malls and trinkets, producer of amusing brightly colored, incongruously shaped but soulless objects like the ones shoppers fight over on Amsterdam and Columbus Avenues, objects that flaunt, like these books, their translucency, covered in vermiform plastic, made of degraded and nondegradable materials, sad ludic crutches for the blasé and the bored. If it were not immoral to take from charity in order to give to theory, the title of Brett Easton Ellis's *Less Than Zero* might perversely invite us to see in it a metafictional confession. The passage of the train-station novel to the dime-store novel is a total success. Ben Yagoda has emphasized its inadequacies,[17] Barth has demonstrated the planetary distance that separates it from the infinitely more serious and coherent "minimalisms" of Newman, Stella, and Beckett;[18] let us add that there exists as great a distance between current minimalisms and the stunning economies of writers as different as Carver, Donald Barthelme, or Richard Brautigan. A reminder, in case we needed one, of what separates asceticism from indigence.

Critique of Everyday Life

William S. Wilson has proposed the following analysis of Ann Beattie's style:

Irony, that annihilates appearances in the name of a higher reality, implies a larger distance between surface and depth than Beattie can afford; so that she tears down the structure of implications that constitute the necessary bedrock of irony and indulges in ironies on irony itself.[19]

Consistent, for a "minimalist" who fears the corrosive effects of irony on surfaces isolating from the true questions posed by the real, such a strategy is not the only possibility when faced with the threats of the quotidian. Donald Barthelme, an "ironist saved from drowning,"[20] shows that, even though it moves one away from realism, irony is not a bad option. His entire body of work illustrates John Ashbery's line by broaching the "surface that is not superficiality but visible core."

In an interview, McElroy testifies to having once heard Grace Paley introduce Donald Barthelme as a "reporter and a poet":

Sounded odd, but maybe she meant that Donald in a way records daily life (reports back) while at the same time, in the midst of our debasement of language and the feelings and thoughts that language is supposed to help us to have, he leads us to hold to our language, like our honor.[21]

Surprising, of course, since although he wrote four novels (*Snow White, The Dead Father, Paradise,* and *The King*), Donald Barthelme was above all a short story writer whose novels could legitimately be considered montages or developments of his stories. After 1964, he published nine collections of short texts. *Sixty Stories* and *Forty Stories* form a kind of anthology, chosen by their author, of the publications that meant the most to him. Among his books, one is for children (*The Slightly Irregular Fire-Engine*), and another, *Guilty Pleasures,* groups together texts midway between fiction and social commentary, satires, parodies, montages mocking various aspects of American culture. The major irony of Barthelme's work is the fact that he always published in *The New Yorker.* Barthelme was like the worm at the core of this Big Apple institution, the bacillus within Koch's city, the sophisticated voice that lent its subversive intonations to *City Life* and to its *Sadness.*

For these stories, published in the pages of a magazine chock full of the products of postindustrial society, constitute a prolonged meditation on what Barthelme has termed "junk," trash, the great bazaar of soulless consumption. Sometimes composed of texts and of images that are not "illustrations," the stories send back an echo of the mixture of advertising icons and texts that surrounds them and which provides the space on which they appear. "Unspeakable practices," or "unnatural acts," it is no doubt the unexpected and artificial aspects of his "intermedia" practice that first grab our attention. His father was an architect, follower of the great modernists of his art, and he himself did layouts for magazines, having, according to his own admission, always harbored the dream of becoming a painter. Barthelme is most fascinated by the rubbish of our consumer culture, by the garbage of a post-Gutenberg world, by that which our world both feeds upon and destroys itself by. We are surrounded by metastases of images and signs, the language is gangrened by intransitiveness and by the evanescence of dialogues in which one can no longer read anything more than a vague and ritual exchange value. Barthelme has provided a name, "dreck," and a translation in his fiction, for the debris of our civilization, to these disconnected tatters of language: references to everyday objects abound there, as do those to brand names, to the fragments of matter and of discourse with which the West doggedly persists in furnishing the world. In general, his short stories are vast collages of discourse and of objects, a salmagundi of styles, fragments, and quotations that are either explicit or stolen from the communal intertext; irony and parody are their dominant modes. The choice of values can be read under the complex working of stylistic valences. But it is less a matter of the modernist vision of *Stilmischung* according to Auerbach than the result of a slightly desperate belief: the variety and abundance of this world are at once a form of plenitude and the sign of its absence, the proliferation of signs and of things does not necessarily make sense. As Molesworth writes:

The realm of brand names, historical allusions, "current events," and fashionable topics exists in a world whose fullness results from the absence of any strong hierarchical sense of values, and the casual randomness of such things both blurs and signals how any appeal to a rigorous, ordering value system would be futile.[22]

So that, contemplating ruins and disorder (a thematic concern illustrated by Steiner, Percy, Wurlitzer, or Hawkes), Barthelme began to think that a certain benefit might be found in their assembly and their collage. Even if this may mean becoming the victim of a culture's castoffs, one might as well organize them and make of them grist for one's critical mill. Barthelme thus proposes to deal with the "leading edge of the trash phenomenon."[23] If cities can be heated with everything their inhabitants throw out, why might one not find a similar energy in the rubbish heaps of language and iconography? If high art is always the replacement of indifference by attention, as Davenport contends, it is always possible to devote oneself, as Walker Percy recommends in his turn, to "dialectical tastings of the familiar,"[24] to recycle rejects, to make them once again into objects worthy of interest, to recompose them and to give them back some meaning through art.

Thus César crushes the dead carcasses of cars, and Californians build statues out of whatever drifts the tide has brought in. Perhaps the function of the artist in this context is as Ezra Pound defined it in "Hugh Selwyn Mauberley": "wringing lilies from the acorn."[25] Yet it would be pointless and, no doubt, wrong to see in these examples of epistemological and moral uncertainty the renewal, or the renewed prolongation, of the aesthetic questions posed by modernism. The tears that easily well up in the eyes of the characters of Barthelme's stories ("Views of My Father Weeping" [*City Life*], for example) do recall the angst provoked in the moderns by the effects of the First World War and by the shattering of the certainties of the West as it left behind forever a less complex world; but the texture of Barthelme's writings forces us to ask whether it results from having granted all cultural seriousness a kind of playful recess, or from the reformulation of modernist preoccupations under parodied forms, whether these stories only constitute a kind of "revisited" modernism, or are the products of an art that only owes part of its effects to modernism. One certainly finds in his works the same desire to present rather than to interpret or express, to show rather than tell, but this desire is reduced to the absurd. His "minimalism" owes more to Beckett than to the writers we have just mentioned. A new sense of parody is added to the modernist feel for collage, and the recognition of the death of a genre is accompanied by its recreation according to new terms. Whereas the modernist short story willingly closes in on itself and becomes self-referential, the texts of Barthelme do not share this confidence in themselves or in their power. No resolution crowns a practice that is surely autonomous but that self-destructs through the distance between its formal elements, the recourse to antithesis, to paradox, to internal contradiction, to dead-end dialogues. To quote Barthes, meaning is "suspended," and to borrow another analysis, that which is called into question is the very possibility of the symbolic process.[26]

In the sixties, seventies, and eighties, the textual collages of Pound, Joyce, and Eliot, the iconic collages of Braque, Ernst, and Gris, of the constructivists or of Picasso, the montages of Griffith, Eisenstein, and Dos Passos can no longer produce the same effects nor carry the same meanings. Nonetheless, Barthelme does not dismiss the principles that had inspired them. The dislocation of the contemporary real is no less great, the imaginary museum has not been reduced; what has changed is that what appeared to the moderns as rupture and scandal, deep abnormality, break, loss of cultural and social values, eventually appeared, with the advent of the sixties, as the equivalence of a new world of awareness, as norm, as an averred modality of being. Nostalgia for the lost unity of the world, of narratives, and of literary forms is perhaps not lessened, the longing for wholeness is hardly less idealized. Yet the fragmentation of the social eventually allows only for recourse to degraded forms. Collage is then no longer an attempt to reconstitute a whole whose value was confirmed both by an aesthetic gesture and by the reference to a possible unity—whether it limited itself to the singularity of myth or to the irre-fragable presence of the work—but a means of simultaneously declaring one's desire for this unity and one's awareness of the impossibility ever to find it. Barthelme's short stories present themselves as empty, conventional, and arbitrary forms that provide sanctuary for fragments of other forms that are not necessarily borrowed from the same field (news, fairy tales, advertisements, shreds of dialogues culled from the street and from living rooms). In this way, the text forces together discourses reputed to be incompatible, the voice carries mutually hostile tones, and a plastic approach to the written will quite naturally come to be coordinated with the use of images that are no longer "extratextual" since they make up an important part of the "text" itself.

In an interview, Barthelme employs an image that helps us to understand the nature of his enterprise:

Barnacles growing on a wreck or a rock. I'd rather have a wreck than a ship that sails. Things attach themselves to wrecks. Strange fish find your wreck or rock to be a good feeding ground; after a while you've got a situation with possibilities.[27]

This vision of a shelter-structure that provides a refuge for a thousand species evokes the produced effect quite well. In the final analysis, there is no qualitative difference between the devices Barthelme uses to produce a text and those that make room for the image at the heart of written texts: the embedding of varied discursive structures at the heart of an arbitrary matrix is comparable. Barthelme's text is always a collage, but we do not need to give the term its strictest iconic dimension here: the cliché, the fragment of accepted discourse is always already an icon. The paratactic series that constitute "The Rise of Capitalism" testify to this ("My daughter demands more Mr. Bubble for her bath. The shrimp boats lower their nets. A book called *Humorists of the XVIIIth Century* is published . . ."); so do the final lines of "The Viennese Opera Ball":

More than six hundred different kinds of forceps have been invented. Let's not talk about the lion, she said. Wilson looked over at her without smiling and now she smiled at him. This process uses a Lincoln submerged arc welding head to run both inside and outside beads automatically. The rate of progress during the first stage will determine the program to be followed in the second stage. The *Glamour* editor whose name was Titti Beale "moved in." What's your name girl? she said coolly. Carola Mitt, Carola Mitt said. The Viennese Opera Ball continued.[28]

The very title of the collection in which this story figures is a montage: *Come Back, Dr. Caligari* at once recalls *Come Back, Little Sheba* by the dramatist William Inge and the film that made the "doctor" famous. Barthelme produces his texts through a systematic rape of conventions and rules, whether technical principles or untouchable logics, taking metaphors and semantic rules absolutely literally. Thus "the hospital refused to give him a disease"[29] results from a logical inversion; "The bull begins to ring, like a telephone,"[30] an apparently surrealist sentence is "naturally" engendered by the pun on "ring"; a sentence like "A number of nightingales with traffic lights tied to their legs flew past me"[31] owes its existence to something Nabokov called "the great somehow of dreams." "The New Music" fearlessly announces: "Went to the grocery store and Xeroxed a box of English muffins, two pounds of ground veal and an apple. In flagrant violation of the copyright act."[32] This violation, as we can see, is not the only one: Barthelme is bent on cutting off all possibilities of agreement between the objects of this world and the usual logic that tries to order them, convinced that the reigning "order" is not much superior. Objects only agree according to the laws of a language whose semantics has been devastated by careless and imprudent use, of which there remains only the crumpled corset of a syntax that no longer knows which poor old verbal flesh to hold.

Voracity and Veracity

In *Some Instructions to My Wife,* Stanley Crawford gives the floor to an accomplished paranoiac, a sort of cross between Kosinski's Mr. Chance and a lightning-struck Benjamin Franklin whose lists of "things to do" were proliferating out of control. The maniacal discourse that borrows from gardening all of the mad allegories that organize these instructions digs down to the most trivial recesses of the everyday. The metaphorical logic of a logophagous madman keeps converting the real. The texts of Stanley Elkin and of Max Apple do not possess this crazed character's sick fascination with a universe whose inventory would channel the threatening diversity. In Elkin's works, the approach to the everyday swings from "less is more" to the resounding utterance of a convinced "more is more and less is less." For him, as for Charles Newman, veracity is always inferior in its effects to voracity, and, as Alexander Theroux has Dr. Crucifer say in *Darconville's Cat,* "nothing exceeds like excess."[33]

Saturating the text with images in *A Bad Man* and *The Franchiser,* where Elkin exploits the world of commerce, allows us to read the beauties of the real, to redeem its flat appearances in order to give them meaning in a new key. His business, as Frank Kermode would put it, is to conduct readers outside the sphere of the manifest. Whether images come to life there by means of a realistic coalescence of hidden resemblances or by means of a fantastic bringing together of differences, the union of "being and of being as it is apprehended," in phenomenological terms, is at the origin of a new literary ontology of the perceived world, at once logical and chaotic, to which Proust and other compulsive translators of the real have accustomed us. Only the systematic excesses of a metaphorical vision appear equipped to combat the entropy of language. Elkin's descriptions seem founded on the belief that objects and phenomena, under the ardor of a gaze, overspill the margins of the normal, incorporate the strange through osmosis, and that to follow the paths of metaphor to their very end is the only way to explain these halos. The radical nature of this attitude is due to its desire for a constant improvement of perception, for the willful embellishment of all objects. Its limit appears in an image such as "brushstrokes like single-hued rainbows,"[34] where the comparison itself exceeds a comparant invited to moderate its ambitions. In *The Franchiser*, the multiple sclerosis that plagues Ben Flesh is the official cause of the narrative's metaphoric hungers: "This M.S. is no respecter of feelings. It blitzkriegs the nerves, gives your hair a headache. You think there are splinters in your eyes and the roof of your mouth has sunburn" (277).

The accidental synesthesias produced by the disease legitimate the mutations of the real. The defamiliarization of the everyday is permanent, systematic, and total. In Flesh's hotel room, "there was a two-headed lamp on the nightstand. There were electric sockets like surprised hobgoblins. There was a plastic wastebasket the color of chewing gum. There was a telephone exactly the shade of ham in a sandwich, with a red message bulb blossoming from it like a tumor" (311–12). Strangely suspended between hyperrealism and Lautréamont's "silk-gazed octopus," Flesh's "translations" are his personal way of making the Other new and close, of integrating the external into the logic of his preoccupations. In the same way, Boswell, the brilliant sycophant (*Boswell*), Bouvard and Pécuchet rolled into one, reduces the personality of the greats of his world to the banality of his references; the ease of his "translations" clearly reinforces the thematics of appearance. It is a quality of the gaze that renders the banal radically other. A maximal distancing of the possible within the familiar, Elkin's quotidian illustrates what Gianni Totti has called the "poessible," the poetic possibilities of everything that routine has made invisible. "Seeing beneath the obvious" is his method. And, although Flesh and Feldman, the eponymous "Bad Man," are enamored of the "manageable ordinary" (221), although they seek "small satisfactions" just as Cézanne sought "small sensations," although they try to be as "ordinary, routine as the other guy," Elkin exposes the indispensable imaginative tactic by stressing that "the play goes to the man who makes necessity delicious" (104). His aims: "to overturn the applecart of ordinary expectation and grammar"; his means: a language that he wants to be "fierce."

As William Gass has stated in his introduction to *The Franchiser*. "Elkin composes a song from the clutter of the country, a chant out of that 'cargo of crap' that comprises our culture. . . . The city, itself, is his Smithsonian, and there is real lust in his love for it."[35] To which the novel's narrator replies, "He has guessed the appeal. Thus the appeal of surrealism and odd juxtaposition" (165). Through sheer linguistic virtuosity, Elkin cheats boredom, "the ultimate childhood disease"; he makes of all the "monuments of the mercantile" "new Sphinxes and new Pyramids . . . new wonders of the world" (162). Perhaps because he remembers that list was once tied to desire and "lust" in English, he marvels and delights in the enumeration of product names, brand names, logos, slogans, empty signs of which the accumulation of forms and of sounds alone fascinate him. If, as he believes, "people need junk," if "there's a hunger for the secondhand, the used, the abused" (267), then it is important to make them find in this way some forgotten equivalences by becoming the creative exalter of a literature that marshals the "lovely close-order drill of ordinary life" (61), in which "romance is as real as heartburn." An "archaeologist of the daily," (186) he struggles against its mediocrities and paralyses by transcending them, thanks to a very personal aesthetic — lyricism, the baroque and precision all at once — that brings to light the treasures buried within the waste. Fascinated by the "strange displacements of the ordinary," Stanley Elkin is a great poet; no translation could do justice to the beauties of the world of everyday people with whom Flesh associates, people described in the following almost Whitman-like passage found in *The Franchiser*.

These are the people I work with, who work for me, these are my partners, the world's put-upon, its A.W.O.L.'d and Article 15'd and Captain's Masted, its chain-ganged and undesirably discharged, all God's plea-bargained, all His sharecropper'd migratory-worked losers. His scummy, heavily tail-finned Chevrolet'd laid-off. Last hired, first fired. This is company picnic we're talking, softball, bratwurst, chug-a-lug'd beer. The common-law husbands of all high-beehived, blond-dyed, wiry waitresses and check-out girls. (292)

In Elkin's work, urban kitsch is at once the primary matter whose spread and abundance are transmuted by a prodigious art and the most solid truth of American culture, if one knows how to read it right. His works must be read in the same way that Flesh reads his world: "famous man signatures and logos, all its *things*, all its *crap*, the true American graffiti, that perfect queer calligraphy of American signatures, what gave it meaning and made it fun" (270). If we do so, we will better understand a remark made by Jayne Anne Phillips in *Machine Dreams* ("You never see the everyday the way you might")[36] as well as the celebrations of the everyday and the conventional also found in Richard Ford's work; a page of *The Sportswriter* becomes lyrical in its description of a mail-order catalog. Phillips manages to extract the poisonous beauties of *Black Tickets* from sordid experiences in urban jungles and the desert of West Virginian towns. From the specialized languages of all types of professionals (from "The Bailbondsman," to the grocers and assorted business owners who people *Criers and Kibitzers, A Bad Man,* or *The Living End,* the radio man in *The Dick Gibson Show* and a huge selection of lawyers, prostitutes, and representatives of the law) whose universe he appropriates along with their universe of discourse, Elkin invents worlds in which every detail is true, but worlds that are also pushed closer to the fantastic with each sentence.

Far from resorting to a dull display of surfaces generally taken at their face value, "realisms" of this sort metamorphize the banal, the trivial, and trash through their sheer energy, proving not only that the ordinary contains the extraordinary but also that the ordinary *is* extraordinary; they know that the secrets of an art of the everyday can only be found in the intensification of a verbal universe. Their authors are not poets by the mere fact of their being "accountants of the inadmissible" (Jacques Besse), but because they know how to handle the diverse excesses that ground literariness, starting with the frame with which all works surround their "painting" of the real. These lessons have been diversely learned by Barthelme, who, in "Sentence," "provides a figure for boredom,"[37] or by such a novel as Cynthia Buchanan's *Maiden,* a kind of shop girl saga in which the language makes itself unbearable through a double extreme of silliness and superficiality. Conversely to the photographic qualities of reportage shown by the minimalists, the slogan that dominates the most successful recourses to the everyday seems to have been taken from Mallarmé: "When creating literature, speak unlike the newspapers."[38]

"Magic Kingdoms"

"To present letters patent of nobility": for once, the verbatim reading of a conventional expression could serve to characterize the attitude of novelists who extract from the vulgar its most glaring emblems in order to make them into high and beautiful icons through writing. Elkin has, in any case, given ambiguous homage to Walt Disney in a cruel novel about his *Magic Kingdom,* a veritable challenge to sentimentalism whose seemingly inexploitable topic (incurable children are granted their dying wish in visiting the kingdom of the fake) nonetheless succeeds in avoiding its pitfalls and dangers. Once again, we find there an interrogation of the mysteries of the organism and of illness that haunted the form of *Searches and Seizures*[39] and the themes of *The Franchiser*, the exceptional combination of hidden tenderness and of scandalously courageous irony that set their tone, the examples of a double definition given by Elkin in his dissertation on Faulkner: "Comedy is the failure of expectation, tragedy the failure of hope."[40]

In "I Look Out for Ed Wolfe" (*Criers and Kibitzers*), there was some question of "a strange band of entrepreneurs and visionaries, men desperately but imaginatively failing."[41] It is to these people that Max Apple—whose novel *Zip* closely resembles those of Elkin—has devoted the core of his work to this day, using the most glaring symbols of the commercial environment in order to draw the line between the always vital powers of myth and its puny incarnations. One can follow step by step the genesis of Apple's *The Propheteers* by reading the short stories of *The Oranging of America* and *Free Agents*. The "orange" that is covering America is the color of the roofs of Howard Johnson motels, a symbol of the commercial structures transfigured on the first page of *The Franchiser*. Johnson is a businessman who thinks of himself as a pioneer, comparing himself to Lewis and Clark, an organizer of space and time, those two "agents" that announce the collapse of Ben Flesh's empire when the opening of his best motel coincides with an unfortunate change of the maximum speed limit on American highways, thereby placing his establishment out of reach of automobile drivers. However, whereas Elkin subordinates his characters' business enterprises to the hazards of personal situations (financial and genetic inheritance), Apple makes them depend on the search for a balance between prophecy and profit, as is shown by the sardonic title of his latest novel. Johnson and Margery Post—heiress to the C. W. Post empire, that militant vegetarian who put breakfast cereal on every table—intend to fight the settling of the Disneys in Orlando, Florida. The Disney brothers serve to illustrate a central dichotomy. Walt is the visionary, the prophet; his brother Roy is the entrepreneur, the profiteer. Walt is fascinated by the animation of surfaces; Roy ("Will," in this case, to fit the circumstances and in order to provide some "will" for a brother who lacks this characteristic) is obsessed by the profitability of talent.

After having explored the world of each of his protagonists in "The Oranging of America" (Howard Johnson), "Walt and Will" and "The Disneyad" (*Free Agents*), and "Vegetable Love" (*The Oranging of America*), Apple brings together several old and irreconcilable ambitions in *The Propheteers*: dream and rest for Walt Disney and Howard Johnson, peace of mind, purity and retreat from the world for C. W. Post and his daughter, the longing to build empires, philanthropy and maximal profit (Post, Johnson, and "Will" Disney), the declaration of "universal" messages exclusively founded on American mythology and the Protestant work ethic. The novel takes shape around some disturbing oxymorons: C. W. Post's proselyte quietism, his heiress's lethargic energy, Howard Johnson's somnolent activism and mobility, Walt's apathy and Will's grasping appetite. Pierre-Yves Pétillon would find there a striking example of the double theme of sleep and flight to which he refers in his readings of American literature in *La Grand'Route*. In this way, the most desperate, the most unremarkable, and the most popular objects and images of American everydayness are given imaginary depth and vigor. New "mythologies" according to Barthes's definition. By digging meticulously among the obsessions hidden beneath the genesis of artifacts that lack depth, by revealing the violences and nightmares contained by the shallow surfaces of roofs, cardboard boxes, and colorful drawings, Apple refers, in a less jarring, less dark, but equally eloquent manner, to the terrifying upheavals with which Nathanael West shook up his novels "in the form of comic strips," linking the grotesque eruptions of the anger of crowds whose dreams have been frustrated to the cynical and hollow rehashing of official dogmas.

The same devastating irony is at work in Apple's other narratives: whether it is a matter of presenting yogurt as a modern form of Old Testament manna ("Vasirin Kefirovsky"), the nostalgia of old service stations ("Gas Stations"), the gesticulations of Norman Mailer as the self-proclaimed genius of the twentieth century ("Inside Norman Mailer"), or the clownishness of Gerald Ford ("Patty-Cake, Patty-Cake, a Memoir"), there is not a single image in circulation that does not fall under the smiling severity of his blows.[42] The most worn-out clichés take on new youth under Apple's pen: the gentle, self-satisfied voice that he gives to lovers of pizza and starchy fast food ("Carbo-Loading," "Pizza Time")[43] adds to their puffiness; the monomanias of those who sing the praises of real estate ("My Real Estate") and of stock-market speculation ("Selling Out"),[44] the snobbery of lovers of fashionable topics (from "Post-Modernism" to "The National Debt"[45] which both remind us of Barthelme) magnify the sometimes touching absurdity of a trite faith in everyday objects whose true measure no distance will allow us to take accurately. Nevertheless, in his cautiously constructed narratives (if Elkin provides all the symphonic excesses of the orchestra, Apple turns to more subtle musics), Apple, like Elkin and Barthelme, manages to make use of that which one might see as literarily unusable, to "recycle," one might say, the waste matter of the discourse and objects of postindustrial society. He astutely brings together old dreams and contemporary pseudorealizations and invites us to judge the gaps between them: on the site where Ponce de Leon believed he had found Paradise and the Fountain of Youth, "Milton Cambell, 437 years later, built Orlando's first drive-in movie," and, in the narrative present tense, the Disney brothers ("close as testicles") and Johnson ("he contemplated the map [of his establishments] and saw that it was good") vie with each other in demiurgic imagination in order to install there the respective horrors of their Gingerbread House for bulimics and the alienated.[46] If one chooses to protect oneself from the hordes of tourists with an electrified fence, as Margery Post does, one also has to take stock of the fact that the childish crowd would rather crush up against this unexpected attraction than take in the surprises of the programmed walk through the unfinished "Magic Kingdom": Apple's satire gives itself the means of its cruelty.

Studying the most important writers of the period, it appears that, on the whole, a double movement governs the dominant relationships of energy to "dreck." For some, the social and linguistic "dreck" in which are summed up the decay of a culture, the artifices and manipulations of consumer society, a debased language "approximately fantastic" and "lightly wonderful," as Barthelme hilariously says in *Overnight to Many Distant Cities,* and rigged relationships, must be combated with high writing, a reaction of the potential energy of language against its entropic decline. We have discussed the works of Hawkes and Gass, in which the virtues of an uncompromising poetic writing are confirmed on every page, where, as René Char might say, "the words that will arise know of us all that we do not know of them."[47] Davenport and McElroy, in their own way, have undertaken the reactivation of abandoned lexical funds; for McElroy and Pynchon, it is the exploration of unprecedented syntaxes. In many of their works, the poetics come to deny the indignity of language and a thematic of ruins that the aesthetic of the fragment often supports. In works by others, it seems possible to generate new energies through the trivial and the devalued: the writings of Donald Barthelme, Pynchon, Sorrentino, Apple, Gaddis, and Elkin deploy all their powers attempting to show just this; these are works for which the mediocre inventory of the world as it is (a new form of constraint) constitutes a challenge and a point of departure. Nor does this mark the limit of possible exploitations of an impoverished real: Carver and the most convincing "minimalists" prove that writing that figures the threats of emptiness and flaws can be illuminating; in their frontal attacks against a language that is in and of itself the oppressor, Burroughs and William Melvin Kelley can promote its destruction more than its accepted usage. But, in each of these cases, an important step has been taken: the liveliness of the language not only establishes itself as superior to that of a world dominated by systems, entropy, the counterfeit, the fake, the simulacrum, and the loss of values, but proposes itself as an instrument of salvation. In such a context, any strictly mimetic attitude could only confirm "the fallacy of imitative forms" denounced by Yvor Winters, by reinforcing the images and the discourses of the anemic and the adulterated. But at its best moments contemporary American fiction knows how to forget a form of suspicion that, by stunting the field of possibilities, would only be an obstacle, in order to make of the *awareness* of suspicion the source of its excesses, of its bypasses, and of its heuristic explorations; pragmatic, perhaps, in this, it knows enough not to retreat from the risk of compromise if such is the cost of its excesses. After all, as the philosopher Richard Rorty recently noted, glossing quite involuntarily the views of George Steiner, "literary or poetic moments occur periodically when things are going badly." It is the honor of literature, then, to look for ways of transcending a world that Samuel Beckett saw as "the famished measure of man and his meager second-class restaurant culture broth."[48]

Chapter 13
The Mouth and the Ear:
The Avatars of Voice

The musician eye moves from one octave to another, grinds the colors, mixes the laughs . . .
— Jean Malrieu, *Acres of Sun*

As French popular irony would have it, people with a sore throat have a beautiful "writing voice." Allowed to push this paradox further, we could add that such a thing is, for such ends, indispensable. "Beautiful" or not, but present, palpable, insistent, "voice" often distinguishes literary writing from literacy's more functional uses, which, nonetheless, can barely do without it. For each book has "its" voice, or "its" voices, an imprint stolen from fingers, at once a signature and a driving force. The first pages of a work set the tone, the accent, the rhythm, define the tessitura, shading, and amplitude; all fictions thrive on vocal mixtures and vocal struggles. "Who is speaking," "from where," "why," "how," and "to whom"? To answer fully these questions, to penetrate the enigma of their interlacing, would mean considerably to dispel the illuminating obscurity of fictions, at the risk of dimming their glow.

As a consistent formalist, Bakhtin emphasizes the consubstantiality of "polyphony" or of "polyglossia" in the novel, identifies the "official monotone" as its major enemy, insists that the plurality of voices is indispensable to the fruitful revelations of conflicts. According to Bakhtin, there cannot be one voice only in the novel, since it is defined by these cohabitations that are properly *political*, mottlings and marblings where questions of power and of its subversion are played out. "Ventriloquism" would threaten to kill the work integrally constructed in the first person were it not for the phenomena of rebound, of echo, of opposition that the novel organizes against other voices, whether public or secret.

In fiction, voice is often the litmus test, revealing the strongest literary personalities, the touchstone of originality. Although my primary intention here is to present voices whose intensity, volume, modulations, and grain push fiction beyond formal retreats, force it past the dead ends of a literature enervated by suspicion, in short, to highlight the importance of what I will call "voices of texture," of the "voice that sees" of which Michael Stephens has written so well,[1] it is worth taking a moment to observe what can happen to the "voices of structure," a function of narrative devices to which Bakhtin accords the greatest importance.

Voice and Structure

"Hypocrite reader . . ."

No regime is more obviously close to voice than that of the vocative. And, in all its avatars, the vocative is the first mode of the dialogical. The greatest "postmoderns" of past centuries, Cervantes, Sterne, Diderot, and Melville understood this so well that they resorted to the apostrophe in order to establish the novel as a "conversation." In the second parts of *Don Quixote, Jacques le fataliste,* and *Tristram Shandy,* the narrator agrees to depend on the reader for his identity as well as for the warm welcome reserved for his speech. By means of the tentative or imperative — according to readings — "Call me Ishmael" of *Moby-Dick,* Melville draws up a more complex contract with the reader.

The advantages of intimacies established in this way are not lost on contemporary fiction. In the 1960s, old images and the return of the ballad and the tale in the popular arts made other borrowings attractive. The invitation to listen to the great prose-writers, but also the friendly closeness provoked by the "Come gather round, friends, and I'll sing you a song" of Seeger and Dylan, heirs to an ancient folk tradition, the coming together of narrator and listener for chats by the fireside (from the pioneers to Roosevelt) or around the confessional couch, elevated the oral to the status of a privileged mode of writing. In an almost emblematic fashion, the only character in Robert Stone's *Dog Soldiers* to pull Hicks from the ruts of autism is named John Converse. *Slaughterhouse-Five,* dedicated to the narration of the unspeakable, opens with an eloquent "Listen"; Salinger's heirs often turn to the "you" that gives shape to Holden Caulfield's confession in *The Catcher in the Rye,* the same "you" that had already opened *Huckleberry Finn,* and that, profoundly changed, serves again as recipient of the story that gives its title to Gass's *In the Heart of the Heart of the Country.* Not until page 8 of Wurlitzer's *Flats* does the character say "Call me Omaha," but the repetition of the Melvillian opening is obvious, underlined as it is by a number of variants: "Call me Cincinnati," "Call me Duluth."[2] The same line is watermarked under the opening statement of *The End of the Road*: "In a sense, I am Jacob Horner,"[3] and Barth, a perfect representative of the tacit conversational dimension of metafiction, structures most of his narratives in the mode of a dialogue with the reader, who is enlisted as a receptive accomplice wise to the ironic commentaries made throughout the story. In Wurlitzer's work, the swing-wing identity of the speaker entails just as many recenterings and failings on the part of his "alias, his brother." In writings by Barth, all doubts concerning identity are generously shared. I do not know if, in writing *Gravity's Rainbow*, Pynchon borrowed the vocative games that characterize Hawkes's *The Lime Twig*, along with the noxious, muggy atmosphere of a squalid London gutted by war. But, outside of the fact that certain pages of the two novels appear interchangeable, Pynchon, in places, heightens the resemblance by creating strange complicities through the use of pronouns: for example, the sections where Dr. Points-man or Roger Mexico combine internal focalization with the intermit-tent use of a "you" that shifts the lived experience onto the reader.[4] One then thinks of the unusual elaboration of Henscher, the transitory narra-tor of *The Lime Twig*.[5] Elsewhere, multiple series of "you bet's" and "you see's" are scattered throughout the narrative, producing a direct com-plicity between the reader and the narrator over the shoulder of the char-acter on stage, a trick that is often supported by the phatic winks of famil-iar locutions and the tics of popular speech (Well; uh-uh; natch; you see, Jackson?); elsewhere still, Pynchon initiates downright "introductions" of the character to the reader. More obvious and more programmed still are the fusions of character, narrator, and reader to which Coover re-sorts in *Pricksongs and Descants*. "The Panel Game" dangerously combines roles, and the voice of "The Leper's Helix," this voice that writes in the desert, first brings together asymptotically a "him," a "you," a "we" and a "me" before twisting them into a tangled strand.

Masteries and Surprises of Dialogue

Nathalie Sarraute notes that dialogue:

which tends more and more, in the modern novel, to take the place left by action, does not adapt itself easily to the forms imposed by the traditional novel. For it is above all the outward continuation of subterranean movements which the author — and with him the reader — must make at the same time as the character, from the moment they form until the moment when, having been forced to the surface by their increasing intensity, to reach the other person and protect them-selves from exterior dangers, they cloak themselves in the protective capsules of words.[6]

At times, Elkin takes up this last image in describing dialogue as dental "plaque." In "The Condominium," Preminger, who is less talented at "conversation than Main the "bailbondsman" in the story of the same name, distinguishes carefully between the two oral modes, as though to stress the artifice of the situation of dialogue in fiction:

What, you think it's hard? This kind of talk? You think it's hard to do? It's *easy*. It makes itself up as you go along. You think it's conversation? It's dialogue. Conversation is hard, I don't do conversation.[7]

As for Main, he knows that dialogue should be "the outward continuation of subterranean movements": "Mr. Crainpool, do you hear this dialogue? . . . The nearer the bone you go, lifewise and deathwise, the saltier the talk. Peppery. You could flavor meat with our exchanges."[8] And Elkin himself rids similar exchanges of the artifices of their transcription by giving back to the dialogues themselves the imaginary nerve and bone structure, the truly organic energy that motivates their enunciation. If "voice is imagination's DNA,"[9] then the syllable is the unit that brings the breath of sound to words, even to images and emotions. For Elkin, this direct take implies the disappearance of the prostheses — he said, she said — that fed the suspicion of the New Novelists. In his novels, people talk as they would shoot, fight, or hit; dialogue *figures*, with no need for annotated commentary, the struggle of voices for power. One can read just as much information in the failures to respond and the drops in regime as in the paroxystic stridency and rhythm of flights of oratory that he describes as "altiloquent." No qualification is provided as follow-up for the elements of a dialogue that is left to the expression of its own energy. Excess makes itself heard but does not draw attention to itself. Speech is the setting of its own theater.

This directly performative aspect of the structure of dialogue is spectacularly illustrated in "Métier: Why I Don't Write Like Franz Kafka" (by William S. Wilson, a fervent practitioner of the dialogue form) where the very scene of the taping of an interview is relayed as a taped conversation. The confrontations between discourses organized on the page by Barthelme's stories, the "fiction for print, tape, live voice" of Barth's *Lost in the Funhouse* provide other examples, as though in response to certain objections made by Sarraute three pages later in her famous essay:

[Contemporary novelists] ostentatiously renounce the subterfuges used ingenuously by writers of the old school (. . . which consisted in constantly varying their formulas), and expose the monotony and clumsiness of this device by repeating tirelessly, with affected negligence or naïveté, "said Jeanne," "said Paul," "said Jacques," the only result being to fatigue and irritate the reader all the more. (101)

This temptation is at times turned to the advantage of innovative strategies. Far from constituting a form of "negligence" or affectation, and far from "fatiguing" the reader, such manipulations of the structures of "voice" in fiction produce surprising effects, and by revealing habit by contrast, by dramatizing the artifice, they raise questions about the true basis of the meaning provided by dialogues and voice. No "message," no information is evidently contained within the following almost intransitive exchange lifted from Thomas Farber's *Curves of Pursuit*:

"Meaning what? Did you hear me?"
"Did I hear you? Of course I heard you. How could I not hear you?"
"Well, then?"
"Well, then, what?"
"You know what."
"No I don't."
"Yes you do."
"This is ridiculous," she said, stalking out of the room, slamming the door.[10]

But both the angry steps and the door speak, replacing all discursive precision. One is reminded of Wilson, correcting one of his characters, who is talking about a voice-activated tape recorder: "Don't use voice as an adverb, it's a noun."[11] In "Tails" (*Love and Will*), Stephen Dixon, a great master of dialogue, delights in generating an argument according to the language's rhythm, and in "Said," he takes pleasure in reminding us of the limits of an art at which he excels:

He said, she said.
She left the room, he followed her.
He said, she said.
She locked herself in the bathroom, he slammed the door with his fists.
He said.
She said nothing.
He said.
He slammed the door with his fist, kicked the door bottom.
She said, he said, she said.
[etc.][12]

In a similar fashion, rhythmic superimpositions make Barth's brief "glossolalic" paragraphs signify ("Glossolalia," *Lost in the Funhouse*), and they do more than illustrate the apparent themes by revealing, like a Galton photograph, the sacred matrix of the scansion, the true voice of the text that emerges from the dialogue between the juxtaposed fragments. It is thus demonstrated that discourse can rely solely on rhythm and syntax and that vocabulary is of lesser importance. Dialogue is the privileged site of these moments of realization, but it is sometimes supported by a constant recycling of identical and limited narrative givens. This is certainly true in Dixon's work, but also in a text such as Lopatin's "Our Perfect Partners." Plot is absent, the deep voice of the text displaces itself from what the characters say to the strange echoes awakened in us by their words; everything confirms the narrator's suspicion: "It was then that I realized that never should you always believe everything you hear" [*sic*].[13] Within the dialogues, two pages of Moira Crone's "Defining Affairs" go so far as to replace all of the substantives the reader is expecting with different ones that are in no way pertinent to the context. Yet, our comprehension of the text is not altered by this in the least: "June agreed that my dialysis was accurate. . . . Her newest love had run off with a true triangle, he an andrologist, she a rich, rich harness."[14] Changing the words and inserting other unexpected ones might very well scarcely alter the effects of a dialogue that remains recognizable by its syntactic armor. Paul Ricoeur maintains that "language is less and less the work of man. The power of speech is no longer what we appropriate for ourselves but rather that which appropriates us." Echoes make sure that one is reminded of the formula "S + n," thanks to which Oulipo gave new life to classic texts, as well as of the preoccupations of the American "L-A-N-G-U-A-G-E Poets": voice, constrained by language, must find the means of using it in order to set itself free. The dialogue with language is always powerful enough to save even the most personal discourses from ventriloquism.

Characters, People, Personae: Voices

William Gass defines character as fiction's "source of verbal energy on the page" which "the rest of the text serves to qualify."[15] The character itself is then the locus of the voice that characterizes it, of a part of the creator's voice and of the text's voice that, in terms suited to Gass, listens to itself and dictates to itself. We shall see the privileged relationships Gass establishes between voice and literary creation, but his remark is helpful in judging, among a handful of examples, those that structurally unite the character's voice to others in order to constitute the narrative and to propel it forward.

Partially taken up in *The Twofold Vibration*, the text of Federman's *The Voice in the Closet* itself takes up on several occasions the text of a poem published in 1967 in *Among the Beasts/Parmi les monstres*. This is to say that the voice that seeks itself there and gives its energy to the narrative is obsessive. From the hiding place that allowed the author to escape from the Nazis during a raid in which he lost his parents and two sisters, this voice speaks to someone named "federman," "featherman," and "quillman" at the same time: "spring" as well, of a story that does not belong to him. In fact, it is possible to identify four different voices employed in the weaving of this text; they are indicated by distinct uses of pronominals: the first person records "the facts," the second invents what the first records, the third is the person to whom the events "invented" by the second occur. Finally, a fourth voice — as suggested by Barth, with whom Federman was then teaching in Buffalo — oversees the collaboration of the other three voices and "produces" the book we are reading. The "voice" that speaks from its "closet" would like to tell the "truth" concerning Federman's horrific childhood experience about which, having become a writer, he has attempted to testify many times — following the example of Vonnegut on the bombing of Dresden in *Slaughterhouse-Five* — without ever succeeding. But, no more than he, the voice does not succeed in starting the story. The text is driven by the succession of his aborted attempts, his failures to tell, his repetitions, the accusations hurled at its creator, returning insistently to the poem, its first try. We see that there is no character, unless we reconstitute it from the voice of the various grammatical persons, and that the "source of verbal energy" defines the character and drowns it at the same time.

Aesthetically less radical and altogether different in its themes, *Sometimes I Live in the Country,* a novel by Frederick Busch, another "Jewish author," manipulates the trials of voice in order to signify a crisis of identity. Petey's adventures are narrated in the third person, but by means of internal focalization. Facts are missing in this elliptical text that only gives us access to thoughts, reactions, and shreds of perception as they appear to the young boy and as they assume in his mind a subjective importance that does not necessarily accord with their importance in the economy of the narrative. Everything happens as though the Jamesian technique of point of view in *The Turn of the Screw* or *What Maisie Knew* had granted itself the daring and the means of a more contemporary language; in this way, the text would follow through on the modernist critique of perception as illustrated by the first two sections of *The Sound and the Fury,* in which the voices also swirl around a central black hole.

Flats, by Rudolph Wurlitzer, owes everything to the tonalities of the great flattening-out of being as dramatized by Beckett. Wurlitzer's meditations on space and landscapes, both natural and interior, are his own but he turns to the Franco-Irishman in order to adorn his great smooth planes with the shallow reliefs of impoverished voices cautiously in search of themselves. There is no "action" aside from the perpetual redistribution of mediocre unwanted objects, the incessant rearrangement of stunted relations, the quest for new positions by errant, hiccuping voices. Even the presence of what we do not dare call "protagonists" threatens to disappear at any point. Identities are only a function of carefully studied regimes of enunciation; "Omaha keeps sinking into the first person like warm mud. . . . The third person handles the changes, keeps me from getting popped. I don't want to knock the third person. I like to travel there. It avoids stagnations and the theatrics of pointing to myself."[16] The novel is made up of this collection of instants in which identity collapses or tries to be reborn as a threat. A schizophrenic writing responds to the surrounding paranoia. And, always, the voice becomes a repository of possibilities:

Omaha needs to draw this moment out a little, to hang on to this voice. I just got here, the action will always come, I'm getting into the voice. . . . I'm over my head. I need a task. A task would give a focus, prevent distractions. To keep on is a task. The first person causes despair, blows Omaha's cover. . . . Although hopefully no motives have crept in pushed by the mad need to speak. (23–25)

Emotion could trigger the logics of action in which one's being would drown since, unable as it is to resist even the flow of an enriched speech, it can no more envisage the necessity of choices, movements, ruptures, duration, projects, or of generalization. This narrative blueprint constantly fights the forces that might organize it; and within this struggle, voice is a questionable ally. For even speech is the harbinger of the worst subjections to an external logic — "Somewhere, in one of us, control lurks" (28) — and the novel is no more than this delicate navigation between speech that provides being and speech that takes it away. The narrator of *Flats*, in a state of abeyance, constantly wants to put off a confrontation with the real that his fragile identity could not survive; he would rather "maneuver among the politics of displacement" (29). It is likely that the number of actors is less than that of the names he gives them, that to each internal voice corresponds the creation of other down-and-out alter egos, that the many "Call me's" summon ephemeral new christenings in order to escape the narrativity of time, that it is thanks to the distancings of the third person, which deals, as "from the outside," with unclaimed acts, that the first person finally survives, in the midst of white noises, in a strange and sinister light.

Speaking of *White Noise*, Don DeLillo creates a list of devices by which, according to him, "irony enters the voice. Nasality, sarcasm, self-carica-ture. . . ."[17] As we will soon see, there is quite an amusing case of nasality in Gaddis's *JR*; but Steven Millhauser's novels owe one of the secrets of their success to their use of the two latter effects of voice. As in *JR*, the principal protagonist of *Edwin Mulhouse* and of *Portrait of a Romantic* is an absurdly precocious and brilliant child. The biographical novel of Edwin Mulhouse, age 11, by Jeffrey Cartwright, age 12, earned Millhauser the Médicis Etranger literary prize. Edwin dies after having completed an autobiographical novel entitled *Cartoons*: where we begin to see that to the author's fascination with childhood, as translated by the precision of the overlapping voices, which relays the child's fascination with violence and death, corresponds a further fascination, of no less importance, with literature. In fact, among the voices of the book, more secret but just as audible as the embittered and frustrated voice of Edwin or that, awkwardly adult and pompous, of Jeffrey, one can hear other murmurs that are the ironic sighs of the structure.

It is indeed the great Nabokov and his *Pale Fire* that one should hear echoing beneath the *mises en abîme* of the biographical form, but also James Boswell and Henry James since Boswell's biography of Samuel Johnson appears just beneath the surface, and because James's biographer, Leon Edel, bears the parodic brunt of a novel when it steals the major divisions of his monumental work ("The Early Years," "The Middle Years," "The Late Years"). The satire, therefore, is not carried exclusively through the tone of voices that are very exact in their constraint and their stiffness, but also through the importing of voices from elsewhere. It is these other voices, as much as the remarkable, uncompromising representation of an overly mythologized universe, that save the world of childhood from the clichés of popular culture, from the mush of preconceptions, and from the stereotypes of psychology and sociology. In Millhauser's works, these high voices save from mere cuteness a love of the miniature magnificently demonstrated by the stories of *In the Penny Arcade*. The same can be said of *Portrait of a Romantic*, in which the author pursues his demystifications by concentrating on the immense troubles of adolescence, problems not unconnected to those experienced by Salinger's Holden Caulfield and Glass children. But the irony here is more integrated to the voice, the sarcasm and self-criticism make themselves heard beneath Arthur Grumm's "romantic" sighs, a character whose name evokes "grimm" and stormy visions: "If only I could create a world superior to this world, which would annihilate it and replace it."[18] The "sufferings of young Grumm" between the ages of twelve and fifteen are not narrated until he is twenty-nine, but Jeffrey Cartwright's pompous tone is matched here by one both grandiloquent and sententious, that of a boy poorly fed with stuffy literatures through which breathes the boredom of a blasé youth who borrows his voice from them. Millhauser thus shows that there are varieties of "ventriloquism" that in no way prohibit dialogue in fiction.

Moreover, Max Apple does not hesitate to describe his coming to writing as an extension of the ventriloquist's delights in voice. In "The American Bakery," fiction eventually replaces the soulless dummy that fascinated the narrator as a child. But we will judge with what precautions Apple distinguishes between the two types of voice in order to preserve the indispensable dialogue:

It took another twenty years for me to cast my voice again, this time into stories rather than dummies. It's a weak analogy, I know, and yet fiction seems sometimes like my dummy, like that part of myself that should get all the best lines. I want to be the straight man so that the very difference between us will be a part of the tension that I crave in each sentence, in every utterance of those wooden lips redeemed from silence because I practiced. Yet the voice from the silence, the otherness that fiction is, doesn't need any metaphoric explanations. It's true that I tried ventriloquism, but it was my fascination with the English language itself that made me a writer.[19]

Certainly it is not insignificant that Apple contrasts English with Yiddish in this essay, since, as a Jewish writer, he shares with Elkin the ability to take pleasure in making light of a language that was not his mother tongue. Finding one's voice becomes complicated by the distances from a medium that, as the examples of Conrad and Nabokov would indicate, has its own additional charms. However, Apple links to these "voices of structure," which give birth to the games of the dialogic, a "voice of texture," which, according to him, constitutes almost the entire meaning:

An awkward hesitant clumsy sentence emerges. I nurse it, love it in all its distress. I see in it the hope of an entire narrative, the suggestion of the fullness of time. I write a second sentence and then I cross out that first one as if it never existed. This infidelity is rhythm, voice, finally style itself. It is a truth more profound to me than meaning, which is always elusive and perhaps belongs more to the reader. (90)

In this case, voice is not only an important dimension of meaning, it is the truth of a fiction that, at its origin, is breath: "[These stories and novels] to you are entertainment; to me breath" (91). This conception of voice as the *matter* of their texts is illustrated by the following authors, from its most pragmatic to its least utilitarian of uses.

Voice and Texture

The Oral Tradition: In the American Grain

Of the American oral tradition, and particularly of the tall tale, from the incredible stories that weave their popular canvas with exaggerations and larger-than-life inventions, the bragging of Davy Crockett and Sut Lovingood, to the testimony of Mark Twain, contemporary writers have retained more than the thematic distancing from the real. Their debts are heavy indeed: from the grotesque acrobatics of Dr. Seuss's cat in *A Political Fable* and the farce of *Gloomy Gus* to Herman Mack's strange feast in *Car* by Harry Crews, during which he devours a 1971 Ford Maverick, to the kidnapping of Christ in Robbins's *Another Roadside Attraction,* and to

Tyrone Slothrop's overflowing sexuality in *Gravity's Rainbow,* the list of fictions requiring more than the usual dose of "suspended disbelief" is not exactly short. Characters that are undeniably larger-than-life march in giant steps across the novels of Jim Harrison, Thomas McGuane, *All We Need of Hell* by Crews, and even Jay McInerney's *Ransom.* Not entirely lacking in a swaggering machismo, these latter works do not all resort, however, to the effects of voice that authenticate and renew the American oral tradition; rather, it is the closing words of "Quenby and Ola, Swede and Carl" (*Pricksongs and Descants*) or a lack of syntax in a Faulkner novel that reveal their secrets. First, the short story. Many possible stories are mixed together here; it ends: "And, from far out on the lake, men in fishing boats, arguing, chattering, opening beer cans. Telling stories."[20] As to the novel, its brilliant French translator, M.-E. Coindreau, nonetheless had some difficulty with Addie Bundren's statement in Faulkner's *As I Lay Dying:* "That was when I learned that words are no good; that words dont ever fit even what they are trying *to say at.*"[21] And yet, in this last expression lie the reserves of aggressive energy that make American orality such a distinctive phenomenon. The taste for stories, the abandonment to the flow of speech, and greedy wordiness can perhaps only be understood in their finality of *contact,* no matter how violent. Speech binds because the voice projects itself, independently of its message, following the example of that thread of words that traverses another page of Faulkner and constitutes the sole reconciliation of the Bundren family members: "[W]e had to use one another by words like spiders dangling by their mouths from a beam, swinging and twisting and never touching."[22] Has there ever been a more beautiful representation of the phatic? The thread of the voice holds, the web of the voice saves.

It is no surprise then that a fiction suspicious of messages and narrative prostheses should resort to voluminous outpourings of verbal incontinence in order to signify the difficulty of relations that a sort of modesty forbids to make explicit or that a lack of awareness renders impenetrable, no surprise that it should replace difficult communication with the hookings of voice. Mouldie, the marathon speaker in Andrée Connors's *Amateur People,* is perhaps, along with the characters of Elkin and McGuane, Brautigan's Jesse in *A Confederate General,* and several others, the greatest word-spewer since Dr. Matthew-Mighty-grain-of-salt-Dante-O'Connor in Djuna Barnes's *Nightwood.* Reading his delirious monologues is all the more useful since the most beautiful among them are addressed to . . . snowflakes: veritable "snow jobs" or "blue streaks," the ejaculations of buffoons serve to illustrate the discontinuous and material character of speech. Mouldie gradually becomes "a verbal train going down now, unstoppable," fills "up the holes with talk," and free associates in order to fill the embarrassing gaps of a day "in jeopardy," to patch up the "marvels and awards" of an existence "in danger of being tattered and tram-pled."[23] The staging of the representation of a voice responds to the existential void; the difficulty of being finds refreshment in the poetic flights of the actor.

Toward Performance

If I possess any sort of principle in criticism, it is that one must seek the purity of genres above all. Theater on one side, or poem on the other, but I prefer and desire that, in distributing very carefully the devices of these two genres, in the manner of all our masters and those of all other eras, we bring a conversation or even flights of fancy into the midst of our descriptions: and that [. . .] we place contents and dialogue simply side by side, allowing an atmosphere to circulate between them that itself becomes part of the work.[24]

By its nature, fiction scarcely responds to Mallarmé's "critical principles" or to his demands for "purity," but his tolerances describe quite well the "circulation of atmosphere" that "itself becomes part of the work" en-gendered by the whirlwind of voices; in fact, their theatricality pulls a number of fictions in the direction of performance. Neither Pynchon (especially in *Gravity's Rainbow*, but also in *V.* and *The Crying of Lot 49*) nor Coover (in *The Public Burning* as in *A Political Fable*) resists the tempta-tion of mixed genres (songs, ballads, theater, sketches, monologues) in which voice takes center stage. Moreover, the gift of gab of their charac-ters and narrators is often the only sign of their presence; their imperial voice amply takes up the space of description and of narrative, it makes "circulate" between "contents and dialogues" — themselves privileged — the "atmosphere" that neither the extravagance of the "facts" nor the bizarreness and idiosyncracies of the plot would suffice to explain. As Michael Stephens, an expert on the matter (one should read his admi-rable *Season at Coole,* with its anarchic tangles of great, drunken, mad Irish voices) would say, these authors "seed [their] prose with the voice of their characters";[25] at the same time, one must enter their fiction by means of their voices: penetrating it through character or plot would render the reading more opaque. By centering the fiction on voice, the emphasis switches from representation to presentation, becomes gestural; the body becomes soul, the content dialogizes, the dialogue becomes content, performance replaces representation; reading is spectacle and listening.

For Norman Mailer, this energy of the voice alone largely succeeds in explaining "why we are in Vietnam." The voice of the disc jockey who handles the narration reverberates with the almost object-free aggressivi-ties of a mythical bear hunt; it takes the place of the soundtracks of *Apocalypse Now* or of *Platoon* in which the music is mixed with the noise of bombs and helicopters. Voice carries all the weight of a questionable search for an object, for an interlocutor upon whom to impose the high tides of speech. Voice is an actor and a setting, and the figure of the disc jockey appears frequently, with his outpourings of sonic stuffing that are an invitation to both "delirium" and "unreading" (*dé-lire*), that move our attention from the eye to the ear. Voice is central to Jaffe's *Mole's Pity*. The reading of these novels implies that "the eye listens" in a manner that Claudel would scarcely have appreciated. Many passages from *Americana* (DeLillo) organize into a sonic background the voices of characters and those of the disc jockey, an undifferentiated brew that becomes almost osmotic with the landscape:

With us all the way had been Sullivan's three-antenna marine-band hi-fi portable radio, a never-ending squall of disc jockey babytalk, commercials for death, upstate bluegrass Jesus, and as we drove through the cloverleaf bedlams and past the morbid gray towns I perceived that all was in harmony, the stunned land feeding the convulsive radio, every acre of the night bursting with a kinetic unity, the logic beyond delirium.[26]

Behaviors and desires are in turn modeled by the voices that shape the environment; the discursive swerves of music and "information" that seem to be used as syringe or padding bring about the temptation to perform a "happening": "I want to piss on all the trees, tumble down hills, chase jackrabbits, climb up rooftops, crucify myself on TV aerials."[27] Semyavin's disillusioned remark in *Gravity's Rainbow* is not far off: "Information. Because you think drugs and women aren't enough?"[28] This writing of paroxysm is the favored channel of the mania that makes up Neal Cassady's *The First Third* or Hunter Thompson's *Fear and Loathing in Las Vegas*. Drugs had already played a large part in opening wide the verbal sluices of the conversationalists in Ginsberg's "Howl":

Yacketayakking screaming vomiting whispering facts and memories and
anecdotes and eyeball kicks and shocks of hospitals and jails and wars,
whole intellects disgorged in total recall for seven days and nights with
brilliant eyes . . .[29]

In *Panama* (McGuane), the actual crucifixion of Chet on Catherine's door is not out of keeping with the story: since, contrary to previous novels, in which the form was due to the author's understanding, perched above and beyond his central protagonists, none of whom were allowed to tell their own stories, here it is Chet Pomeroy who is speaking, and the living process of his narrative stands out on each page. Space, action and writing are intimately connected to voice here. In Thomas Glynn's *Temporary Sanity*, the manuscript that Jarrell thinks he sees in his rearview mirror burning behind him in the ditch resembles in its shape the legendary roll of paper on which Kerouac is supposed to have typed *On the Road*. Cassady's endless logorrhea (the "Moriarty" of Kerouac, the "secret hero" of Ginsberg's poem), his uninterrupted and uninterruptible phrases of connected/disconnected words, his erratic overflows of speech into the closest microphone or the closest ear, are reflections of his famous driving virtuosity; espousing the curves of the imaginary as the driver does those of the terrain, stopping only to catch its breath and refuel, the punctuationless sentence of the "word-spewer" becomes a softly articulated ribbon; if one crosses over the lines or fails to see unexpected turns in the headlights, one runs the risk of accidents, of the collapse into a sudden awkward silence. His "choo-choo nonsense"[30] is definitely seen as a means of "transport," a path toward a verbal trance that transforms consciousness into space. The wobbly phrases, the runaway sentences and the foggy or surrealizing descriptions, the dislocated narratives of *Panama* respond to the here, there and anywhere of a disorganized existence.

Speaking more generally, in McGuane's novels, the simultaneity of the narratives, the superimposing of narrative levels, the non sequiturs heighten our perception of the flow that is waiting to burst forth. In *Ninety-two in the Shade*, what Skelton calls his "frenetic glibness" corresponds to the intensity of his desires.[31] The marathoners of speech answer the sprinters of retort; in *The Bushwhacked Piano*, Nick is described as "a hundred percent idiot born standing up and talking back." He never stops rebelling through abrupt, violent, powerful speech against what he can only call "snivelization," in order to describe the whining of a "civilization of snivellers."[32] In *The Sporting Club*, Vernor Stanton wants to "foment discord"; gifted with a rare capacity for demolishing the social, he also has an "unfathomable capacity for wrecking himself"; truth be told, the relationship maintained by his voice with these two fundamental activities is paradoxical: his floodlike discourses systematically erode all "normal" dialogue along their unchecked path. He fascinates his victims: "Why don't you stop talking, darling. Because I am obliged to recognize the great pleasure that it brings to others."[33] In the same way, the passion for speech without logical barriers does not allow one to take hold of the real and, with the flow, all identity ceases. For a certain fiction of wandering and quest, the real has, to a great extent, disappeared; speech has replaced it as a field of investigation; if it was ever legitimate to indulge in homonymic winks, these are the places in which to find one's way ("chercher sa voie") and to find one's voice ("chercher sa voix") have become indissociable.

Obviously, among everything that enables these "new" installments that fiction "brings from another world" (Carver) to be delivered safely, some prefer the "stamp" to the "letter"; or sometimes, if you like, they prefer the seal of the butcher ("Metzger") guilds who gave their impetus to the post of Thurn and Taxis, as *The Crying of Lot 49* reminds us; in this case, they borrow their voices from semiprivate languages, from these languages for the initiated that professional jargons are.

The attraction that "novelists of manners" (O'Hara, Marquand, Cozzens, Cheever, or Updike) felt in regard to these specialized worlds provided them with themes, settings, and ideas. Elkin's taste for their vocational language inspires him to borrow it from them. The phenomenon has long been apparent in American theater — from Arthur Miller's *Death of a Salesman* to David Mamet's *Glengarry Glen Ross* — where, in a general fashion, as C. W. E. Bigsby has observed, the character of the salesman dominates as a bearer of language. Elkin, himself the son of a traveling salesman, feels a deep respect for the theatrical quality of their sales pitches.[34] Almost all of his characters have the voice of these little everyday heroes, along with something to sell. And if Hellequin, devil king of genies, gave his name and his colors to Harlequin's coat, one might propose to call "Art-Elkin" his flamboyant manipulations of speech.

Elkin's characters are unusual in that they are at once harlequins and pierrots, Coco the Clowns and white clowns, and in that the reversal of perspective that gives such moments of poignancy and liberation to *commedia* and to circus acts is often internalized into a dialogue of voices. The "I" of the protagonists, along with their social life, disdains conversation with others and prefers a brutal variety of dialogue — and even of monologue — as the seizing and losing of power. Capable of sudden shifts in register, of an excessive lyricism and an eloquent reserve, they simultaneously project themselves and perceive themselves in the act of their discourse, they come to light through unexpected inversions, they discover their strengths through their weaknesses, their despair in the turn of a baroque gesture, of a skid along a word, their desire at the moment of finding its limits, their frightened face beneath the loveliest masks, and their epiphanies always cavort with death. With the randomness of a joke, of a simple pun (a furrier who wants to "call the pelisse"), their universe falters, their aggressive face is revealed, their confidence dissolves. Language reveals dizzying perspectives at the same time as it allows characters to keep them under control. In their world, everything is reversible; paradoxes and oxymorons communicate their incompatibilities to a vocabulary that indifferently transforms substantives into verbs, verbs into substantives, and nouns into adjectives, as well as to a syntax characterized by the permanent alteration of utterances by clauses, parentheses and dashes, a constant temptation to invert vectors.

In Elkin's work, the locutory is never merely locutory, and illocution and perlocution are in strong evidence everywhere. Beyond the act of speech, it is speech *as* act that dominates, at the same time as the act of speech, known in its strength and its efficacy — "selling," seductive, or polemical — constantly intensifies in acts effected by speech *on* speech. The feeling that speech can do anything and the certainty that its power is subjected to a formal condition reign over the text: that it distances itself as much as possible from all that it is ordinarily judged capable of doing. At the end of the virtuosity and the eloquence of the sales talks, or in this case, of a magistrate's discourse, Alexander Main's belief is always lurking more or less explicitly: "Here, this is the pertinent language, I think . . . blah blah de dum blah de dum."[35] Alliterations, neologisms, excessive metaphorization, generic singulars, hyperbolic plurals, strings of conjunctions, application of the genitive to inanimate objects: anything goes in order to help the voice escape from an imprisoning referentiality and to remove adherence through hypnotism and fascination.

Moreover, Elkin is not alone in exploiting the resources of specialized languages to feed the voices of his texts. In *Ancient History* and elsewhere (the film vocabulary of *Lookout Cartridge*, of biology in *Plus* . . .), McElroy uses the lexical universe of science for two contradictory reasons: specialized discourses offer both the advantage of exact notations and of "an improbability rich in information in a literary context."[36] The reader is simultaneously forced to acknowledge the role played in one's comprehension of the world by nonliterary codes and to discover the ways in which to resolve literarily the problems posed by the text. The voice of *Ancient History* is split between a sort of hunger for a vocabulary that would colonize the unknown and its blatant distrust of metalanguages. "Cy" is in search of new voices to express the emotions of childhood, his needs for friendship; the novel's tension is in great part born of the gap between the voice that he possesses and the one he seeks; this gap almost constitutes the work's true "action." This performative character of voice emerges even more clearly in another novel based on a scientific vocabulary: *Ratner's Star*, in which, according to DeLillo himself, the "characters don't just open their mouths to say hello. They have to make the action part of the remark. 'My mouth says hello.' 'My ears hear.' " And he adds that in *End Zone*, "some of the characters have a made-up nature. They are pieces of jargon. They engage in wars of jargon with each other."[37] At the extreme point of vocal performance, the question of power is thus raised.

Voice and Power

The short stories of *Criers and Kibitzers, Kibitzers and Criers* refer without end to questions of power and of its absence; one of these stories, "A

Poetics for Bullies," is a how-to guide on tyranny for teenagers. "Kibitz-ing," which mixes the letters of *blitz* and *krieg* in a falsely suggestive man-ner, is the verbal aggression characterized by the idea of "putting one's oar in," and Elkin constantly elaborates on the list of examples he pro-poses. But it is in *The Dick Gibson Show* that the oral wrestling match is most spectacular, that the relations of the voice to violence and to power are most darkly drawn. Like Reed in *Mumbo Jumbo*, Apple in *Zip*, and Coover in *The Public Burning*, Elkin pushes the voices of popular culture beyond all "literary decency" in this work (LeClair). Push outdoes shove and performance is pushed to putsch.

The ambition of Dick Gibson (alias Marshall Maine), radio man, is to become a voice without a place, out of time, so good and recognizable that it would "*define* life, [his] name a condition," whose pedigree would read "Dick Gibson of Nowhere, of Thin Air and the United States of America sky."[38] He aspires to become the "ordinary" voice of America, a voice that, a significant paradox, will "incarnate" the country without resorting to myth, although the ironic structure of the story takes up the traditional mythic phases of departure, initiation, and return. His voice will struggle against the voices of listeners who call him, and that, as he discovers, in no way resemble his ideal. A woman's incessant voice, Bob Hope's monologues show him the true measure of his capacities at the same time as they increase his fascination with the powers of voice. He "is a sucker for the first person singular" (92), he wants "to learn to move dispassionately into the silence," to tame it, to shape it (105). Hav-ing become a "magic" voice on armed forces radio during the Second World War, he remarks its power more brutally, turns it to his own ad-vantage by obscenely vituperating the military universe on the air, then repents.

The second part of the novel muddles together the voices of listeners who recount their stories live. A confrontation with one of the people he presents will lead to the central test: his nemesis's name is Edmond Behr-Bleibtreau, a psychologist. Whereas Gibson only lives for the feeling of control he gets from being the central voice of his show, Behr-Bleibtreau, a shock kibitzer, steals his thunder. He interrupts, stirs up oppositions, provokes. He turns the harmonious concert of voices into a free-for-all, transforms the "debate" into the opposite of the planned dialogue, em-phasizes the isolation of voices to the detriment of their constructive unity, briefly stated, he takes power, transforming himself, to use an expression of McElroy's, into a sort of "silence" into which others then willingly throw themselves. Gibson only manages to save the voice that is being stolen from him because of an incident, which is also violent, and the end of the second part finds him using his voice because he still has it, because it's still *his*—uniquely inflected, Gibson-timbreed, a sum of private frequencies and personal resonances, as marked as his thumbs—because the show must go on and he must be on it. (229)

The choices left to him are to remain "what [he says] on the radio" (209), to become "a character as other people were amoral" (208), or to abandon his ideals in order to satisfy his immediate needs. The third part is the field of his wanderings and hesitations, that of a voice that can no longer "place" itself; it is infected by the voices he receives, loses its own tone: a return to the clichés of the raw data of a real that a different voice no longer manages to constrain into meaning. The cry that liberates Boswell at the end of Elkin's first novel ("Down with the Club!")[39] is no longer strong enough to liberate Gibson from the banality of things.

This hymn to voice, to its power, and its violences is a contemporary of a study similar in its themes and cruelty. Philip Roth's "On the Air" places the traditionally somewhat forced voice of the author at the service of a story that also has the world of radio broadcasting as its setting.[40] The grotesque does battle with the obscene, diverts all the effects of voice toward physical confrontations of such violence that an expected slip transforms, for the Jewish protagonists, "programs" into "pogroms," thus providing the short story with its thematic framework. At the end of a Rabelaisian "carnivalization" (Bakhtin), the voice reveals the evil of the forces of destruction lurking beneath comic situations, returning all its intensity to their subversive power.

Indeed, in this agonistic perspective, darkness seems to be linked to voice. The threat seems slight enough in the early pages of DeLillo's *Players,* when an unknown voice bursts out of nowhere and undertakes to express for us its feelings about motels. The threat becomes more frightening when, in the midst of a nocturnal and disintegrated world from which all communication has disappeared, there appears in the heavy silence of hushed or smothered voices, and as though to compensate for an insecure masculinity, the capital "I" of a cannibal voice that dreams of domination: "I, Zizendorf," "I, the Editor."[41] The paradox of the voice of *The Cannibal* that confers omniscience upon the first person narrator is not a slight one. Omniscience but not omnipotence. Since, in spite of the maxims that fall heavily upon the shoulders of the neo-Nazi's "subjects" up to the last sentence of Hawkes's novel ("She did as she was told"), in spite of a bulimia of power that can be read in the crests of a voice, and perhaps by reason of the book's strange genesis (drafted in the third person, its switch to first-person narrative only occurred later), an even stronger voice comes to counter the commentaries of the fanatic who plans to secure his power through writing and through voice. The very excesses of Zizendorf's voice sketch just beneath the surface the accents of another voice, which Hawkes baptizes the narrative's "black intelligence," a secret, clandestine, and seemingly resistant voice that places between the spectacle of the horror and our eyes that "glasspane" beneath which Baumbach wrote that Hawkes slid his text. It is a voice born of the novel's structure, but also of the ups and downs of a forced tone.

The same is true in Hawkes's *Second Skin* of the voice of the "Skipper," whose bragging and complacency ("I am a tiger," "lover of my sanguine and harmless self")[42] betray the weaknesses of another "leading" voice. In Hawkes's work, the voice that wants to climb too lofty summits from which to contemplate its domains tends to break, or at least to crack up, to let appear the rhizomes of its dangerous cracklings, to reveal its gaps in the hymns to its own power. In this world, "more" is "less," and power that declares itself as such is shown to be vulnerable. The authority figures, the tyrannical narrators (the "Sheriff" in *The Beetle Leg*; Cyril in *The Blood Oranges,* master-weaver of the great erotic tapestries of the narrative; the driver of the crazy vehicle in *Travesty*; the "Master" arranger of the suspicious ceremonies in *Virginie: Her Two Lives*) manage to escape in this way, in the best of cases, the nastiness or the disdain that the reader would shower upon them if it were not for the pathetic fragility that can be read beneath the glaze that stiffens their voice. The voice that subverts their bombasts is the honor of a fiction about which one sometimes fears that it is born of the fascination they exert. It slips among the voices of these novels, whose number seems to exceed that of the actors. This dark voice also runs through Hawkes who, on the one hand, confesses to having "first wanted to be Lenny Bruce, then a preacher, then a salesman, and finally, master of the universe," and on the other hand, knows that the "goal of imagination is not simply to fantasize — self-gratification through dreaming — but to help the individual to see things as they really are."[43]

William Melvin Kelley and Ishmael Reed place their faith as novelists in a completely different kind of "black voice." In *Dunford Travels Every Wheres,* the racial struggle passes through voice. Kelley's novel presents itself as an attempt at liberation from an actual state of "slavery": the inability of African Americans to reject the condescension and manipulation of Euro-American culture and language; they can only fight back by employing the resources of their own idiom. Kelley's language, in retaliation, dissimulates a great part of its meaning from all exclusive practitioners of Euro-American, even if it is only toward the end of the book that Chig becomes aware of the subversive and emancipatory power of his voice. Reed does not forgo using this strategy by infusing the voice of his various "demons" into the text of his narrative collages. Their esotericism constantly recalls the obscure and ancient foundations of black culture through a complex set of harmonics and double meaning; this is a veritable "vernacular dance" that allows the voice to branch the reader off toward the world of jazz, voodoo, witchcraft, and legend, as well as toward the themes and images of high culture (Knights Templars, freemasonry, surrealism, Jungian psychoanalysis) or of a more broadly shared popular culture. This guffawing, skewed voice thus relays Bob Kaufmann's "Abominist Manifesto," whose taste for reinterpreting history has had an important influence on Reed. Just as "the devil was created by the Church to avoid paper work," Reed's voice alone manages to sow panic in conventional rhetoric. No control, no context hastily put in place to contain his beautiful anarchies can conquer their subversive cacophonies: the muse of "allegory" upon whom Reed calls, tumbled after many dishonest propositions, has never known such dishevelment. American feminists, logically, resent it.

Voice and Collective Identity

I do not know what Grace Paley thinks of Reed's work, but I would wager that it might vary between a solid refusal of his machismo and admiration for a writer who knows how to channel with such verve the community voices to which she devotes many pages of her own fiction. When her first collection of short stories appeared (*The Little Disturbances of Man*), it was Paley's unique "voice" that caught people's attention. She has now published about four dozen short stories, of varying quality, but throughout this work there circulates the song of a writing that has been called *a capella* (Baumbach) before it even confessed: "Song is one of the famous methods for continuing or entrenching happiness."[44] Perhaps this image of a voice alternately drowning in and emerging from a chorus, that lifts itself without the aid of rhetorical brass by stealing the restrained intensities of the woodwinds and the strings, by borrowing the unmatched cadences and accents of the rhythm section to compose her fictions, might serve to present Paley's work further. This image will no doubt contrast with another aspect of this voice that stems from the warm personality, passionate to the point of burning but also willingly abrasive and vituperating, of a politically engaged woman, scarcely more patient with compromises than with the powers-that-be. Paley's voice, like the gaze in one of the short stories from *Later the Same Day* that hides behind tears, can veil itself; it can, like Hawthorne in "Young Goodman Brown," hide itself behind Faith, its main alter ego, it can raise itself for curses or take on the accents of a prophet: these are not the reasons for which I will say that this voice is, above all, "religious." Such a characterization might seem surprising to those who know that, on occasion, this voice has denounced "those three monotheistic horsemen of perpetual bossdom and war: Christianity, Judaism, and Islam."[45] But one will guess the use that I am making of this term if, by staying in a musical register, one kindly reads the "symphony" of her voices in a slightly literal way and discovers all that "blends" them into a voice that is only "unique" in its quality.

Paley's stories are characterized by the dispersion of the voice and of the enunciative source. Not only because, as one character says, her "momness is diffuse" or that her poems, "sketches" of her stories, appear as dialogues with herself, but because the ends of her writing consist in opening each word up to the word of the other. "Why should *I* always tell the story? I like the other to tell the story."[46] Less the "other" person than the "Other" or others, actually, as the substitutions of narrative point of view willingly complicate themselves through combinations of speech. Paley explicitly places the dialogical back at the center of the fictional act, confident that these sweeps of crossed projectors will better illuminate the world. It is in this way that her women — mothers, daughters, grand-mothers, neighbors, and shopkeepers — find refuge in a regime of voices that protects them from outside aggressions — counterattack not being excluded, God knows — they allow the voice of the other to come inside: another woman, man, child, voices of the innumerable skin colors and suit colors of the streets of Brooklyn and the Bronx; all at the same time, the voices of Faith or Alexandra develop themselves, welcoming the out-side words and subjecting themselves to their own irony, which saves them — another "enormous change at the last minute" — from the stiff sermons of a feminism lacking in distance. These dislocated presences express the tensions and the unions of the communal; her dialogues are confrontations as much as collaborations. For Paley, voice is "a noisy taking in and a loud giving back."[47] A master of the art of dialogue, she does not insist on directing the debates, convinced that their music sig-nifies the "floating truth" of "the little disturbances of man" indepen-dently of their conclusions. "Speaking to one another as the books of any author will do arguing the past and future of technical authority, ghosts invented for melody's sake. Its tune the time sings all our stories are set to it."[48]

Perhaps "Faith" is more of a persona than a character, although Paley would certainly deny this. But when her voice comes down from the trees from which she comments on the world of the playground ("Faith in a Tree," *Enormous Changes*), she humbly abandons control of her image in order to give it to the voice of the other. More than by the reversal of point of view, we are struck by her astonishing capacity to melt and fuse together the spheres of the public and the private, to pass from intimisms to broad exteriors, and one is reminded of the art of her good friend Tillie Olsen, who, in *Tell Me a Riddle,* drowns and redraws the boundaries of the personal within the great concert of collective voices. For this rea-son, Linsey Abrams is able to connect the name of Grace Paley to that of

Louise Erdrich, whose "communal story" — *Love Medicine,* which would represent for the Chippewa Indians what Paley's stories represent for her world — likewise mingles together "dozens of lives like so many switchboard wires crossing time and space."[49]

Grace Paley is all voice. Her "verbalosity," as she says, aims to combat a "dead" language in which we seem to have forgotten the truth that lies hidden in the oral ("Dreamer in a Dead Language"). "There are a lot of kids," she adds, "who have never heard a nursery rhyme; they can't write because there is nothing in their ear."[50] Like Gass, another fan of voice, who claims in *On Being Blue* that, "people who can't speak have nothing to say," that "it's one more thing we do to the poor, the deprived: cut out their tongues . . . allow them a language as lousy as their lives,"[51] Grace Paley wants to give voice to the dailiness of this world, to make us hear "the soft-speaking tough souls of anarchy."[52] Ernst Bloch once spoke of Seurat's "Sundayness"; the art of Grace Paley stipples her pages in shimmering garb that everyone's voice wears even on weekdays.

It is understandable that the elaboration of such "communal voices" interests above all the writers who belong in one way or another to the "margins" of American society, to ethnic or national minorities, since they promote consciousness-raising through the suggestion of collective identities. As Michael Stephens writes, "voice is just as ethnic as geographic or regional,"[53] and *Black Tickets,* written by Jayne Anne Phillips from a simple range of voices, partially pulls a region of the Appalachians from the obscurity to which it had been relegated by space and history. In Phillips's work, as in that of African American or Native American writers, the characters, somewhat in the manner of *Jacques le fataliste,* are most often voices before having more developed personalities, as if that which is shared should precede that which separates. To hear N. Scott Momaday (*House Made of Dawn*) read his Kiowa stories, to read Erdrich's *Love Medicine* or the works of Toni Cade Bambara is to take the measure of what a collective fullness of voice can be; it is to understand that voice is the main axis of the fictional grouping of identities mistreated by history. In both legend and the blues, the individual voice is the bearer of a tradition much larger than itself.

Toni Cade Bambara's use of black language knows no equal. Harsher and more crudely energetic, less in debt to social origins that would have smoothed out its unevenness, her writing is to that of Toni Morrison what the rough country sheets of our grandmothers are to the somewhat artificial and vaguely synthetic fabrics of our own. The short stories of *Gorilla, My Love* and of *The Sea Birds Are Still Alive* preceded her only novel, *The Salt Eaters.* The latter places its title between myth and everyday reality since "to eat salt" is an antidote for snakebites as well as an image of capitulation before the serpent of evil, who changes into a statue of salt. The narrative, torn between the radical discourse of Velma Henry (which threatens, at least in places, to transform the work of this political militant and feminist into a didactic novel) and the occultism practiced by Minnie Ransom (who brings back the voices of the Bible and of voodoo from the depth of the ages), is in itself an interweaving of antagonistic discourses; but the resolutions of this text, which "holds together" in large part thanks to a dizzying use of the vernacular, are scarcely due to the belief that would carry off one or the other of the positions in presence. It is the music of the voices that serves as a passage between the two worlds, that resolves the contradictions raised by the incandescent lyricism, the visionary, prophetic, and at once familiar tone of Minnie against the theories of her relative, "the staunch Marxist-Maoist-Dialectical-Historic-Materialist who is always plenty short mouthed about the buzhwahh elements in the improvisations," whom Cecile refers to as a "hard-nosed scientific bullshit detector."[54] Music in the strict sense — "These crazy folks need some saying-it-music"[55] — also serves as an intermediary, but the uncommon rhythm and precision of the voices that clash and carry the entire narrative are the secret of Bambara's successes. Her books are like indirect documentaries that do not work so much through topical exploration of the problems raised by the characters as through the exploration of a communal tonality; in "My Man Bovanne" (*Gorilla, My Love*), one can read with delight the way in which dance, music, and irresistible verbal exchanges manage to turn the conflict between generations to old Hazel's profit.

But such techniques are not reserved for African American writers whom one would relegate again in this way to a new literary ghetto, this time using the expedient of forms. If it is true that Reed or Major, who have no desire to stay there, resort to them, one can point out as counterexamples the vocal scores rendered complex by the Caribbean environment of *Continental Drift* (Banks) or the astonishing interlacing of black voices that constitutes *Far Tortuga*. This novel by Peter Matthiessen is punctuated in rare places by the words of a narrator who has been reduced to the role of a coryphaeus but whose presence seems to illustrate this precept of Wurlitzer's *Nog*: "There are times when the voice of the narrator or the presence of the narrator should almost sing out."[56] In the case in point, the voices are lowered to murmurs or raised to screams by means of a typography in three bodies. In addition, more than one white writer has been unable to resist the attraction of the blues or of jazz, which offer their privileged narrative forms to authors concerned with disengaging themselves from old structural constraints. Such is the case of Ron Sukenick (*Long Talking Bad Conditions Blues, The Endless Short*

Story) and even, in a less expected fashion, of Frederick Busch in *Too Late American Boyhood Blues.*

In Search of a Voice

Voice is also a heuristic mode in the search for personal identity once contemporary authors become preoccupied with the effect of the quality of a language on the relationships that it is possible to maintain with the world. If one can continue to hear a desire for enrichment of the common heritage ("the words of the tribe" of his master) beneath Valéry's remark when he professes to "value what a writer does only in so far as it strikes me as being of the order and having the efficacy of a step forward in the field of language,"[57] the more personal continuation given to this concern by the purist grammarian of Pascal Quignard indicates that an increased precision of speech tends to radically modify the nature of the links between one being and the Other:

> I[eurre] justified himself thus. That by refining taste, by putting in place day after day a refinery of language much like an oil refinery, one was providing thought with a perception and an agility that had become rare. That one was granting to perception a broader, more complex field, and that in this sense one was developing a less rudimentary real, less compartmentalized by abrupt, crude oppositions cutting in two or in three.
>
> He added — correctly, it seemed to me — that since a logical argument always contained syntax, the most elementary sentences forced thought to violent, quite impoverished convictions, almost tests of strength.[58]

The metamorphosis of Jethro Furber in *Omensetter's Luck* (Gass), his "change of heart," is directly tied to the changes in his voice; his relationship with the kind of absolute Other that is Brackett Omensetter only lasts under the guise of "tests of strength" because this tormented black reverend is inhabited by violent voices of imprecation and frustrated desire that forbid him all contact with the accolades promised by the strange given name of a "wide and happy" Adamic man. As for Henry Pimber, he is incapable of giving voice to his "love and sorrow" to the point of suffering lockjaw. Gass points out that, over the course of the successive manuscripts of the novel, Furber's voice progressively came to occupy a place as preponderant as unexpected: in the original project, his role was in fact insignificant. That which had conceived itself only in terms of interlacing voices (the choric commentary of Israbestis Tott, the flux of Pimber's awareness, the crossed conversations of the inhabitants of the village of Gilean, Ohio) gradually enriched itself from the central tangle of interior voices that Furber must attempt to undo in order to accept the idea of any contact with the "natural": the fulminations of Saint Augustine and of Saint Jerome, the living words from Pike's tomb, the phantasmal lasciviousness of a bridled sensuality, the echoes of childhood, the strict and Manichean sermons of the preacher.

The essential character of an "utterance" that would find in the depths of personality a true voice's modes of hooking up with others leads us to compare the fate of Henry Pimber to a failed self-analysis, that of Jethro Furber to one that succeeds. Pimber never manages to find a language of his own and the narrative voice must constantly interject itself between him and the reader. His unconscious is not open to our perception and his speech never attains the richness of invention and the verbosity that finally allow Furber his "change of heart." His puns remain fabricated and awkward, he only has at his disposal the voices of the ordinary in order to confront the extraordinary presence that interrogates him. This will bring about his death. As for Furber, he gives painful birth to his voice thanks to the conversational shuttle that confronts him with two fathers: a father in language — Pike, the old preacher lying in the churchyard — whose name provides him with the imaginary supports necessary for his free associations, and Omensetter himself, a foil of natural authority, free of the discourses that hinder Furber. The latter descends to the very core of himself in order to gather the brute signifiers that will constitute his own voice at the end of a long delirium. At first isolated from the reality of the world in which he lives by thick walls of outside voices, Furber, summoning hosts of onomatopoeias, anaphoras, puns, and noises, reconstructs reality through a complex dialectic of the interior and the exterior, the past and the present, sounds and meanings. As fast as his voice gains strength, at first disorganized by phonetic jugglings, abrupt changes of subject, rhythmic games of limericks and gratuitous couplets, then reconstructed by the artifices of metaphor and the art of the actor, he becomes aware that words that are pronounced are "superior," that they "maintain a superior control" over the real, that they "touch without being touched," that they are "at once the bait, the hook, the line, the pole, and the water in between."[59]

A comparable dramatization of the "intensification of a verbal universe" that characterizes all fiction for Frederick Karl is at the heart of McElroy's *Plus*, as we have seen. Except for the fact that the phase of forgetting and of deconstructing the "ready-to-say" of languages does not apply to IMP Plus, who is straightaway deprived through surgery of the very memory of the possibility of a voice. His own voice, which we hear coming to life, growing, and increasing in size and assurance over the course of instants, lives on the feedback of reactions to stimuli, adds bit by bit to the variety of its accents, its possibilities and nuances, going so far as to rediscover the distances indispensable to humor and irony. The voice of *Plus* moves us through the meticulously figured conditions of its birth, it has the sober beauties of the laborious emergence of self-awareness.

IMP Plus was deprived of a voice. Yet others would like to get rid of theirs. For voice, in contemporary fiction, can just as easily reveal itself to be an affirmation of personality, power, and presence, as show a desire for retreat and absence, tend as it can toward the silence that its stubborn nature refuses. This is the dual temptation of the blank Beckettian voices, illustrated in the United States by the novels of Wurlitzer and by certain texts of Coover's ("The Sentient Lens" and "Seven Exemplary Fictions," in *Pricksongs and Descants, Spanking the Maid*), the double movement of the voice that speaks to Stig Dagerman as soon as he understands that "our need for consolation is too great to be satisfied":

My power is formidable as long as I can set the force of words against that of the world, for he who constructs prisons expresses himself less well than he who builds freedom. . . . But my strength will know no more bounds the day I will have only my silence to defend my inviolability, for no axe can have a hold over living silence.[60]

This "living silence" then replaces plot and characters; the remarks made by the voice, its subject, become its very presence, its silences, its cadences, and its flux. "I can't go on, I must go on," say both Beckett and Wurlitzer, with the latter substituting only "keep on" ("I can't keep on. I have to keep on.")[61] for Beckett's famous "go on" of which Wurlitzer preserves the blankness of a tense that is less a present than a state deprived of past and future. In *Flats,* we can hear the strange echo of a line of Davenport's in *Flowers and Leaves*: "[They] had learned, / finding their sentences controvertible, not to speak."[62] The total stripping of voices that oscillate from the first to the third person in order to avoid being surprised in any one place is the point of departure for an *a minima* reconstruction of speech. An "infinite conversation" of which Maurice Blanchot thus defines the terms of the alternative by situating the voice at the precise point where choice is refused: "To speak or else to kill. Speech does not consist in speaking, but, first, in maintaining the movement of the 'or else.' "

The voice that does not "find itself" has no other choice than silence to preserve its purity, to resist the polluting invasions of outside languages, all kinds of "Americana" that Brand, in DeLillo's novel, wants to have cleaned out of his skull:

My brain needs cleaning out. I think the way I talk. The way I'm trying not to talk anymore. You can help me get rid of the slang. You have my permission to correct me whenever I fall back into the old drug argot or military talk. One of the things I've figured out for myself here in exile is that there's too much slang in my head. It's insidious. It leads to violence. You can help, Davy. I want to be colorless.[63]

Babbles

We're often repulsed by the "Tower of Babble" in which we live.[64] But from beneath the apparently general denunciation emerges a certain fascination of the kind found in Elkin's work, for example. Others question it in different terms, regretting, as Cynthia Ozick does in *The Cannibal Galaxy*, "the purity of babble, inconceivable in this valley of interpretation."[65] DeLillo tells us that the "unspeakable"

points to the limitations of language. Is there something we haven't discovered about speech? . . . Maybe this is why there's so much babbling in my books. Babbling can be frustrated speech, or it can be a purer form, an alternative speech.[66]

The suggestiveness of this enigma haunts a novel precisely entitled *Babble* by Jonathan Baumbach, who claims to have staged the only scene in American literature "with a baby-hero." And the problem is so strongly felt by DeLillo that he admits to having once written a short story that ended with the spectacle of two babies babbling in a car: "I felt these babies *knew* something. They were talking, they were listening, they were *commenting*, and above and beyond it all they were taking an immense pleasure in the exchange."[67] The mystery of unknown voices is obviously the source of the appeal of Barth's "Glossolalia," which substitutes a fascination with the mythical knowledge of a group of misunderstood prophets for Davenport's natural objects: "This glossolalia of leaves and vortex of wrens / Works beneath our dialogue."[68] "Glossolalia is interesting because it suggests there is another way to speak, there's a very different language lurking somewhere in the brain," continues DeLillo,[69] whose interest in jargons, incomplete sentences, childish chatter, grunting, foreign accents, dialects, and onomatopoeia provides part of Pammy and Lyle's voices in *Players*. For him it represents the expression of a certain "intimacy of language." The appalling English spoken by Cynthia Buchanan's "maiden" and her friends is properly revolting (*Maiden*). This novel despairs so much over the vulgar, scrawny, plastic-coated language of its protagonists that at points certain dialogues can be replaced by "blah blah blah," with no great loss. The idiotic clichés, platitudes, and trashy concerns of Fortunée Dundy would make her the ideal correspondent for Nathanael West's Miss Lonelyhearts. And yet, the very energy of these voices manages to hold together the pages of this anthology of silliness, in the same way as some popular songs and more than one opera libretto escape condemnation for minor brain damage inflicted upon the public through the contagious grace of their chorus or the noble transport of their arias. That "windbag" Horse Badorties (Kotzwinkle, *The Fan Man*) punctuates his lost hippie discourse with unbearable verbal tics; his adventures have no more coherence than his thoughts, while his language strangely resembles the place from which he is speaking in the first paragraph:

I am all alone in my pad, man, my piled-up-to-the-ceiling-with-junk pad. Piled with sheet music, with piles of garbage bags bursting with rubbish and encrusted frying pans piled on the floor, embedded with unnameable flecks of putrefied wretchedness in grease. My pad, man, my own little Lower East Side Horse Badorties Pad.[70]

Still, his incredible voice makes the novel one of the funniest to be found.

For Gaddis, on the other hand, anarchic chatter provides at once a thematic commentary on the decay of values — with cacophonies being read as transgressions against the idealized background of a "pure" language[71] — and a structural framework — with the highly identifiable different voices of his protagonists serving as the precious reference points in which his enormous novels are otherwise lacking. The voice becomes the guide through these thick forests, the tics in speech indicating the speaker's identity. Such a technique is also adopted by Harold Jaffe: in *Mole's Pity*, the reader's ear identifies the characters whose voices sweep along the entire spectrum from the wooden language of bureaucrats to the various levels of surrealism of the marginal characters. But whereas in *The Recognitions* an authorial voice always provides a yardstick by which to measure the gaps, its appearances in *JR* are so rare that the lines in which it does appear scarcely represent more than a few dozen within this 726-page novel. What dominates here in this "supreme masterpiece of acoustical collage"[72] is babble, chatter, blather, idle talk, the "noise" that invades DeLillo's *White Noise*. Gaddis's genius is to have succeeded in giving a symphonic dimension to Barthelme's "dreck," while making it carry, in spite of everything, the crushing weight of a plot so complex that it requires several readings to master. But then, the plot does not much matter, since the essential resides elsewhere.

This brings to mind the American judge who, when asked to define pornography, replied "I know it when I see it." I hope I shall be forgiven for saying that Gaddis's answer when he was asked to define the "ear" that allows him to set up the rhythm and balance of his monster conversations lies along the same line, even if he embellishes it with a few examples: "Stanley Elkin has an ear; C. P. Snow doesn't. You see what I mean."[73] And an ear is something that the people JR calls on the telephone need: his voice comes through badly, muffled as it is by the filthy handkerchief he holds over the receiver to try to give deeper, more respectable tones to his voice — that of an eleven-year-old kid with approximate English. In effect, from the phone booths of his Long Island school or from the nearby drugstore, thanks to a five-dollar investment made by his class during an educational field trip to Wall Street and ten dollars in cash, JR (Junior) Vansant will stand behind the irresistible rocketing of a financial empire destined to crumble as quickly as it was born. Not because of mistakes made directly by the little genius himself but because of vices in organization and communication within the small-time "structures" that he has set up. One day, answering the phone for JR's only partner, a third party nonchalantly goes ahead with a sale that is as massive as it is unwise. So much for the roughshod résumé of a plot as voluminous and involved as the accounts of conglomerates speculating on Wall Street. Need one add that Gaddis's vast reflections on value, swindling, art, and the Protestant work ethic find their natural expansion here?

"I mean how do I even know whose voice they are talking . . . where this company spokesman makes this statement which I don't even know who it is,"[74] says JR, giving voice on page 646 to the reader's ongoing feeling and defining our relationship to characters that are in fact "mouthpieces," "spokesmen," "bearers of the word" as one can be staff or flag bearer, a carrier of luggage or signs, heavy objects or unwieldy phrases. Gaddis immerses us headfirst in a "universe of discourse" that has never before borne its name so well. The insane logic of unmediated oral communication is applied integrally to the form. The effect this has is not unlike the fear that seizes someone who replays a tape recorded with sentences that were thought to be clearly constructed, only to find coughs, hesitations, digressions, temporary gaps never mended, open brackets in search of closure and finding none in sight, ruptures in syntax. The voices are the sole presence, the only "handlebar of the mind" (Breton) through a complex tale in which the stage can only be guessed at from behind a curtain of words, should one even choose to put together the fragments we are granted. Carriers of all the information there is, the voices rise up, pass by, and move on, vanish in the hubbub of the crowd, and are lost in radio static and signal interference. Commentary, when perchance it occurs, is nothing more than an inventory; even the presence of idle secretaries is something that must be decoded: "The voices came together, separated, rose above the grating of emery boards, and fell with the ringing of a telephone" (154). Interminable telephone conversations generalize at the level of the whole book the modus operandi of Cocteau's *The Human Voice*. Hearing only half of the conversation, the reader has to reconstruct the missing half that often contains information essential to an understanding of events. Information always arrives in a tangential way, on the rebound or as an echo from beneath the rubble of exchanges in which the phatic element plays the largest part. A shambles of interjections, swearing, and elocutionary crutches spreads out over the even greater mass of voices unrelated to the characters:

broadcast voices ooze from a radio buried in the debris of a room that, as in an Ionesco play, is ceaselessly filled by aleatory crowds, an avalanche of brand names, advertisements, and publicity spots. Communication is blocked by the layered accumulation of extraneous discourses: getting lost in their superposed strata is an everpresent threat.

JR is pure presentation. Access to these languages that come into contact without understanding each other and are torn apart by the interruptions and quid pro quos that result from ambiguity (the ambiguity is often sexual or scatological, so as to emphasize at the same time the unrealizable desires for communion and the "crap" of which their expression is made) — this access, then, is sometimes that of the witness, the innocent participant assailed on all sides by incomprehensible jabberings. Elsewhere, by the logic of telegraphic communication, the voice can literally transport the reader from one end of the line to the other, in the manner of the wild Rabelaisian project for the transporting of bodies over distance by the freezing of sound, the Frigicom project, in which one of the protagonists has invested. The scene flips without warning from the room in which we find the first speaker to one in which we find the person at the other end of the line. A character that had disappeared three pages earlier is suddenly heard at the other end of a telephone that is off the hook in an office where a passing character has brought us with no narrative ado whatsoever. Thus our impression of a certain seamlessness in this universe. When the voice does speak, space and time are constituted around it; when it is silent, they vanish. Three minutes of conversation in an office will fill five pages. Later a couple falls asleep; their eyes close on the suspension marks of an interrupted sentence; in the following sentence, or a new clause of the same sentence, it is already morning. People meet, people part; a paragraph break can contain ten days.

The voice in Gaddis is not there to modify or enrich a form, nor to reside in it: it *is* the form, and only the many fragments of literary quotations floating through these scenes of disaster are there to remind us that once there were others. This being the case, the reader can no longer feed his suspicion of the text, since to a great extent he is writing it. Through the voice of Gibbs, Gaddis shows us this at least twice. Once in reaction to Bast ("Ask them to bring one God damned bit of effort want everything done for them . . ." [290]); and the other to explain more calmly to Amy that you "can't say what a book's about before it's done that's what any book worth reading's about, problem soving" (499).

Voice-as-Matter

Through their various modes of excess, Gaddis's novels illustrate the desire for that "perpetual orgy of a literature to get lost in" discussed by

Flaubert.[75] Echoing him in *The History of Madness,* Foucault tells us, in substance, that in a world in which it is known that freedom and happiness will not come through politics, language and signs remain the only resource in which freedom can really "rage." Witness this paragraph from *Americana* where it is the voice that seduces rather than the completely unimportant message:

In the evening we sat in the camper on Howley Road and listened to the radio. . . . I did not listen to the news, merely to the words themselves, the familiar oppressive phrases. . . . The words . . . soon seemed to generate an existence of their own, to demand an independence, to live in a silhouette of meaning more subtle, more cunning than the intelligence which bred them might ever know. We listened quietly for a while. The announcer said he had accidentally read the previous day's dispatch.[76]

It is not so much that the voice and words become a sort of artificial paradise as that, as we shall see, the materiality of sound and of sentences is able to become a source of eroticism and inebriation. They are "creamy and delicious," as Steve Katz tells us, whose drunk-on-words voices spread themselves from the first to the last page of his books. Rather, they seem to be the only remaining means of access to the physical and spiritual truth of a world that is strangled by the neck brace (or *minerve*) of paralyzing discourses that have nothing to do with the owl-like wisdom of *Pilgermann,* Russell Hoban's wise bird. As for John Hawkes's "owl," it quickly turned into an executioner.[77]

The materiality of the voice, true fuel of the body and of being itself, is privileged by Wurlitzer, who has the narrator of *Flats* say: "I've used up all I have to say. That's Halifax speaking. We both want to use up all we have to say. Memphis had nothing to say. Omaha had little to say. The engine throbs on and off" (64). When all is said and done, he will "miss the voices more than the bushes" (66), for the exhaustion of the voice occurs after that of the real:

It is one of the rare, almost universal principles that, in man, air is inhaled, then, once it has been used for otherwise serious purposes, it is exhaled through a voice that amuses itself by saying anything at all, with the intention of breathing.
"Oh!" said Ieurre . . . "words, are used-up air!"[78]

It may well be possible that the "stuff" of Hunter Thompson's heroes (*Hell's Angels, Fear and Loathing in Las Vegas*) and Tom Wolfe's (*The Right Stuff*) consists solely in the energy of their voices, in that kind of hyper-narrativity where language narrates itself in addition to everything else, where the form of the voice becomes its content, where its exhaustion expresses the limits of experience. The result being an expressionism of lexical and syntactical inventions, a kind of supernarrativity, as one speaks of "postcombustion" or of "overdrive." In these "journalists' " works, the verbal electricity of the narrative voice submerges all descriptive functions. Ironically, the ultimate intransitivity of a voice wallowing in its rhythms to allow the waves themselves to speak has much in common with the inflamed preaching done by hordes of fundamentalist preachers who are invading American airwaves and the pages of *Americana,* melting down reason through their burning rhetoric whose style of delivery and tone make the formulas they are proposing interchangeable; and their only attempt at gaining support is through the massage of a voice unencumbered by the logics of any real argument: so go the trances induced by the chantings of "storefront churches." Anti-intellectualism finds its natural recourse here, and Mailer's voice is often that of a "stage desperado" (Mark Schechner), tough and righteous at one and the same time. Drawing its voices from the depths of a culture, the "new journalists' " (how time flies!) expressionism signals the secret return of a discredited mimesis. This attitude has its own pathetic side. The dry burned-out voice causes all the more suffering for having once been full. In Cassady, Mailer, Thompson, Wurlitzer, DeLillo, or Price, whenever the voice becomes hoarse, breaks, or runs dry, the whole being is threatened with extinction. For in their works the voice is never a simple mode of transportation for information, a channel of communication: it is an outpouring of "substance" to fill the abysmal lack, a bit like the sweet young girls in Remedios Varos's tapestry mentioned by Pynchon at the beginning of *The Crying of Lot 49,* "embroidering a kind of tapestry which spilled out the slit windows and into a void, seeking hopelessly to fill the void."[79] What a strange relationship to the real in these captures and feedings by regurgitation: the return of Faulkner's spider.

"The Stuff Dreams Are Made Of": The Voice That Dreams

No matter how material, the body is a "house of breath," as the title of a novel by William Goyen puts it (*The House of Breath*). Goyen's fundamental poetics could be defined by the title of a collection of short stories: *Had I a Hundred Mouths.* And his late *Arcadio* was less a "disincarnated" voice, as has been said, than a substitute, a guarantor of unity for a hermaphroditic body in search of its identity, the lyric and despairing witness of an obscurity that envelops and isolates. The singer and his voice melt into the listener and his thoughts, replacing the impossible physical contact that, for mere mortals, is the ultimate place of the most fertile spiritual collisions. The musicality of Goyen's novels, related to that found in William Spackman's and Edmund White's, originates in the vaporization of a beloved and encumbering flesh, the "stuff," in answer to Prospero, of which "dreams are made." The dreaming voice becomes caresses in their works; it tries to make the words be forgotten through its songs.

And yet our attention is constantly pulled, by certain writers less inclined to dismiss matter altogether, toward the relations between the dream, erotic or otherwise, and words. To each master his due, and to Nabokov the dizzying affirmation — a thousand times more eloquent than the Freudian ties of metaphor and metonymy to the condensations and displacements of *Traumarbeit* (another revenge of the assailant of the "Viennese delegation"?) — according to which "tropes are the dreams of speech."[80]

A sensuality of the voice, an erotic of the word are at the origin of two curios in William Gass's works. Gourmand readers, who will not be deaf to the cuddly and cajoling voice of the beautiful Babs, are referred to *Willie Masters' Lonesome Wife*; and those who are not insensitive to the subtle tastes and the accents of a color are referred to *On Being Blue*. For all Babs's insistence that she is only a "necklace of sounds, after all — nothing more than that really — an arrangement, a column of air that rises and falls," and that "behind the laughing porcelain of teeth" she hears the "terror of terminology,"[81] the "babble" suggested by the name of this woman with the multicolored body (the book's pages are of four different colors) is rather the murmur of brooks carrying little pebbles that Gass tells us are the words themselves that he likes to roll around on his tongue. From "babble" to "pebble" Gass tells us the joys of an "inexpressible state of soliloquy," the physics of "lip-movers," the happiness of a voice fashioned or received, of "that which dwells in words."[82] This verbologist's relationship to words is like that of the oenologist to wine — knowing as the other does that the "soul" is found in the "swirl of the mouth"; he is to words what the seducer is to women. He recalls one of Elkin's "condominium" scenes in which the concert of voices around the swimming pool is a prelude to other minglings ("The men's voices fertilize the women's. Their sounds fuck."),[83] or the couplings of the more somber voices in "Lechery" or "Country" (Jayne Anne Phillips's *Black Tickets*), or Furber's soliloquy in *Omensetter's Luck* that "made love to discreet verbs, easy nouns, delicate conjunctions." He also recalls, in passing, the truly eighteenth-century verve of Michel Chaillou's *Rêve de Saxe*: "He practices verbal coitus. The sperm is his words, his ejaculatory mania, his way of inseminating a sentence, of talking an adjective into a fling, of persuading a verb to screw a complement."[84]

Having arrived in the Land of Oz, Dorothy turns to Toto and says with a straight face: "I have a feeling we're not in Kansas anymore!"[85] Those who penetrate the fictional country of Jerome Charyn experience just such an unexpected feeling of disorientation. Everything seems so normal that the voice signaling "the strange" must come from our dreams. During the sixties, Charyn participated in the "voice project" at Stanford University with John Hawkes. It is remarkable that the "power" of the voice should have equally fascinated two writers who share an identical anxiety. If Charyn turned his preoccupations with power as such toward his detective tetralogy,[86] one of the essential mainsprings of his "fabulation" lies in the music and the rhythm of an inimitable voice. Charyn attributes the "magic realism" of his novels to the fact that for him the text is a dream state. The child in him, having remained a *flâneur,* a gleaner of images and dreams, and having become, it would seem, a slave to writing, does nothing other than fall back into the arms of Morpheus every time he sits down at his desk. Writing, for Charyn, amounts to sleepwalking. Just as he assigns to the twists and turns of his novels the role of subverting the narrative structures of the genres from which they are borrowed, so he assigns to voice the role of dissolving the image of the real that threatens to reflect itself in the words, as well as the task of lending his universe the fabulous blur that substances smeared on the lens can give to camera shots. The "real" being too important to be abandoned to the realists, a personal synthesis of stylistic experiences and of moral perspective allowed him to bring to life a comic and subversive voice that reveals and deforms at the same time. Not that the nightmare is ever far from the dream, according to this logic. The voice sometimes caws, goes hoarse, and cracks, signaling the swerves of an imaginary along whose path horrifying ruts and ditches—holocausts, the loss of loved ones, or fascism—defy the providential balance of the sleepwalker.

Finally, in the deepest part of the dream, in the hollow of the wakened sleep of hypnosis, the unknown voice of language itself can be born. In *Mary Stuart's Ravishment Descending Time* by Georgiana Peacher, a text pushed to the limit, like *Finnegans Wake* to which it owes so much, the voice of an unconscious that laughs and plays with the frames and the signs of fiction is freed by self-hypnosis. And so, even though one can think that "prose becomes fiction when we are seduced by the voice of the writer into believing anything,"[87] the urgency of a voice stripped of all surroundings (for having devoured them) wants to pull us along by leaps and bounds toward the prairies of live poetry, a poetry in which Joë Bousquet who, in spite of his crucifixion responded to its calls, saw nothing other than the "speech of speech."

But the day is drawing to a close, and the greener pastures that lie further in this direction are, sadly, not ours to explore.

Part III
The Age of American Fiction

Chapter 14
The Age of American Fiction

Ists and isms are rather a growing weariness.
— Emerson, 1841

Regarding works of art, it is wise to keep an eye on the company they keep but to allow their civil status to fluctuate slightly.
— Julien Gracq, *En lisant, en écrivant*

Phony Genres . . .

This essay opened with an observation: the categories by which one tried to control American postwar novels (Fall in! Attention!) appeared unable to hold back the flood of new fictions. These pages would like to loop the loop, to complete the collapse of these ancient pigeonholes through the dispersal of groups and the scattering of genres, to restore the long view to perspectives and free play to the present, to highlight again the confusion that the present work wanted to provoke, the diversity that it wanted to render: rather than pursue improper categorization under various "isms" which only replace knowledge with synecdoche, it would seem preferable to me to spend time in the company of artists in order to listen to their voices instead of assigning them a role. In literature, there are times when justice might demand that we open each volume of a living writer as if it were their first, in order to avoid burdening with debt the liberties lived therein. In this way, suspicion, which came to bear on representations lacking in distance and on automatic affiliations, also affects literary historiography.

Returning to the profound differences that have appeared in the production of ethnic and social groups previously read through the constraint of grids that were more sociological than literary, I would like to complete by means of various testimonies the illustration of this growing and frequently expressed desire to escape the stereotypes, this refusal of the "amputations," as Clarence Major has put it, that expectations provoke. Alice Walker, whom one can hardly suspect of refusing the identity of a black woman, writes the following in *In Search of Our Mothers' Gardens*— a remark that was scarcely heard, it would appear: "Writing should move away from sociology, toward greater concern for ambiguities, complexities, contradictions. Away from exploration, toward mystery and prophecy."[1] In the name of this responsibility of vision, and in reaction to a paternalistic, collective, and normative review—with just a whiff of ideological fashion — of several black women novelists that had appeared in *The New York Times,* Lynne Sharon Schwartz also writes: "[These] gifted writers . . . should be free to present black males, or any other groups for that matter, as their own visions and not social conditions dictate. In an age of image worship, let us remember that literature is not public relations." Perhaps one will find this kind of recommendation useless, since obviously, even from a strict political point of view, the strength of an extraordinary imagination does more to recommend an author and that author's class, sex, or race, than the hackneyed or pious refrains of threepenny critical tracts. Yet this would sell short the astonishing pressure exerted by intellectual conformism that, although it varies its credo with disturbing frequency, continues to inform authorized criticism all the more vigorously. To be black, like Mason, the protagonist of *My Amputations,* and like him to "exceed" (in two senses, yes, completely: to go beyond *and* to tire out) the accepted attitude, means to expose oneself to the jeers of one's own social group, to the "interrogation" conducted by a public that has come looking for the simple confirmation of its ideological certainties. In this day and age, to be a woman and to write without "writing woman"[2] does not better one's chances of entry into the literary pantheons. On the other hand, one gets forgiven one's petty mediocrities as long as one's intentions are good, that is to say, in fashion. "Good intentions" continue to characterize "good literature." It is only because her "sociological quota" has been filled in other respects, and because she owes no aesthetic explanations to anyone, that Paule Marshall can calmly assert — *horresco referens!*— that "language is the only homeland" of the writer.

Thus, it is *against* all expected publishing formulas that the most interesting "minority" authors write. Far from complying with the accepted thematics and image encouraged by the ideological environment, they convince by reason of their art, strictly speaking, by reason of their ability to dust off and energize the tradition. As a black man, Reed speaks in the name of other minorities; a red thread of Indianism runs through Major's imagination in *Painted Turtle: Woman with Guitar.* Bambara pulls her world from the conventional ghettos. Morrison, born in Ohio, takes us beyond the "South," where her voices are born, toward the even more distant southern magics of Latin America.[3] Their technical sophistication does not distinguish them from their fellow brothers and sisters of the social majority which they are undisturbed to join within a militant aesthetic minority. The combined genres of Rolando Hinojosa (interviews punctuate *Dear Rafe,* an "epistolary novel"), the formal audacities of Clarence Major, the new historiography of David Bradley, the legendary restructurings of Leslie Marmon Silko, the hybridization of memory in the work of Maxine Hong Kingston, the linguistic combat of William Melvin Kelley, the proliferation of narrators in the work of Louise Erdrich: the escape from thematic ghettos is effected through the audacity of forms. In *Elbow Room,* James Alan McPherson openly discusses narrative categories, the true stakes of his writing that, as his title confesses, is made to feel cramped by ideological clichés:

Narrator is unmanageable. Demonstrates a disregard for form bordering on the paranoid. Questioned closely, he declares himself the open enemy of conventional narrative categories. When pressed for reasons, narrator became shrill in insistence that "borders," "structures," "frames," "order," and even "form" itself are regarded by him with the highest suspicion. Insists on unevenness as a virtue. Flaunts an almost barbaric disregard for the moral mysteries, or integrities, of traditional narrative modes. . . . In order to save this narration, editor felt compelled to clarify slightly, not to censor but to impose at least the illusion of order. This was an effort toward preserving a certain morality of technique. Editor speaks here of a morality of morality, of that necessary corroboration between unyielding material and the discerning eye of absolute importance in the making of a final draft.[4]

Similarly, the most efficacious militant feminists are not the strident (Marge Piercy) or simplistic (Marilyn French) ones, who limit themselves to pamphlet writing, but rather those who distance themselves the most from sanctioned discourses through the grace and vigor of their poetics (Marianne Hauser, Toni Morrison, Mary Caponegro, Rikki Ducornet, or Marilynne Robinson), by creatively mixing genres (myth, fiction, personal biography in the work of Kingston, Silko, Walker, or Erdrich), or by grounding their irony and critique on the placing in perspective (at times metafictional) of dominant discourses (Joanna Russ, Grace Paley, Ntozake Shange). None of these characteristics, it must be said, is necessarily peculiar to their sex. Ironically, the most convincing literary successes from a feminist point of view belong to the older generation among our contemporaries, to women little concerned with orthodoxy in these matters: Marianne Hauser, Ursule Molinaro, and Georgiana Peacher, in their distinguished discretion, do more for "l'écriture féminine" than the battle's more mediatized "specialists." Yet we should remain aware that Alan Friedman's *Hermaphrodeity,* for example, is also devoted, in an equally convincing manner, to the blurring of sexual boundaries, to blowing to pieces the "male grammar" denounced by his sister feminists, making it impossible to differentiate between Millie (man) and Willie (woman) Niemann (his name is nobody). In addition, if one is bent on applying sexual difference as a literary parameter, how are we to group together without artifice, in the gay American domain, the raw lyric harshness and violence of John Rechy's novels and the controlled, somewhat "artistic" lyricism of that admirable stylist Edmund White? With what artificial boundaries would it then be necessary to beset the works of Coleman Dowell, Goyen, Burroughs, or Purdy? How can one not distinguish the experimentations of Audre Lorde (*Zami: A New Spelling of My Name*, 1982) from the commonplaces and vulgarities of Rita Mae Brown?

When it comes to geographic affiliations, one must be just as wary of the comforts of well-tried labels. Grace Paley stresses this ironically when she says that "all American writers are regional writers, even if they sometimes feel they don't belong to the right region," and then defines herself as "a regional writer from New York" before declaring, in the same breath, that the great river into which regional currents flow is not American literature but world literature.[5] Howard Mosher, whose whole being is tied to New England, as may also be the case for John Irving, Carolyn Chute, or Thomas Williams, nonetheless insists on saying, as hunters and fishermen do, that a region is no more than a *jumping-off place*, "a starting point from which they strike out in so many different directions that the term 'regional' seems to have no application to their work at all."[6] If the South has preserved, to certain ears, its particularity of tone, this is because its fiction, as Lewis Simpson tells us, "has retained its autonomy within American literature by making the very loss of its subject its subject."[7] This is not new; the remark can nonetheless still be of some use in the case of Cormac McCarthy, John W. Corrington, or Marion Montgomery. Yet it remains a fact that Barry Hannah is aesthetically closer to McGuane or to Harrison, that Richard Ford has more affinities with Harrison or with Jayne Anne Phillips than with Fred Chappell or William Humphrey, that Harry Crews sometimes approaches the grotesque aspects of a Terry Southern, whose name indicates no real regional membership. The Southern tradition of nostalgia and remembrance is just as typical today of the works of certain Northwestern writers (Kittredge, Brautigan). William Kennedy may well be the bard of Albany; but the beauties of his work imply some loyalties in which myth plays an infinitely greater part than the real.

Is all this the effect of an increasing homogenization of American culture? Or is it that the pulverization of our times invites one's attention back to the sturdier forms and frames of images from the olden days?

More probably, it is a consequence of obsolescent aesthetics, at the same time as distances are taken from all attempts at direct representation, when creations of fictional worlds converge, fictional worlds in which forms and language lead the dance, fictional worlds just as impatient with established thematics as with genres canonized by tradition.

The "Novel" Beyond Suspicion

The irony is delightful: in order to denounce such a "confusion of genres" — that which makes the production of a "document" the primary motivation of a literary work — contemporary fiction resorts to another sort of confusion, one that is both lucid and fertile. Everything occurs as though fiction no longer defined itself as a genre but as genres, as though Henry James's *fluid puddings* had once again complicated their recipes.

In the course of the preceding chapters, we have witnessed the wrecking of recognized subgenres: in the middle of his career, Brautigan waged systematic war on them by opposing them two by two; Thomas Berger relies on their individual use the better to go beyond them; in *Arthur Rex*, he transforms the Round Table into a magic square by prolonging the effects of the relationship of Lancelot and Guinevere; even metafictions become the object of critical usage (Sorrentino). The detective novel has suffered at the hands of Pynchon, Kotzwinkle, Brautigan, Crawford, Charyn, Carkeet, Auster, and others. The Western bears the brunt of *The Beetle Leg, The Hawkline Monster, Little Big Man,* or *Yellow Back Radio Broke-Down*; the historical novel bears that of *The Public Burning, Ragtime, The Adventures of Mao,* and *The Chaneysville Incident.* The pastoral is spared neither by McElroy, nor by Olson or Hawkes. Exotic landscapes have difficulty withstanding the "Mount Pastiche" and "Lake Lobotomples" of Crawford's *Travel Notes.* Tales and legends provide the sticks with which Coover, Barthelme, Elkin, Barth, and Berger beat them. Such parodies, destructions, and oppositions are neither gratuitous nor purely negative. Making use against the grain of the effects of the "rebarbarization" of serious literature according to Shklovsky, they bring to light the narrative means, the contradictory traditions of these conventional narratives; they explain the reasons for which myth remains or does not remain possible, the conditions in which it can be harmful or useful, making use of their conclusions in order to refine our comprehension of complex phenomena that do nothing less than affect our modes of apprehending the real and color our interpretations of the world. Once again they demonstrate, certainly, that "in families of the mind, as in some others, gifts and loans do not necessarily inspire gratitude";[8] but, such layings bare bring forgotten connections to light, make plain unknown resemblances, authorize exchanges, allow experiments in hybridization to be undertaken that make up for the cruelty of certain grafts by producing original and marvelous blossomings.

The recent tinkering with vocabulary by various and sundry authors in order to point out the dissolution of earlier dividing lines can be seen as a sign of the tensions to which contemporary fiction is subjected: "mystory" (Walker), "hysterical novel" (Bradley), "faction" (Mailer), "docudramas" (Reed), "critifiction"; with increasing frequency, subtitles modify and specify that which the "novel" no longer always manages to say. A random look on my bookshelf reveals: "writing" (Brautigan), "fictions" (Coover), "a sort of love story" (Robbins), "chronicles" (Anne Rice), "monologue" (Sonia Pilcer), "dream" (Acker). One can argue without great risk that the literary period studied here is dominated by such responsibility taken for hybrid genres; they characterize the times better than any other: cross(ed) words, crossed modes of a new type of "crucifiction." From the cohabitation of criticism and poetry in *Pale Fire* to the blurring of the boundary between fiction and history in *The Armies of the Night*; from the osmoses between biography, autobiography, and fiction — diversely illustrated by Millhauser, Baumbach, Vonnegut, and Sukenick — to the internecine wars of Brautigan; from the mutual fertilizations of mythology and realism in the works of Kennedy, Morrison, or Boyle to the mixtures of the fabulous, the fantastic, and daily life in the works of Ingalls, Ted Mooney, or Hoban; from the stories in the form of hypotheses of Pynchon to the speculative fiction of Denis Johnson or Steve Erickson and to the science fictions of Gibson or Mooney, from the "probable" to the "possible," the very notion of genre becomes porous. In 1986, a young Indian living in the United States named Vikram Seth published a "novel in verse": *The Golden Gate*. Old-style realism crossbreeds and enriches itself through "fabulism": in derealized times, it is perhaps a means of survival for mimesis, which might simply be adapting itself to new conditions; it is also often the trace of a refusal to reach the real through paths that have been well-trodden or booby-trapped. Within remarkable works, a whole novelistic range emerges from the storehouses of literary memory, from the gothic to the sentimental novel, passing through the picaresque and the epistolary; the circus, jazz, pop music, serials, the press, recipes, and how-to guides all blend together there with no great trouble.[9] A taste for the kitsch of a period lacking aesthetic direction? Functional eclecticism for plural times in which the memory and nostalgia industry casts its trinkets upon the present in order to avert our uncertain gazes from the future? The dehierarchization of the "postmodern" as a baroque moment? It would be pointless to silence the questions suggested here by offering hasty replies, to conclude our efforts at opening up with untimely blockages.

Better to limit oneself to observations: aside from the fact that "novels" and collections of shorter pieces are mingled together here, it no longer appears even reasonable to continue to speak in general terms of the "novel," in spite of the constitutive "generophagic" nature of this anti-genre according to Bakhtin. Moreover, when it comes to a French view of American works, confidence in these generic terms has never been immense: when "novel" (*roman*) distances itself as much as possible from the "romance"; when it calls itself a "novel" in order to signify something quite different from the "short story" (*nouvelle*); when "novella" does not mean "short novel" any more than it does "long short story"; when *récit* in French places a stylistic emphasis on the texts that it defines, and when its equivalent— "narrative" —places a historic emphasis on its own texts; when, finally, each passing designation makes Meininger's law appear all the more striking and more appropriate, according to which semantic baggage travels badly, then one scarcely dreams of making any explanation convincing that would rely on etymologies, the relationships and the harmonics of these taxonomic vagabonds. But to read William Gass is not to read a "novelist": it is to submit oneself to the experience of a writing that retains the same foundations in a "novel" (*Omensetter's Luck*), in "short stories" (*In the Heart of the Heart of the Country*), in "essays" (*Habitations of the Word*), in a "philosophic inquiry" (*On Being Blue*); to express his greatness while basing one's argument on one of these "genres" only would be to mislead the reader. With great humility, Guy Davenport has justified his "assemblages of history and necessary fiction." Immediately desirous of repudiating the classic instances of the novel, John Hawkes offers a gripping corpus to those who would wish to explore the thin line that is reputed to separate fiction from poetry. Charyn is as powerfully "mythopsychotic" in *Metropolis* as in his novels; Kennedy is not different in *O Albany!* from the author of his fictional trilogy. Finally, William S. Wilson bases all his activity as a writer on the refusal to give to his essays the conclusions he denies to his fictions, just as he refuses to give to his fictions the openness he is loathe to remove from his essays.

Fiction, the Soul of the Novel

Whatever the case, these tensions are constitutive elements of the "novel" that will always wriggle out of straitjackets, as Bakhtin has shown. From the start, the novel was bastardy, mixed ink, parasite, excrescence, curiosity, drift; it covered its dubious pallet with a set of respectable linens from which it never extricated itself: travel narrative, pseudo-autobiography or journalism for Defoe, more or less direct epistles and confessions in the works of Laclos or Richardson. The bourgeois, who was thus served by being offered the instrument of vast social frescoes where, in due time, he would be able to find, in case of ideological need, illustrations of both "human nature" and "the nature of things," nonetheless proved most ungrateful for quite some time: even in the Victorian age, there were still some with enough good sense to attribute, on the scale of values of an evangelical review— the "spiritual barometer" linking death ("minus seventy") to glory ("plus forty") — a grade of "minus forty" to novel reading. This is because, already, more than the "novel," which pledged allegiance, formally or thematically, to the structure of an industrial society and a Newtonian universe, "fiction" was coming under fire: lie, imaginary loves and adventures, sham stories embellished by titillating and reprehensible digressions, the "resident madwoman" (as the French call imagination) on a binge; in short, as in the eyes of Smollett, "the index of Catholicism." The novel gradually became acceptable because it stubbornly borrowed its flashy rags from other genres, asserted itself as the vague resurgence of an "elsewhere," the doppelgänger of some Other, and, pro forma, wore the conventional masks. Certain romantics could still see the introduction of poetic verse into novels as an official mark guaranteeing the product's authenticity.

One might as well say that to express the least opinion on the "hybridization of genres in fiction," even American, even contemporary, amounts, *grosso modo,* to claiming that yellow is yellow, that circles are round, or that fog is foggy. The fact that the object in question has *borrowed* color, forms, or vapors in order to indulge in other clandestine practices thanks to them changes absolutely nothing. Even if "novel" is not contained by "fiction," which nevertheless overflows it, even if the novel as a historic genre was able for a time to suggest that it was possible to draw its boundaries, it owes to Proteus both the impreciseness of its being and its salvation. The current recourse to the term "fiction" signals that we have finally freed ourselves from the feeling of sinning through the practice of the unreal; but the word "novel" is still very much in use as soon as the question of labeling comes up. Let us give thanks to Bakhtin for having on its behalf vaunted precisely what the novel was: a place where "one can find everything," a place not unlike a department store. But, since he was not heard, since "novel" tends to perpetuate for our time what it was assumed to mean in its realist and naturalist phases, since American publishing — often against the authors' wishes — persists in applying this label to forms whose only dream is of distancing themselves from its mimetic connotations, since the semantic heritage is heavy, in other words, and since most contemporary writers do not have the feeling that the false innocence of this designation can resist suspicion, even while rigging it up in the epithet "new," we shall speak here of "the age of American *fiction*" in order to refer to the movement most representative of literary creation in prose in the United States since 1960. To speak of the "new novel," with the writers of suspicion, is to have more confidence in the overhauling of an existing genre than in its vigors and its powers to transform. To speak, beyond suspicion, of "fiction" is, to speak improperly, "to venture forth," if one is willing to read beneath this verb a personal and transitive strength, along with an intransitive sense: to explore, certainly, oneself and the world, but also "to make an adventure of oneself."

As he refined his analyses of the "embedding" of forms and genres in the novel, Bakhtin, as a matter of fact, reached conclusions that sound like definitions of the creative gestures presented in this book. Let us listen to him distinguish, among the interaction of genres at the heart of the novel, "incorporated" genres and "framing" genres: the former insert into the structure "short stories, lyrical songs, poems, dramatic scenes," "verse, aphorisms, maxims," while the latter provide structure such as "confession, the diary, travel notes, biography, the personal letter . . ."[10] Let us note, in particular, an effect of some importance: in the case of "incorporated genres," Bakhtin observes that in principle "any genre could be included in the construction of the novel, and in fact it is difficult to find any genres that have not at some point been incorporated into a novel by someone" (320–21). But he goes on to add something of great importance here: "Such incorporated genres usually preserve within the novel their own structural integrity and independence, as well as their own linguistic and stylistic peculiarities" (321). On the other hand, "framing genres," those genres that determine structure and "are fundamental to the novel's development," also introduce into the novels "their own languages" — note this plural that can only apply to that by which "genres" is affected:

but these languages are primarily significant for making available points of view that are generative in a material sense, since they exist outside literary conventionality and thus have the capacity to broaden the horizon of language available to literature, helping to win for literature new worlds of verbal perception, worlds that had been already sought and partially subdued in other — extraliterary — spheres of linguistic life. (323)

In terms that are at once more precise and more directly important here, in this second case, the ways in which their languages are used are "indirect, conditional, distanced." All these forms "signify a relativizing of linguistic consciousness in the perception of language borders — borders created by history and society, and even the most fundamental borders (i.e., those between languages as such)" (323). Reading this, are we not led to believe that the novel has always known "suspicion" even when its authors were not aware of it? Today, those who want to live and to write with such awareness prefer to underline *both* this manner of winning "new worlds of verbal perception" *and* this other manner of objectifying "language as such"; in order to do this and to break free from a heritage that appears from that time onward as an aberration, an illusion, or a hypocrisy, they refer to their activity under the name of "fiction." It is thus demonstrated that "they shoot novels, don't they?"

Rather than smuggling in deviously constitutive ambiguity, as Charles Newman summarizes it below, contemporary fictions choose to acknowledge the contraband activities they indulge in and, if forced to take refuge in one or the other, opt for the second:

The novel has always exemplified an uneasy cohabitation between the empirical and the fictional impulses, which Ortega defined as the conflict between "scientific psychology" and "imaginary psychology." The empirical grants the appearance of actuality, while the fictional indulges in the appearance of ideal system.[11]

In his own time, Montaigne, commenting on the poet who wanted "to give heaviness even to smoke," knew that "our discourse has capacity enough to provide the stuff for a hundred other worlds, and then to discover their principles and construction! It needs neither matter nor foundation; let it run free: it can build as well upon the void as upon the plenum, upon the inane as upon the material."[12]

Beyond suspicion, "novel" can no longer be anything more than a taxonomic remanence, the light of an extinguished star that still reaches the earth. Its energy is always with us. The "novel" is indeed dead, bequeathing to us its eternal youth, escaping the shackles of the term in which one tried to imprison it. Its spirit, fiction, floats free, above the best American prose of our time, forgetful of a body rejected because of its wrinkles. To weep for this "dear departed," one would have to be of little faith indeed.

Fictions

"Fiction" reigns, therefore. Anarchist that it is, the instrument and reverse of power, it does not cease emphasizing the artifices that make our world "hold," that give it its coherence and the diversity of its "meanings." Its orderings are "an act of mind which brings together like two hands that buzzing blooming confusion of which James spoke, and some sublimely empty abstract system like that which Euclid once devised . . . brings them together till they clap."[13] Ortega y Gasset already surprised himself by wondering whether "human life at its most human" was not "a work of fiction," insofar as it transcended the reality of nature. Not that it is simply a matter, henceforth, of placing our trust in words in order to entrap the dream. Particularly in a literary tradition where the heirs of Pym forever strive to distinguish some meaningful forms within the senselessness of great white spaces, the activity of fiction consists more than ever, and simultaneously, in laying bare the frames inherited from experience and in escaping them while discerning, suggesting, or building new models. What still remains of "realism" within this activity, the latter owes to the confessions of a society that can now only hide its mediocrities from its own eyes thanks to the opiate discourses wherein the fictionist stalks its patterns. Fiction, in the United States, scarcely attempts to *formulate* the dream any more, let alone the American one; it lays bare the ways in which this very fiction gives shape and order to the formlessness of a disorder, banalizes it, therefore, does away with its exceptionalism.

For the "immachination" that Pynchon discovers at the heart of his worlds, we must try to substitute readings that are consciously "immachinated." Such is the price of lucidity. Berger tries to make of each of his novels an "independent existence," a new reality that he hopes the reader will then approach "without the luggage of received ideas, *a priori* assumptions, sociopolitical axes to grind, or feeble moralities in search of support."[14] Similarly, Coover seeks to "debunk these bogus mythmakers once and for all."[15] If, as the anthropologist Clifford Geertz would argue, societies, like lives, contain their own interpretation, if it is enough to find it in order to have access to and weigh upon it, then, and at the same time, such explanations are an invitation to make them into books that provide their own rules of operation and that make their authors wonder about the imperative demand that makes them write them. Thus, William S. Wilson says that he composes fictions "in order to prove falsehoods, which a scientist cannot do," and citing Polanyi, he adds that it is a question of a "systematic course in teaching myself to hold my own beliefs."[16] The strength of a model, externally imposed or internally adopted or experienced, is the object of the explorations of fiction. For McElroy, "fiction is a model of the way in which life consists in its possibilities, and of the fact that they are always linked in one way or another, whether the artist controls their relations or not."[17] After all, refuting this or that model by opposing another, or one's own conception, presents no lesser risk of succumbing to a model. Thus, Don DeLillo believes that "over the years it's possible for a writer to shape himself as a human being through the language he uses. I think written language, fiction, goes that deep. He not only sees himself but begins to make himself or remake himself."[18] The ambivalence and ambiguity of the writer's relationship to fiction are the object of a passage in a short story by Millhauser: the marvellous, impossibly beautiful "snowmen" of *In the Penny Arcade* possess the infinite plasticity of fictions, their cunning and perverse powers.

But it was precisely a feature of that second day, when the art of the snowman appeared to reach a fullness, that one could no longer be certain to what extent the act of seeing had itself become infected by these fiery snow-dreams. . . . But once the idea of "snowman," already fertile with instances, had blossomed to include animals, new and dizzying possibilities presented themselves, for there was suddenly nothing to prevent further sproutings and germinations; and it was then that I began to notice, among the graceful white figures and the daring, exquisite animals, the first maples and willows of snow. . . . I think it was the very thoroughness of these successes that produced in me the first stirrings of uneasiness, for I sensed in our extravagant triumphs an inner impatience. Already, it seemed to me, our snowmen were showing evidence of a skill so excessive, an elaboration so painfully and exquisitely minute, that it could scarcely conceal a desperate restlessness. . . . Exhausted by these prodigies, I sought to pierce the outward shapes and seize the unquiet essence of the snow, but I saw only whiteness there.[19]

The thaw returns, and with it, almost a relief in seeing an end brought to these fleeting petrifications of that which should remain moving; the melting of the snow is

a protest against the solemnity, the rigidity, of our snowmen. What has seemed a blossoming forth of hidden powers, that second afternoon, suddenly seemed a form of intricate constriction. It was as if those bird-filled maples, those lions, those leaping ballerinas and prancing clowns had been nothing but a failure of the imagination. (131)

The true beauties appear when these snowmen, "weary with consummation, swerved restlessly away" (131), then "distorted, elongated, disturbingly supple figures began to replace our punctilious imitations" (132). Elsewhere, Millhauser has his "romantic" say that a work of fiction "is a radical act of the imagination whose sole purpose is to supplant the world," and not to imitate it.[20] Certainly, the dominant characteristic of his protagonist would lead us to take his remark with a grain of salt; but, on the whole, as demonstrated in "Cathay" or in "In the Penny Arcade" (in *In the Penny Arcade*), this substitution is in no way idealistic; on the contrary, it consists in showing the role of the artifice that subtends any kind of real by creating artifices (automats, clockworks, snow figures, or miniatures), and that, in turn, avow their nature in the very gesture that constitutes them as real. The modification of relations between the recourse to the possible and the recourse to the probable tears fiction away from the "novel" for good. Whatever might remain of realism is systematically marshaled into the service of the imaginary against the real as it is perceived.

Naturally, these practices are not distinguishable from a meditation on the power of fictions and, from the characters of Coover who are their victims or who manipulate them, to those of James Purdy, "memoirists," whose more or less illusory "versions" constantly seek to impose themselves in an authoritarian way on everyone, there would be a long list of the exploitations, avoidances, ruses, and deliriums to which a radical and laicized antinomianism has recourse in order to break the received readings of reality. Whether paranoiac (Pynchon) or libertarian (Coover), fictions declare themselves necessary; whether they threaten or strip away, they are omnipresent in a world that fiction no longer seeks merely to imitate, but whose forces fiction enrolls with a view to diverting them. In order to prevent these "new versions" from solidifying, Pynchon places them in tension, in equilibrium, in counterweight. Pynchon knows how to do everything, and his dazzling stylistic and hermeneutic *patchworks* do not allow one motif or one color to dominate. Coover masters all voices, and no voice is so powerful that he does not undermine it with the interferences of another. Writing, henceforth, knows that it can no longer reflect. But the advent of fiction confers upon it a different set of powers. Two provocative reactions will help size them up, as we are about to conclude. A voice asks the narrator of a short story by William S. Wilson "what these stories reflect";[21] and we have seen earlier what response he provided and the reasons why he "doesn't write like Franz Kafka."

"Why do you write?" someone asked Coover one day. His answer produced the following verses:

Because fiction imitates life's beauty, thereby inventing the beauty life lacks.
Because fiction, mediating paradox, celebrates it.
Because God, created in the storyteller's image, can be destroyed only by his maker.
Because in its perversity, it harmonizes the disharmonious.
Because in the beginning was the gesture, and in the end to come as well: in between what we have are words.
Because, of all the arts, only fiction can unmake the myths that unman men.
Because the pen, thought short, casts a long shadow (upon, it must be said, no surface).
Because the world is re-invented everyday and this is how it is done.
Because truth, that elusive joker, hides himself in fictions and must therefore be sought there . . .[22]

Not so long ago, someone wondered about "a difficult but definite desire: how, in the fading away of the contemporary Real, to avoid the return of the psychological novel as well as the aporia of the impossible narrative, and how to continue to tell stories that are those of the world in general?"[23] The question was French. Perhaps, once this book has been closed, one will be tempted to seek some elements of the answer in today's American fiction. After all, the aporia, whose depth a thousand paradoxes strived to measure over the centuries, is not a new one. Nourished by language and moved by language, inventor of language, manipulator of language, nourished by the world, sifter of the world's riches, and inventor of the world, creator and creature whose tongue, indissociably — because some prodigious "immachination" ironically decided thus — tastes, speaks, and is spoken at one and the same time, the contemporary writer would perhaps recognize herself or himself in the image of this small child: It is said that, as a boy, Krishna was denounced by his playmates for having eaten a fistful of dust. His mother, while scolding him, made him open his mouth. On the tongue of her son, she saw then, poised, the entire universe: the Earth, and standing on the sphere, very tiny, herself, scolding her child. And him: fearless; his mouth wide open.

Notes

Preface

1. Jean-Paul Sartre, *What Is Literature?*, trans. Bernard Frechtman (London: Methuen, 1967), 18.

2. Paul Valéry, *Tel Quel*, trans. Stuart Gilbert (Princeton, N.J.: Princeton University Press, 1970), 123.

3. In addition, Gérard Cordesse's book, *La Nouvelle Science-Fiction américaine* (Paris: Aubier, 1984), brings the topic superbly up to date.

4. See in particular: Tony Tanner, *City of Words: American Fiction, 1950–1970* (New York: Harper and Row, 1971); Raymond M. Olderman, *Beyond the Wasteland: A Study of the American Novel in the 1960s* (New Haven: Yale University Press, 1972); Alan Wilde, *Horizons of Assent: Modernism, Postmodernism, and the Ironic Imagination* (Baltimore: Johns Hopkins University Press, 1981), and *Middle Grounds: Studies in Contemporary American Fiction* (Philadelphia: University of Pennsylvania Press, 1987); Jerome Klinkowitz, *Literary Disruptions: The Making of a Post-Contemporary American Fiction* (Urbana: University of Illinois Press, 1975); Patrick O'Donnell, *Passionate Doubts: Designs of Interpretation in Contemporary American Fiction* (Iowa City: University of Iowa Press, 1986); Frederick R. Karl, *American Fictions, 1940–1980: A Comprehensive History and Critical Evaluation* (New York: Harper and Row, 1983).

Chapter 1

1. Pierre Dommergues, *L'Aliénation dans le roman américain contemporain, 1940–1965* (Paris: Bourgois, 1969), and *Les USA à la recherche de leur identité* (Paris: Grasset, 1967); Rachel Ertel, *Le roman juif américain* (Paris: Payot, 1980).

2. As was remarked by Frederick R. Karl in *American Fictions, 1940–1980* (New York: Harper and Row, 1983), 90.

3. Grace Paley, *Later the Same Day* (New York: Farrar, Straus, and Giroux, 1985), 89.

4. In *La Grand'Route* (Paris: Seuil, 1979).

5. See Alexis de Tocqueville, *Democracy in America*, trans. Henry Reeve (London: Longmans, Green, and Co., 1875), chapters 22–24 of the first book.

6. So much so that James Fenimore Cooper rewrote descriptive passages for the British publication of his novels.

7. Tocqueville, *Democracy in America*, chapters 22 and 23 respectively.

8. Robert Coover, "On Reading 300 American Novels," *New York Times Book Review*, 18 March 1984, 37.

9. As, for example, in Michel Terrier's *Le Roman américain, 1914–1945* (Paris: Presses Universitaires de France, 1979). The move is similar to that of Jean Béranger and Maurice Gonnaud in *La Littérature américaine jusqu'en 1865* (Paris: Colin, 1974).

10. The redskin/paleface distinction is borrowed from Philip Rahv, former editor of the *Partisan Review*: indigenous, virile, and "natural" literature, as opposed to that of writers turned toward Europe, toward culture, toward a genteel tradition that is enervated and rotten with sophistication.

11. Claude-Edmonde Magny, *L'Age du roman américain* (Paris: Seuil, 1948).

12. On reading the commentaries of Vidal, John Gardner, or Bellow on recent productions, one thinks of Louis-Ferdinand Céline: "Nobody does the breast stroke once they've seen the crawl! . . . There's no 'studio day,' there can't be no 'Raft of the Medusa' once they've seen 'Déjeuner sur l'Herbe'! D'ya get it, Colonel? . . . Those 'backward types' defend themselves, that's for sure! . . . A thousand convulsions, and they're nasty, aggressive, unapproachable!" (*Entretiens avec le professeur Y*, [Paris: Gallimard, 1955], 86).

13. See Chapter 4, "Evolutions."

14. Cormac McCarthy was on the shelves in the sixties, Styron as early as 1951.

15. On this point, see André Bleikasten, "Un romancier à façon" in *Delta*, no. 23.

16. Styron was among François Mitterrand's guests at his inauguration in 1981.

17. Allen Guttman, *The Jewish Writer in America: Assimilation and the Crisis of Identity* (New York: Oxford University Press, 1971), 226.

18. A similar danger, one that exists whenever fiction is considered as a space directly open to collective demands and affirmations, also threatens the most militant feminist literature. As a victim of its own success, this literature encourages, through its subjects and themes, the recognition of negative stereotypes and harmful generalities that it claims to combat (and in so doing, *nolens volens*, reinforces and supports them).

19. Nathalie Sarraute, *The Age of Suspicion*, trans. Maria Jolas (New York: George Braziller, 1963), 41.

20. Warner Berthoff, *A Literature without Qualities: American Writing since 1945* (Berkeley: University of California Press, 1979), 28.

21. See the end of Chapter 4, "Evolutions."

22. Paul Valéry, *Tel Quel*, trans. Stuart Gilbert (Princeton, N.J.: Princeton University Press, 1970), 115.

23. William Gaddis, *The Recognitions* (New York: Harcourt, Brace and Co., 1952), 230.

24. Interview with Gilbert Sorrentino, *Review of Contemporary Fiction* 1.1:6.

25. Robert Coover, "On Reading 300 American Novels," *New York Times Book Review*, 18 March 1984, 1.

26. Ibid., 38.

27. Ibid.

28. Gustave Flaubert, *Correspondence* (Paris: Gallimard, coll. "Bibliothèque de la Pléiade," 1973), 1: 344.

29. In his preface to the first book published by New Directions in 1936.

30. Coover, "On Reading 300 American Novels," 38.

31. Georges Devereux, *De l'angoisse à la méthode* (Paris: Flammarion, 1980), 191.

Chapter 2

1. Or his analyst? A number of remarks in the novel suggest that Holden's confession arises from therapy. The obsessive/insistent questions that punctuate Walter Abish's *How German Is It* do not seem far off.

2. J. D. Salinger, *The Catcher in the Rye* (New York: Bantam, 1964), 172.

3. Vladimir Nabokov, *Lolita* (New York: Vintage, 1991), 9.

4. "Traveling along the good names," says the narrator of *Trout Fishing in America* in "The Lake Josephus Days" (New York: Dell, 1967), 78.

5. Susan Sontag, *Against Interpretation* (New York: Farrar, Straus, and Giroux, 1966).

6. An earlier incarnation of *Lolita* was entitled *The Magician*.

7. At a conference held in New York in 1985, John Barth, clearly irritated by Alain Robbe-Grillet, who was expressing his preference for Vladimir Nabokov among American writers, retorted that his favorite French writer was Samuel Beckett!

8. Tim Hunt, *Kerouac's Crooked Road* (Hamden: Archon, 1981), 2.

9. As noted by Philippe Mikriammos: "Eléments pour un portrait de l'artiste en journaliste," *Essais*, vol. 1 (Paris: Bourgois, 1981), 254.

10. Nathalie Sarraute was generous enough to forgive me my hijacking of her title, since she had stolen hers from Stendhal. Literature is a den of thieves.

11. In conversation with the author.

12. Coover devoted an important article to him in Ted Solotaroff's *New American Review*, no. 11: "The Last Quixote."

13. William Gaddis, *The Recognitions* (Cleveland: World Publishing, 1962).

14. The term is all the more appropriate in that it refers to a color of artificial paint as well as to alchemy, primary themes in the novel.

15. Paul Valéry, *Tel Quel*, trans. Stuart Gilbert (Princeton, N.J.: Princeton University Press), 75.

16. Nathalie Sarraute, *The Age of Suspicion*, trans. Maria Jolas (New York: George Braziller, 1963), 99.

17. Jacques Derrida, *Dissemination*, trans. Barbara Johnson (Chicago: University of Chicago Press, 1981), 11.

18. Introduction to S. Elkin and S. Ravenel, eds., *Stories from the Sixties* (New York: Doubleday, 1971), 12.

19. "An Interview with John Hawkes," *Wisconsin Studies in Contemporary Literature* 6 (1965): 149.

20. John Hawkes, "Notes on the Wild Goose Chase," *Massachusetts Review* 3.4 (Summer 1962): 786.

21. Ibid., 787.

22. Ibid., 786.

23. Ibid.

24. Sarraute, *The Age of Suspicion*, 140.

25. John Hawkes, *The Passion Artist* (New York: Harper and Row, 1979), 83.

Chapter 3

1. Aristotle, *Poetics* 24.10.

2. Richard Stern, *A Father's Words* (New York: Arbor House, 1986).

3. See also Chapter 10, "Images/Noises," below.

4. In the course of a leap unequaled since the 1920s, a decade in which "ads," radio, film, fashion, and the advent of credit and of scriptural currency, the expansion of chain stores had, in the wake of another war, worn down the notion of place, value, difference, and economic reality.

5. In *Amérique* (Paris: Grasset, 1986).

6. Stephen Wright, *Meditations in Green* (New York: Farrar, Straus, and Giroux, 1983).

7. Philip D. Beidler, *American Literature and the Experience of Vietnam* (Athens: University of Georgia Press, 1982), 4.

8. David Halberstam, *One Very Hot Day* (Boston: Houghton Mifflin, 1967), 127.

9. In this vein, Charles Durden reports the transformation of a "big pig" into an "enemy freight animal," and Beidler's *American Literature and the Experience of Vietnam* intelligently covers this question.

10. As André LeVot has shown in "Contre l'entropie: les stratégies de la fiction américaine postmoderniste," *Ranam* 10 (1977): 298–319.

11. Paul Valéry, *Monsieur Teste*, trans. Jackson Mathews (Princeton, N.J.: Princeton University Press, 1973), 47.

12. Nathalie Sarraute, *The Age of Suspicion*, trans. Maria Jolas (New York: George Braziller, 1963), 139.

13. Letter to Paul Verlaine, 1866; quoted in Henri Mondor, *Propos sur la poésie* (Monaco: Editions du Rocher, 1953), 21.

14. Sarraute, *The Age of Suspicion*, 57.

15. Moreover, the tendencies toward descriptive delirium on the part of Balzac or of late Dickens, criticized in their time, only now begin to appear in criticism, with the "postmodernist" gaze, like all others, happily colonizing the past in order to bring forth a "tradition" that justifies the present.

16. Charles Newman, *The Post-Modern Aura* (Evanston, Ill.: Northwestern University Press, 1985), 98.

17. "Babylon was a whore. *Ô La Reine aux fesses cascadantes.*" Saul Bellow, *Mr. Sammler's Planet* (New York: Viking, 1970), 163.

18. Gore Vidal, "American Plastic: The Matter of Fiction," *New York Review of Books*, 15 July 1976, 31–39.

19. Gustave Flaubert, *Correspondance* (Paris: Gallimard, Coll. "Bibliothèque de la Pléiade," 1973), 1: 762.

20. Richard Brautigan, *Trout Fishing in America* (New York: Dell, 1967), 26.

21. Tom Robbins, *Even Cowgirls Get the Blues* (New York: Bantam Books, 1984), 144 and 1.

22. Brautigan, *Trout Fishing in America*, 111.

23. Stern, *A Father's Words*, 15.

24. Sarraute, *The Age of Suspicion*, 13.

25. The expression is Wesley A. Kort's.

26. John Barth, "The Literature of Exhaustion," *Atlantic*, August 1967, 29–34.

27. André Chénier, "L'invention: Poème," in *Anthologie de la poésie française*, ed. R. Kanters and M. Nadeau (Paris: Rencontre, 1967), 306. (My trans.)

28. John Barth, "The Literature of Replenishment," *Atlantic Monthly*, January 1980, 65–71.

29. Ronald Sukenick, *The Death of the Novel and Other Stories* (New York: Dial, 1969), 47.

30. H. G. Wells, "Digression about Novels," in *Henry James and H. G. Wells*, ed. Leon Edel and Gordon N. Ray (Urbana: University of Illinois Press, 1958), 220.

31. Ronald Sukenick, *Statements* (Brooklyn: Fiction Collective, 1975), 7–8.

32. Philip Stevick, "Sheherazade Runs out of Plot, Goes on Talking; the King, Puzzled, Listens," *TriQuarterly* 26 (Winter 1973).

33. See Chapter 4, "Evolutions," below.

34. Sukenick, *The Death of the Novel and Other Stories,* 41.

35. Pascal Quignard, *Carus* (Paris: Gallimard, 1979), 135.

36. Grace Paley, *Later the Same Day* (New York: Farrar, Straus, and Giroux, 1985), 74.

37. Susan Sontag, *Against Interpretation* (New York: Farrar, Straus, and Giroux, 1966).

38. Ronald Sukenick, *In Form: Digressions on the Act of Fiction* (Carbondale: Southern Illinois University Press, 1985), 32.

39. Gilbert Sorrentino, *Imaginative Qualities of Actual Things* (New York: Pantheon, 1971.

40. Donald Barthelme, "The Explanation," *City Life* (New York: Farrar, Straus, and Giroux, 1970), 77.

41. Barthelme, *City Life,* 24.

42. Sukenick, *Death of the Novel and Other Stories,* 42.

43. George Chambers, *Ø Null Set* (Brooklyn: Fiction Collective, 1977), 25.

44. John Hawkes, *Travesty* (New York: New Directions, 1976), 27.

45. Sukenick, *In Form,* 33.

46. Ishmael Reed, *Yellow Back Radio Broke-Down* (Garden City, N.J.: Doubleday, 1969), 36.

47. Among his critics are John Barth, in particular, who has accused him of resorting to the technique of *jambazo,* as well as his friend William Gass, Max Apple, and others.

48. John Gardner, *On Moral Fiction* (New York: Basic Books, 1978), 126.

49. See Chapter 12, "Cultural Tradition and the Present II," below.

50. Christopher Lasch, *The Culture of Narcissism* (New York: Norton, 1978).

51. Tom Wolfe nicknamed the seventies "the me decade." Lasch's next book was entitled *The Minimal Self: Psychic Survival in Troubled Times* (New York: Norton, 1984).

52. Lasch, *The Culture of Narcissism,* 96.

53. Ibid., 97.

54. "Culture, Criticism, and Unreality," "The Myth of the Postmodern Breakthrough," and "The Politics of Anti-Realism," in Gerald Graff, *Literature Against Itself* (Chicago: University of Chicago Press, 1979).

55. Graff, *Literature Against Itself,* 8.

Chapter 4

1. David Leavitt, as quoted by Michiko Kakutani, "Defining a Generation of Writers," *New York Times,* 21 April 1986, C17.

2. A wonderful publisher that, unfortunately, has failed since these lines were written.

3. Under Reagan's presidency, a study estimated that more than 13 percent of the American population was illiterate.

4. Charles Newman, *The Post-Modern Aura* (Evanston, Ill.: Northwestern University Press, 1985).

5. Ibid., 95.

6. Jean-François Lyotard, *Le Postmoderne expliqué aux enfants* (Paris: Galilée, 1986).

7. Guido Almansi, "Le Haricot postmoderniste," *Fabula* 1 (March 1983):133.

8. Stéphane Mallarmé, quoted in Henri Mondor, *Propos sur la poésie* (Monaco: Editions du Rocher, 1953), 143–44.

9. Newman, *The Post-Modern Aura*, 36.

10. John Leggett, "Lasting Ephemera," *New York Times Book Review*, 6 October 1985, 22.

11. See the last chapter of this book.

Chapter 5

1. Nathalie Sarraute, *The Age of Suspicion*, trans. Maria Jolas (New York: George Braziller, 1963), 126.

2. See "Epic and Novel" in *The Dialogic Imagination*, ed. Michael Holquist, trans. Caryl Emerson and Michael Holquist (Austin: University of Texas Press, 1981). Elsewhere, Bakhtin speaks of "those organizational categories which it is in the novel's nature to resist." The novel would be defined, then, precisely by the impossibility of integrating it into pre-existing categories.

3. Flann O'Brien, *At Swim-Two-Birds* (London: Granada, 1982), 33.

4. Ibid., 139.

5. See Lucien Dällenbach, *Le Récit spéculaire* (Paris: Seuil, 1977).

6. Robert Coover, *Pricksongs and Descants* (New York: Dutton, 1969), 78.

7. Ibid., 77.

8. Robert Scholes, *Fabulation and Metafiction* (Urbana: University of Illinois Press, 1979), 2 and 3.

9. Claude Simon, *Discours de Stockholm* (Paris: Minuit, 1986).

10. In Dillard's *Teaching a Stone to Talk* (New York: Harper and Row, 1982).

11. Alan Singer, *A Metaphorics of Fiction* (Tallahassee: University Press of Florida, 1983), 25.

12. Gilbert Sorrentino, *Review of Contemporary Fiction* 1:23.

13. Ibid.

14. Robert Steiner, Presentation at the Congrès de l'Association française d'études américaines/Conference of the French Association for American Studies, Dourdan, May 1986.

15. Zavarzadeh defines "transfiction" as "the type of narrative constructed on . . . a baring of literary devices: unmasking narrative conventions and turning them into counterconventions in order to shatter the illusion of reality which is the aesthetic function of the totalizing novel." In *Mythopoeic Reality* (Urbana: University of Illinois Press, 1976), 38–40.

16. Scholes, *Fabulation and Metafiction*.

17. James Joyce, *Letters*, vol. 1, ed. Stuart Gilbert (New York: Viking, 1966), 241.

18. Readers may refer to Tanner's excellent book *City of Words* (New York: Harper and Row, 1971) for an author-by-author analysis of fiction from the sixties and seventies.

19. Jonathan Baumbach, *The Return of Service* (Urbana: University of Illinois Press, 1979), 1.

20. Richard Ford, *The Sportswriter* (New York: Vintage, 1986), 43.

21. Ibid., 36.

22. Gordon Lish, "Picture," *Raritan* 6.1 (Summer 1986): 109.

23. See Dillard's remarkable short work *Living by Fiction* (New York: Harper and Row, 1982).

24. James Purdy, *Malcolm* (New York: Farrar, Straus, and Cudahy, 1959), 91.

25. Donald Barthelme, "Sentence," in *City Life* (New York: Farrar, Straus, and Giroux, 1970) and "The Dolt," in *Unspeakable Practices, Unnatural Acts* (New York: Farrar, Straus, and Giroux, 1968); Robert Coover, "Beginnings," in *In Bed One Night and Other Brief Encounters* (Providence, R.I.: Burning Deck, 1983); Stephen Dixon, "Fourteen Stories," in *Fourteen Stories* (Baltimore: Johns Hopkins University Press, 1980).

26. Grace Paley, "A Conversation with My Father," in *Enormous Changes at the Last Minute* (New York: Farrar, Straus, and Giroux, 1974).

27. Clarence Major, *Reflex and Bone Structure* (New York: Fiction Collective, 1975), 112.

28. Ibid., 17.

29. Jerome Charyn, *The Tar Baby* (New York: Holt, Rinehart and Winston, 1973), 3.

30. These are islands of apparent interest to contemporary fiction writers, since Kurt Vonnegut (*Galapagos*) and Annie Dillard ("Life on the Rocks," *Teaching a Stone to Talk*) both choose to meet Darwin there as well.

31. Charyn, *The Tar Baby*, 9.

32. He also appears often in works by Guy Davenport and William S. Wilson, and he is at the center of Bruce Duffy's *The World As I Found It* (New York: Ticknor and Fields, 1987) and David Markson's *Wittgenstein's Mistress* (Ellwood, Ill.: Dalkey Archive Press, 1988).

33. In *Horizons of Assent* (Baltimore: Johns Hopkins University Press, 1981) and *Middle Grounds* (Philadelphia: University of Pennsylvania Press, 1987).

34. David Carkeet, *I Been There Before* (New York: Harper and Row, 1985), 103.

35. Richard Brautigan, *Trout Fishing in America* (New York: Dell, 1967), 66.

36. Tom LeClair and Larry McCaffery, eds., *Anything Can Happen* (Urbana: University of Illinois Press, 1983), 2.

37. Coover, *Pricksongs and Descants*, 20.

38. I discuss this aspect of the novel in "The Pen and the Skin: Inscription and Cryptography in John Hawkes's *Second Skin*," *Review of Contemporary Fiction* (Fall 1983): 167–76.

39. Dillard, *Living By Fiction*, 21.

40. In Jerome Klinkowitz, *The New American Novel of Manners* (Athens: University of Georgia Press, 1986). The study focuses on Yates, Wakefield, and McGuane.

41. Andrée Connors, *Amateur People* (New York: Fiction Collective, 1977), 122.

Chapter 6

1. Paul Valéry, *Tel Quel*, 1:175; and *Odds and Ends*, trans. Stuart Gilbert (Princeton, N.J.: Princeton University Press, 1970), 120.

2. This will be discussed in the last section of the work. One can also refer to Françoise Sammarcelli's invaluable doctoral study of *LETTERS* entitled "La Chambre aux échos: L'Intertextualité dans l'oeuvre de John Barth," University of Paris VIII, 1989. The game of letters, from the alphabet primer to Freitag's triangle, is abundantly explored in Sammarcelli's work.

3. We will return to Curtis White in our discussion of "high culture."

4. Joseph McElroy, in Tom LeClair and Larry McCaffery, eds., *Anything Can Happen* (Urbana: University of Illinois Press, 1983), 246.

5. Ludwig Wittgenstein, *Philosophical Investigations,* trans. G. E. M. Anscombe (New York: Macmillan, 1958), 11.

6. "The Panel Game" appears in Robert Coover, *Pricksongs and Descants* (New York: Dutton, 1969).

7. See Patricia Waugh, *Metafiction: The Theory and Practice of Self-Conscious Fiction* (London and New York: Methuen, 1984), 54: "All the possible functions of language — emotive, referential, poetic, conative, phatic and finally metalingual — whirl about him."

8. Thomas LeClair, *Contemporary Literature,* no. 21 (1980): 15–37.

9. See Jean-François Lyotard, *The Postmodern Condition: A Report on Knowledge, Theory and History of Literature,* vol. 10, trans. Geoff Bennington and Brian Massumi, foreword by Fredric Jameson (Minneapolis: University of Minnesota Press, 1984).

10. I borrow the notion of "frames" from Erving Goffman's *Frame Analysis* (New York: Harper and Row, 1974).

11. Valéry, *Tel Quel,* 45.

12. An identical horizontal diamond structure shapes Sukenick's novel *Out.* The paragraphs gradually become thicker, reaching their greatest dimension in the middle of the book before becoming blunter and tapering down again, until reaching the final paragraph of one line. In this way, typographical form is given over to space and to escape; both themes dominate the book and provide it with its title.

13. Arthur Rimbaud, "After the Flood," *Complete Works,* trans. Paul Schmidt (New York: Harper and Row, 1975), 219.

14. Cf. infra, *On Being Blue* (New York: Godine, 1976).

15. Gilbert Sorrentino, *Splendide-Hôtel* (Elmwood Park, Ill.: Dalkey Archive, 1973), 13.

16. On this early paradigm of American literature, see Claude Richard's rich and penetrating work, *Lettres américaines* (Aix-en-Provence: Alinéa, 1987). (Translation forthcoming from the University of Pennsylvania Press.)

17. In *TriQuarterly,* no. 26 (1973).

18. Ronald Sukenick, *98.6* (New York: Fiction Collective, 1975), 26.

19. Richard Brautigan, *Revenge of the Lawn* (New York: Touchstone, 1971), 170.

20. Harold Jaffe, "Underbelly (1)" and "Underbelly (2)" in *Mourning Crazy Horse* (New York: Fiction Collective, 1982).

21. Jaffe, *Mourning Crazy Horse,* 178.

22. Remark attributed to Flaubert by Jules de Goncourt and Edmond de Goncourt, *Journal* (17 March 1861). One is reminded of another innovator in a different medium, Jean Renoir, who, in speaking of his filmed metatheater, blandly confessed: "I'm not all that interested in subjects . . ."

23. If only for the planetary divergences between the two authors concerning their appreciation and use of metaphor; if only for the fact that Sorrentino travels a parallel route in following the shades of the color orange.

24. This is how Terry Southern's *Blue Movie* should be read.

25. James Purdy, *Malcolm* (New York: Farrar, Straus, and Cudahy, 1959), 76.

26. Alexander Theroux, *Darconville's Cat* (Garden City, N.J.: Doubleday, 1981), 576.

27. Mikel Dufrenne, *Le Poétique* (Paris: Presses Universitaires de France, 1973).

28. In *The Floating Opera,* Barth introduced this technique as a means of comparing possible narratives. With *Lost in the Funhouse,* he confesses to wanting to give a "multimedia" dimension to fictions composed for "print, tape, live voice."

29. The formulations are Ihab Hassan's.

30. Steve Katz, preface, *Saw* (New York: Alfred A. Knopf, 1972), v. The book is made up of four "reports" numbered 17, 11, 3, 7, and also includes "explanations" ranging from A to D. The last section is entitled "The First Chapter."

31. This work appears in Eugene Wildman, *Experiments in Prose* (Chicago: Swallow Press, 1969).

32. Steve Katz, *Creamy and Delicious* (New York: Random House, 1970).

33. Don DeLillo, *Ratner's Star* (New York: Knopf, 1976).

34. In LeClair and McCaffery, *Anything Can Happen,* 81.

35. Ibid., 82.

36. Larry McCaffery and Sinda Gregory, *Alive and Writing* (Urbana: University of Illinois Press, 1987), 174.

37. Robert Coover, *Whatever Happened to Gloomy Gus of the Chicago Bears?* (New York: Linden Press, 1987), 92.

38. See the following chapters.

39. In *Close-Up* 15: 1 (Winter 1985). In this same issue, one can read Barthelme on baseball, Coover on soccer, and John Irving on wrestling. Significantly, Irving's article, written by a man who wrestled for years and possesses the most thorough knowledge of his topic, offers the least interesting analysis of the sport's ties to fiction. On the other hand, what a feast Paul Fournel, an intellectual and a champion of Lady Literature alone, provides for us in *Les Athlètes dans leur tête* (Paris: Ramsay, 1988).

40. Only in the last few years, we have seen the publication of W. P. Kinsella's *Iowa Baseball Confederacy,* Donald Hays's *Dixie Association,* Eric Greenberg's *The Celebrant,* Paul Hemphill's *Long Gone,* and Philip O'Connor's *Stealing Home.*

41. Judy Lopatin, "Etiology of the New War," in *Modern Romances* (New York: Fiction Collective, 1980), 116.

42. Richard Brautigan, *A Confederate General from Big Sur* (New York: Grove, 1964).

43. Philippe Djian, *37.2 le matin* (Paris: Barrault, 1989).

44. Lopatin, *Modern Romances,* 119.

45. Ibid., 154.

46. Ibid., 217.

47. Rob Swigart, *Little America* (Boston: Houghton Mifflin, 1977), 92.

48. This device was also employed in Anne Gorreta's *Sphynx* (Paris: Grasset, 1986).

49. Swigart, *Little America,* 3, 4.

50. Ibid., 87.

51. Kurt Vonnegut, *Slaughterhouse-Five* (New York: Dell, 1969), 30 and 157.

52. Barry Hannah, *Airships* (New York: Alfred A. Knopf, 1978), 80.

53. By antinomianism, I mean here not the strict theological doctrine but its effects on ideology: from the conviction that divine forgiveness frees one not only from Mosaic law but also from the recognition of other laws, we easily pass to the conviction that secular laws and the rules governing behavior could not control anyone who knows he is in close communion with the truth. The righteousness of the "holier-than-thou" finds its prime origin here.

54. Tom Robbins, in McCaffery and Gregory, *Alive and Writing,* 231.

Chapter 7

The expression "Connoisseurs of Chaos" in the chapter title is borrowed from Wallace Stevens.

1. Judy Lopatin, *Modern Romances* (New York: Fiction Collective, 1980), 214.

2. "It is quite obvious, however, that reality is not their main interest, but form, always, form invented by others, and from which a magnetic force makes them unable ever to break away" (Sarraute, *The Age of Suspicion*, trans. Maria Jolas [New York: George Braziller, 1963], 137).

3. Robert Coover, *A Political Fable* (New York: Viking, 1980), 58.

4. Georges Devereux, *De l'angoisse à la méthode* (Paris: Flammarion, 1980), 191.

5. Andrée Connors, *Amateur People* (New York: Fiction Collective, 1977), 44.

6. See David Porush, *The Soft Machine: Cybernetic Fiction* (New York: Methuen, 1985).

7. Annie Dillard, *Living by Fiction* (New York: Harper and Row, 1982), 24. Tom Robbins reads another lesson here: in their incompatibility, organized religion and spirituality can be substituted for the original terms of the theorem . . . (in Larry McCaffery and Sinda Gregory, eds., *Alive and Writing* [Urbana: University of Illinois Press, 1987], 233).

8. *New York Times Book Review*, 29 October 1972, 4.

9. Walker Percy, *Love in the Ruins* (New York: Farrar, Straus, and Giroux, 1971).

10. Jerry Bumpus, "Our Golf Balls," in *Things in Place* (New York: Fiction Collective, 1975), 14–23.

11. William Gibson, *Neuromancer* (London: Grafton, 1986), 204.

12. Ibid., 285.

13. Warner Berthoff, *A Literature Without Qualities* (Berkeley: University of California Press, 1979), 102.

14. Ibid., 110. Berthoff is quoting Orwell's *Inside the Whale*.

15. Nathalie Sarraute, *The Age of Suspicion*, trans. Maria Jolas (New York: George Braziller, 1963), 102. Subsequent references appear parenthetically in the text.

16. Thomas LeClair, *Dallas Times Herald/Lone Star Review* (June 1981): 3.

17. Joseph McElroy in Tom LeClair and Larry McCaffery, eds., *Anything Can Happen* (Urbana: University of Illinois Press, 1983), 248.

18. These observations by Christian Delacampagne in *Le Monde* originally referred to Lukács.

19. Gérard Cordesse, *La Nouvelle Science-Fiction américaine* (Paris: Aubier, 1984).

20. In the *Columbia Literary History of the United States* (New York: Columbia University Press, 1988).

21. Denis Johnson, *Fiskadoro* (New York: Knopf, 1985), 46.

22. Bruce Herzberg, "Illusions of Control: A Reading of *Gravity's Rainbow*" (Ph.D. diss., Rutgers University, 1978), iii.

23. In *Omensetter's Luck*, Furber also falls victim to the binarism of his thought (William Gass, *Omensetter's Luck* [New York: New American Library, 1966]).

24. Thomas Pynchon, *The Crying of Lot 49* (Philadelphia: J. B. Lippincott, 1966), 170.

25. Anne Battesti's wonderful work, "*Gravity's Rainbow:* L'Ecriture de la bifurcation" (diss., University of Orléans, January 1994) has recently filled that gap.

26. See *Language, Thought and Reality: Selected Writings of Benjamin Lee Whorf*, ed. J. B. Carroll (Cambridge: MIT Press, 1956).

27. Pynchon, *The Crying of Lot 49*, 4.

28. J. D. Salinger, *Raise High the Roof Beam, Carpenters* (New York: Penguin, 1963), 51.

29. Nathanael West, *Miss Lonelyhearts* (New York: New Directions, 1970), 9.

30. In Pynchon's logic, the fact that the epileptic bites his tongue at the point of cutting off language could have become more than a metaphor: designation of a gesture indispensable to a consciousness without paranoia. In Denis Johnson (*Fiskadoro*), mutilation is prevented by inserting a candle between Chung's teeth: the flame of a candle is small compared to the great bedazzlements of the seizure; but language is saved.

31. On this question, see Steven Weisenburger, "Paper Currencies," *Review of Contemporary Fiction* 2:2 (1982).

32. James Purdy, *Malcolm* (New York: Farrar, Straus, and Cudahy, 1959), 114.

33. For a good summary of the problems raised by an "anthropic" reading of the cosmos, see *Discover* (May 1987).

34. Joseph McElroy, "Neural Neighborhoods," *TriQuarterly* 34 (Fall 1975): 216.

35. In LeClair and McCaffery, *Anything Can Happen*, 242.

36. Pynchon, *The Crying of Lot 49*, 95.

37. In LeClair and McCaffery, *Anything Can Happen*, 242.

38. Frederick R. Karl, *American Fictions, 1940–1980* (New York: Harper and Row, 1983), 190.

39. In LeClair and McCaffery, *Anything Can Happen*, 248.

40. Ibid., 239, 248.

41. Ibid., 238.

42. In a different mode, as we will see, and for reasons more psychological than epistemological, this is also what Georgiana Peacher attempts in *Mary Stuart's Ravishment Descending Time*.

43. In LeClair and McCaffery, *Anything Can Happen*, 240.

44. Joseph McElroy, *Plus* (New York: Knopf, 1977), 138. Subsequent references appear parenthetically within the text.

45. In LeClair and McCaffery, *Anything Can Happen*, 241.

46. Joseph McElroy, *Lookout Cartridge* (New York: Knopf, 1974).

47. The expression is from George Stade, *New York Times Book Review*, 2 February 1975, 9.

48. McElroy, *Lookout Cartridge*, 197.

49. William S. Wilson, *Why I Don't Write Like Franz Kafka* (New York: Ecco Press, 1977), 39.

50. Ibid., 38.

51. Wilson, *Why I Don't Write Like Franz Kafka*, 67.

52. DeLillo, in LeClair and McCaffery, *Anything Can Happen*, 85.

53. Ibid., 86. Thus, Thomas Farber, in *Curves of Pursuit*, borrows a relational model from mathematics. Plot is devalued. In its place we find the spirals of the form and their superimposed returns. The relationship between the two brothers becomes a meditation on the forms produced by the evolution in space of connected and moving poles. This is a less experimental variation than it might seem. More powerfully, Coover employs this device to shape the "leper's helix" (*Pricksongs and Descants*).

54. In *The Book of Revelations*, Swigart stages the problems of communication between humans when Cassie succeeds in talking to dolphins and killer whales.

55. Don DeLillo, *White Noise* (New York: Penguin Books, 1986), 12.

56. This has become a central question for the excellent critic of contemporary

fiction, Thomas LeClair. The reader is referred to his articles mentioned elsewhere. But "big" novels are also part of the American tradition, from *Modern Chivalry* to *Moby-Dick* and Thomas Wolfe.

57. As quoted in Marcus Cunliffe, *The Literature of the United States*, 4th ed. (New York: Penguin, 1986), 105.

58. Patrick O'Donnell, *Passionate Doubts: Designs of Interpretation in Contemporary American Fiction* (Iowa City: University of Iowa Press, 1986), 73.

59. Robert Coover, *The Water-Pourer: An Unpublished Chapter from* The Origin of the Brunists (Bloomfield Hills, Mich.: Bruccoli-Clark, 1972), 3.

60. LeClair, *Lone Star* (June 1981): 3.

61. George Steiner, review of William Gaddis's *JR*, *New Yorker*, 26 January 1976, 106. See also, *On Difficulty* (Oxford: Oxford University Press, 1979).

62. Karl, *American Fictions*, 3.

Chapter 8

1. Hayden White, *Metahistory* (Baltimore: Johns Hopkins University Press, 1973) and *Tropics of Discourse* (Baltimore: Johns Hopkins University Press, 1978); Dominick LaCapra, *Rethinking Intellectual History* (Ithaca, N.Y.: Cornell University Press, 1983), and with S. L. Kaplan, *Modern European Intellectual History* (Ithaca, N.Y.: Cornell University Press, 1982).

2. Vincent Descombes, *Modern French Philosophy*, trans. L. Scott-Fox and J. M. Harding (Cambridge: Cambridge University Press, 1980), 110.

3. Robert Scholes, *Fabulation and Metafiction* (Urbana: University of Illinois Press, 1979), 208–9.

4. Norman Mailer, *The Armies of the Night* (New York: Signet, 1968), 179.

5. Harold Jaffe, *Mole's Pity* (New York: Fiction Collective, 1979).

6. In conversation with the author.

7. Joseph McElroy, in Tom LeClair and Larry McCaffery, eds., *Anything Can Happen* (Urbana: University of Illinois Press, 1983), 238.

8. James Purdy, *Malcolm* (New York: Farrar, Straus, and Cudahy, 1959), 136.

9. Raymond Federman, "Self-Reflexive Fiction," in ed. Emory Elliott, *Columbia Literary History of the United States* (New York: Columbia University Press), 1149.

10. Raymond Federman, "From the Chronicle of a Disaster," *Blatant Artifice*, vol. 2 (1986): 97.

11. Federman, "Self-Reflexive Fiction," 1149.

12. Barry Hannah, *Ray* (New York: Penguin, 1980), 45.

13. Kurt Vonnegut, *Slaughterhouse-Five* (New York: Dell, 1969), 23.

14. Hannah, *Ray*, 41.

15. Richard Condon, *The Abandoned Woman* (New York: Dial Press, 1977), 3.

16. Robert Alter, in *Dialogue* 7:3 (1976): 45 *et seq.* and 52.

17. Remark made during the Conference of the Association for American Studies in Philadelphia, 1984.

18. Agota Kristof, *Le Grand Cahier* (Paris: Seuil, 1986).

19. In "A Conversation on *The Blood Oranges* between John Hawkes and Robert Scholes," *Novel* 5 (1972): 205.

20. Joseph McElroy, *Ancient History* (New York: Knopf, 1971).

21. Frederic Tuten, *The Adventures of Mao During the Long March* (New York: Citadel, 1971), 68.

22. John Barth, *LETTERS* (New York: Putnam, 1979).

23. Tuten, *Adventures of Mao,* 29.

24. Ibid., 9–10.

25. Warner Berthoff, *A Literature Without Qualities* (Berkeley: University of California Press, 1970).

26. Obviously, "reconstruction" refers to the period following the surrender at Appomattox as well as to the philosophical concept. Everything occurs as though the logic of the historical text were modeling itself after that of the establishment of institutions in the defeated South. The historian as carpetbagger. Bradley made this remark at the Conference of the Association for American Studies in Philadelphia in 1984 during a discussion with Ishmael Reed and John Flanagan.

27. On the question of an inherent "fiction" in "historical narrative," readers are referred to Michel de Certeau, *L'Ecriture de l'histoire* (Paris: Gallimard, 1975) and to the works of Paul Veyne.

28. See the following chapter.

29. Davenport, *The Geography of the Imagination* (San Francisco: North Point Press, 1981).

30. In an interview with R. Stein, "Baseball on Their Minds," *New York Times Book Review,* 1 June 1986, 53.

31. Robert Coover, *The Universal Baseball Association, J. Henry Waugh, Prop.* (New York: New American Library, 1968), 45.

32. Robert Coover, *Whatever Happened to Gloomy Gus of the Chicago Bears?* (New York: Linden Press, 1987), 10.

33. Coover, *The Universal Baseball Association,* 224.

34. Joseph McElroy, "Neural Neighborhoods," *TriQuarterly* 34 (Fall 1975): 215.

35. Remark made at the Conference of the Association for American Studies in Philadelphia, 1984.

36. Pascal Quignard, *Carus* (Paris: Gallimard, 1979), 204.

37. I have further explored this question in "Clio Doesn't Live Here Anymore," *Delta* 8 (May 1979).

38. Interestingly, Hawkes knew little about Germany; and Abish had never been there before the publication of his book. So much for the documentary aspect.

39. Wolfe, after having demonstrated by the expressionistic techniques of his pseudo-journalistic narratives that the "real" is constituted in language, returns in *The Bonfire of the Vanities* to a vaguely Sartrian aesthetic, even claiming a certain naturalism. It is as though, entering into the novel, he were renouncing writing. A tribute to anti-intellectualism.

40. Don DeLillo, *Libra* (New York: Viking, 1988), 181.

41. Federman, "Self-Reflexive Fiction," 1149.

42. Hugh Henry Brackenridge, *Modern Chivalry* (New York: American Book Company, 1937), 431.

Chapter 9

1. These stories appear in Coover's *Pricksongs and Descants.*

2. Rachel Ingalls, *I See a Long Journey* (New York: Simon and Schuster, 1985), 128.

3. George Santayana, *Interpretations of Poetry and Religion* (Cambridge: MIT Press, 1986), 38.

4. William Gaddis, *The Recognitions* (Cleveland: World Publishing, 1962), 632.

5. Annie Dillard, *Living by Fiction* (New York: Harper and Row, 1982), 28.

6. Op. cit., 33.

7. Craig Hansen, *Paradoxical Resolutions* (Urbana: University of Illinois Press, 1982), 69.

8. Don DeLillo, *Americana* (New York: Penguin, 1989), 154.

9. Thomas Berger, *Arthur Rex* (New York: Delacorte, 1978).

10. John Updike, as quoted in Hansen, *Paradoxical Resolutions,* 74.

11. Larry McCaffery, "The Fictions of the Present," *Columbia Literary History of the United States,* ed. Emory Elliott (New York: Columbia University Press, 1988), 1171.

12. Toni Morrison, lecture at Princeton University, January 1987.

13. *Jazz* (1992) vies for the title.

14. Stanley Elkin, *Searches and Seizures* (New York: Random House, 1973), 120.

15. Robert Coover, *A Night at the Movies* (New York: Simon and Schuster, 1987), 73.

16. Toby Olson, *The Life of Jesus* (New York: New Directions, 1976), 151.

17. Jerome Charyn, *Pinocchio's Nose* (New York: Arbor House, 1983), 152.

18. Nathanael West, *The Day of the Locust* (New York: New Directions, 1950), 179.

19. Richard Brautigan, *The Hawkline Monster* (New York: Simon and Schuster, 1974), 16.

20. John Barth, "Welcome to College—and My Books," *New York Times Book Review,* 16 September 1984, 36.

21. John Barth, "Dunyazadiad," in *Chimera* (New York: Random House, 1972), 19.

22. Barth, *Chimera,* 194.

23. John Barth, *Lost in the Funhouse* (Garden City, N.J.: Doubleday, 1968), 177.

24. John Barth, quoted in Craig Hansen Werner, *Paradoxical Resolutions: American Fiction Since James Joyce* (Urbana: University of Illinois Press, 1982), 146.

25. Werner, *Paradoxical Resolutions,* 147.

26. This sentiment is frequently echoed in Kathy Acker's work.

27. Russell Banks, quoted in Werner, *Paradoxical Resolutions,* 48.

28. Charles Molesworth, *Donald Barthelme's Fiction* (Columbia: University of Missouri Press, 1983), 31.

29. Robert Coover, *The Universal Baseball Association, J. Henry Waugh, Prop.* (New York: New American Library, 1968), 225. Subsequent references appear parenthetically in the text.

30. Robert Coover, "On Reading 300 American Novels," *New York Times Book Review,* 18 March 1984, 37.

31. Ibid.

32. Robert Coover, *The Public Burning* (New York: Viking, 1977), 191.

33. Ibid., 191.

34. Claude Lévi-Strauss, *Anthropologie structurale* 1:231, cited in Vincent Descombes, *Modern French Philosophy,* trans. L. Scott Fox and J. M. Harding (Cambridge: Cambridge University Press, 1980), 107. In *Modern French Philosophy,* Descombes explains the equivalence in the following way: "The semiological theorem of the exteriority of the signifier has thus a political corollary. The self-styled 'political ideologies' of our societies are, very precisely, myths, and their symbolic efficacy (the trust of the faithful, the adherence of the masses), is no guarantee of their correspondence with the reality which they claim to describe. . . . If it is true that the signifier is exterior to the subject, then the various political discourses of

industrial society are analogous to the mythical narratives of so-called primitives" (106–7).

35. Robert Coover, "The Dead Queen," *Quarterly Review of Literature* 8 (1973): 304–13.

36. Descombes, *Modern French Philosophy*, 137.

37. Pascal Quignard, *Carus* (Paris: Gallimard, 1979), 208.

38. Andrée Connors, *Amateur People* (New York: Fiction Collective, 1977), 46.

39. William H. Gass, "Emerson and the Essay," in *Habitations of the Word* (New York: Simon and Schuster, 1985), 21.

Chapter 10

1. Thomas LeClair, "The Best American Fiction," *Dallas Times Herald/Lone Star Review* (June 1981): 3, 8.

2. Nathalie Sarraute, *The Age of Suspicion*, trans. Maria Jolas (New York: George Braziller, 1963), 72–73.

3. Claude-Edmonde Magny, *L'Age du roman américain* (Paris: Seuil, 1948), trans. Eleanor Hochman as *The Age of the American Novel: The Film Aesthetic of Fiction Between the Two Wars* (New York: Frederick Ungar, 1972).

4. See Alan Spiegel, *Fiction and the Camera Eye: Visual Consciousness in Film and the Modern Novel* (Charlottesville: University Press of Virginia, 1976).

5. Susan Sontag, *Against Interpretation* (New York: Farrar, Straus, and Giroux, 1966), 12.

6. The expression is Faulkner's.

7. In Larry McCaffery and Sinda Gregory, eds., *Alive and Writing* (Urbana: University of Illinois Press, 1987), 216–17.

8. In Tom LeClair and Larry McCaffery, eds., *Anything Can Happen* (Urbana: University of Illinois Press, 1983), 84–85.

9. In McCaffery and Gregory, *Alive and Writing*, 217.

10. Don DeLillo, *Americana* (New York: Penguin, 1989), 263.

11. See Claude Richard's article on this in Marc Chénetier, ed., *Critical Angles* (Carbondale: Southern Illinois University Press, 1986), 77–104.

12. On the same theme, see Frederick R. Karl, *American Fictions, 1940–1980: A Comprehensive History and Critical Evaluation* (New York: Harper and Row, 1983), 315–16.

13. Jonathan Baumbach, *The Life and Times of Major Fiction* (New York: Fiction Collective, 1987), 122.

14. Don DeLillo, *Running Dog* (New York: Knopf, 1978), 225.

15. In LeClair and McCaffery, *Anything Can Happen*, 84.

16. Baumbach, *The Life and Times of Major Fiction*, 51.

17. From this point of view, Jerome Klinkowitz's book *The New American Novel of Manners* (Athens: University of Georgia Press, 1986) offers some good analyses.

18. Bruce J. Friedman, *A Mother's Kisses* (New York: Simon and Schuster, 1964).

19. DeLillo, *Americana*, 294.

20. In LeClair and McCaffery, *Anything Can Happen*, 84–85.

21. Barbara Guest, *Seeking Air* (Santa Barbara, Calif.: Black Sparrow, 1978), 62.

22. Kenneth Gangemi, *The Interceptor Pilot* (London: Marion Boyars, 1980), 49.

23. Rudolph Wurlitzer, *Slow Fade* (New York: Knopf, 1984).

24. Joseph McElroy, *Lookout Cartridge* (New York: Knopf, 1974).

25. DeLillo, *Americana*, 266.

26. Ibid., 6.
27. DeLillo, *Running Dog*, 156.
28. Ibid., 80.
29. In LeClair and McCaffery, *Anything Can Happen*, 244.
30. Cf. Chapter 13, "The Mouth and the Ear," below.
31. DeLillo, *Americana*, 214.
32. Philip Roth, "On the Air," *New American Review* 10 (1970): 17–49.
33. DeLillo, *Americana*, 377.
34. One summer while I was writing this book, I heard a young Austrian woman on the Brittany coast: she was sitting down, watching the changing multicolored sails on the green of the ocean, against the blue of the sky; movement, colors, nothing was missing. Her conclusion carried the proof of a believer: "It's like television."
35. Interview with Grace Paley, *Delta* 14 (May 1982): 35–36.
36. In *Gisants* (Paris: Gallimard, 1986).
37. Charles Molesworth, *Donald Barthelme's Fiction* (Columbia: University of Missouri Press, 1983), 30.
38. Bruce Jay Friedman, *A Mother's Kisses* (New York: Simon and Schuster, 1964), 71.
39. Ibid., 71.
40. Richard Ford, *The Sportswriter* (New York: Vintage, 1986), 290.
41. I borrow the expression from Kosinski's "The Art of the Self," in *Passing By: Selected Essays, 1962–1991* (New York: Random House, 1992).
42. Jerzy Kosinski, *Being There* (New York: Harcourt, 1971), 5.
43. Jerzy Kosinski, *The Devil Tree* (New York: Harcourt Brace Jovanovich, 1973), 157.
44. In *Mourning Crazy Horse* (New York: Fiction Collective, 1982), 145.
45. In conversation with the author.
46. Jerome Charyn and François Boucq, *The Magician's Wife*, trans. of *La Femme du magicien* (New York: Catalan, 1987). This work received the award for the Best Comic Strip at the Festival d'Angoulême in 1986. Charyn continues to work on new developments within this genre by which he is fascinated.
47. Harold Jaffe, *Mole's Pity* (New York: Fiction Collective, 1979), 159.

Chapter 11

1. Milan Kundera, *The Book of Laughter and Forgetting*, trans. Michael Henry Heim (New York: Knopf, 1980), 186.
2. Paul Valéry, *Rhumbs*, trans. Stuart Gilbert (Princeton, N.J.: Princeton University Press, 1970), 235, 239.
3. William S. Wilson, *Why I Don't Write Like Franz Kafka* (New York: Ecco Press, 1977), 39.
4. Rob Swigart, *Little America* (Boston: Houghton Mifflin, 1977).
5. Tom Robbins, *Even Cowgirls Get the Blues* (New York: Bantam, 1977), 256.
6. Ibid., 82 and 101.
7. F. Scott Fitzgerald, "My Generation," *Esquire* 70.4 (1968): 119.
8. Roger Sale, *Literary Inheritance* (Amherst: University of Massachusetts Press, 1984).
9. Paul Metcalf, *Genoa* (Highlands, N.C.: J. Williams, 1965), dustjacket. What a

marvelous metaphor referring to the embroidered shrouds of the dead: the game of writing on the warp of the ancestors.

10. Ibid., 71.

11. Annie Dillard, *Pilgrim at Tinker Creek* (New York: Bantam Books, 1975).

12. Henry David Thoreau, *Walden* (New York: Modern Library, 1950), 141.

13. Dillard, *Pilgrim at Tinker Creek*, 227.

14. Ibid.

15. In *Le Magazine littéraire* (September 1986): 38.

16. Guy Davenport, *Tatlin!* (New York: Scribner's, 1974), 250, 203.

17. Letter to Robert Creeley (3 March 1950).

18. Edward Gibbon, *The Decline and Fall of the Roman Empire* (New York: The Modern Library, 1932), 212.

19. Barbara Guest, *Seeking Air* (Santa Barbara, Calif.: Black Sparrow, 1978), 176.

20. Curtis White, *Heretical Songs* (New York: Fiction Collective, 1980), 20.

21. Ibid., 70 and 68.

22. Franklin Mason, *Four Roses in Three Acts* (New York: Fiction Collective, 1981).

23. Ibid., 35.

24. Similar motivations and formally identical manipulations could in fact be found in the science fiction and the "speculative fiction" of the 1970s and 1980s.

25. T. Coraghessan Boyle, *Water Music* (New York: Penguin, 1981), 153.

26. Evan S. Connell, *A Long Desire* (New York: Holt, Rinehart and Winston, 1979). Subsequent references to this edition appear parenthetically in the text.

27. See Charles Caramello, *Silverless Mirrors* (Tallahassee: Florida State University Press, 1983).

28. Kenneth Gangemi, *The Volcanoes from Puebla* (London: Marion Boyars, 1979), 181.

Chapter 12

1. Grace Paley, *Later the Same Day* (New York: Farrar, Straus, and Giroux, 1985), 36.

2. Kurt Vonnegut, *Mother Night* (New York: Bard, 1971), 150.

3. Samuel Butler, *Erewhon* (New York: AMS Press, 1968), 53.

4. Paul Valéry, *Tel Quel*, trans. Stuart Gilbert (Princeton, N.J.: Princeton University Press, 1970), 153.

5. Tobias Wolff, ed. *Matters of Life and Death* (Green Harbor, Mass.: Wampeter Press, 1983).

6. In a remarkable article on the questions asked by minimalism (*New York Times Book Review*, 28 December 1986).

7. Raymond Carver, "On Writing," in *Fires* (Santa Barbara: Capra Press, 1984).

8. I devoted a study to this question in *Critical Angles* (Carbondale: Southern Illinois Press, 1986).

9. Carver, "On Writing," in *Fires*.

10. Raymond Carver, "The Art of Fiction," introduction by Mona Simpson, *Paris Review* 88 (1983): 221.

11. And Charles H. Newman has said it in an excellent article, "What's Left Out of Literature," published in the *New York Times Book Review*, 12 July 1987, 1+.

12. Robert Coover in *Mississippi Review* 40–41 (Winter 1985): 10.

13. Richard Ford, *The Sportswriter* (New York: Vintage, 1986), 61.

14. Kim A. Herzinger, "On the New Fiction," *Mississippi Review* 40–41 (Winter 1985): 20.

15. Ibid.

16. Newman, "What's Left Out of Literature," 1+.

17. Ben Yagoda, "No Time Like The Present, *New York Times Book Review*, 10 August 1986, 1+.

18. John Barth, "A Few Words About Minimalism," *New York Times Book Review*, 28 December 1986, 1–2+.

19. William S. Wilson, "Ann Beattie's Implications," *Mississippi Review* 40–41 (Winter 1985): 94.

20. As described by Charles Molesworth in his book, *Donald Barthelme's Fiction* (Columbia: University of Missouri Press, 1983), while imitating the title of one of Barthelme's stories ("Robert Kennedy Saved from Drowning," in *Unspeakable Practices, Unnatural Acts*).

21. In LeClair and McCaffery, *Anything Can Happen*, 247.

22. Molesworth, *Donald Barthelme's Fiction*, 11.

23. Donald Barthelme, *Snow White* (New York: Bantam, 1967), 97.

24. Walker Percy, as quoted by Gail Godwin, "The Devil's Own Century," a review of Percy's *The Thanatos Syndrome* in the *New York Times Book Review*, 5 April 1987, 1+.

25. Ezra Pound, "Hugh Selwyn Mauberley," in *Selected Poems of Ezra Pound* (New York: New Directions, 1957), 61.

26. See M. Couturier and R. Durand, *Donald Barthelme* (London: Methuen, 1982), 38.

27. In LeClair and McCaffery, *Anything Can Happen*, 34.

28. Donald Barthelme, *Sadness* (New York: Farrar, Straus, and Giroux, 1972), 144; and *Come Back, Dr. Caligari* (Boston: Little, Brown and Co., 1964), 94.

29. Donald Barthelme, "The Dragon," in *Guilty Pleasures* (New York: Farrar, Straus, and Giroux, 1974).

30. Donald Barthelme, "The Wound," in *Amateurs* (London: Routledge, 1977), 17.

31. Donald Barthelme, "The Glass Mountain," in *City Life* (New York: Farrar, Straus, and Giroux, 1970), 63.

32. Donald Barthelme, *Great Days* (New York: Farrar, Straus, and Giroux, 1979), 21.

33. Alexander Theroux, *Darconville's Cat* (Garden City, N.J.: Doubleday, 1981).

34. Stanley Elkin, *The Franchiser* (Boston: David R. Godine, 1988), 61. Subsequent references to this edition appear parenthetically in the text.

35. William Gass, introduction to Elkin's *The Franchiser*, x.

36. Jayne Anne Phillips, *Machine Dreams* (New York: Dutton, 1984), 16.

37. Donald Barthelme, "Sentence," in *City Life*.

38. Letter to Jean Moréas, quoted by Henri Mondor, *Propos sur la poésie* (Monaco: Editions du Rocher, 1953), 15.

39. See my "Organisme, organicisme et écriture dans *Searches and Seizures*," *Delta* 20 (February 1985).

40. Stanley Elkin, "Religious Themes and Symbolism in the Novels of William Faulkner" (Ph.D. diss., University of Illinois, 1961), 368.

41. Stanley Elkin, *Criers and Kibitzers, Kibitzers and Criers* (New York: New American Library, 1973), 38.

42. These stories appear in Max Apple, *The Oranging of America* (New York: Grossman Publishing, 1976).

43. In Max Apple, *Free Agents* (New York: Harper and Row, 1984).

44. In Apple, *The Oranging of America.*

45. In Apple, *Free Agents.*

46. Max Apple, *The Propheteers* (New York: Harper and Row, 1987), 122, 150, and 41.

47. René Char, "Ma feuille vineuse," *Sept saisis par l'hiver* in *Oeuvres complètes* (Paris: Gallimard, coll. "Bibliothèque de la Pléiade," 1983), 534.

48. Samuel Beckett, *Disjecta: Miscellaneous Writings and a Dramatic Fragment,* ed. Ruby Cohn (New York: Grove Press, 1984).

Chapter 13

1. Michael Stephens, *The Dramaturgy of Style* (Carbondale and Edwardsville: Southern Illinois University Press, 1986).

2. Rudolph Wurlitzer, *Flats* (New York: Dutton, 1970), 8, 89, and 110.

3. John Barth, *The End of the Road* (New York: Bantam Books, 1969).

4. See, in particular, Thomas Pynchon, *Gravity's Rainbow* (New York: Viking, 1973), 49–51.

5. Henscher dies in chapter 3, an unwonted fate for a first-person narrator . . . See Pierre Gault, *John Hawkes: La parole coupée* (Paris: Klincksieck, 1984).

6. Nathalie Sarraute, *The Age of Suspicion,* trans. Maria Jolas (New York: George Braziller, 1963), 98.

7. Stanley Elkin, *Searches and Seizures* (New York: Random House, 1973), 214.

8. Ibid., 25.

9. Stephens, *The Dramaturgy of Style,* 9.

10. Thomas Farber, *Curves of Pursuit* (New York: G. P. Putnam's Sons, 1984), 123.

11. William S. Wilson, *Why I Don't Write Like Franz Kafka* (New York: Ecco, 1977), 61.

12. Stephen Dixon, "Said," *Boundary* 2.8 (Spring 1980): 99.

13. Judy Lopatin, *Modern Romances* (New York: Fiction Collective, 1980), 152.

14. Moira Crone, *The Winnebago Mysteries and Other Stories* (New York: Fiction Collective, 1982), 32.

15. William Gass, *Fiction and the Figures of Life* (New York: Vintage, 1972), 34–54.

16. Wurlitzer, *Flats,* 22. Subsequent references appear parenthetically in the text.

17. Don DeLillo, *White Noise* (New York: Viking, 1985), 86.

18. Steven Millhauser, *Portrait of a Romantic* (New York: Knopf, 1977), 84.

19. Max Apple, *Free Agents* (New York: Harper and Row, 1984), 85. Subsequent references appear parenthetically in the text.

20. Robert Coover, *Pricksongs and Descants* (New York: Dutton, 1969), 166.

21. William Faulkner, *As I Lay Dying* (New York: Vintage, 1987), 157.

22. Ibid., 158.

23. Andrée Connors, *Amateur People* (New York: Fiction Collective, 1977), 31, 33, 52.

24. Letter from Mallarmé to Anatole France, dated 15 May 1876, in Henri Mondor, *Propos sur la poésie* (Monaco: Editions du Rocher, 1953), 119.

25. Stephens, *The Dramaturgy of Style*, 89.
26. Don DeLillo, *Americana* (New York: Penguin, 1989), 214.
27. Ibid.
28. Pynchon, *Gravity's Rainbow* (New York: Viking, 1973), 258.
29. Allen Ginsberg, *Howl*, ed. Barry Miles (New York: Harper and Row, 1986), 3.
30. Neal Cassady, *The First Third And Other Writings* (San Francisco: City Lights Books, 1971), 79.
31. Thomas McGuane, *Ninety-two in the Shade* (New York: Penguin, 1980), 104.
32. Thomas McGuane, *The Bushwhacked Piano* (New York: Warner, 1973).
33. Thomas McGuane, *The Sporting Club* (New York: Penguin, 1979), 46, 50, 43.
34. But all jargon has its limits. *The Rabbi of Lud* discovers there a means of access to community identity.
35. Elkin, *Searches and Seizures*, 101.
36. Joseph McElroy, in Tom LeClair and Larry McCaffery, eds., *Anything Can Happen* (Urbana: University of Illinois Press, 1983), 241.
37. Don DeLillo, in LeClair and McCaffery, *Anything Can Happen*, 81.
38. Stanley Elkin, *The Dick Gibson Show* (New York: Random House, 1971), 334 and 11. Subsequent references appear parenthetically in the text.
39. Stanley Elkin, *Boswell* (New York: Random House, 1964).
40. Philip Roth, "On the Air," *New American Review* (August 1970).
41. John Hawkes, *The Cannibal* (New York: New Directions, 1949), 15, 22, 23.
42. John Hawkes, *Second Skin* (New York: New Directions, 1964), 3 and 1.
43. In conversation with the author.
44. Grace Paley, *Leaning Forward* (Penobscot, Maine: Granite Press, 1985), 8.
45. Grace Paley, "The Story Hearer," *Later the Same Day* (New York: Farrar, Straus, and Giroux, 1985), 144.
46. Interview with Grace Paley, *Delta* 17: 29.
47. Paley, *Leaning Forward*, 39.
48. Ibid., 66.
49. Linsey Abrams, "A Maximalist Novelist Looks at Some Minimalist Fiction," *Mississippi Review* 40–41 (Winter 1985): 24–30.
50. Interview with Grace Paley, in *Delta* 21 (May 1982): 14.
51. William Gass, *On Being Blue* (New York: Godine, 1976), 25.
52. Paley, *Later the Same Day*.
53. Stephens, *The Dramaturgy of Style*.
54. Toni Cade Bambara, *The Salt Eaters* (New York: Vintage, 1981), 64.
55. Ibid.
56. Rudolph Wurlitzer, *Nog* (New York: Random House, 1968), 34.
57. Paul Valéry, *Rhumbs*, trans. Stuart Gilbert (Princeton, N.J.: Princeton University Press, 1970), 240.
58. Pascal Quignard, *Carus* (Paris: Gallimard, 1979), 69–70.
59. William Gass, *Omensetter's Luck* (New York: Plume, 1966), 113.
60. Stig Dagerman, *Notre besoin de consolation est impossible à rassasier* [Our need for consolation is too great to be satisfied] (Actes Sud, 1984).
61. Wurlitzer, *Nog*, 121.
62. Davenport, *Flowers and Leaves* (Flint, Mich.: Bamberger Books, 1991), 23.
63. DeLillo, *Americana*, 121.
64. I borrow this expression from the title of Michel Pierssens's book published by the Editions de Minuit: *La Tour de Babil*.
65. Cynthia Ozick, *The Cannibal Galaxy* (New York: Knopf, 1983), 148.

66. In LeClair and McCaffery, *Anything Can Happen*, 84.

67. Ibid.

68. Davenport, *Flowers and Leaves*, 106.

69. DeLillo in LeClair and McCaffery, *Anything Can Happen*, 84.

70. William Kotzwinkle, *The Fan Man* (New York: Dutton, 1987), 9.

71. See Johan Thielemans, "The Energy of an Absence," in Marc Chénetier, ed., *Critical Angles* (Carbondale: Southern Illinois Press, 1986).

72. William Gass, "Authors' Authors," *New York Times Book Review*, 5 December 1976, 102.

73. In conversation with the author.

74. William Gaddis, *JR* (New York: Knopf, 1975), 646. Subsequent references to this edition appear parenthetically in the text.

75. In a letter dated 1858 to Mlle. Leroyer de Chantepie.

76. DeLillo, *Americana*, 267–68.

77. John Hawkes, *The Owl* (New York, New Directions, 1977).

78. Quignard, *Carus*, 304.

79. Thomas Pynchon, *The Crying of Lot 49* (Philadelphia: J. B. Lippincott, 1966), 21.

80. Vladimir Nabokov, *Ada or Ardor: A Family Chronicle* (New York: McGraw Hill, 1969).

81. William H. Gass, *Willie Master's Lonesome Wife* (Evanston, Ill.: Northwestern University Press, 1968).

82. See William H. Gass, *Habitations of the Word* (New York: Simon and Schuster, 1985).

83. Stanley Elkin, *Searches and Seizures* (New York: Random House, 1973), 285.

84. Michel Chaillou, *Rêve de Saxe* (Paris: Ramsay, 1986), 146.

85. Pynchon uses this quotation from *The Wizard of Oz* as the epigraph to the third part of *Gravity's Rainbow*, "In the Zone."

86. The abandonment of the first-person narrator indicates the voice's loss of intimate sonorities; the evolution that brings him back to first-person narration "with a vengeance" is interesting: from *The Catfish Man* on, this voice finds its rights anew, with the narrator assuming for his part the role of the author.

87. Stephens, *The Dramaturgy of Style*, 28.

Chapter 14

1. Alice Walker, *In Search of Our Mothers' Gardens* (New York: Harcourt Brace Jovanovich, 1983).

2. In a thematic sense. I have tried to explore the mysteries of "l'écriture féminine" in contemporary American fiction in "A la recherche de l'Arlésienne," *Revue française d'études américaines* (November 1986).

3. Similarly, we have seen that the Spanish-speaking and Caribbean world invades the fiction of Banks, Johnson, or Mooney.

4. James Alan McPherson, *Elbow Room* (Boston: Little, Brown & Co., 1977), 215.

5. During the "Contemporary American Literature Day" held at the Paris Museum of Modern Art by the Society of Friends of M.-E. Coindreau (4 May 1985).

6. Howard Frank Mosher, *New York Times Book Review*, 17 August 1986, 8.

7. Lewis P. Simpson, "Southern Fiction," in *Harvard Guide to Contemporary American Writing* (Cambridge: Harvard University Press, 1979), 156.

8. Stéphane Mallarmé in Henri Mondor, *Propos sur la poésie* (Monaco: Editions du Rocher, 1953), 2.

9. Following the example of the joyous cinematographic confusion created by "The Phantom of the Movie Palace" in Robert Coover's *A Night at the Movies* (New York: Simon and Schuster, 1987), which leads to the idea "of sliding two or more projected images across each other like brushstrokes, painting each other with the other, so to speak, such that a galloping cowboy gets in the way of some slapstick comedians and, as the films separate out, arrives at the shootout with custard on his face; or the dying heroine, emerging from montage with a circus feature, finds herself swinging by her stricken limbs from a trapeze, the arms of weeping lover in the other frame now hugging an elephant's leg; or the young soldier, leaping bravely from his foxhole, is creamed by a college football team, while the cheerleaders, caught out in no-man's-land, get their pom-poms shot away. . . . He knows there's something corrupt, maybe even dangerous, about this collapsing of boundaries, but it's also liberating, augmenting his film library exponentially." (23)

10. M. M. Bakhtin, "Discourse in the Novel," in *The Dialogic Imagination,* ed. Michael Holquist, trans. Caryl Emerson and Michael Holquist (Austin: University of Texas Press, 1981), 320. Subsequent references to this work appear parenthetically in the text.

11. Charles Newman, *The Post-Modern Aura* (Evanston, Ill.: Northwestern University Press, 1985), 138.

12. Michel de Montaigne, *Essays* 3.11, trans. M. A. Screech (London: Penguin, 1991), 1161.

13. William Gass, *The World Within the Word* (New York: Knopf, 1978), 270.

14. In *Dictionary of Literary Biography* (1980): 12.

15. In *News of the American Place Theatre* 5.1 (November 1972): 2.

16. William S. Wilson, in Tom LeClair and Larry McCaffery, eds., *Anything Can Happen* (Urbana: University of Illinois Press, 1983), 62.

17. Joseph McElroy, in LeClair and McCaffery, *Anything Can Happen,* 246.

18. Don DeLillo, in LeClair and McCaffery, *Anything Can Happen,* 82.

19. Steven Millhauser, *In the Penny Arcade* (New York: Knopf, 1986), 129. Subsequent references to this work appear parenthetically in the text.

20. Steven Millhauser, *Portrait of a Romantic* (New York: Knopf, 1977), 28.

21. William S. Wilson, "Métier," *Why I Don't Write like Franz Kafka* (New York: Ecco Press, 1977).

22. Robert Coover, "In Answer to the Question 'Why Do You Write?' " in *Traduire* 131 (March 1987): 11–13.

23. Raymond Bellour, *Le Magazine littéraire,* no. 248 (December 1987): 90.

Index